Intellectual Property and Access to Medicines in Africa

A major target of Goal 3 of the Sustainable Development Goals adopted by the United Nations in 2015 is the elimination of 'the epidemics of AIDS, tuberculosis, malaria and neglected tropical diseases' and combating 'hepatitis, water-borne diseases and other communicable diseases'. Intellectual property (IP) has been identified as one of the factors impeding access to affordable medicines in developing countries, especially in relation to the HIV pandemic.

This book examines the scope of the existing flexibilities in international IP law for promoting access to medicines. It analyses the factors accounting for the underutilisation of the flexibilities in Africa and the measures that African countries may adopt to address the IP barriers to access to medicines. It explores the regional strategies that Africa can adopt to resolve the tension between IP regimes and access to medicines. It also highlights how trade liberalisation and regional integration can play crucial roles in enhancing the use of TRIPS flexibilities, local pharmaceutical manufacturing and access to medicines in Africa.

By adopting qualitative research methods to investigate how African countries may effectively use IP to serve public health purposes through the stratagem of regional integration, this book will be a valuable contribution to the existing literature on IP.

Olasupo Owoeye, LL.B, PhD, is a Senior Lecturer in Law at the RMIT University, Melbourne, Australia.

Routledge Research in Intellectual Property

Intellectual Property and Access to Medicines in Africa
A Regional Framework for Access
Olasupo Owoeye

Intellectual Property Branding in the Developing World
Tshimanga Kongolo

Intellectual Property Policy, Law and Administration in Africa
Exploring Continental and Sub-Regional Co-Operation
Caroline Bongiwe Ncube

Intellectual Property Rights and Competition in Standard Setting
Objectives and Tensions
Valerio Torti

Re-Thinking Intellectual Property
The Political Economy of Copyright Protection in the Digital Era
YiJun Tian

The Development of Intellectual Property Regimes in the Middle East
David Price

Intellectual Property, Community Rights and Human Rights
The Biological and Genetic Resources of Developing Countries
Marcelin Tonye Mahop

Intellectual Property in Global Governance
The Crisis of Equity in the Knowledge Economy
Chidi Oguamanam

For more information about this series, please visit: https://www.routledge.com

Intellectual Property and Access to Medicines in Africa

A Regional Framework for Access

Olasupo Owoeye

Routledge
Taylor & Francis Group
LONDON AND NEW YORK

First published 2019
by Routledge
2 Park Square, Milton Park, Abingdon, Oxon OX14 4RN

and by Routledge
605 Third Avenue, New York, NY 10017

First issued in paperback 2021

Routledge is an imprint of the Taylor & Francis Group, an informa business

Publisher's Note
The publisher has gone to great lengths to ensure the quality of this reprint but points out that some imperfections in the original copies may be apparent.

British Library Cataloguing-in-Publication Data
A catalogue record for this book is available from the British Library

Library of Congress Cataloging-in-Publication Data
Names: Owoeye, Olasupo, author.
Title: Intellectual property and access to medicines in Africa: a regional framework for access / by Olasupo Owoeye.
Description: Abingdon, Oxon; New York, NY: Routledge, 2019. | Series: Routledge research in intellectual property | Based on author's thesis (doctoral – University of Tasmania, 2014) issued under title: Patents for pharmaceuticals and access to affordable medicines: towards an all-encompassing access paradigm for Africa. | Includes bibliographical references and index.
Identifiers: LCCN 2019005010 | ISBN 9781138343382 (hardback)
Subjects: LCSH: Drugs—Africa—Patents. | Pharmacy—Law and legislation—Africa. | Patents (International law)
Classification: LCC KQC391.M44 O954 2019 | DDC 346.604/86—dc23
LC record available at https://lccn.loc.gov/2019005010

ISBN 13: 978-1-03-224114-2 (pbk)
ISBN 13: 978-1-138-34338-2 (hbk)

Typeset in Galliard
by codeMantra

To my adorable wife, Busayo, for the great sacrifices and the unending support, and our children; Dara, Ogo and Ayanfe

Contents

Preface

The Agreement on Trade Related Aspects of Intellectual Property Rights (TRIPS Agreement) was adopted as one of the annexes to the Marrakesh Agreement Establishing the World Trade Organization in 1994. The TRIPS Agreement is the first international treaty to substantially harmonise the legal framework for intellectual property (IP) protection across the globe by providing certain minimum standards of IP protection to which all countries signatory to it must conform. In the field of patents, the TRIPS minimum standard requirement necessitated the extension of patents to all fields of technology including pharmaceuticals, which formerly were outside the ambit of patent protection in many developing countries. The TRIPS patent regime also contains provisions that make the requirements for compulsory patent licensing more rigorous than what obtains under the Paris Convention on the Protection of Industrial Property. These developments have raised significant concerns across the globe as to the implications of patent protection on access to patented pharmaceutical products.

Africa suffers the highest disease burden in the world, and the African public health crisis is further aggravated by the global access to medicines challenge. Significant commentaries and analyses have been presented on how the international legal regime for patent protection has made access to medicines extremely onerous in Africa. This work appraises the international regime for patent protection with particular emphasis on the TRIPS Agreement and its flexibilities for advancing national and public interest. The work takes the view that the existing flexibilities, though somewhat controversial in practical terms, provide a sufficient safeguard for ensuring that national and public interests are not unduly compromised. The work examines how the human rights jurisprudence in the context of health and development may be used to further justify a purposive interpretation of the TRIPS Agreement. The work posits that the access to medicines problem in Africa is not due to the implementation of overtly strong IP legislations or policies; it is largely due to the fact that the continent lacks the ability to locally produce drugs for her populace. Another significant problem is the fact that Africa has not really embraced intra-continent free trade. The book highlights the importance of having an African free-trade area as this will not only provide a strong base for the maximum use of the TRIPS flexibilities, but it may also facilitate the process of developing a significant pharmaceutical manufacturing capacity in the continent.

Olasupo Owoeye, LL.B, PhD
Melbourne
23 January 2019

Acknowledgements

I appreciate my wife Oluwabusayo, without whose steadfast love and unending sacrifices for the family, I would have been unable to undertake this project. I thank my parents and siblings for their continuing encouragement and unwavering support. I am grateful to Prof Dianne Nicol and Dr Jane Nielsen of the University of Tasmania for their valuable insights on the issues covered in this book. I am also grateful to Prof Ruth Okediji of the Harvard Law School and Prof Peter Drahos of the Australian National University for their comments on the initial draft of the work. Special thanks to my colleague, Dr Dominic Dagbanja of the University of Western Australia, for his continual encouragement.

Cases

African court on human and peoples' rights and African commission

Inter-American court on human rights

WTO cases

International tribunal

Legislations

Treaties & declarations

1 Introduction

For African nations, as with other countries in the Global South, one of the most significant public health problems is the availability of affordable treatment and medicines especially for people who are HIV-positive.[1] The 2014 Ebola outbreak in West Africa is an eloquent testimony to how a public health emergency in even the most remote part of the world may have a ricochet effect on global public health.[2] Africa bears a significant disease burden. Up to two billion people (26% of the global population) currently lack access to medicines, with a significant proportion of them living in developing countries.[3] The incident of tuberculosis (TB) cases amongst people living with HIV in Africa was found to be up to 72% in 2017.[4] The WHO African region has the highest global malaria burden and the region accounts for 90% of malaria deaths globally.[5] Africa, especially eastern and southern Africa, remains the world's most affected region by the HIV/AIDS pandemic.[6] A major target of Goal 3, relating to health and well-being, of the Sustainable Development Goals adopted by the United Nations in 2015 is the elimination of 'the epidemics of AIDS, tuberculosis, malaria and neglected tropical diseases' and combating 'hepatitis, water-borne diseases and other communicable diseases'.[7]

The advent of the Agreement on Trade Related Aspects of Intellectual Property Rights (TRIPS Agreement) has brought about a new era of intellectual property governance that is widely believed to have further compounded the

1 See E George, 'The Human Rights to Health and HIV/AIDS: South Africa and South-South Co-operation to Reframe Global Intellectual Property Principles and Promote Access to Essential Medicines' (2011) 18 *Indiana Journal of Global Legal Studies* 168.

2 See O Owoeye & J Oduwole, 'Development, Access to Medicines and the Ebola Virus Epidemic in West Africa' (2017) 24 *Journal of Law and Medicine 722*, 731

3 Access to Medicines Foundation, The 2016 Access to Medicine Index: Methodology 2015 p. 6 available at http://apps.who.int/medicinedocs/documents/s22176en/s22176en.pdf.

4 World Health Organization, Tuberculosis Report 2018, p. 27.

5 World Health Organization, World Health Statistics 2017, p. 30.

6 See UNAIDS, Global AIDS Update 2016, p. 1.

7 Sustainable Development Knowledge Platform: Sustainable Development Goal 3 available at https://sustainabledevelopment.un.org/sdg3 accessed 27 January 2019.

global access to medicines challenge.[8] The TRIPS Agreement however contains a number of safeguards designed to ensure that the protection of intellectual property rights does not stifle competition or impede access to essential products. These safeguards are generally tagged the 'TRIPS flexibilities'.

Intellectual property has been identified as one of the factors impeding access to affordable medicines in developing countries especially in relation to the HIV pandemic.[9] The emergence of regional free trade agreements imposing standards that far exceed the requirements of the TRIPS Agreement may also make it more difficult for countries that depend on foreign imports to enjoy access to affordable medicines.[10] The TRIPS flexibilities have not been fully implemented or utilised in many African countries,[11] and there have been concerns on whether the TRIPS flexibilities are flexible enough to enable developing countries to adopt measures to protect public health and public interest.[12] The United Nations High-Level Panel on Access to Medicines for instance recommended a review of the TRIPS compulsory licensing flexibility in its 2016 report.[13] While least developed countries are currently exempted from implementing the substantive provisions of the TRIPS Agreement till July 2021[14] with a further extension to waive patents for pharmaceuticals until 2033,[15] the extent to which these existing waivers are likely to be of significant benefit to least developed countries will depend largely on their ability to harness the opportunities offered by the current waivers.

8 M A Oliveira, J A Bermudez, G C Chaves & G Velásquez, 'Has the Implementation of the TRIPS Agreement in Latin America and the Caribbean Produced Intellectual Property Legislation that Favours Public Health?' (2004) 82 *Bulletin of the World Health Organization* 815–821; M T Islam, 'TRIPS Agreement and Public Health: Implications and Challenges for Bangladesh' (2011) 17 *International Trade Law and Regulation* 10–38; D Nicol & O Owoeye 'Using TRIPS Flexibilities to Facilitate Access to Medicines' (2013) 91(7) *Bulletin of the World Health Organization* 533–539.

9 M El Said & A Kapczynski, *Access to Medicines: The Role of Intellectual Property Law and Policy.* Working Paper prepared for the Third Meeting of the Technical Advisory Group of the Global Commission on HIV and the Law, 7–9 July 2011.

10 B K Baker, 'Trans-Pacific Partnership Provisions in Intellectual Property, Transparency, and Investment Chapters Threaten Access to Medicines in the US and Elsewhere.' (2016) 13 (3) *PLoS Medicine* 1–7; O Owoeye, O Olatunji & B Faturoti, 'Patents and the Trans-Pacific Partnership: Do the Existing Flexibilities offer much to LDCs in the East African Community?'. (2017) *International Trade Journal* 1–22 doi:10.1080/08853908.2017.1386143.

11 O Owoeye, 'International Patents Law and Public Health: Revisiting the TRIPS Compulsory Licensing Regime and the Doha Paragraph-6 System' (2015) 37 (12) *European Intellectual Property Review* 782, 794–795.

12 Abbott, 'The WTO Medicines Decision' (2005) 99 *American Journal of International Law* 317; H E Anderson Jr, 'We Can Work It Out: Co-operative Compulsory Licensing as the Way Forward in Improving Access to Anti-Retroviral Drugs' (2010) 16 *Boston University Journal of Science and Technology Law* 167, 168–169.

13 UN Secretary-General's High-Level Panel on Access to Medicines Report September 2016 p. 27.

14 Council for TRIPS: Extension of the Transition Period under Article 66.1 For Least Developed Country Members IP/C/64 (Decision of the Council for TRIPS of 11 June 2013).

15 Council for TRIPS: Extension of the Transitional Period under Article 66.1 of the TRIPS Agreement for Least Developed Country Members for Certain Obligations with Respect to Pharmaceutical Products IP/C/73 (6 November 2015).

1.1 Patents and access to medicines

Patents provide exclusive ownership and exploitation rights in respect of inventions possessing a degree of novelty, some scintilla of inventiveness over what is already known and having significant utility value.[16] Patent protection is very important to ensure inventors are able to recoup the cost of their investments and also obtain economic rewards for their labour. There is, however, no unequivocal evidence to support the proposition that patents promote innovation in all cases.[17] Nonetheless, in protecting patent rights there is always the need to ensure a good balance is struck with social policy goals especially in relation to access to essential goods. The makers of the TRIPS Agreement seemed to have taken this view into consideration in ensuring the inclusion of certain flexibilities in the TRIPS Agreement.

Prior to the advent of the TRIPS Agreement, the international intellectual property rights (IPRs) system only provided for national and international registration of rights.[18] The TRIPS Agreement remains the most far-reaching effort towards the harmonisation of global IPRs.[19] Before the TRIPS Agreement came to be, most developing countries did not extend patent protection to pharmaceutical products, thereby allowing generic firms to enter the market and sell medicines at considerably lower prices than originator pharmaceutical companies, whilst driving prices of the original drugs down by the competitive force they exert in the market.[20]

However, with the advent of TRIPS, all WTO countries became bound to grant patents for pharmaceutical inventions to meet their obligations under the Agreement.[21] This is because TRIPS requires WTO Member States to make patents available in all fields of technology to the extent that the invention to be patented meets the criteria for patentability. It has been observed that the primary objective for bringing IPRs protection within the WTO framework was not to make it more consistent with international trade rules but to strengthen and harmonise the protection of intellectual property (IP) on a global scale as

16 See W Cornish & D Llewelyn, *Intellectual Property: Patents, Copyright, Trade Marks and Allied Rights* (London Sweet & Maxwell, 6th ed., 2007) 179.

17 See generally M J Burstein, 'Exchanging Information Without Intellectual Property' (2012) 91 *Texas Law Review* 227.

18 The Paris Convention for the Protection of Industrial Property and the Berne Convention for the Protection of Literary and Artistic Works do not impose uniform standards for IP protection. Rather, they require countries to grant nationals of countries signatory to the conventions the same rights they accord their own nationals. Article 4 of the Paris Convention particularly provides that the registration of a particular work in a member country will give the work priority in all other member countries.

19 C M Correa, *Intellectual Property, WTO and Developing Countries: The Trips Agreement and Policy Options* (TWN 2000) 1.

20 E Ghanotakis, 'How the US Interpretation of Flexibilities Inherent in TRIPS Affects Access to Medicines for Developing Countries' (2004) 7(4) *Journal of World Intellectual Property* 563, 565.

21 Ibid., 566.

a result of the growing concerns of the most economically advanced and industrialised nations about losing technological leadership to newly industrialising countries in Asia and Latin America.[22]

It has also been argued that the difficulty with access to medicines in developing countries has nothing to do with patent protection under the TRIPS Agreement but with problems such as the absence of free trade and effective economies of scale.[23] There is however a connection between patents on pharmaceuticals, which empower patent holders to set high prices for their products, and the availability of these drugs in poor countries that lack the capacity to provide access through public healthcare systems.[24] Whilst it would be wrong to suggest that the TRIPS Agreement is the sole cause of the global access to medicines concern, it is undoubtedly a significant part of the problem. This is because the TRIPS patent regime has made it more difficult for countries to address measures that were available to them prior to the emergence of the minimum standards for IP protection set by it. For instance, the countries that used to refuse to grant patents for pharmaceutical products were unable to continue the practice due to the provision of TRIPS Article 27 that patents shall be available in all fields of technology provided the inventions are patentable.

In recognition of the possible effects of the TRIPS Agreement on access to medicines in developing countries, the WTO Ministers adopted the Doha Ministerial Declaration on TRIPS Agreement and Public Health in November 2001. The WTO Ministers noted that IP protection was important for the development of new medicines but nonetheless acknowledged the concerns about its effects on prices. The WTO Ministers affirmed in this Declaration the position that the TRIPS Agreement should be interpreted and implemented in a way supportive of the right to protect public health and promote access to medicines for all. The Ministers went further by giving the Council for TRIPS a mandate to find an expeditious solution to the problems that countries with little or no pharmaceutical manufacturing capacity might encounter in utilising the TRIPS compulsory licensing provision. The solution eventually came with the adoption of the Decision of 30 August 2003, on Implementation of Paragraph 6 of the Doha Declaration on the TRIPS Agreement and Public Health. The decision has now been incorporated into the TRIPS Agreement with the adoption of the Protocol Amending the TRIPS Agreement in 2005. The amendment entered

22 S Bartelt, 'Compulsory Licenses Pursuant to TRIPS Article 31 in the Light of the Doha Declaration on the TRIPS Agreement and Public Health'(2003) 6 (2) *Journal of World Intellectual Property* 284, 285; See also P Drahos with J Braithwaite, *Information Feudalism: Who Owns the Knowledge Economy?* (The New Press, 2002) 61–73.

23 N Pires de Carvalho, *The TRIPS Regime of Patent Rights* (Kluwer Law International, 2nd ed., 2005) 337.

24 R Roumet, 'Access to Patented Anti-HIV/AIDS Medicines: The South African Experience' (2010) *European Intellectual Property Review* 137.

into force on 23 January 2017.[25] Countries that are yet to accept the TRIPS Protocol may, however, still use the Doha Paragraph-6 system by relying on the Doha Paragraph-6 Implementation Decision.

1.2 The TRIPS flexibilities

The basic flexibilities guaranteed by TRIPS in relation to patents can be found in Articles 1.1, 6, 8.1, 27.2, 30 and 31. The flexibilities guaranteed by these sections are as follows:

- a Article 1.1 provides that members shall be at liberty to determine the appropriate method of implementing the agreement in their national laws.
- b Article 6 gives members the prerogative to determine the exhaustion doctrine that best suits their needs by removing issues relating to the exhaustion doctrine from the ambit of the TRIPS dispute settlement framework.
- c Article 8.1 empowers members to adopt measures to protect public health and interest to the extent that the measures adopted are consistent with the TRIPS Agreement.
- d Article 27.2 allows the exclusion from patentability of inventions where preventing the commercial exploitation of such inventions is necessary to protect health or the environment.
- e Article 30 empowers members to provide limited exceptions to the exclusive rights conferred by patents provided the exceptions do not unreasonably prejudice the normal exploitation of the patent or the legitimate interest of the patent owner.
- f Article 31 allows the compulsory licensing of patented inventions under certain circumstances.

However, the focus of this work is on the TRIPS Agreement provisions on compulsory licensing and parallel importation and their implications for health and development in Africa in the context of the access to medicines debate. This is because compulsory licensing and parallel importation are probably the most practical means of addressing the access to medicines problem.

The TRIPS data exclusivity regime is equally a major issue. States usually require pharmaceutical companies to submit clinical tests data to health regulatory authorities before granting market approval for new drugs to safeguard public health.[26] Article 39.3 of TRIPS requires WTO members to protect such test data against unfair commercial use. It imposes a data exclusivity regime for drugs test data. There is, however, currently a significant controversy between developed and developing countries on the degree of legal protection to

25 WTO, Amendment of the TRIPS Agreement, www.wto.org/english/tratop_e/trips_e/amendment_e.htm accessed 28 January 2019.

26 See J A DiMasi, R W Hansen & H G Grabowski, 'The Price of Innovation: New Estimates of Drug Development Costs' (2003) 22 *Journal of Health Economics* 151.

be afforded test data submitted for market approval of new drugs.[27] The TRIPS test data protection regime is also examined in relation to its connection with compulsory licensing.

Compulsory patent licensing is one of the ways a patent right can be derogated from under the TRIPS Agreement. Exhaustion of rights on the other hand means that IPRs are exhausted or terminated, as far as trade in the goods is concerned, once the goods have been released in the market by the right owner or with the owner's consent. The implication of this is that the IPRs invested in the goods become exhausted, for the purposes of commerce, once they have been released into the market and third parties can parallel import such products by buying in cheap markets for sale in markets where the products might come at a higher price from the manufacturer. This approach to trade in IP products is popularly known as parallel importation. Parallel importation is one other flexibility allowed by Article 6 of the TRIPS Agreement which provides that nothing in the Agreement shall be used to address the issue of exhaustion of rights. The issue of exhaustion is therefore left to the discretion of members. The extent to which these flexibilities serve a useful purpose from a legal standpoint in addressing the access to medicines problem and the legal framework the African continent can explore in taking advantage of these flexibilities warrant detailed examination.

Arguably, the available flexibilities in the TRIPS Agreement should be interpreted in a way that gives force to them as against interpretations that are likely to make them otiose. The relevant human rights provisions in international law are relied upon to advance this argument. Efforts to adopt the flexibilities allowed by TRIPS to protect national interest and access to medicines have always elicited acrimonious debate and serious opposition, particularly from pharmaceutical companies and the US government, who usually contend that such measures run afoul of the TRIPS Agreement.[28] This book posits that a case can be made for a liberal and effective interpretation of the TRIPS flexibilities by using international human rights law perspective when interpreting IP laws, especially in cases involving pharmaceuticals. Patents are said to pose the largest barrier for firms based in least developed countries that are interested in the production of newer pharmaceutical products such as those meant for HIV/AIDS or pandemic flu treatment.[29] The WTO has extended the deadline for least developed countries to grant or enforce patents for pharmaceuticals till January 2033 for least developed countries. This might increase interest in considering the possibilities for local production of pharmaceuticals in such countries.[30]

27 See S Matilal, 'Do Developing Countries Need a Pharmaceutical Data – Exclusivity Regime?'(2010) *European Intellectual Property Review* 268.

28 P Boulet, C Garrison, & E t'Hoen, *Drug Patents under the Spotlight* (Médecins Sans Frontières, 2003).

29 S Moon, *Pharmaceutical Production and Related Technology Transfer* (World Health Organization, 2011) 8.

30 Ibid.

1.3 IP and access to medicines: an African free trade remedy

The field of IP law has always recognised the need to balance private property rights with the public interest in having reasonable access to and enjoying the benefits of scientific invention. Hence, Lord Hoffmann's trenchant observation in *Biogen Inc. v Medeva Plc*:

> It is inevitable, in a young science like electricity in the 19th century or flying at the turn of the last century or recombinant DNA technology in the 1970s, that dramatically new things will be done for the first time. The technical contribution made in such cases deserves to be recognised. But care is needed not to stifle further research and healthy competition by allowing the first person who has found a way of achieving an obviously desirable goal to monopolise every other way of doing so.[31]

This balance was undoubtedly part of the reasons for having a compulsory licensing regime in the TRIPS Agreement. The TRIPS compulsory licensing regime, the Doha Declaration of November 2001, the Implementation Decision of August 2003 and the Protocol Amending the TRIPS Agreement all contain provisions of significant importance to the IP law and access to medicines debate. Some provisions such as those found in Articles 1.1, 6, 8.1, and 27.2, 30 and 31 of TRIPS also confer some power on states to adopt some measures in national interests.

Recommendations have been made in the existing literature on options that may be explored to address the access to medicines challenge. Kathleen Liddell observes that there have recently been a number of initiatives and proposals designed to improve the fairness of the patents system.[32] Recent proposals also include compulsory patent licensing, patent pools,[33] research prizes[34] and the Health Impact Fund,[35] which Liddell described as '*extremely ambitious, requiring substantial donations of money from national government, a special administrative body to analyse the clinical value of inventions and voluntary participation*

31 *Biogen Inc. v Medeva Plc* [1997] RPC 1 citing R P Merges and R R Nelson 'On the Complex Economics of Patent scope' (1990) 90 *Columbia Law Review* 839.

32 K Liddell, 'The Health Impact Fund: A Critique' in T Pogge, M Rimmer & K Rubenstein (eds.), Incentives for Global Public Health: Patents Law and Access to Essential Medicines (Cambridge University Press, 2010) 155, 156.

33 See D Nicol and J Nielsen, 'Opening the Dam: Patent Pools, Innovation and Access to Essential Medicines' in T Pogge, M Rimmer & K Rubenstein (eds.), *Incentives for Global Public Health: Patents Law and Access to Essential Medicines* (Cambridge University Press, 2010) 235.

34 See W W Fisher & T Syed, 'A Prize System as a Partial Solution to the Health Crisis in the Developing World' in T Pogge, M Rimmer & K Rubenstein (eds.), *Incentives for Global Public Health: Patents Law and Access to Essential Medicines* (Cambridge University Press, 2010) 181.

35 See T Pogge, 'The Health Impact Fund: Better Pharmaceutical Innovations at Much Lower Prices in T Pogge, M Rimmer & K Rubenstein (eds.), *Incentives for Global Public Health: Patents Law and Access to Essential Medicines* (Cambridge University Press, 2010) 135.

of patent owners'.[36] Adusei observes, in relation to the access to medicines problem in Africa, that elaborate provisions in the statute books do not in themselves promote access to medicines unless those flexibilities are effectively utilised and he proceeds to recommend the exploitation of diverse regulatory mechanisms to promote access to antiretroviral medicines.[37] A study in the area has also suggested reforming the prevailing international paradigm for patent protection in the context of the WTO.[38]

The establishment of an African Economic Community or free trade area can boost the chances of developing a viable local manufacturing capacity in the continent. In this regard, the Treaty Establishing the African Economic Community can provide a useful guide towards mapping out the framework for an African Economic Community. Equally pertinent is the technology transfer package that is meant to come with the TRIPS Agreement. Although the extent to which developing and least developed countries can benefit from technical assistance and technology transfer under the TRIPS Agreement remains to be seen,[39] an economic coalition strategy under the African Union Commission may make it possible for African countries to negotiate technology transfer and licensing agreements that will boost industrial development in the continent.

1.4 The aim of this contribution

The effect of patent protection on access to medicine has already been studied extensively from a range of different standpoints. The TRIPS Agreement sets out a minimum standard of regulation. However, as rightly observed by Bernieri,[40] divergences of interest among different groups of countries with different degrees of development were and are still present in the dynamics of international regulation of IPRs. Whilst developed countries predicate the claim for higher IPR protection on the need to provide incentives for innovation, the less privileged nations tend to oppose stringent IPR protection on the basis that such tight measures will have severe effects on their ability to have access to medicine at affordable prices. The need to have access to medicines at affordable costs is undoubtedly a global issue albeit the severity of the problem is more prominent in developing countries.

36 Ibid.

37 P Adusei, 'Exploiting Patent Regulatory "Flexibilities" to Promote Access to Antiretroviral Medicines in Sub-Saharan Africa'(2011) 14(1) *Journal of World Intellectual Property* 1–20.

38 P Adusei, *Patenting Pharmaceuticals and Development in Sub-Saharan Africa* (Springer, 2013).

39 A M Pacon, 'What Will TRIPS Do For Developing Countries?' in F Beier and G Shricker (eds.), *From GATT to TRIPS – The Agreement on the Trade Related Aspects of Intellectual Property Rights* (VCH 1996) 329; D Matthews, 'TRIPS Flexibilities and Access to Medicines in Developing Countries: The Problem With Technical Assistance and Free Trade Agreements' (2005) *European Intellectual Property Review* 420.

40 R C Bernieri, 'Intellectual Property Rights in Bilateral Investment Treaties and Access to Medicines: The Case of Latin America' (2006) 9(5) *Journal of World Intellectual Property* 548, 572.

This work brings fresh perspectives into the patents and access to medicines problems as they affect the African continent. The work examines the TRIPS compulsory licensing regime and its connection with test data protection to assess the legal flexibilities and impediments to making pharmaceuticals available at affordable rates. The work also examines the TRIPS provision on exhaustion of IPRs and the benefits it may offer countries seeking access to patented pharmaceuticals at affordable rates. The legal frameworks for the rights to health and development in international law are considered to determine whether they can be relied on to provide further legal force to the case for a broad interpretation of the TRIPS flexibilities. Accordingly, the work argues that there is need for Africa to harness her resources together and take full advantage of all available options in WTO law and the general field of public international law in order to be able to provide real solutions to her access to medicines challenge. The book examines the implications of TRIPS-plus provisions in regional trade agreements and how they may affect access to medicines. The book underscores the importance of an African Free Trade Area or Economic Community, which will place the continent in a better position to effectively take advantage of the available options in public international law. The book notes the challenges the establishment of an African Economic Community might entail and recommends pursuing the goal of opening up Africa to free trade within the existing arrangement in the African Union.

The objective of the work is to identify the problems with the current legal regime in respect of pharmaceutical patents and the best way to remedy these without necessarily prejudicing the interest of the patent holders. This objective is addressed via the following components.

a An evaluation of the TRIPS regimes for compulsory licensing, test data protection, parallel importation, exhaustion of rights and an analysis of the extent to which these may ameliorate the plight of poor countries.
b A consideration of the relevance of international human rights law in interpreting the TRIPS flexibilities.
c A discussion of the implications of regional trade agreements for access to medicines in Africa.
d A discussion of the significance of an African Free Trade Area in maximising the benefits of the TRIPS flexibilities and promoting access to medicines in Africa.

This work investigates how Africa can adopt regional strategies to resolve the tension between intellectual property regimes and access to medicines. The work examines how African countries may effectively use IP to serve public health purposes through the stratagem of regional integration. The book explores the strategies and measures that may be adopted through regional framework in Africa to utilise the various TRIPS flexibilities and international human rights law to promote access to medicines and domestic pharmaceutical manufacturing in Africa.

Bibliography

Abbott F M, 'The WTO Medicines Decision' (2005) 99 *American Journal of International Law* 317.
Access to Medicines Foundation, *The 2016 Access to Medicine Index: Methodology* 2015.
Adusei P, *Patenting Pharmaceuticals and Development in Sub-Saharan Africa* (Springer, 2013).
Adusei P, 'Exploiting Patent Regulatory 'Flexibilities' to Promote Access to Antiretroviral Medicines in Sub-Saharan Africa' (2011) 14(1) *Journal of World Intellectual Property* 1.
Anderson H E Jr, 'We Can Work It Out: Co-operative Compulsory Licensing as the Way Forward in Improving Access to Anti-Retroviral Drugs' (2010) 16 *Boston University Journal of Science and Technology Law* 167.
Baker B K, 'Trans-Pacific Partnership Provisions in Intellectual Property, Transparency, and Investment Chapters Threaten Access to Medicines in the US and Elsewhere' (2016) 13 (3) *PLoS Med* 1–7.
Bartelt S, 'Compulsory Licenses Pursuant to TRIPS Article 31 in the Light of the Doha Declaration on the TRIPS Agreement and Public Health' (2003) 6 (2) *Journal of World Intellectual Property* 284.
Bernieri R C, 'Intellectual Property Rights in Bilateral Investment Treaties and Access to Medicines: The Case of Latin America' (2006) 9(5) *Journal of World Intellectual Property* 548.
Boulet P, Garrison C, & t'Hoen E, *Drug Patents under the Spotlight* (Médecins Sans Frontières, 2003).
Burstein M J, 'Exchanging Information Without Intellectual Property' (2012) 91 *Texas Law Review* 227.
Cornish W & Llewelyn D, *Intellectual Property: Patents, Copyright, Trade Marks and Allied Rights* (London Sweet & Maxwell, 6th ed., 2007).
Correa C M, *Intellectual Property, WTO and Developing Countries: The Trips Agreement and Policy Options* (TWN 2000).
Council for TRIPS: Extension of the Transition Period under Article 66.1 for Least Developed Country Members IP/C/64 (Decision of the Council For Trips of 11 June 2013).
Council for TRIPS: Extension of the Transitional Period under Article 66.1 of the TRIPS Agreement for Least Developed Country Members for Certain Obligations with Respect to Pharmaceutical Products IP/C/73 (6 November 2015).
DiMasi J A, Hansen R W & Grabowski H G, 'The Price of Innovation: New Estimates of Drug Development Costs' (2003) 22 *Journal of Health Economics* 151.
Drahos P with Braithwaite J, *Information Feudalism: Who Owns the Knowledge Economy?*, (The New Press, 2002).
El Said M & Kapczynski A, *Access to Medicines: The Role of Intellectual Property Law and Policy*. Working Paper prepared for the Third Meeting of the Technical Advisory Group of the Global Commission on HIV and the Law, 7–9 July 2011.
Fisher W W & Syed T, 'A Prize System as a Partial Solution to the Health Crisis in the Developing World' in T Pogge, M Rimmer & K Rubenstein (eds.), *Incentives for Global Public Health: Patents Law and Access to Essential Medicines* (Cambridge University Press, 2010) 181.
George E, 'The Human Rights to Health and HIV/AIDS: South Africa and South-South Co-operation to Reframe Global Intellectual Property Principles and Promote Access to Essential Medicines' (2011) 18 *Indiana Journal of Global Legal Studies* 168.
Ghanotakis E, 'How the US Interpretation of Flexibilities Inherent in TRIPS affects Access to Medicines for Developing Countries' (2004) 7(4) *Journal of World Intellectual Property* 563.

Islam M T, 'TRIPS Agreement and Public Health: Implications and Challenges for Bangladesh' (2011) 17 *International Trade Law and Regulation* 10.

Liddell K, 'The Health Impact Fund: A Critique' in T Pogge, M Rimmer & K Rubenstein (eds.), *Incentives for Global Public Health: Patents Law and Access to Essential Medicines* (Cambridge University Press, 2010).

Matilal S, 'Do Developing Countries Need a Pharmaceutical Data – Exclusivity Regime?'(2010) 32(6) *European Intellectual Property Review* 268.

Matthews D, 'TRIPS Flexibilities and Access to Medicines in Developing Countries: The Problem with Technical Assistance and Free Trade Agreements' (2005) 27(11) *European Intellectual Property Review* 420.

Merges R P & Nelson R R, 'On the Complex Economics of Patent Scope' (1990) 90 *Columbia Law Review* 839.

Moon S, *Pharmaceutical Production and Related Technology Transfer* (World Health Organization, 2011).

Nicol D & Nielsen J, 'Opening the Dam: Patent Pools, Innovation and Access to Essential Medicines' in T Pogge, M Rimmer & K Rubenstein (eds.), *Incentives for Global Public Health: Patents Law and Access to Essential Medicines* (Cambridge University Press, 2010).

Nicol D & Owoeye O, 'Using TRIPS Flexibilities to Facilitate Access to Medicines' (2013) 91(7) *Bulletin of the World Health Organization* 533.

Oliveira M A, Bermudez J A, Chaves G C, Velásquez G, 'Has the Implementation of the TRIPS Agreement in Latin America and the Caribbean Produced Intellectual Property Legislation that Favours Public Health?' (2004) 82 *Bull World Health Organ* 815.

Owoeye O, 'International Patents Law and Public Health: Revisiting the TRIPS Compulsory Licensing Regime and the Doha Paragraph-6 System' (2015) 37 (12) *European Intellectual Property Review* 782.

Owoeye O & Oduwole J, Development, 'Access to Medicines and the Ebola Virus Epidemic in West Africa' (2017) 24 *Journal of Law and Medicine* 722.

Owoeye O, Olatunji O, Faturoti B, 'Patents and the Trans-Pacific Partnership: Do the Existing Flexibilities offer much to LDCs in the East African Community?'. (2017) *International Trade Journal* 1–22 doi:10.1080/08853908.2017.1386143 accessed 27 January 2019.

Pacon A M, 'What Will TRIPS Do For Developing Countries?' in F Beier & G Shricker (eds.), *From GATT to TRIPS – The Agreement on the Trade Related Aspects of Intellectual Property Rights* (VCH 1996) 329.

Pires de Carvalho N, *The TRIPS Regime of Patent Rights* (Kluwer Law International, 2nd ed., 2005) 337.

Pogge T, 'The Health Impact Fund: Better Pharmaceutical Innovations at Much Lower Prices' in T Pogge, M Rimmer & K Rubenstein (eds.), *Incentives for Global Public Health: Patents Law and Access to Essential Medicines* (Cambridge University Press, 2010) 135.

Roumet R, 'Access to Patented Anti – HIV/AIDS Medicines: The South African Experience' (2010) 32(3) *European Intellectual Property Review* 137.

Sustainable Development Knowledge Platform: Sustainable Development Goal 3 available at https://sustainabledevelopment.un.org/sdg3 accessed 27 January 2019.

UNAIDS, Global AIDS Update 2016.

UN Secretary-General's High-Level Panel on Access to Medicines Report September 2016.

World Trade Organization, Amendment of the TRIPS Agreement, www.wto.org/english/tratop_e/trips_e/amendment_e.htm accessed 28 January 2019.

World Health Organization, Tuberculosis Report 2018.

World Health Organization, World Health Statistics 2017.

2 The TRIPS compulsory licensing regime and access to medicines

2.1 Introduction

The compulsory licensing regime established under the Agreement on Trade Related Aspects of Intellectual Property Rights (TRIPS Agreement) has been the subject of immense controversy. This is chiefly due to the various requirements attached to its use that make it difficult to take advantage of the system without being accused of running afoul of the TRIPS Agreement.[1] The use of compulsory licences has always been attended with significant opposition by the parties owning the intellectual property rights (IPRs) in the products being compulsorily licensed. This makes it increasingly difficult to identify with real certainty circumstances under which compulsory licences may be issued without attracting significant opposition from companies with intellectual property (IP) intensive services. Indeed, discussions about the relevance of compulsory licences remain largely multifaceted and highly topical.[2] This chapter provides an insight into the TRIPS compulsory licensing regime.

Compulsory licensing can be defined as an authorisation by the government to use patented products without the consent of the holder of the patent right.[3] Compulsory licenses allow a country to use a patented article without the permission of the right holder at a lower royalty rate imposed by the government.[4]

1 N Ansari, 'International Patent Rights in a Post-Doha World' (2002) 11 *International Trade Law Journal* 57, 60; J Burton-Macleod, 'Thai Compulsory Licenses Redefine Essential Medicines Debate' in T Pogge et al. (eds.), *Incentives for Global Public Health: Patents Law and Access to Essential Medicines* (Cambridge University Press, 2010), 406.

2 R A Epstein & F S Kieff, 'The Licensing of Intellectual Property: Questioning the Frequency and Wisdom of Compulsory Licensing for Pharmaceutical Patents' (2011) 78 *University of Chicago Law Review* 71.

3 See H Hestermeyer, *Human Rights and the WTO: The Case of Patents and Access to Medicines* (Oxford University Press, 2007) 239.

4 C M Ho, 'Patent Breaking or Balancing?: Separating Strands of Fact from Fiction under TRIPS' (2009) 34 *North Carolina Journal of International Law & Commercial Regulation* 371, 373.

Compulsory licences can be granted for use by the government, by its agents or by third parties.[5] Thus, private individuals or corporate bodies may also have compulsory licences issued in their favour. Compulsory licences may be issued for a range of purposes, including meeting the demand for a patented product in a domestic market, enhancing competition by aiding the growth of domestic competitors, or facilitating the development or establishment of a domestic market.[6] Compulsory licensing may also be used to protect the public interest especially in cases of public health emergencies or to act as a safeguard against abuses that may arise from the monopoly rights conferred by patents.[7] Thus, compulsory licences can be used to control abuse of market power especially where the innovator is using IPRs to impose higher prices and restrict access to new technologies.[8]

Article 31 of the TRIPS Agreement, which provides for compulsory patent licensing, states that goods made pursuant to a compulsory licence must be predominantly for the domestic market. The concern is that countries lacking a manufacturing capacity in the pharmaceutical sector will be deprived of the ability to use the TRIPS compulsory licensing provision, in particular where it is being sought for the purposes of manufacturing generic versions of medicines that are the subject of patent protection. The WTO Ministers acknowledged this as a major issue deserving special attention in the Doha Declaration on TRIPS and Public Health (the Doha Declaration) and mandated the Council for TRIPS to find a solution to the problem. This led to the adoption of the Decision of 30 August 2003 on Implementation of Paragraph 6 of the Doha Declaration on the TRIPS Agreement and Public Health (the Implementation Decision) and culminated in the adoption of the Protocol Amending TRIPS.

This chapter traces the history of compulsory licensing of patents and how it became part of the TRIPS Agreement after a series of intensely negotiated deliberations. The circumstances that culminated in the emergence of the Doha Declaration, the Implementation Decision and Protocol Amending TRIPS are then discussed to provide an insight into the legal framework for the use of compulsory licensing by countries without local manufacturing capacity in the pharmaceutical sector.

2.1.1 Compulsory licensing in historical context

IP has been an instrument of public policy used by States since the 14th century to enhance technology transfer through the mechanisms of incentives and local

5 N Pires de Carvalho, *The TRIPS Regime of Patent Rights* (Kluwer Law International, 2nd edition, 2005) 315.

6 See Hestermeyer, above n 3.

7 W Cornish & D Llewelyn, *Intellectual Property: Patents, Copyright, Trade Marks and Allied Rights* (London Sweet & Maxwell, 6th ed., 2007) 295.

8 Jack Brodsky, 'The Health of Ebay: The Impact of Ebay on the Future of TRIPS-Like Pharmaceutical Compulsory Licenses in the United States' (2015) 41 *American Journal of Law & Medicine* 656, 660.

working requirements.[9] Historically, the world's first patent legislation was enacted in Venice in 1474.[10] It reads:

> WE HAVE among us men of great genius, apt to invent and discover ingenious devices; and in view of the grandeur and virtue of our City, more such men come to us from divers parts. Now if provisions were made for the works and devices discovered by such persons, so that others who may see them could not build them and take the inventor's honor away, more men would then apply their genius, would discover, and would build devices of great utility and benefit to our Commonwealth.
>
> Therefore:
>
> BE IT ENACTED that, by the authority of this Council, every person who shall build any new and ingenious device in this City, not previously made in this Commonwealth, shall give notice of it to the office of our General Welfare Board when it has been reduced to perfection so that it can be used and operated. It being forbidden to every other person in any of our territories and towns to make any further device conforming with and similar to said one, without the consent and license of the author, for the term of 10 years. And if anybody builds it in violation hereof, the aforesaid author and inventor shall be entitled to have him summoned before any magistrate of this City, by which Magistrate the said infringer shall be constrained to pay him [one] hundred ducats; and the device shall be destroyed at once. It being, however, within the power and discretion of the Government, in its activities, to take and use any such device and instrument, with this condition however that no one but the author shall operate it.[11]

As is evident from the above extract, the law established a system of granting 10-year monopoly rights to inventors of new arts and machines. Its aim was to encourage new inventions for the common good, but at the same time an attempt was made to introduce a balance by allowing the government to take and use any of these new inventions, subject to the condition that no one but the patentee should operate them.

The English patent system has its roots in State patronage or royal privileges.[12] Thus, although English patents were already being granted prior to the passage of the Statute of Monopolies in 1624,[13] that statute was the first substantive English legislation dealing with patent law. Its main purpose was to check abuse of the King's royal prerogative to grant monopolies as its first section rendered all mo-

9 S Sell, 'Intellectual Property at a Crossroads: The Use of Past in Intellectual Property Jurisprudence: Intellectual Property and Public Policy in Historical Perspective: Contestation and Settlement' (2004) 38 *Loyola of Los Angeles Law Review* 267, 273.

10 Hestermeyer, above n 3, 22.

11 Patent Statute of Venice 1474.

12 Cornish & Llewelyn, above n 7; T B Nachbar, 'Monopoly, Mercantilism, and the Politics of Regulation' (2005) 91 *Virginia Law Review* 1313, 1320–1321.

13 C Dent, '"Generally Inconvenient": The 1624 Statute of Monopolies as Political Compromise' (2009) 33 *Melbourne University Law Review* 415, 420.

nopolies illegal, with the later sections making exceptions. Patents for inventions were one such exception. Section 6 of the statute provided that the declaration that all monopolies are contrary to the 'Laws of the Realm' shall not apply to:

> ...Letters Patents and Grants of Privilege for the Term of fourteen Years or under, hereafter to be made, of the sole Working or Making of any manner of new Manufacture within this Realm, to the true and first Inventor and Inventors of such manufactures, which others at the Time of making such Letters Patents and Grants shall not use, so as also they be not contrary to the Law, nor mischievous to the State, by raising Prices of Commodities at home, or Hurt of Trade, or generally inconvenient...[14]

Although the 1624 Statute of Monopolies did not mention compulsory licensing, it did prohibit the use of patents in a way that was '*mischievous to the State, by raising Prices of Commodities at home, or Hurt of Trade, or generally inconvenient*', grounds which today constitute the basic rationale for the grant of compulsory licences. The use of the monopoly rights granted by the statute in a way that is prejudicial to trade or 'generally inconvenient' would result in the forfeiture of the rights conferred given the tenor of Section 6 of the Statute of Monopolies. Thus, under the statute, where the monopoly rights conferred by patents result in anticompetitive prices or abuse of market power, the right conferred would be forfeited and the invention could be exploited by others.

The next reported patent legislation after the English Statute of Monopolies was the French patent law of 1771.[15] The first reported attempt to legislate compulsory licensing in the US was in the form of an unsuccessful bill presented before the US congress in 1790, proposing the issuance of compulsory licences should a patentee refuse to provide adequate supply of the patented invention or charge inordinate prices.[16] The US eventually passed its first patent law in 1773. Patent laws subsequently spread to other nations. Machlup and Penrose reported that patent legislations:

> ...were enacted in Austria in 1810, Russia in 1812, Prussia in 1815, Belgium and the Netherlands in 1817, Spain in 1820, Bavaria in 1825, Sardinia in 1826, the Vatican State in 1833, Sweden in 1834, Wiirttemberg in 1836, Portugal in 1837, and Saxonia in 1843.[17]

In the international scene, business leaders in the 19th century began to press for higher standards of patent protection for the outcomes of corporate research and

14 Statute of Monopolies 1624, (UK) James 1, s 6.

15 F Machlup & E Penrose, 'The Patent Controversy in the Nineteenth Century' (1950) 10(1) *The Journal of Economic History* 1, 3.

16 E T Penrose, *The Economics of the International Patent System* (Baltimore: Johns Hopkins Press, 1951) 165–166.

17 Machlup & Penrose, above n 15, 3.

development that attended the industrial revolution.[18] This eventuated in the emergence of the Paris Convention for the Protection of Industrial Property (originally concluded by eleven countries) which formed a foundation for subsequent international patent rights agreements. At the 1873 Vienna Congress, one of the preliminary negotiation rounds for the Paris Convention, it was resolved by the parties that compulsory licences should be available where required in the public interest.[19]

Compulsory licensing did not, however, appear in the Paris Convention until the conclusion of the 1925 Revision Conference of The Hague.[20] Today, the Paris Convention confers substantive IP protection on the works of inventors in foreign countries and allows a government to grant a third party the right to use the patent without the consent of the patentee in order to prevent an abuse of the system.[21] Article 5(A) (2)-(4) of the Paris Convention provides the framework for compulsory licensing under the Convention in the following terms:

> each country of the Union shall have the right to take legislative measures providing for the grant of compulsory licenses to prevent the abuses which might result from the exercise of the exclusive rights conferred by the patent, for example, failure to work.[22]

The language of Article 5A(2) suggests that the only ground for compulsory licensing explicitly recognised by the Paris Convention is failure to work the patent locally.

Local working requirements oblige the patentee who desires to maintain exclusive rights to exploit the patented invention to do so by manufacturing the patented product or applying the patented process in the country granting the patent right.[23] Although there was no provision for compulsory licensing in the international patent system until 1925, history reveals that the system always recognised the need for qualifying the rights conferred on patentees in order to prevent abuse through mechanisms such as forfeiture or some other form of restriction on the rights conferred.[24] Rather than an outright forfeiture of patent rights, the compulsory licensing regime today under the TRIPS Agreement makes it possible for patentees to still get some compensation for the 'unauthorised' exploitation of their inventions through a compulsory licence.[25]

18 Sell, above n 9, 291.

19 Penrose, above n 15, 47.

20 M Halewood, 'Regulating Patent Holders: Local Working Requirements and Compulsory Licenses at International Law' (1997) 35 (2) *Osgoode Hall Law Journal* 243, 266.

21 Paris Convention for the Protection of Industrial Property, opened for signature 20 March 1883, 161 CTS 409 (entered into force 6 July 1884) Article 5 (A) (2).

22 Ibid.

23 B Mercurio & M Tyagi, 'Treaty Interpretation in WTO Dispute Settlement: The Outstanding Question of the Legality of Local Working Requirements' (2010) 19 *Minnesota Journal of International Law* 275, 281.

24 Before 1925, the only remedy for non-working pursuant to the Paris Convention was forfeiture by virtue of Article 5 Paris Convention, 1883, Article 5 Paris Convention (Brussels Revision, 1900), Article 5 Paris Convention (Washington Revision, 1911).

25 Article 31(h) of the TRIPS Agreement provides that the patentee shall be adequately remunerated whenever a compulsory license is granted.

2.1.2 Compulsory licensing under TRIPS: the negotiations

An understanding of the TRIPS compulsory licensing regime requires an examination of the circumstances that led to its emergence. The TRIPS Agreement became part of the agenda for the GATT Uruguay Round for trade discussion partly through the significant influence of two important American lobbying groups: the Intellectual Property Committee (consisting of chief executive officers from selected economically influential American-based multinational corporations) and the International Intellectual Property Alliance.[26] At the launch of the Uruguay Round at Punta del Este in September 1986, the US and Japan submitted proposals covering all IPRs to the Round's preparatory committee whilst parallel proposals from Brazil and Argentina opposed the inclusion of IP in the new Round.[27] At the end of the September 1986 Punta del Este negotiations, the 'trade-related aspects of intellectual property rights, including trade in counterfeit goods', were part of the Ministerial Declaration on the Uruguay Round of 20 September 1986.[28]

During the 1989 TRIPS Negotiating Group's deliberations, compulsory licensing was already at centre stage with Brazil and Korea making a strong case for its inclusion.[29] The US, in tandem with the European Community, sought to limit the use of compulsory licensing by Member States and to impose the payment of remuneration to the patent holder in each case where a licence was granted.[30] The US initially sought to expressly limit the use of compulsory licensing to cases of antitrust violation and national emergency. Thus, Article 27 of the Draft Agreement on Trade Related Aspects of Intellectual Property, Communication from the US stated:

> Contracting Parties may limit the patent owner's exclusive rights solely through compulsory licenses and only to remedy an adjudicated violation of competition laws or to address, only during its existence a declared national emergency.[31]

The above provision was undoubtedly very restrictive, and it was opposed by developing countries that viewed the proposals presented by the developed

26 S K Sell, 'Post-TRIPS Developments: The Tension between Commercial and Social Agendas in the Context of Intellectual Property' (2002) 14 *Florida Journal of International Law* 193, 194; P Drahos with J Braithwaite, *Information Feudalism: Who Owns the Knowledge Economy?* (The New Press, New York, 2002) 91.

27 See D Gervais, *The TRIPS Agreement: Drafting History and Analysis* (Sweet and Maxwell, Thomson Reuters 3rd edition, 2008) 11.

28 *GATT Ministerial Declaration on the Uruguay Round*, GATT/WTO Doc MIN (86)/W/19 (Ministerial Declaration of 20 September 1986).

29 Gervais, above n 27, 16.

30 See E T Penrose, 'The Economics of the International Patent System', in F. Abbot et al, *The International Intellectual Property System: Commentary and Materials* (Kluwer Law International, The Hague, Part 1, 1999) 635.

31 *Draft Agreement on Trade Related Aspects of Intellectual Property, Communication from the US*, GATT Doc. No. MTN.GNG/NG11/W/70 (11 May 1990).

countries as being overprotective of IPRs with little regard for the interest of consumers.[32] As observed by Gold and Lam:

> In particular, developed and developing countries argued over whether it was necessary to engage in negotiations with the patent holder prior to issuing compulsory licenses granted in the public interest. It was this argument that set the stage for the current article 31 of TRIPS...[33]

Compulsory licensing was thus viewed by most developing countries as an indispensable weapon to prevent the abuse of patent rights whilst enhancing competition in domestic markets.[34] During the TRIPS negotiations, India, in particular, argued that members should be free to specify the grounds for granting compulsory licences and the automatic grant of such licences should be available to developing countries in sectors of critical importance to them.[35] To counter this, a 'prior negotiation' requirement was included in TRIPS requiring those seeking compulsory licences to have made reasonable efforts to negotiate voluntary licences.[36]

At the end of 1991, India still refused to accept the TRIPS 'package' because it was concerned about the restrictions on compulsory licensing especially where the patent was not 'worked' in the country conferring the right.[37] This was heavily influenced by the fact that India had a very strong generic pharmaceutical manufacturing industry which would be significantly affected by the TRIPS minimum standards for IP protection. Writing on how India came to accept the TRIPS package, Chopra thus observed:

> Later, however, due to an economic slowdown in the late 1980s, India reversed its anti-IP stance. Fearing trade barriers to its exports, withdrawal of textile tariff concessions, suspension of economic aid, etc., India signed the Trade-Related Aspects of Intellectual Property Rights (TRIPS) Agreement on April 15, 1994, and subsequently, on January 1, 1995, it became a member of the World Trade Organization (WTO).[38]

32 See A M Pacon, 'What Will TRIPS Do for Developing Countries?' In F Beier, & G Schricker (eds.) *From GATT to TRIPS – The Agreement on Trade Related Aspects of Intellectual Property Rights, IIC Studies: Studies in Industrial Property and Copyright Law* (VCH Verlagsgesellschaft mbH, Munich, 1996).

33 E R Gold & D K Lam, 'Balancing Trade in Patents, Public Non- Commercial Use and Compulsory Licensing', (2003) 6(1) *Journal of World Intellectual Property* 5, 16.

34 See Pacon, above n 32.

35 See GATT Secretariat, *Synoptic Tables Setting out Existing International Standards and Proposed Standards and Principles*, MTN.GNG/NG11/W/32/Rev.2, 99–103 (February 1990).

36 See Article 31(b) TRIPS Agreement.

37 Gervais, above n 27.

38 See Madhavi "Mira" Chopra, Of the Big Daddy, the Underdog, the Mother Hen, and the Scapegoats: Balancing Pharmaceutical Innovation and Access to Healthcare in the Enforcement of

It has been observed that the extent of the working obligations imposed on a patentee was one of the most controversial issues in negotiating the Agreement. This is evident in the language of compromise contained in Article 27.1 of TRIPS,[39] which provides that patents shall be available and the rights enjoyable without discrimination as to whether the products are imported or manufactured locally. Whilst this provision seems to expressly oust the ability of Members to refuse to grant patents or to issue compulsory licences for failure to work locally, the position, as shown below, is less straightforward than it might appear.

What eventually emerged at the end of the negotiations was Article 31 of the TRIPS Agreement, which represented a compromise between the conflicting interests of the developed and developing countries. Developing countries accepted TRIPS, no doubt hoping it would give them better access to international trade through the WTO[40] and probably thinking it would allow greater flexibility in the national interest, given the TRIPS recognition of social policy goals and certain exceptions to patents rights.[41] It is generally believed that TRIPS does attempt to strike a balance between the interest of society in spurring innovation through economic incentives as well as the desires of users for liberal access, and that compulsory licensing is one of the ways for achieving this balance.[42] Compulsory licensing under TRIPS can be a means of striking a balance between the interest of the right holders and the social objectives of protecting access provided the necessary structures for its effective utilisation exist.

The TRIPS compulsory licensing regime provides clear parameters for the grant of compulsory licences which are arguably not only strong enough to check any potential or real abuse of the patent system but also sufficient to address a public health emergency. The problem, it appears, is with the strict interpretation of the TRIPS Agreement generally favoured by pharmaceutical companies. Mace has argued that, given the drafting history of the TRIPS compulsory licensing regime, a more plausible interpretation of Article 31 is that it was meant to discourage the intentional infringement of pharmaceutical patents and prevent the use of compulsory licensing in a way unreasonably favourable to domestic interests.[43]

Compulsory Patent Licensing in India, its Compliance with TRIPS, and Bayer V. Natco (2015) 13 *Santa Clara Journal of International Law* 333, 341–342.

39 C M Correa, *Trade Related Aspects of Intellectual Property Rights: A Commentary on the TRIPS Agreement* (Oxford University Press, 2007) 318.

40 R L Gana (Okediji), 'The Myth of Development, the Progress of Rights: Human Rights to Intellectual Property and Development' (1996) 18 *Law & Policy* 315, 334; D P Harris, 'Carrying a Good Joke Too Far: TRIPS and Treaties of Adhesion' (2006) 27 *University of Pennsylvania Journal of International Economic Law* 681, 724–738; A Reich, 'The WTO as a Law Harmonising Institution'(2004) 25 *University of Pennsylvania Journal of International Economic Law* 321, 362.

41 D Borges Barbosa et al., 'Slouching Towards Development in International Intellectual Property' (2007) *Michigan State Law Review* 71, 110.

42 G Scott, 'A Protocol for Evaluating Changing Global Attitudes toward Innovation and Intellectual Property Regimes' (2011) 32 *University of Pennsylvania Journal of Intellectual Property Law* 1165, 1250.

43 A C Mace, 'TRIPS, EBAY, and Denials of Injunctive Relief: Is Article 31 Compliance Everything?' (2009) 10 *Columbia Science and Technology Law Review*, 232, 248–249.

In sum, Article 31 of TRIPS provides the framework for compulsory licensing under the Agreement, although via the phrase 'use without authorization'. Under Article 31, compulsory licences can be used to advance social policy goals by making essential goods available at affordable rates where the manufacturer is unwilling or unable to do so at a rate within the purchasing power of the populace of a country. This was reinforced by the Doha Declaration of 2001, the Implementation Decision of 2003 and the Protocol Amending TRIPS.[44] In particular, the Implementation Decision provided for legal changes to make it easier for countries without manufacturing capacity to import cheaper generics made under compulsory licensing.

It has however been posited by a commentator that 'the actual implementation of compulsory licensing for the public good has been disappointing and its true potential is largely unrealised'.[45] This statement is hardly contestable having regard to the fact that virtually all countries that have made use of compulsory licences to address their public health problems have found a way into the US Special 301 trade-sanction list and countries without pharmaceutical manufacturing capacity may find it extremely difficult to meet the requirements for using the system to import products manufactured for them by other countries. On the other hand, there is equally the argument that while compulsory licensing may provide short-term solution to challenges relating to the availability of medicines at affordable prices, it can be a real impediment to pharmaceutical innovation.[46] A discussion of the requirement of compulsory licensing is nonetheless instructive in evaluating how the TRIPS Agreement addresses the issue.

2.2 The scope of compulsory licensing under TRIPS Article 31

Article 31 of the TRIPS Agreement defines the scope for compulsory licensing under the Agreement by allowing the use of the subject matter of a patent without the authorisation of the right holder, including use by the government, or third parties authorised by the government where the law of that Member allows it. The TRIPS Agreement provides that each case of compulsory licensing shall be considered on its merits.[47] Thus, Members cannot make laws that empower them to automatically issue compulsory licences as a matter of course.[48] The requirement that every application for a compulsory licence shall be considered

44 See Section 2.3.

45 D R Cahoy, 'Breaking Patents' (2011) 32 *Michigan Journal of International Law* 461, 466.

46 B A McDonald, V Ugryumov, & D Kolesnikov, 'Compulsory Licensing of Pharmaceutical Patents in the Russian Federation Threatens Foreign & Domestic Drug Developers' (2018) *AIPLA Quarterly Journal*, 1, 10.

47 *Marrakesh Agreement Establishing the World Trade Organisation*, opened for signature 15 April 1994, 1867 UNTS3 (entered into force 1 January 1995) Annex 1 C (*Agreement on Trade Related Aspects of Intellectual Property Rights*, Article 31(a).

48 See Pires de Carvalho, above n 5, 318.

on its own merits entails taking into account the peculiar facts of each case in determining whether the licence is to be issued or not and the value of remuneration to be paid.

With the exception of semiconductor technology which can only be the subject of compulsory licensing in the event of public non-commercial use or anticompetitive practice,[49] the TRIPS Agreement does not explicitly limit the grounds on which a compulsory licence may be granted. It has been argued that the fact that Article 31 does not define the grounds for the grant of compulsory licences does not mean they can be granted on frivolous grounds as they are meant for use only in exceptional circumstances when serious reasons exist for the grant.[50] This interpretation cannot, however, be supported by Article 31(b) which requires that a voluntary licence be sought from the right holder before a compulsory licence can be pursued. Further, Article 31(b) only waives the prior negotiation requirement in cases of national emergency, circumstances of extreme urgency and for public non-commercial use. Accordingly, the TRIPS Agreement does not limit compulsory licensing to these grounds. It appears, to the extent that a voluntary licence negotiation has been unsuccessful, a party may apply for a compulsory licence under the TRIPS Agreement even if the circumstances are not exceptional. All that is required is to adhere strictly to the conditions expressly set out in Article 31.

It has also been argued that Article 30 of the TRIPS Agreement places a limit on the right of Members to issue compulsory licences as Article 30 requires Members to ensure compulsory licensing does not 'unreasonably conflict with a normal exploitation of the patent'.[51] To determine whether Article 30 of TRIPS places some restriction on the issuance of compulsory licences pursuant to Article 31(b), it is important to carefully consider the provision of Article 30 of the TRIPS Agreement. Article 30 of the TRIPS Agreement provides thus:

> **Article 30 – Exceptions to Rights Conferred**
> Members may provide limited exceptions to the exclusive rights conferred by a patent, provided that such exceptions do not unreasonably conflict with a normal exploitation of the patent and do not unreasonably prejudice the legitimate interests of the patent owner, taking account of the legitimate interests of third parties.

49 TRIPS Agreement above n. 51 Article 31(c).

50 See Article 31(b) TRIPS Agreement; Pires de Carvalho, above n 6, 317; In the words of the author: 'Compulsory licenses are exceptions to patent rights and, as such, should be kept exceptional. In the light of Article 7, and taking into account paragraph 4 of the Preamble, the balance between rights and obligations cannot be obtained by diminishing the rights of the patent holders without accruing to the collective interests of society. In other words, the individual rights of patent owners may not be diminished for the benefit of individuals only. Only social and collective interests justify the grant of compulsory licenses'.

51 B A McDonald, V Ugryumov, & D Kolesnikov, 'Compulsory Licensing of Pharmaceutical Patents in the Russian Federation Threatens Foreign & Domestic Drug Developers' (2018) *AIPLA Quarterly Journal* 1, 19.

The first important point to note on whether Article 30 imposes further restrictions on Article 31 of the TRIPS Agreement is the fact that Article 31 is a provision that deals with exceptions to the exclusive rights conferred by patents other than those addressed by Article 30. Hence, Article 31 specifically states that its provisions deal with "Other Use Without Authorization of the Right Holder". This position was further confirmed by the WTO Panel in Canada – Pharmaceutical Patents, where the Panel thus observed:

> Articles 30 and 31 are linked together by the opening words of Article 31 which define the scope of Article 31 in terms of exceptions not covered by Article 30.[52]

It is also important to note that footnote 7 to Article 31 of the TRIPS Agreement states that 'other use' under that Article 'refers to use other than that allowed under Article 30'.[53] Article 30 of the TRIPS Agreement is generally believed to apply to experimental use and 'Bolar' exceptions. As succinctly put by Carlos Correa, exceptions available under Article 30 'may include, for instance, acts of experimentation and the request for marketing approval of a pharmaceutical product before the expiration of the patent (known as the "Bolar exception")'.[54] Consequently, Article 30 of the TRIPS Agreement does not impose further conditions on the grant of compulsory licences under the TRIPS Agreement beyond the conditions set out in Article 31 of the Agreement.

The party seeking a compulsory licence under the system must first initiate efforts to obtain authorisation from the patent owner on reasonable commercial terms and conditions and it may only apply for a compulsory licence where such efforts have not been successful within 'a reasonable period of time'.[55] The TRIPS Agreement does not contain a definition of what constitutes 'reasonable commercial terms' or a 'reasonable period of time' and it has been suggested that this should be within the purview of national law and practices.[56] Some commentators have argued that the expression sets an objective standard and its interpretation should be subject to two tests.[57] First, no offer should be considered reasonable if it does not cover the production and distribution cost of the patented product in the host country. Secondly, terms cannot be commercially favourable if they provide the host country with a deal that is unequivocally

52 Panel Report, Canada – Pharmaceutical Patents, Paragraph. 7.90.

53 TRIPS Agreement Article 31, footnote 7.

54 C M Correa, *Implications of the Doha Declaration on the TRIPS Agreement and Public Health* (World Health Organization, 2002) 28.

55 TRIPS Agreement Article 31(b).

56 Correa *Trade Related Aspects of Intellectual Property Rights: A Commentary on the TRIPS Agreement* (n 39), 320; Pires de Carvalho, above n 5, 319.

57 See e.g. R A Epstein & F S Kieff, 'The Licensing of Intellectual Property: Questioning the Frequency and Wisdom of Compulsory Licensing for Pharmaceutical Patents' (2011) 78 *University of Chicago Law Review* 71, 74.

more favourable *'than those that have been negotiated in voluntary markets by other countries within the same economic class as the host country'*.[58]

Whilst the first test seems to fall within the definition of reasonable commercial terms, the same cannot be said of the second. Two countries can be in the same 'economic class', in the sense of being grouped as either developed or developing, and still have different standards of living. Since TRIPS has left the question of 'reasonable commercial terms' undefined after the intensely negotiated Uruguay Round deliberations, it will be most appropriate not to set a general standard for the term as what can be a reasonable commercial term in one context may not be so in another. Indeed, it has been opined that the definition of 'reasonable commercial terms' and conditions is deliberately vague to allow each case to be determined on its merits.[59] It is therefore more desirable to leave this within the purview of national law and practices. A Member may, however, dispense with prior negotiations in cases of national emergency, extreme urgency or public non-commercial use provided that the right holder is promptly notified of the authorisation in the case of public non-commercial use and within a reasonable time in all other cases.[60]

The use of an invention made under a compulsory licence is required to be limited to the purpose for which it was authorised, and in the case of semiconductor technology such use should be for public non-commercial purposes or to restrain anticompetitive practices.[61] This implies that there must be a purpose for seeking the compulsory licence; such purpose could include the failure or unwillingness to make the goods available in sufficient quantity in the country where the licence is sought or failure to work the patent locally. Rights acquired under the compulsory licensing regime are required to be non-exclusive[62] and non-assignable.[63] The licensee is thus barred from transferring the licence or sub-licensing.[64] The right of the patent holder to continue to exploit their invention is therefore still at large.

One of the most significant limitations on compulsory licensing is found in Article 31(f), requiring that use shall be authorised predominantly for the supply of the domestic market of the Member authorising such use.[65] Since the language of the provision is that the use must 'predominantly' be for the supply of local market, this does suggest that a 'non predominant' part can be exported.[66] This is nonetheless one of the most controversial provisions of Article 31, and, as noted above, its implications for countries without significant pharmaceutical

58 Ibid.
59 See Hestermeyer above n 3, 246
60 TRIPS Agreement, Article 31(b).
61 TRIPS Agreement, Article 31(c).
62 TRIPS Agreement, Article 31(d).
63 TRIPS Agreement, Article 31(e).
64 See Pires de Carvalho above n 5, 328.
65 TRIPS Agreement Article 31(f).
66 F M Abbott, 'The WTO Medicines Decision: World Pharmaceutical Trade and the Protection of Public Health' (2005) 99 *American Journal of International Law* 317, 319.

manufacturing capacity led to the eventual adoption of the Protocol Amending the TRIPS Agreement.[67]

The requirements relating to prior negotiations and manufacturing for domestic use may not apply with respect to use permitted to remedy a practice determined after judicial or administrative process to be anticompetitive.[68] This stands to reason as the judicial or administrative process would afford parties concerned the opportunity to be adequately heard on their respective rights before an order is given. Article 31 imposes a further limitation on compulsory licensing, that the licence must terminate when the circumstances that led to its issuance cease to exist and are unlikely to recur.[69]

In addition, Members must ensure that the compulsory licensee pays adequate remuneration to the right holder having regard to the economic value of the authorisation.[70] The TRIPS Agreement does not define what constitutes 'adequate compensation', thereby leaving considerable room for it to be interpreted in line with the national law of the party concerned.[71] It has been suggested that licensees in developing countries should compensate on the basis of their relative economic development, and subsequent compensations should take account of economic growth.[72] It is submitted that it should, however, be sufficient to leave the quantum of compensation to be determined within the purview of the relevant domestic law and practice provided judicial or administrative review of the 'adequacy' of the remuneration paid is available.

Where a compulsory licence is issued to remedy an anticompetitive practice, the need to correct anticompetitive practices may be taken into account in determining the amount of remuneration payable.[73] Compulsory licences can also be granted to remedy problems associated with dependent patents where a patent ('the second patent') cannot be exploited without infringing another patent ('the first patent').The owner of the first patent may be entitled to a cross-licence to use the invention in the second patent and the compulsory licence in the first patent shall be non-assignable except with the assignment of the second patent.[74]

This provision applies to dependent patents that cannot be worked without the exploitation of earlier patents. Such circumstances are likely to arise more frequently in the area of biotechnology and are particularly relevant to pharmaceutical patents as such patents usually build on earlier patents.

67 See Section 2.3.3.

68 TRIPS Agreement Article 31(k).

69 TRIPS Agreement Article 31(g).

70 TRIPS Agreement Article 31(h).

71 See Correa above n 37, 322.

72 D R Cahoy, 'Confronting Myths and Myopia on the Road from Doha' (2007) 42 *Georgia Law Review* 131,143.

73 TRIPS Agreement Article 31(k); By Article 31(i) & (j), the legal validity of any decision relating to compulsory licensing shall be subject to judicial or administrative review by a distinct higher authority in the country issuing it. Any decision relating to remuneration for granting compulsory licensing shall equally be subject to judicial or administrative review.

74 TRIPS Agreement Article 31(l).

2.2.1 Local working requirements and TRIPS

One issue that has generated significant controversy is whether failure to meet local working requirements (which is a ground for granting compulsory licences under the Paris Convention), can be a valid ground for compulsory licensing under TRIPS. The argument that the TRIPS Agreement does not recognise local working requirement as a ground for compulsory licensing is based on the provision of TRIPS Article 27(1) which states that patents shall be available 'without discrimination as to the place of invention, the field of technology and whether products are imported or locally produced'. The pertinent question is whether this provision overrides compulsory licensing under the Paris Convention. Article 2(1) of TRIPS seems to confirm the fact that Members' rights under the Paris Convention are still very much at large as it provides that Members shall 'comply with Articles 1 through 12, and Article 19, of the Paris Convention (1967)'.[75] Article 2(2) further provides that nothing in the TRIPS Agreement shall derogate from existing obligations that Members may have to each other under the Paris Convention.

Consequently, it has been argued that TRIPS Article 27.1 does not prohibit Members from imposing a working requirement in relation to patents. Rather, what it prohibits is Members obliging patentees to work the patent in their territories; thus importation would be sufficient evidence of compliance with working requirement.[76] Further, by including international exhaustion of rights in TRIPS,[77] developing countries would seem to have forfeited the right to rely on the local working requirement which would have been available under the Paris Convention.[78] Alternatively, some commentators have expressed the view that although the TRIPS Agreement incorporates two seemingly contradictory provisions, the fact remains that Article 5(A), (2) of the Paris Convention dealing with local working requirements has been unequivocally incorporated into the TRIPS Agreement. Consequently, a holistic approach to the interpretation of the relevant provisions would therefore support the conclusion that the right of States to impose local working requirements is still very much at large under the TRIPS Agreement.[79]

It is submitted, however, that the language of Article 27.1 of TRIPS clearly prohibits countries that are signatory to TRIPS from imposing local working requirements in relation to the grant of patents. The resulting question is whether such countries may, where they are parties to the Paris Convention, rely on the local working requirements in the Paris Convention to derogate from the language of Article 27.1. It does appear that the combined effect of Articles 2.1 and 2.2 of TRIPS is to preserve the rights and obligations of parties under the Paris Convention.

75 See M Halewood, 'Regulating Patent Holders: Local Working Requirements and Compulsory Licenses at International Law' (1997) 15(2) *Osgoode Hall Law Journal* 243, 255.

76 Pires de Carvalho, above n 5, 196.

77 The concept of exhaustion of rights is explored in Chapter 5.

78 Pires de Carvalho, above n 5, 198.

79 Mercurio and Tyagi above n 23, 275, 325–326.

Two cases involving local working requirements have come before the WTO Dispute Settlement Board. In the first case, *Brazil-Measures Affecting Patent Protection*,[80] the US disputed the legitimacy of Article 68(1) (I) (II) of the Brazilian Industrial Property Code of 1996, which contains a local working requirement. In the second case, *United States-US Patent Code*,[81] Brazil contended that Chapter 18 of the US Patents Act which requires local working of patented inventions obtained with federal assistance runs afoul of the TRIPS Agreement, and Articles III and XI of the GATT 1994. Both cases were settled between the two parties outside the WTO dispute resolution system and as a result, the WTO Dispute Settlement Board has not had an opportunity to make a pronouncement on the validity of local working requirement under the TRIPS Agreement.

Kevin McCabe notes that local working requirements are unpopular for manufacturers, particularly in the field of biotechnology. He argues that companies from developed countries seldom manufacture patented products in developing countries and imposing local working requirements would force them to have a facility in virtually every country, a situation that would be quite burdensome and onerous for foreign companies.[82]

While it will be impracticable to attempt to compel companies to work their inventions in every country, it should nonetheless be open to countries to grant a compulsory licence for inventions that are not being worked in their territories where they deem that to be in their national interest. A manufacturer who feels such compulsory licence will be significantly injurious to their interest must therefore be willing to prevent compulsory licensing by working the patents locally.

The pertinent question is whether there is a conflict between Article 27.1 of TRIPS and Article 5(A) (2) of the Paris Convention. It is clear that Article 5(A) of the Paris Convention explicitly allows countries to impose local working requirements on foreign rights holders while the provision ofTRIPS in Article 27.1 prohibits countries from refusing patents on the basis of failure to manufacture locally. Article 27.1 of the TRIPS Agreement prohibits the use of local working requirements. It is therefore important to consider whether WTO Members that are signatory to the Paris Convention still reserve their right to impose local working requirements as a ground for patent protection without running afoul of their obligations under the TRIPS Agreement.

Leges posteriors priores contrarias abrogant is a principle of statutory interpretation to the effect that a latter statute shall be deemed to overrule any earlier statute that contradicts it.[83] This principle seems to have received legislative articulation in international law by virtue of Article30(2) and (3) of the *Vienna*

80 *Brazil-Measures Affecting Patent Protection*, WTO DocWT/DS199/1 (8 June 2000).

81 *United States-US Patent Code*, WTO Doc WT/DS224/1 (7 February 2001).

82 K W McCabe, 'The January 1999 Review of Article 27 of the TRIPS Agreement: Diverging Views of Developed and Developing Countries toward the Patentability of Biotechnology' (1998) 6 *Journal of Intellectual Property Law* 41, 62.

83 B A Garner (ed.) *Black's Law Dictionary* (Thomson Reuters 9th ed., 2009) 1843.

Convention on the Law of Treaties which provide that when all parties to an earlier treaty are also parties to a later treaty and the later treaty does not specify that it is subject to or not to be considered as incompatible with the earlier treaty, then the earlier treaty shall only have the force of law to the extent permitted by the later treaty. Article 30(4) of this Treaty goes further, to provide that when the parties to the later treaty do not include all the parties to the earlier one, as between States Parties to both treaties, the later treaty shall prevail to the extent that it is not subject to the earlier treaty. On the other hand, as between a State party to both treaties and a State party to only one of the treaties, the treaty to which both States are parties governs their mutual rights and obligations.[84]

Having regard to the fact that Article 2 of TRIPS expressly provides that Members shall not derogate from existing obligations under the Paris Convention, it follows that by virtue of Article 30(2) of the *Vienna Convention on the Law of Treaties*, TRIPS Members that are signatory to the Paris Convention reserve the right to use lack of local working requirements as a ground for granting compulsory licences. While there is a clear contradiction between the TRIPS Agreement and the Paris Convention in relation to the right to impose local working requirements for patents, it does seem that the principle that a latter law supersedes any contrary provision in an earlier law does not apply here. This is because of the saving provision in TRIPS Article 2.1 which clearly obliges Members of the WTO to comply with the relevant provisions of the Paris Convention in relation to Parts 1 through IV of TRIPS. Article 2.2 further reinforces the position that nothing in Parts 1 to IV of the TRIPS Agreement shall derogate from existing provisions under the Paris Convention. It is thus submitted that the right of countries to impose local working requirements have been sufficiently preserved, either intentionally or through sheer inadvertence, at least in so far as parties who are signatory to the Paris Convention are concerned.

2.2.2 TRIPS compulsory licensing regime – pre-Doha developments

One of the major challenges posed by Article 31 of TRIPS was the inability of States with no significant pharmaceutical manufacturing capacity to take advantage of the system as Article 31 does not make provision for such States.[85] This was due to the requirement in Article 31 that products manufactured pursuant to a compulsory licence should be 'predominantly' for the supply of domestic markets.

In 1997, South Africa enacted the Medicines and Related Substances Control Amendment Act No. 90 1997 to empower the government to use parallel importing[86] and compulsory licensing to create generic versions of patented drugs

84 *Vienna Convention on the Law of Treaties*, opened for signature 23 May 1969, 1155 UNTS 331 (entered into force 27 January 1980) Article 30 (4).

85 See TRIPS Agreement, Article 31(f).

86 Medicines and Related Substances Control Amendment Act No. 90 1997.

to combat the HIV epidemic in the country. This was a very significant public health concern in the country at the time. The reaction of the US Government was to place South Africa on the US trade-sanction 301 Watch List, and a patent infringement action was instituted against the South African government by the Pharmaceutical Manufacturer's Association (PMA) and 39 pharmaceutical companies.[87] The crux of their argument was that the South African law discriminated against pharmaceutical patents and thus fell afoul of TRIPS Article 27, which requires that patents be made available without discrimination as to the field of technology.[88] Prior to 2001, similar attempts by Brazil and Thailand to use the compulsory licensing regime had also received stiff opposition from the US.[89] These developments incensed AIDS and human rights activists all over the world, and the public pressure they generated led to the reduction of AIDS drugs prices by pharmaceutical companies and an executive order from the US that allowed the use of compulsory licences for Sub-Saharan Africa.[90] The US executive order stated that:

> the United States shall not seek, through negotiations or otherwise, the revocation or revision of any intellectual property law or policy of a beneficiary sub-Saharan African country...that regulates HIV/AIDS pharmaceuticals or medical technologies....[91]

Thus, as a result of public outcry, international moral outrage and the immense support South Africa received from different non-governmental organisations, the US reversed its position on the South African legislation[92] and the pharmaceutical companies discontinued the legal proceedings brought against South Africa.[93] The South African legislation thus remains part of the laws relevant to pharmaceutical patents in the country.

Another development that also raised public health concerns over the TRIPS patent regime was the circulation of anthrax-contaminated letters in the US in 2001 following the terrorists' attacks on the World Trade Centre.[94] The US

87 See Pharmaceutical Manufacturers Association of South Africa: In re Ex Parte President of the Republic of South Africa and Others (CCT31/99) [2000] ZACC; 2000 (2) SA 674; R Roumet, 'Access to Patented Anti-HIV/AIDS Medicines: The South African Experience' (2010) 32 *European Intellectual Property Review* 137.

88 P Drahos with J Braithwaite, *Information Feudalism, Who Owns the Knowledge Economy?* (The New Press, New York 2002) 6.

89 H Jin, 'Reality and Potentiality: Compulsory Patent Licensing in China from a Comparative Perspective' (2009) 31 (2) *European Intellectual Property Review* 93, 96.

90 See Ansari above n 1, 61.

91 Text of the Africa /HIV/AIDS Executive Order 13155 (May 10, 2000).

92 B C Mercurio, TRIPS, 'Patents and Access to Life-Saving Drugs in the Developing World' (2004) 8 *Marquette Intellectual Property Review* 211, 224.

93 R Roumet, 'Access to Patented Anti-HIV/AIDS Medicines: The South African Experience' (2010) 32 *European Intellectual Property Review* 137.

94 Ansari, above n 1, 63.

government hinted that it might parallel import or issue a compulsory licence for Ciproflaxin (an anthrax antidote) should Bayer (the patentee/manufacturer) refuse to sell the drug below market cost.[95] Bayer was thus compelled to grant the US government a significant concession by reducing the price from $1.86 per pill to $0.95 per pill.[96] The use of a developing country's negotiation strategy by the US against Bayer thus suggests that the US might be inclined to maintain double standards on the issue of compulsory licensing especially where its national interest is involved.[97]

The South African PMA case, the public health concerns emanating from the TRIPS patent regime and the inquiries by UN agencies into the link between IP and public health led the TRIPS Council to convene a special session in 2001.[98] The growing concern that the relevance of compulsory licensing under TRIPS might be whittled down by the threat of retaliatory measures by developed countries and multinational drug firms led to the meeting of the TRIPS Council on 20 June 2001. It was then agreed by all parties concerned that the HIV/AIDS epidemic was an obvious emergency in many developing countries deserving the invocation of TRIPS Article 31.[99] These developments culminated in the adoption of the Doha Declaration at a WTO Ministerial Conference in Doha, Qatar, in November 2001. Section 2.3 discusses the Doha Declaration in more detail.

2.3 The Doha Declaration

The major objective of the Doha Declaration seems to be well encapsulated in its Paragraph 4 which provides:

> We agree that the TRIPS Agreement does not and should not prevent Members from taking measures to protect public health. Accordingly, while reiterating our commitment to the TRIPS Agreement, we affirm that the Agreement can and should be interpreted and implemented in a manner

95 Cornish & Llewelyn above n 7, 295.

96 See K Bradsher, 'A Nation Challenged: The Cost; Bayer Agree to Charge Government a Lower Price for Anthrax Medicine', *New York Times*, Oct. 25, 2001 at B7.

97 See to a similar effect Cornish & Llewelyn, above n 7,295; D P Harris, 'TRIPS' Rebound: An Historical Analysis of How the TRIPS Agreement Can Ricochet Back against the United States', (2004) 25 *Northwestern Journal of International Law* 99, 153–154.

98 WTO News: Moore: Countries must feel secure that they can use TRIPS' flexibilities www.wto.org/english/news_e/news01_e/dg_trips_medicines_010620_e.htm accessed 25 January 2019; Erika George, 'Struggle, Identity, and the Collective: The Human Right to Health and HIV/AIDS: South Africa and South-South Cooperation to Reframe Global Intellectual Property Principles and Promote Access to Essential Medicines' (2011) 18 *Indiana Journal of Global Legal Studies* 167, 188; N Al-Ali, 'The Egyptian Pharmaceutical Industry After TRIPS – A Practitioner's View' (2003) *Fordham International Law Journal* 26, 274, 291.

99 World Trade Organisation, *Governments share interpretations on TRIPS and public Health* (2001) available at www.wto.org/english/news_e/news01_e/trips_drugs_010620_e.htm accessed 25 January 2019.

> supportive of WTO Member's right to protect public health and, in particular, to promote access to medicines for all.
>
> In this connection, we re-affirm the right of WTO Members to use to the full, the provisions in the TRIPS Agreement, which provide flexibility for this purpose.[100]

The Doha Declaration, whilst maintaining commitments in the TRIPS Agreement, recognises the right of Members to grant compulsory licences and to determine the grounds upon which such licences are granted.[101] Members are allowed to determine what constitutes a national emergency or other circumstances of extreme urgency, with cases of HIV/AIDS, tuberculosis, malaria and other epidemics being recognised as representing national emergency or circumstances of extreme urgency.[102] The Declaration also affirms the right of each Member to establish its own regime for exhaustion of IPRs subject to the most favoured nation's clause and national treatment provisions of TRIPS Articles 3 and 4.[103]

At Doha, the Council for TRIPS was given a mandate to find an expeditious solution to the problem that might be encountered by Members without significant manufacturing capacity as a result of the requirement that goods made under compulsory licensing must predominantly be for the supply of domestic market.[104] The Declaration reaffirms the commitment of developed country Members to promote technology transfer to least developed country Members in line with TRIPS Article 66.2.[105] The Ministers at Doha also agreed that the least developed countries shall not be obliged to comply with Sections 5 and 7 of the TRIPS Agreement until 1 January 2016 without prejudice to their right to seek further extension under Article 66.1 and the Council for TRIPS was given the mandate to give effect to this.[106] The Doha Declaration has therefore confirmed the position that Member governments must interpret and implement TRIPS in a way that is compatible with public health by enhancing access to medicines. The implication of this is that unnecessarily onerous interpretation must not be preferred in relation to the provisions of TRIPS especially where public health is involved.

Some commentators have already argued that the title of the Doha Declaration suggests that:

> the provision should be limited solely to those patents that deal with the gravity of the public health problems afflicting many developing countries,

100 *Doha Ministerial Declaration on the TRIPS Agreement and Public Health*, WT/MIN(01)/Dec/2 (20 November 2001) (14 November 2001) Paragraph 4.

101 Ibid., Paragraph 5(b).

102 Ibid., Paragraph 5(c).

103 Ibid., Paragraph 5 (d); see also Section 4.2.1.

104 Ibid., Paragraph 6

105 Ibid., Paragraph 7.

106 Ibid.

especially those problems resulting from HIV/AIDS, tuberculosis, malaria and other epidemics'.[107]

It should, however, be noted that TRIPS only considers national emergencies as constituting a ground for the grant of compulsory licences without necessarily meeting the requirement of prior negotiations.[108] There is nothing in the Doha Declaration that suggests it is meant to apply only to grave public health problems. As a matter of fact, the WTO Ministers in their declaration explicitly support the right of Members to interpret the Agreement in a way that will promote access to medicines for all. To limit the application of the Doha Declaration or compulsory licences to cases of grave public health crises would impose unduly onerous requirements that cannot be supported either by the TRIPS Agreement or the Doha Declaration. It is submitted therefore that any measure that genuinely seeks to protect public health in any way can be brought within the purview of the Doha Declaration, the Implementation Decision and the Protocol Amending the TRIPS Agreement.

2.3.1 Doha Paragraph-6 Implementation Decision – the negotiations

The mandate to find an 'expeditious' solution to the problem countries with insignificant pharmaceutical manufacturing capacity might encounter in using compulsory licences under TRIPS led to series of negotiations on how to implement Paragraph 6 of the Doha Declaration. The core issues that received preponderant consideration in negotiations were 'scope of diseases', eligible countries and the Article(s) of TRIPS that would be affected by the solution.[109] Developing countries viewed limiting the solution to particular diseases as reneging on the Doha Declaration, which recognises public health problems 'especially' those resulting from 'HIV/AIDS, tuberculosis, malaria and other epidemics'.[110] What therefore eventually emerged in the decision implementing the Paragraph-6 solution (the Implementation Decision) was a definition of public health problems that directly incorporates the scope covered by Paragraph 1 of the Doha Declaration.[111] Paragraph 1 of the Doha Declaration is stated to cover

107 R A Epstein & F S Kieff, 'The Licensing of Intellectual Property: Questioning the Frequency and*University of Chicago Law Review*

108 See C M Ho, 'Unveiling Competing Patent Perspectives' (2009) 46 *Houston Law Review* 1047, 1082.

109 F M Abbott, 'The WTO Medicines Decision: World Pharmaceutical Trade and the Protection of Public Health' (2005) 99 *American Journal of International Law* 317, 327.

110 See *Communication from the African, Caribbean and Pacific Group of States* (ACP), WTO Doc. IP/C/W401 (May 28, 2003).

111 Paragraph 1 of the WTO Implementation Decision on Paragraph 6 of Doha Declaration on TRIPS and Public Health defines 'Pharmaceutical Product' as 'any patented product ... needed to address the public health problems as recognized in paragraph one of the Declaration'.

all public health problems afflicting developing and least developed countries. It is submitted that any public health problem in any developing country is within the wide ambit of the provision.

With respect to the eligible countries under the system, the US and EU's interest in limiting the prospective exporting and importing countries seemed to have been borne out of a general desire to limit the use of the system.[112] Thus, an initial proposal by the US sought to limit the eligible exporting countries to developing countries.[113] The US also explored the possibility of basing entitlement to use the system on national income, on the ground that a country having sufficient financial capacity does not need to import cheap drugs.[114] Developing countries, on the other hand, insisted that the criteria for eligibility should be based on insufficient or lack of manufacturing capacity in the pharmaceutical sector, as stated in Paragraph 6 of the Doha Declaration.[115]

It has been observed that the EU seemed to have been principally concerned about protecting prices in developed countries from erosion by low-priced imports through diversion of products manufactured under the system from the markets for which they are intended.[116] To address this concern, the Decision imposes a number of stringent safeguards to prevent the diversion of products manufactured under the system.[117] The Implementation Decision, as adopted, recognises insufficient or lack of manufacturing capacity as determining eligibility to use the system with least developed countries being presumed to lack such manufacturing capacity.

Another highly contentious part of the negotiations was the Article of the TRIPS Agreement that would be used to support the solution in the Implementation Decision.[118] Developing countries, NGOs and the WHO desired a solution based on Article 30 of TRIPS as this would remove the need for a compulsory licence in the country exporting under the system.[119] Article 30 empowers Members to provide limited exceptions to the exclusive rights conferred by patents to the extent that such exceptions do not unreasonably prejudice the normal exploitation of the patent. The pharmaceutical patent holders, however, viewed an Article 30-based approach as incapable of providing adequate

112 F M Abbott, 'The WTO Medicines Decision: World Pharmaceutical Trade and the Protection of Public Health' (2005) 99 *American Journal of International Law* 317, 327.

113 *Second Communication from the US*, WTO Doc. IP/C/W/358 (July 2002).

114 See USTR Press Release, US Announces Interim Plan to Help Poor Countries Fight HIV/AIDS and Other Health Crises in Absence of WTO Consensus (20 December 2002).

115 See South African Nonpaper, *Substantive and Procedural Elements of a Report to the General Council Under Paragraph 6 of the Declaration on the TRIPS Agreement and Public Health*, WTO Ref. Job(02)/156 (4 November 2002).

116 See Abbott above n 60, 337.

117 *Implementation of Paragraph 6 of the Doha Declaration on the TRIPS Agreement and Public Health*, WTO Doc WT/L/540 (2 September) (Decision of 30 August 2003) Paragraph 2.

118 Ibid., 338.

119 *Communication from Brazil on Behalf of Bolivia, Brazil, Cuba, China, Dominican Republic, Ecuador, India, Indonesia, Pakistan, Peru, Sri Lanka, Thailand and Venezuela*, WTO Doc. IP/C/W/355 (June 2002).

safeguards against third-party activity which would make it difficult to draw a dividing line between actions taken to meet the legitimate needs of importing countries and those taken predominantly for profit at the expense of the patentee's rights.[120] The African Group initially proposed using Articles 30 and 31 to provide a comprehensive solution to the problem[121] but subsequently favoured an amendment or waiver of Article 31(f) of TRIPS.[122] The Decision as adopted provides for a waiver of Article 31(f) but does make some allowance for the advocates of an Article 30-based solution by providing that it is without prejudice to the rights that Members may otherwise have under the Agreement.

2.3.2 The Implementation of Paragraph 6 of Doha Declaration

On August 30, 2003, the WTO General Council adopted the Implementation Decision. The Decision sets out the framework to be adopted where a country without a significant manufacturing capacity seeks to take advantage of the system. The Implementation Decision applies only to pharmaceutical patents. To this end, Paragraph 2 of the Decision provides:

> The obligations of an exporting Member under Article 31(f) of the TRIPS Agreement shall be waived with respect to the grant by it of a compulsory licence to the extent necessary for the purpose of production of a Pharmaceutical Product(s) and its export to an eligible importing Member(s)...

'Pharmaceutical Product' is defined in the Decision as any patented product, or product manufactured through a patented process, of the pharmaceutical sector (including active ingredients necessary for its manufacture and diagnostic kits needed for its use) needed to address the public health problems as recognised in Paragraph 1 of the Declaration.[123] Only least developed countries and other Members with little or no manufacturing capacities are entitled to take advantage of the system.[124] Least developed countries are to be determined in line with UN classification.[125] Countries other than the least developed countries are required to prove lack of manufacturing capacity. Proof of insufficient or no manufacturing capacity is either by the Member showing that it has no manufacturing capacity in the pharmaceutical sector or that the Member has no sufficient manufacturing capacity to meet its needs.[126] The Implementation

120 *Second Communication from the United States*, WTO Doc. IP/C/W/358 (July 2002).

121 *Communication from Kenya on Behalf of the African Group*, WTO Doc. IP/C/W/351 (June 2002).

122 *Elements of Paragraph 6 Solution, Communication from Kenya as Coordinator of the African Group*, WTO Doc. IP/C/W/389 (Nov. 14, 2002).

123 *Implementation of Paragraph 6 of the Doha Declaration on the TRIPS Agreement and Public Health*, WTO Doc WT/L/540 (2 September) (Decision of 30 August 2003) Paragraph 1(a).

124 Ibid., Paragraph 2 (ii).

125 Ibid., Paragraph 6.

126 Ibid., Annex to the Decision.

Decision does not give a clearer guidance on how countries are to prove the degree of manufacturing capacity they possess. It is thus submitted that an assertion by a country that it lacks a manufacturing capacity should suffice until validly rebutted by any party disputing it. The country exporting under the system is not required to comply with the Article 31(f) requirement of manufacturing predominantly for the supply of domestic market.[127] Thus the exporting country can manufacture drugs for export to a foreign market in line with the terms set out in the Decision.

The eligible importing country is obliged to notify the Council for TRIPS of its intention to import under the system. The notification shall specify the quantities of the products needed, confirm that the importing Member has little or no manufacturing capacities for the product and that it has granted or intends to grant a compulsory licence in accordance with Article 31 of TRIPS.[128] The notification, however, does not have to be approved by a WTO body.[129] It has been argued that the notification requirement for importing countries does not apply to least developed countries.[130] This, however, cannot be a correct interpretation of the law. The combined effect of Paragraph 1(b) and 2(a) of the Implementation Decision as well as Paragraph 1(b) and 2(a) of the Annex to the TRIPS Agreement is to make it abundantly and unequivocally clear that all eligible importing countries, whether least developed or not, are bound by the notification requirement. Least developed countries are exempted from proving lack of sufficient manufacturing capacity as there is a legal presumption that they lack such capacity. The eligible exporting country is equally bound to notify the Council for TRIPS of the grant of the licence and the conditions attached to it. The notification is also required to contain the name and address of the licensee, the product and the quantity for which the licence has been granted, the beneficiary country(ies) and the duration of the licence.[131]

The importing country is obliged to grant a compulsory licence in line with Article 31 of TRIPS and the Implementation Decision where the product to be imported is patented in its territory.[132] In a similar vein, the exporting country is also obliged to grant a compulsory licence for the product.[133] However, only the

127 World Trade Organization, *Implementation of Paragraph 6 of the Doha Declaration on the TRIPS Agreement and Public Health*, WTO Doc WT/L/540 (2 September) (Decision of 30 August 2003), Paragraph 2; Annex to the *Protocol Amending the TRIPS Agreement*, WTO Doc No. WT/L/641 (8 December 2005) (Decision of 6 December 2005) Article 31bis (3).

128 World Trade Organization, *Implementation of Paragraph 6 of the Doha Declaration on the TRIPS Agreement and Public Health*, WTO Doc WT/L/540 (2 September) (Decision of 30 August 2003) Paragraph 2 (a).

129 Ibid.

130 See M Kennedy, 'When Will the Protocol Amending the TRIPS Agreement Enter into Force?' (2010) 13(2) *Journal of International Economic Law* 459, 462.

131 *Implementation of Paragraph 6 of the Doha Declaration on the TRIPS Agreement and Public Health*, WTO Doc WT/L/540 (2 September) (Decision of 30 August 2003) Paragraph 2 (c).

132 Ibid.

133 Ibid.

exporting country is required to pay adequate remuneration to the right holder under the system.[134]

The system contains a number of safeguards to ensure products manufactured under it are not re-exported from the eligible importing country to other countries. Thus, the exporting Member is obliged to produce only the amount necessary to meet the needs of the eligible importing Member(s), the products manufactured under the system must be clearly identified by specific marks or labels and the licensee must provide internet tracking facilities for the products.[135] The importing country is under an obligation to take all reasonable measures to prevent the re- exportation or diversion of products imported under the system and they may seek technical and financial assistance from the developed country Members in discharging this obligation.[136] All WTO Members are under an obligation to provide effective legal means to prevent the unlawful importation into, and sale in, their territories of products manufactured under the system and where a Member considers the measures being taken as insufficient, a review in the Council for TRIPS may be sought.[137]

2.3.3 The Implementation Decision and regional trade agreements

The Decision also encourages the making of regional trade agreements (RTAs) to harness economies of scale and for the purposes of enhancing purchasing power for pharmaceutical products.[138] Thus, where a developing or least developed country is a party to an RTA within the context of the WTO, the country will be allowed to export goods produced or imported under a compulsory licence in that Member to other developing or developed country parties to the RTA that share the same health problem. This is without prejudice to the territorial nature of the patent rights in question provided half of the parties to the RTA are recognised as least developed countries by the UN.[139] It has been argued that the expression '*It is understood that this will not prejudice the territorial nature of the patent right in question*' means the importing RTA Members are bound to issue a compulsory licence for the goods or obtain a voluntary one

134 Ibid., Paragraph 3; Annex to the *Protocol Amending the TRIPS Agreement*, WTO Doc No. WT/L/641 (8 December 2005) (Decision of 6 December 2005) Article 31bis (2).

135 Decision on the Implementation of Paragraph 6 of Doha Declaration on the TRIPS Agreement and Public Health, Paragraph 2 (b); Annex to the TRIPS Agreement Paragraph 2 (b).

136 *Implementation of Paragraph 6 of the Doha Declaration on the TRIPS Agreement and Public Health*, WTO Doc WT/L/540 (2 September) (Decision of 30 August 2003) Paragraph 3; Annex to the *TRIPS Agreement*, WTO Doc No. WT/L/641 (8 December 2005) (Decision of 6 December 2005) Paragraph 3.

137 Implementation of Paragraph 6 of Doha Declaration, above n 120 Paragraph 4; Annex to the TRIPS Agreement, Paragraph 4.

138 Ibid., Paragraph 6.

139 Implementation of Paragraph 6 of Doha Declaration, above n 130, Paragraph 6(i); Annex to the Protocol Amending the TRIPS Agreement, Article 31bis (3).

if the imported goods are patented in their territories.[140] This is, however, not an interpretation that is supportive of the rights of Members to protect public health as it will result in a situation where countries will have to go through a very long and arduous process of obtaining a myriad of compulsory licences that will defeat the essence of the RTA. It is submitted that the IPRs in such goods will cease to exist once they are put in the regional market having regards to the provisions of Article 6 the TRIPS Agreement which deals with the exhaustion of IPRs and Paragraph 6 of the Implementation Decision.[141]

The system recognises the need to promote the development of systems providing for the grant of regional patents in developing and least developed countries and there is an undertaking on the part of the developed country Members to provide technical assistance in conjunction with other relevant intergovernmental organisations to achieve this goal.[142] The Decision emphasises the desirability of promoting the transfer of technology and capacity building in the pharmaceutical sector and Members are to use the system in a way that would promote this objective.[143] This is a particularly significant provision for countries with little or no pharmaceutical manufacturing capacity as it suggests that TRIPS must be interpreted and implemented in a way that enhances their ability to build the technological base for manufacturing. The decision, including its waivers ceases to have force for each Member on the day on which the amendment to TRIPS incorporating its provisions takes effect for that Member.

It has been argued that the valid use of the provision seems to be limited to patents that deal with the gravity of the public health conundrum in many poor countries especially those emanating from epidemics.[144] To limit the use of the provision to cases of grave public health disasters or outbreak of epidemics is to impose undue hardship on less privileged countries and make the use of the system not only an extremely difficult exercise but also largely illusory. Indeed, one is inclined to accept the view that '*to impose a necessity test on Members for all measures in the public interest would go against both the wording and the spirit of the provision*'.[145] There is a General Council Chairperson's statement accompanying the Implementation Decision. The accompanying statement essentially emphasises the need to use the system in good faith and not to pursue industrial or commercial policy objectives. Although all WTO Member countries are eligible to import under the Implementation Decision, 23 developed countries have announced voluntarily that they would not use the system to import. With the

140 See F M Abbott & R V Puymbroeck, *Compulsory Licensing for Public Health: A Guide and Model Document for Implementation of the Doha Declaration Paragraph 6 Decision* (World Bank, 2005) 9.

141 Exhaustion of IPRs is discussed in much detail in Chapter 3.

142 Implementation of Paragraph 6 of Doha Declaration, above n 129, Paragraph 6(ii); Annex to the TRIPS Agreement, Paragraph 5.

143 Implementation of Paragraph 6 of Doha Declaration, above n 129, Paragraph 7; Annex to the TRIPS Agreement.

144 Epstein & Kieff, above n 51, 74.

145 Hestermeyer above n 3, 242.

accession of the EU to the WTO in 2004, another 10 countries have been added to the list from the EU membership. Eleven more said they would only use the system to import in national emergencies or other circumstances of extreme urgency.[146]

It does appear that the conditions imposed for the use of the Doha Implementation Decision are generally hard to meet, and this may explain why only one country has so far been able to import drugs under the system. In sum, it is submitted that the Implementation Decision has provided a means for countries without manufacturing capacity to use compulsory licences for importation from a country that has specially manufactured the products for them. However, the various requirements that must be met are significant disincentives and to that extent it is very doubtful whether the system can be considered a significant achievement in facilitating the import of affordable medicines to countries in need.

2.3.4 The Protocol Amending TRIPS

The Council for TRIPS was initially expected to prepare an amendment to TRIPS, which would substantially incorporate the Implementation Decision into the TRIPS Agreement, by June 2004.[147] The deadline was subsequently extended to March 2005 by the TRIPS Council. In December 2004, Nigeria presented, on behalf of the African group, a proposal on the Implementation of the Decision. The proposal substantially omitted the measures that are required to avoid 'trade diversion' on the ground that they were superfluous and had already been sufficiently covered by other provisions in the TRIPS Agreement.[148] This was, however, criticised by Members such as the US, EU, Canada, Japan and Switzerland, who argued that the proposal amounted to renegotiating the TRIPS Agreement. Consequently, most developed and some developing countries maintained the view that any amendment must be no more than a 'technical translation' of the Implementation Decision.[149] This stands to reason as the mandate of the Council was to make the Implementation Decision a permanent solution through its direct incorporation into the TRIPS Agreement.

The Protocol Amending TRIPS was thus prepared based on the 2003 Implementation Decision and was adopted by the WTO General Council on 6 December 2005. The amendment was to take effect upon acceptance by two-thirds of Member States. The initial 2005 Decision gave Members until December

146 See World Trade Organisation, *Fact Sheet on TRIPS and Pharmaceutical Patents* (2006) available at www.wto.org/english/tratop_e/trips_e/factsheet_pharm02_e.htm#importing (accessed 25 January 2019).

147 World Trade Organization, Decision on the Implementation of Paragraph 6 of Doha Declaration on the TRIPS Agreement and Public Health, Paragraph 11.

148 See World Trade Organization, *Communication from Nigeria on Behalf of the African Group*, WTO Doc IP/C/W/437 (10 December, 2004).

149 See Gervais, above n 27, at 61.

2007 to accept the amendment. The General Council extended the deadline to 31 December 2009[150] and then to 31 December 2011[151] by decisions on 18 December 2007 and 17 December 2009, respectively. On 30 November 2011, the deadline was extended to 31 December 2013.[152] Following a WTO General Council decision of 26 November 2013, the deadline was further extended to 31 December 2015.[153] The General Council of the WTO on 30 November 2015 further extended the deadline for accepting the Protocol Amending the TRIPS Agreement to 31 December 2017.[154] On 23 January 2017, the Protocol Amending the TRIPS Agreement entered into force for the Members that have accepted it[155] following the lodgement of instruments of acceptance by two-thirds of WTO Members.[156] On 30 November 2017, the deadline for acceptance was further extended by the General Council to 31 December 2019 'or until such later date as may be decided by the Ministerial Conference'.[157] The WTO had 164 Members as of 29 July 2016[158] and at the date of writing, 127 Members have accepted the amendment.[159] Members that are yet to accept the amendment may still benefit from the waiver under the 2003 Doha Paragraph-6 Implementation Decision.

The amendment is basically in three parts. There are five paragraphs under Article 31 'bis' (i.e. an additional Article after Article 31). The paragraphs

150 World Trade Organization, *Amendment of the TRIPS Agreement – Extension of the Period for the Acceptance by Members of the Protocol Amending the TRIPS Agreement*, WT/L/711 (21 December) (Decision of 18 December 2007).

151 World Trade Organization, *Amendment of the TRIPS Agreement – Second Extension of the Period for the Acceptance by Members of the Protocol Amending the TRIPS Agreement*, WTO Doc: WT/L/785 (21 December 2009) (Decision of 17 December 2009).

152 World Trade Organization, *Amendment of the TRIPS Agreement – Third Extension of the Period for the Acceptance by Members of the Protocol Amending the TRIPS Agreement*, WTO DocWT/L/829 (5 December 2011) (Decision of 30 November 2011).

153 World Trade Organization, *Amendment of the TRIPS Agreement – Fourth Extension of the Period for the Acceptance by Members of the Protocol Amending the TRIPS Agreement*, WTO Doc WT/L/899 (27 November 2013) (Decision of 26 November 2013).

154 World Trade Organization, *Amendment of the TRIPS Agreement – Fifth Extension of the Period for the Acceptance by Members of the Protocol Amending the TRIPS Agreement*, WTO Doc No. WT/L/965 (Decision of 30 November 2015).

155 See WTO 2017 News Items, WTO IP rules amended to ease poor countries' access to affordable medicines (23 January 2017) www.wto.org/english/news_e/news17_e/trip_23jan17_e.htm accessed 25 January 2019.

156 See Marrakesh Agreement Establishing the World Trade Organisation, opened for signature 15 April 1994, 1867 UNTS 3 (entered into force 1 January 1995) Article X (3).

157 *Amendment of the TRIPS Agreement – Fifth Extension of the Period for the Acceptance by Members of the Protocol Amending the TRIPS Agreement*, WTO Doc No. WT/L/1024 (Decision of 30 November 2017).

158 See World Trade Organisation, *Understanding the WTO: The Organization: Members and Observers* (2013) www.wto.org/english/thewto_e/whatis_e/tif_e/org6_e.htm accessed 25 January 2019.

159 See World Trade Organisation, *TRIPS: TRIPS and Public Health, Members Accepting Amendment of the TRIPS Agreement* www.wto.org/english/tratop_e/trips_e/amendment_e.htm accessed 25 January 2019.

legitimise the export of pharmaceutical products made under compulsory licences to countries lacking production capacity. They also address issues such as the prevention of double remuneration to the patent-owner, RTAs involving least developed countries and the preservation of all existing flexibilities under the TRIPS Agreement. An additional seven paragraphs constitute a new annex to the TRIPS Agreement. The annexure provides a framework for using the system and covers matters such as definitions, notification, avoiding the pharmaceuticals being diverted to the wrong markets, developing regional trade systems and annual reviews in the TRIPS Council. An 'appendix' to the annex covers the assessment of lack of manufacturing capability in the importing country.[160] In sum, the Protocol Amending TRIPS simply incorporates provisions of the Implementation Decision into the TRIPS Agreement. The Implementation Decision and the Protocol Amending TRIPS are collectively referred to hereafter as the Doha Paragraph-6 System.

2.3.5 Compulsory licensing under the Doha Paragraph-6 System

Despite recognition by the TRIPS Council of the legitimate role of compulsory licensing in facilitating access to medicines, the TRIPS compulsory licensing under the Doha Paragraph-6 System has been largely underutilised. Different reasons have been proffered for this and they are all well encapsulated in the following observation of Horace Anderson:

> Commentators have variously attributed this underutilization to the scheme's burdensomeness and lack of implementation flexibility, the scheme's failure to recognize the need for economies of scale for exporting countries, political pressure and norm imposition by the West, failure of antitrust and competition policy, and inadequate existing market and private investment models of development and distribution of public goods.[161]

The reasons for the underutilisation of the system are issues that demand some attention. A number of non-governmental organisations with interest in access to medicines have criticised the system as largely unworkable.[162] A considerable number of commentators have opined that the TRIPS regime for compulsory licensing is very cumbersome, time-consuming and expensive.[163] Does all this

160 See World Trade Organisation, *Press Release: Members OK Amendment to Make Health Flexibility Permanent* (2005) available at www.wto.org/english/news_e/pres05_e/pr426_e.htm accessed 25 January 2019.

161 H E Anderson (Jr.), 'We Can Work It Out: Co-operative Compulsory Licensing as the Way Forward in Improving Access to Anti-Retroviral Drugs' (2010) 16 *Boston University Journal of Science and Technology Law* 167, 168–169.

162 F M Abbott, 'The WTO Medicines Decision: World Pharmaceutical Trade and the Protection of Public Health' (2005) 99 *American Journal of International Law* 317, 317.

163 C Kee, 'Efficiency, Equity and Ethics: Examining the Policy behind Compulsory Licensing and Access To Medicines in Developing Countries' (2007) 18 *Australian Intellectual Property*

criticism mean the system is absolutely unmeritorious and of no significance? Commenting on the issue, Frederick M Abbott opined:

> Clearly, the Decision adopted by the WTO is not a solution to the HIV/AIDS pandemic or the myriad other public health problems confronting developing (and developed) countries. The global response to HIV/AIDS remains a continuing catastrophe and, more generally, billions continue to live with inadequate health care. Nonetheless, the Decision constitutes one helpful piece of a much larger public health puzzle.[164]

In a similar vein, it has been posited that the result of the current debates about the Doha Declaration have been to recognise that there are flexibilities despite the fact that many developing countries have not taken advantage of the flexibilities. This has further increased the divide in the approaches to IP between the highly developed countries and the developing world.[165]

Nuno Pires de Carvalho has argued that the Implementation Decision (and by extension the Protocol Amending TRIPS) is not likely to be of much significance because most developing countries do not have the necessary expertise to understand how compulsory licences work. The Decision does not place small countries in the situation of power as to supply conditions and consequently what Africa and other developing countries need is fair trade and '*not charity disguised under a cosmetic provision which may have no practical impact whatsoever*'.[166]

Whilst one will not dispute the fact that the problem of access to essential medicines is not one emanating solely from the TRIPS Agreement, it will not be correct to maintain that TRIPS has nothing to do with it. The fact that the TRIPS patent regime could raise serious concerns for public health has been recognised right from the introduction of an IP package into the Uruguay Round discussions[167] and the implications of the TRIPS patent regime for public health has been well documented in a number of commentaries.[168]

Journal 39, 62; K Paas, Compulsory Licensing Under the TRIPS Agreement – A Cruel Taunt for Developing Countries? (2009) 31 *European Intellectual Property Review* 609.

164 F M Abbott, 'The WTO Medicines Decision: World Pharmaceutical Trade and the Protection of Public Health' (2005) 99 *American Journal of International Law* 317, 318.

165 C Lawson, 'Who Shall Live When Not All Can Live? Intellectual Property in Accessing and Benefit-sharing Viruses through the World Health Organisation' (2011) 18 *Journal of Law and Medicine* 554, 557.

166 N Pires de Carvalho, *The TRIPS Regime of Patent Rights* (Kluwer Law International, 2nd edition, 2005) 337.

167 See P Drahos with J Braithwaite, *Information Feudalism, Who Owns the Knowledge Economy?* (The New Press, New York, 2002) 147.

168 See M Tsui, 'Access To Medicine and the Dangers of Patent Linkage: Lessons from Bayer Corp v Union of India (2011) *Journal of Law and Medicine* (18) 577; R Roumet, 'Access to Patented Anti-HIV/AIDS Medicines: The South African Experience' [2010] *European Intellectual Property Review* 137; J Burton-Macleod, 'Thai Compulsory Licenses Redefine Essential Medicines Debate' in T Pogge, M Rimmer & K Rubenstein (eds.), *Incentives for Global Public Health: Patents Law and Access to Essential Medicines* (Cambridge University Press, 2010), 406.

There are instances of compulsory licences for domestic usage but there have been negative consequences for countries that issued them. In May 2007, the Brazilian government enacted a decree granting a compulsory licence to enable it to produce or import generics of Efavirenz, a patented HIV drug when negotiations with Merck & Co. for price reduction broke down.[169] This was preceded by similar action taken in respect of Efavirenz and some other HIV drugs in Thailand.[170] These developments elicited significant concerns and controversies from different circles including the US.[171] Merck also issued a statement decrying the Brazilian compulsory licence in the following terms: '*[t]his expropriation of intellectual property sends a chilling signal to research-based companies about the attractiveness of undertaking risky research on diseases that affect the developing world*'.[172] Merck further noted that the decision '*will have a negative impact on Brazil's reputation as an industrialized country seeking to attract inward investment*'.[173] In April 2010, Ecuador issued a compulsory licence for ritonavir, an antiretroviral drug.[174] Ecuador was listed on the USTR Special 301 list for both 2010 and 2011 with the comment that the US '*will continue to monitor recent developments concerning compulsory licensing of pharmaceutical and agricultural chemical production in Ecuador*'.[175] On 9 March 2012, the Indian Controller of Patents granted a compulsory licence for NEXAVAR, a drug used for the treatment of advanced stages of liver and kidney cancer.[176] In the 2012 USTR Special 301 report which was released a month later, India was on the 301 Priority Watch List and the US noted:

> The United States will closely monitor developments concerning compulsory licensing of patents in India following the broad interpretation of Indian law in a recent decision by the Controller General of Patents…

More recently in the 2018 USTR Special 310 report, the US expressed the following concern in relation to India:

> In particular, India has yet to take steps to address longstanding patent issues that affect innovative industries. Companies across different sectors

169 J Cohen, Brazil, 'Thailand Override Big Pharma Patents' (2007) 316 Science 816.

170 Cohen, Brazil, ibid.

171 US Trade Representative, 2007 Special 301 Report 30.

172 Press Release, Merck & Co., Statement on Brazilian Government's Decision To Issue Compulsory License for Stocrin (4 May 2007) www.businesswire.com/news/home/20070504005566/en/Merck-Statement-Brazilian-Governments-Decision-Issue-Compulsory accessed 25 January 2019.

173 Ibid.

174 IP Watch, 'Ecuador Grants First Compulsory Licence, for HIV/AIDS Drug' www.ip-watch.org/2010/04/22/ecuador-grants-first-compulsory-licence-for-hivaids-drug/ accessed 25 January 2019.

175 US Trade Representative Special 301 List 2010 & 2011.

176 Natco Pharma Ltd vs Bayer Corporation, Compulsory Licence Application No 1 of 2011 available at http://ipindiaservices.gov.in/decision/IN-PCT-2001-00799-MUM-39950/INPCT200100799MUM-215758-compulsory_License_12032012.pdf.

remain concerned about narrow patentability standards, the potential threat of compulsory licensing and patent revocations, as well as overly broad criteria for issuing such licenses and revocations under the India Patents Act.

All the examples given above are with respect to the use of compulsory licences predominantly for domestic supply and all elicited significant concerns from the pharmaceutical industry and the US government. It is clear that the use of compulsory licensing is hardly encouraged or well tolerated by the industry. This is because the pharmaceutical companies are a powerful lobby group; hence the Special 301 list and other trade sanctions that may attend a perceived breach of international obligations relating to IP protection.

With respect to compulsory licensing under the Doha Paragraph-6 System, a review of the 2010 Annual Report on the Implementation of the system is instructive. In the course of the 2010 review, the representative of Canada recalled that it was an intensely negotiated decision that had garnered unanimous support from all WTO Members. He noted that his delegation had implemented its Access to Medicines Regime (CAMR) in 2005 to facilitate the export of affordable generic drugs to developing countries. Canada had also been the first, and to date only, WTO Member to ship generic medicines under the waiver. An HIV antiretroviral drug – Apo-TriAvir – had been sent to Rwanda in two shipments by the Canadian pharmaceutical company Apotex Inc. in September 2008 and 2009. He opined that this example clearly showed that Canada's regime and the system were efficient, effective and timely.[177]

In contrast, the representative of India cited three cases in which there had been an attempt to use the Paragraph-6 system unsuccessfully.[178] He argued that compliance with the conditions in Paragraphs 2(a), (b) and (c) of the Implementation Decision, which included the notification requirements and anti-diversion measures, was unnecessary. He further noted that the detailed requirements for suppliers to distinguish products produced under the system, such as pill colouring, labelling and website tracking did not only seem costly and time-consuming but were also a disincentive for generic producers.

He further mentioned that in 2004, the Doctors Without Borders (or Médecins Sans Frontières, hereafter 'MSF') had attempted to place an order with the Canadian company Apotex for a fixed-dose combination drug but had found it too cumbersome. After trying in vain for two years,[179] MSF procured the generic version of the same fixed-dose combination drug, which had been WHO pre-qualified and reasonably priced, from two Indian generic companies. MSF has further argued that the prior negotiation requirement of the Decision will result in protracted delays and the system will be anything but expeditious.[180]

177 *Annual Review of the Decision on the Implementation of Paragraph 6 TRIPS*, WTO Doc. IP/C/57 (10 December 2010).

178 Ibid.

179 Ibid.

180 Médecins Sans Frontières (MSF), *Neither Expeditious, Nor a Solution: The WTO August 30th Decision Is Unworkable. An illustration through Canada's Jean Chretien Pledge to Africa* (report prepared for the XVI International AIDS Conference, Toronto, August 2006) https://

They, in addition, posit that the anti-diversion measures are onerous and great disincentives, and that the notification requirement will open developing countries up to pressure from both the pharmaceutical industry and countries whose practice and policy are against compulsory licensing. Finally, in the view of MSF, the case-by-case approach of the System is not economically viable as generic manufacturers will not produce for export without being sure of getting a viable market for the drugs.[181]

While there are a number of challenges with the Doha Paragraph-6 System, it is still a useful measure in addressing the access to medicines problem of countries without pharmaceutical manufacturing capacity. The objective of the system is not necessarily to solve the global access to medicines problem or to even make medicines available at an affordable rate. Essentially, it is about removing the restriction in TRIPS Article 31(f) by allowing countries with little or no pharmaceutical manufacturing capacity to import goods made under compulsory licences. The system, despite its challenges, is capable of achieving that and this has been demonstrated by the Rwandan import of HIV/AIDS drugs from Canada.

The process of delivering medicines under the Paragraph-6 System, however, is bound to remain onerous and tortuous. The system, it is submitted, is not fashioned to be a measure to facilitate access to affordable medicines. The system is, in practical terms, a measure to ensure countries without pharmaceutical manufacturing capacity are able to have drugs manufactured for them through compulsory licences for imports. The system is therefore not likely to be of much significance in making medicines available at affordable rates in Africa and the way forward is to boost pharmaceutical manufacturing capacity in Africa and reduce substantially the existing barriers to trade within the continent.

2.3.6 Compulsory licensing and the TRIPS waivers for least developed countries

The WTO has approved a number of waivers relating to the implementation of the TRIPS Agreement for least developed countries. Article 66.1 of the TRIPS Agreement thus provides:

> In view of the special needs and requirements of least-developed country Members, their economic, financial and administrative constraints, and their need for flexibility to create a viable technological base, such Members shall not be required to apply the provisions of this Agreement, other than Articles 3, 4 and 5, for a period of 10 years from the date of application as defined under paragraph 1 of Article 65. The Council for TRIPS shall, upon duly motivated request by a least-developed country Member, accord extensions of this period.

---

msfaccess.org/sites/default/files/MSF_assets/Access/Docs/ACCESS_briefing_NeitherExpeditiousNorSolution_WTO_ENG_2006.pdf accessed 25 January 2019.

181 Ibid.

Article 66.1 of the TRIPS Agreement allows for an initial transitional period of 10 years for least developed countries subject to further extensions. During the transitional period under Article 66.1, least developed countries are not required to implement the substantive provisions of the TRIPS Agreement with the exception of the non-discrimination obligations under Article 3 & 4 until they cease to be categorised as least developed or following the expiration of the transitional period, whichever happens earlier. The initial transitional period under Article 66.1 was to expire on 1 January 2006. Apart from the transitional provisions under Article 66, the first waiver for least developed countries came through the Doha Declaration on the TRIPS Agreement and Public Health.[182] Paragraph 7 of the Doha Declaration provides thus:

> We reaffirm the commitment of developed-country members to provide incentives to their enterprises and institutions to promote and encourage technology transfer to least-developed country members pursuant to Article 66.2. We also agree that the least-developed country members will not be obliged, with respect to pharmaceutical products, to implement or apply Sections 5 and 7 of Part II of the TRIPS Agreement or to enforce rights provided for under these Sections until 1 January 2016, without prejudice to the right of least-developed country members to seek other extensions of the transition periods as provided for in Article 66.1 of the TRIPS Agreement.

The WTO Ministers, through the Doha Declaration further instructed the Council for TRIPS to take the necessary steps to give effect to the waiver authorised by the Declaration.[183] The Council for TRIPS, acting on the instruction of the Ministerial Conference decided on 27 June 2002 that least developed country Members would not be obliged to offer patent protection for pharmaceutical products until 1 January 2016.[184] An extension request with respect to the general transitional period under Article 66 was made by least developed Members of the WTO in 2005. Acting on the request for extension, by a Decision dated 30 November 2005, the WTO Council for TRIPS extended the transitional period for least developed country Members to implement the general substantive provisions of the TRIPS Agreement till 1 July 2013. On 5 November 2012, Haiti, on behalf of other least developed country Members of the WTO communicated a request for a further extension of the transitional period under Article 66.1 to the Council for TRIPS.[185] Acting on the request,

182 *Doha Ministerial Declaration on the TRIPS Agreement and Public Health*, WT/MIN(01)/Dec/2 (20 November 2001) (14 November 2001).

183 Ibid.

184 Council for TRIPS: Extension of the Transition Period under Article 66.1 of the TRIPS Agreement for Least Developed Country Members for Certain Obligations with Respect to Pharmaceutical Products IP/C/25 (1 July 2002) (Decision of 27 June 2002).

185 See Council for TRIPS: Request for an Extension of the Transitional Period under Article 66.1 of the TRIPS Agreement IP/C/W/583 (5 November 2012).

the Council for TRIPS, by a decision dated 11 June 2013, further extended the deadline for least developed country Members to implement the provisions of the TRIPS Agreement, with the exception of Article 3, 4 and 5 dealing with the non-discrimination obligations, until 1 July 2021.[186]

In February 2015, Bangladesh, on behalf of least developed country Members communicated a request for a further extension of the transitional period for least developed countries in relation to pharmaceutical patents and test data protection.[187] The communication noted thus:

> The least developed country (LDCs) Members of the WTO represent the poorest and weakest segment of the international community. The economies of least developed country Members are extremely vulnerable, with large segments of their population living in poverty. They bear high burdens of infectious and non-infectious diseases and face numerous challenges in confronting disease and illness. LDCs are disproportionately exposed to the health risks associated with poverty (such as poor and under-nutrition, unsafe water and poor sanitation). Further low-income levels mean that they also struggle to provide their population with prevention, treatment and care. Patent protection contributes to high costs, placing many critical treatments outside the reach of LDCs.[188]

Acting on the request, the Council for TRIPS extended the transitional period for least developed country Members to offer patent protection for pharmaceutical products till 1 January 2033.[189]

2.4 Conclusion

The history of the patent system shows it has always allowed measures for protecting public interests when necessary. Compulsory licensing is one of the public interest measures explicitly recognised in the TRIPS Agreement and it remains an essential component of the TRIPS flexibilities. The Doha Paragraph-6 System allowing countries without manufacturing capacity to import through the use of compulsory licensing is inexorably cumbersome as it involves protracted processes that can result in significant delay and expenses. Rwanda is the only country that has used the System so far and the process of manufacturing and

186 Council for TRIPS: Extension of the Transition Period under Article 66.1 for Least Developed Country Members IP/C/64 (Decision of the Council for Trips of 11 June 2013).

187 Council for TRIPS: Request for an Extension of the Transitional Period Under Article 66.1 of the TRIPS Agreement for Least Developed Country Members with Respect to Pharmaceutical Products and for Waivers from the Obligation of Articles 70.8 and 70.9 of the TRIPS Agreement IP/C/W/605 (23 February 2015).

188 Ibid., Paragraph 1.

189 Council for TRIPS: Extension of the Transitional Period under Article 66.1 of the TRIPS Agreement for Least Developed Country Members for Certain Obligations With Respect to Pharmaceutical Products IP/C/73 (6 November 2015).

shipping HIV drugs to Rwanda was anything but swift. Although the Doha Paragraph-6 System remains relevant to the access to medicines conundrum, it does not provide a liberal framework for making medicines available to countries lacking pharmaceutical manufacturing capacity. This no doubt explains the general lack of enthusiasm with respect to accession to the Protocol Amending TRIPS as it took more than a decade from its adoption for it to enter into force.

Whilst compulsory licensing is bound to remain one of the most significant TRIPS flexibilities, its effective utilisation, however, depends largely on the pharmaceutical manufacturing capacity of the country seeking to use it. It does not seem realistic to expect the existing flexibilities in the international patent system to become more flexible than they already are. The current system is arguably accommodating enough to enable countries with the political will to deliver responsible governance and take full advantage of the system to address their problems. The Doha Paragraph-6 System, despite its cumbersome requirements, can still play a significant role in facilitating access to medicines in Africa if the necessary structures for its effective utilisation are put in place. The use of compulsory licensing for patented drugs by many developing countries has, nonetheless, constantly attracted some significant opposition from the pharmaceutical industry and the US government. This has led to some concerns as to the desirability and efficacy of compulsory licences in the access to medicines context.

The Doha Paragraph-6 System is likely to be more effective as short-term solution where there exists a collaborative licensing scheme for developing countries through the stratagem of a regional trade agreement or economic community. Chapter 3 further appraises the use of compulsory licences to facilitate access to medicines and examines the existing framework for its utilisation in selected African countries. This analysis will allow a more informed appraisal of the compulsory licensing provisions generally, and the Doha Paragraph-6 System specifically.

Bibliography

Abbott F M, 'The WTO Medicines Decision: World Pharmaceutical Trade and the Protection of Public Health' (2005) 99 *American Journal of International Law* 317.

Abbott F M and Puymbroeck R V, *Compulsory Licensing for Public Health: A Guide and Model Document for Implementation of the Doha Declaration Paragraph 6 Decision* (World Bank, 2005).

Al-Ali N, 'The Egyptian Pharmaceutical Industry after TRIPS – A Practitioner's View' (2003) 26 (2) *Fordham International Law Journal* 274.

Anderson (Jr.) H E, 'We Can Work It Out: Co-operative Compulsory Licensing as the Way Forward in Improving Access to Anti-Retroviral Drugs' (2010) 16 *Boston University Journal of Science and Technology Law* 167.

Ansari N, 'International Patent Rights in a Post-Doha World' (2002) 11 *International Trade Law Journal* 57.

Barbosa D B et al., 'Slouching Towards Development in International Intellectual Property' (2007) *Michigan State Law Review* 71.

Bradsher K, A Nation Challenged: The Cost; Bayer Agree to Charge Government a Lower Price for Anthrax Medicine, *New York Times*, Oct. 25, 2001.

Brodsky J, 'The Health of Ebay: The Impact of Ebay on the Future of TRIPS-Like Pharmaceutical Compulsory Licenses in the United States' (2015) 41 *American Journal of Law & Medicine* 656.

Burton-Macleod J, 'Thai Compulsory Licenses Redefine Essential Medicines Debate' in Pogge T et al. (eds), *Incentives for Global Public Health: Patents Law and Access to Essential Medicines* (Cambridge University Press, 2010).

Cahoy D R, 'Breaking Patents' (2011) 32 *Michigan Journal of International Law* 461, 466.

Cahoy D R, 'Confronting Myths and Myopia on the Road from Doha' (2007) 42 *Georgia Law Review* 131.

Chopra M, 'Of the Big Daddy, the Underdog, the Mother Hen, and the Scapegoats: Balancing Pharmaceutical Innovation and Access to Healthcare in the Enforcement of Compulsory Patent Licensing in India, its Compliance with TRIPS, and Bayer V. Natco' (2015) 13 *Santa Clara Journal of International Law* 333.

Cohen J, Brazil, 'Thailand Override Big Pharma Patents' (2007) 316 Science 816.

Cornish W & Llewelyn D, *Intellectual Property: Patents*, Copyright, Trade Marks and Allied Rights (London Sweet & Maxwell, 6th ed., 2007).

Correa C M, *Implications of the Doha Declaration on the TRIPS Agreement and Public Health* (World Health Organization, 2002).

Correa C M, *Trade Related Aspects of Intellectual Property Rights: A Commentary on the TRIPS Agreement* (Oxford University Press 2007) 318.

Council for TRIPS: Extension of the Transition Period under Article 66.1 of the TRIPS Agreement for Least-Developed Country Members for Certain Obligations with Respect to Pharmaceutical Products IP/C/25 (1 July 2002) (Decision of 27 June 2002).

Council for TRIPS: Extension of the Transition Period under Article 66.1 for Least Developed Country Members IP/C/64 (Decision of the Council for TRIPS of 11 June 2013).

Council for TRIPS: Extension of the Transitional Period under Article 66.1 of the TRIPS Agreement for Least Developed Country Members for Certain Obligations with Respect to Pharmaceutical Products IP/C/73 (6 November 2015).

Council for TRIPS: Request for an Extension of the Transitional Period under Article 66.1 of the TRIPS Agreement IP/C/W/583 (5 November 2012).

Council for TRIPS: Request for an Extension of the Transitional Period under Article 66.1 of the TRIPS Agreement for Least Developed Country Members with Respect to Pharmaceutical Products and for Waivers from The Obligation of Articles 70.8 and 70.9 of the TRIPS Agreement IP/C/W/605 (23 February 2015).

Dent C, "'Generally Inconvenient": The 1624 Statute of Monopolies as Political Compromise' (2009) 33 *Melbourne University Law Review* 415.

Drahos P with Braithwaite J, *Information Feudalism, Who Owns the Knowledge Economy?* (The New Press, New York 2002).

Epstein R A & Kieff F S, 'The Licensing of Intellectual Property: Questioning the Frequency and Wisdom of Compulsory Licensing for Pharmaceutical Patents' (2011) 78 *University of Chicago Law Review* 71.

Gana (Okediji) R L, 'The Myth of Development, the Progress of Rights: Human Rights to Intellectual Property and Development', (1996) 18 *Law & Policy* 315.

Garner B A (ed.) *Black's Law Dictionary* (Thomson Reuters 9th ed., 2009).

George E, 'Struggle, Identity, and the Collective: The Human Right to Health and HIV/AIDS: South Africa and South-South Cooperation to Reframe Global Intellectual Property Principles and Promote Access to Essential Medicines' (2011) 18 *Indiana Journal of Global Legal Studies* 167.

Gervais D, *The TRIPS Agreement: Drafting History and Analysis* (Sweet and Maxwell, Thomson Reuters 3rd ed., 2008).

Gold E R & Lam D K, 'Balancing Trade in Patents, Public Non-Commercial Use and Compulsory Licensing', (2003) 6(1) *Journal of World Intellectual Property* 5.

Halewood M, 'Regulating Patent Holders: Local Working Requirements and Compulsory Licenses at International Law (1997) 35 (2) *Osgoode Hall Law Journal* 243.

Harris D P, 'Carrying a Good Joke Too Far: TRIPS and Treaties of Adhesion' (2006) 27 *University of Pennsylvania Journal of International Economic Law* 681.

Harris D P, 'TRIPS' Rebound: An Historical Analysis of How the TRIPS Agreement Can Ricochet Back Against the United States', (2004) 25 *Northwestern Journal of International Law* 99.

Hestermeyer H, *Human Rights and the WTO: The Case of Patents and Access to Medicines* (Oxford University Press, 2007).

Ho C M, 'Patent Breaking or Balancing?: Separating Strands of Fact from Fiction under TRIPS' (2009) 34 *North Carolina Journal of International Law & Commercial Regulation* 371.

Ho C M, 'Unveiling Competing Patent Perspectives' (2009) 46 *Houston Law Review* 1047, 1082.

IP Watch, 'Ecuador Grants First Compulsory Licence, for HIV/AIDS Drug' www.ip-watch.org/2010/04/22/ecuador-grants-first-compulsory-licence-for-hivaids-drug/ accessed 25 January 2019.

Jin H, 'Reality and Potentiality: Compulsory Patent Licensing in China from a Comparative Perspective' (2009) 31 (2) *European Intellectual Property Review* 93.

Kee C, 'Efficiency, Equity and Ethics: Examining the Policy behind Compulsory Licensing and Access to Medicines in Developing Countries' (2007) 18 *Australian Intellectual Property Journal* 39.

Kennedy M, 'When Will the Protocol Amending the TRIPS Agreement Enter into Force?' (2010) 13(2) *Journal of International Economic Law* 459.

Lawson C, 'Who Shall Live When Not All Can Live? Intellectual Property in Accessing and Benefit-sharing Viruses through the World Health Organisation' (2011) 18 *Journal of Law and Medicine* 554.

Mace A C, 'TRIPS, EBAY, and Denials of Injunctive Relief: Is Article 31 Compliance Everything?' (2009) 10 *Columbia Science and Technology Law Review* 232.

Machlup F & Penrose E, 'The Patent Controversy in the Nineteenth Century' (1950) 10(1) *The Journal of Economic History* 1.

McCabe K W, 'The January 1999 Review of Article 27 of the TRIPS Agreement: Diverging Views of Developed and Developing Countries toward the Patentability of Biotechnology' (1998) 6 *Journal of Intellectual Property Law* 41.

McDonald B A, Ugryumov V & Kolesnikov D, 'Compulsory Licensing of Pharmaceutical Patents in the Russian Federation Threatens Foreign & Domestic Drug Developers' (2018) *AIPLA Quarterly Journal*, 1.

Médecins Sans Frontières (MSF), Neither Expeditious, Nor a Solution: The WTO August 30th Decision Is Unworkable. An illustration through Canada's Jean Chretien Pledge to Africa, (report prepared for the XVI International AIDS Conference, Toronto, August 2006) https://msfaccess.org/sites/default/files/MSF_assets/Access/Docs/ACCESS_briefing_NeitherExpeditiousNorSolution_WTO_ENG_2006.pdf accessed 25 January 2019.

Merck & Co., *Statement on Brazilian Government's Decision to Issue Compulsory License for Stocrin* (May 4, 2007) www.businesswire.com/news/home/20070504005566/en/Merck-Statement-Brazilian-Governments-Decision-Issue-Compulsory accessed 25 January 2019.

Mercurio B C, 'TRIPS, Patents and Access to Life-Saving Drugs in the Developing World' (2004) 8 *Marquette Intellectual Property Review* 211.

Mercurio B & Tyagi M, 'Treaty Interpretation in WTO Dispute Settlement: The Outstanding Question of the Legality of Local Working Requirements' (2010) 19 *Minnesota Journal of International Law* 275.

Nachbar T B, 'Monopoly, Mercantilism, and the Politics of Regulation' (2005) 91 *Virginia Law Review* 1313.

Paas K, Compulsory Licensing Under the TRIPS Agreement – A Cruel Taunt for Developing Countries? (2009) 31 *European Intellectual Property Review* 609.

Pacon A M, 'What Will TRIPS Do for Developing Countries?' In F Beier & G Schricker (eds.) *From GATT to TRIPS – The Agreement on Trade Related Aspects of Intellectual Property Rights, IIC Studies: Studies in Industrial Property and Copyright Law* (VCH Verlagsgesellschaft mbH, Munich, 1996).

Penrose E, *The Economics of the International Patent System* (Baltimore, MD: Johns Hopkins Press, 1951).

Pires de Carvalho N, *The TRIPS Regime of Patent Rights* (Kluwer Law International, 2nd edition, 2005) 315.

Reich A, 'The WTO as a Law Harmonising Institution' (2004) 25 *University of Pennsylvania Journal of International Economic Law* 321.

Roumet R, 'Access to Patented Anti – HIV/AIDS Medicines: The South African Experience' (2010) 32 *European Intellectual Property Review* 137.

Scott G, 'A Protocol for Evaluating Changing Global Attitudes toward Innovation and Intellectual Property Regimes' (2011) 32 *University of Pennsylvania Journal of Intellectual Property Law* 1165.

Sell S, 'Intellectual Property at a Crossroads: The Use of Past in Intellectual Property Jurisprudence: Intellectual Property and Public Policy in Historical Perspective: Contestation and Settlement' (2004) 38 *Loyola of Los Angeles Law Review*, 267.

Sell S K, 'Post-TRIPS Developments: The Tension between Commercial and Social Agendas in the Context of Intellectual Property' (2002) 14 *Florida Journal of International Law* 193.

South African Nonpaper, Substantive and Procedural Elements of a Report to the General Council Under Paragraph 6 of the Declaration on the TRIPS Agreement and Public Health, WTO Ref. Job(02)/156 (4 November 2002).

Tsui M, 'Access to Medicine and the Dangers of Patent Linkage: Lessons from Bayer Corp v Union of India' (2011) *Journal of Law and Medicine* (18) 577.

World Trade Organization, '2017 News Items, WTO IP Rules Amended to Ease Poor Countries' access to affordable medicines (23 January 2017) www.wto.org/english/news_e/news17_e/trip_23jan17_e.htm accessed 25 January 2019.

World Trade Organization, *Amendment of the TRIPS Agreement – Extension of the Period for the Acceptance by Members of the Protocol Amending the TRIPS Agreement*, WT/L/711 (21 December) (Decision of 18 December 2007).

World Trade Organization, *Amendment of the TRIPS Agreement – Second Extension of the Period for the Acceptance by Members of the Protocol Amending the TRIPS Agreement*, WTO Doc: WT/L/785 (21 December 2009) (Decision of 17 December 2009).

World Trade Organization, *Amendment of the TRIPS Agreement – Third Extension of the Period for the Acceptance by Members of the Protocol Amending the TRIPS Agreement*, WTO DocWT/L/829, (December 5 2011) (Decision of 30 November 2011).

World Trade Organization, *Amendment of the TRIPS Agreement – Fourth Extension of the Period for the Acceptance by Members of the Protocol Amending the TRIPS*

Agreement, WTO Doc WT/L/899, (27 November 2013) (Decision of 26 November 2013).

World Trade Organization, *Amendment of the TRIPS Agreement – Fifth Extension of the Period for the Acceptance by Members of the Protocol Amending the TRIPS Agreement*, WTO Doc No. WT/L/965 (Decision of 30 November 2015).

World Trade Organization, *Amendment of the TRIPS Agreement – Fifth Extension of the Period for the Acceptance by Members of the Protocol Amending the TRIPS Agreement*, WTO Doc No. WT/L/1024 (Decision of 30 November 2017).

World Trade Organization, *Annual Review of the Decision on the Implementation of Paragraph 6 TRIPS*, WTO Doc. IP/C/57 (10 December 2010).

World Trade Organization, *Communication from Kenya on Behalf of the African Group*, WTO Doc. IP/C/W/351 (June 2002).

World Trade Organization, *Communication from Brazil on Behalf of Bolivia, Brazil, Cuba, China, Dominican Republic, Ecuador, India, Indonesia, Pakistan, Peru, Sri Lanka, Thailand and Venezuela*, WTO Doc. IP/C/W/355 (June 2002).

World Trade Organization, *Second Communication from the United States*, WTO Doc. IP/C/W/358 (July 2002).

World Trade Organization, *Communication from the African, Caribbean and Pacific Group of States (ACP)*, WTO Doc. IP/C/W401 (May 28, 2003).

World Trade Organization, *Communication from Nigeria on Behalf of the African Group*, WTO Doc IP/C/W/437 (10 December, 2004).

World Trade Organization, *Doha Ministerial Declaration on the TRIPS Agreement and Public Health*, WT/MIN(01)/Dec/2 (20 November 2001) (14 November 2001).

World Trade Organization, *Elements of Paragraph 6 Solution, Communication from Kenya as Coordinator of the African Group*, WTO Doc. IP/C/W/389 (Nov. 14, 2002).

World Trade Organisation, *Fact Sheet on TRIPS and Pharmaceutical Patents* (2006) available at www.wto.org/english/tratop_e/trips_e/factsheet_pharm02_e.htm#importing accessed 25 January 2019.

World Trade Organisation, *Governments Share Interpretations on TRIPS and Public Health* (2001) www.wto.org/english/news_e/news01_e/trips_drugs_010620_e.htm accessed 25 January 2019.

World Trade Organization, *Implementation of Paragraph 6 of the Doha Declaration on the TRIPS Agreement and Public Health*, WTO Doc WT/L/540 (2 September) (Decision of 30 August 2003).

World Trade Organization News. 'Moore: Countries must feel secure that they can use TRIPS' flexibilities (June 2001) www.wto.org/english/news_e/news01_e/dg_trips_medicines_010620_e.htm accessed 25 January 2019.

World Trade Organisation, *Press Release: Members OK Amendment to Make Health Flexibility Permanent* (2005) www.wto.org/english/news_e/pres05_e/pr426_e.htm accessed 25 January 2019.

World Trade Organisation, *TRIPS: TRIPS and Public Health, Members Accepting Amendment of the TRIPS Agreement* www.wto.org/english/tratop_e/trips_e/amendment_e.htm accessed 25 January 2019.

World Trade Organisation, *Understanding the WTO: The Organization: Members and Observers* www.wto.org/english/thewto_e/whatis_e/tif_e/org6_e.htm accessed 25 January 2019.

US Trade Representative, Special 301 Report 2007.

US Trade Representative Special 301 List 2010.

US Trade Representative Special 301 List 2011.

USTR Press Release, US Announces Interim Plan to Help Poor Countries Fight HIV/AIDS and Other Health Crises in Absence of WTO Consensus (Dec. 20, 2002).

3 Compulsory licensing and access to medicines in Africa

3.1 Introduction

This chapter presents a critique of the effectiveness of the compulsory licensing regime in the international patent system and its significance to the access to medicines debate. It argues that compulsory licensing remains one of the most powerful measures for protecting public interest in the patent system and its use should not be unduly stifled. The chapter goes further to examine the legal framework for compulsory licensing in selected African countries and the challenges African countries might encounter in the utilisation of compulsory licensing for pharmaceutical patents. The extent to which non-voluntary licences of this nature can facilitate access to medicines in the African continent is also considered.

The chapter takes the view that African countries should not adopt intellectual property (IP) standards that will substantially deprive them of the ability to take full advantage of the Trade Related Aspects of Intellectual Property Rights (TRIPS) flexibilities. It is argued that African countries should harness resources through the African Union to boost local pharmaceutical manufacturing capacity to be able to make maximum use of the compulsory licensing regime. It is noted that the Doha Paragraph-6 system may offer short-term benefits to African countries if the necessary collaborative structures are put in place. The Chapter, however, concludes by arguing that without the ability to manufacture pharmaceuticals locally, the TRIPS compulsory licensing regime in the long term offers no significant advantage to the African continent.

3.2 Justifying compulsory licensing

The policy arguments against compulsory licensing, as observed by a commentator, are that it is inappropriate and inconsistent with innovation and the optimum level of protection of intellectual property rights (IPRs) required in enhancing innovation.[1] Compulsory licensing opponents consider them an

1 C M Ho, 'Patent Breaking or Balancing?: Separating Strands of Fact from Fiction under TRIPS' (2009) 34 *North Carolina Journal of International Law & Commercial Regulation*, 371, 452.

aberration as they derogate from the exclusive rights conferred by patents.[2] Indeed, it has been said that a major problem with compulsory licensing is that it may deter pharmaceutical companies from investing in treatments of ailments that are prevalent in poor countries, thereby leading to a situation where there will be no drugs for which such licences can be granted.[3] There is, however, no unequivocal empirical evidence in support of the assertion that compulsory or non-voluntary licences dampen innovation and it has been argued that such assertions should be considered with some scepticism.[4] Further, this argument does not seem to take cognisance of the fact that compulsory licences do not necessarily result in significant economic losses to IP producers as reasonable compensation is still required under the TRIPS Agreement whenever a compulsory licence is used. The compensation is expected to be on reasonable commercial terms as Article 31(h) clearly provides that '*the right holder shall be paid adequate remuneration in the circumstances of each case, taking into account the economic value of the authorization*'. This shows that whilst the patent holder may not make profit from the enterprise, appropriate measures will be taken to ensure there are, at least, no significant losses. Indeed, the current controversy over the propriety of compulsory licensing eloquently shows that parties do not have uniform views on TRIPS and this underscores the fact that TRIPS was an agreement of compromise.[5]

Another argument against compulsory licensing is that, in practice, it can be abused by governments as it empowers them to select firms that may sell the generic drug at prices that do not reflect the high fixed cost involved in its development.[6] This may not always be the case, however, having regard to the fact that there are sufficient safeguards in the TRIPS Agreement to guard against such abuse.

There is also the view that, apart from being a disincentive for investors to conduct business in countries where they are frequently used, compulsory licensing amounts to coerced wealth transfer as it forces individuals in other countries to bear all the costs of the investment. This is seen as potentially having serious negative implications for consumers outside the country issuing the compulsory licence.[7]

Again, this argument seems to be somewhat exaggerated because it loses sight of the fact that the legal framework for compulsory licensing makes it imperative

2 See D P Harris, 'Carrying a Good Joke Too Far: TRIPS and Treaties of Adhesion' (2006) 27 *University of Pennsylvania Journal of International Economic Law* 681, 724–738, 135.

3 N Ansari, 'International Patent Rights in a Post-Doha World' (2002) 11 *International Trade Law Journal* 57, 65.

4 See J H Reichman with C Hasenzahl, *Non-voluntary Licensing of Patented Inventions* (UNCTAD-ICTSD 2003), 6.

5 See Ho, above n 1, 463–464.

6 R A Epstein & F S Kieff, 'The Licensing of Intellectual Property: Questioning the Frequency and Wisdom of Compulsory Licensing for Pharmaceutical Patents' (2011) 78 *University of Chicago Law Review* 71, 80.

7 Ibid., 81.

that patent owners receive at least a reasonable royalty to ensure there is no diminution in the economic incentive to innovate.[8] Writing in a similar vein, Bagley thus opined:

> Issuing a compulsory license in accordance with TRIPS is not a morally culpable action and is far removed from theft. It is not even defined as stealing under international law and involves compensation to the patent owner. Yet it is too often characterized as theft in a way that appears to give pharmaceutical companies the moral high ground and allows them to play the victim in terms of public relations and inciting governmental action against offending countries.[9]

It has been suggested that from an economic perspective, compulsory licensing could be a good source of additional revenue as non-voluntary licensing would make the drugs more affordable and result in significantly increased sales[10] and patented drugs would be unlikely to be licensed at a commercial rate in developing countries in any case. Another argument against compulsory licensing is that it is basically unnecessary because it would be economically irrational for a patent holder to make unavailable a product that is in popular demand.[11] This argument may, however, not hold in relation to pharmaceuticals, especially when a company seeks to maintain tight control over the availability and pricing of its patented goods across different markets.[12] It is also possible for such products to be in much demand in poor countries but unavailable because only a few people would be able to afford them. In such cases, the compulsory licensing mechanism may be the only practical means the government can explore to protect public health and the welfare of the people.

Besides, in view of the fact that patents come at a significant societal cost, especially in relation to public health, having a mechanism for relaxing the restrictions imposed by patent rights without severely dampening the incentive to innovate is a desideratum.[13] A potential problem that has also resulted in significant opposition to compulsory licensing is the probability of drugs manufactured under a mandatory licence in developing countries finding their way to developed country markets at significantly reduced prices due to differential

8 See A Beckerman-Rodau, 'Balancing Profit Maximization and Public Access to Technology' (2002) 4 *Columbia Science and Technology Law Review* 1, 42.

9 See Margo A Bagley, 'The Morality of Compulsory Licensing as an Access to Medicines Tool' (2018) 102 *Minnesota Law Review* 2463, 2493.

10 See A Beckerman-Rodau, 'Balancing Profit Maximization and Public Access to Technology' (2002) 4 *Columbia Science and Technology Law Review* 1, 43.

11 D R Cahoy, 'Confronting Myths and Myopia on the Road from Doha' (2007) 42 *Georgia Law Review* 131, 143.

12 See P M Danzon & M F Furukawa, 'Prices and Availability of Pharmaceuticals: Evidence from Nine Countries' (2003) 22 *Health Affairs* W3-521.

13 See Cahoy, above n 11, 141.

pricing.[14] This problem, nonetheless, seems to already have sufficient safeguards in the anti-diversion measures provided for in the Implementation Decision.[15]

Despite the significant opposition to the use of compulsory licensing, it still remains one of the mechanisms for preventing an abuse of the patent system.[16] The fear of people opposed to compulsory licensing can be allayed if adequate safeguards are in place to ensure that the exercise of the governmental power to issue compulsory licences is not abused. Compulsory licensing is very germane to the global access to medicines debate and it is submitted that the solution does not lie in unduly restricting the use of compulsory licensing but in ensuring there is integrity in the use of the system.

3.2.1 Compulsory licensing and the access to medicines conundrum

The pertinent question to consider at this point is whether compulsory licences are really a panacea to the access to medicines problem facing people in developing countries, especially in the African continent. Does compulsory licensing offer any pragmatic solution to the global access to medicines problem and is it capable of being of some succour to poor countries in their quest for better health standards for their people? Although compulsory licensing is well recognised in the global patent system, the issuance of such licences is, as already noted, not very common in practice.[17] Some countries may refuse to explore that option as a matter of reputation,[18] which further lends credence to the argument that the Doha Paragraph-6 Implementation Decision was more of a political statement than a pragmatic licensing scheme.[19] Due to the real likelihood of diversion and IP arbitrage, major IP exporting countries continually seek TRIPS-plus provisions when negotiating free trade agreements that have the practical effect of discouraging the use of the system.[20] The most significant use of the Implementation Decision therefore seems to be as a lever in price bargaining or negotiations on patented pharmaceuticals.[21] A good example of using the threat of compulsory licensing in price bargaining is the US Bayer anthrax drug negotiation discussed above.[22]

14 Beckerman-Rodau above n 10, 45.

15 Doha Implementation Decision.

16 See J Subhan, 'Scrutinized: The TRIPS Agreement and Public Health' (2006) 9(2) *McGill Journal of Medicine* 152, 158.

17 A Attaran, 'Assessing and Answering Paragraph 6 of the Doha Declaration on the TRIPS Agreement and Public Health: The Case for Greater Flexibility and a Non-Justiciability Solution' (2003) 17 *Emory International Law Review* 743, 746–747.

18 Ibid., 750.

19 See S Lucyk, 'Patents, Politics and Public Health: Access to Essential Medicines Under the TRIPS Agreement' (2006) 38 *Ottawa Law Review* 191, 194.

20 H E Anderson (Jr.), 'We Can Work It Out: Co-operative Compulsory Licensing As the Way Forward in Improving Access to Anti-Retroviral Drugs' (2010) 16 *Boston University Journal of Science and Technology Law* 167, 185.

21 Ibid.

22 See Section 2.2.2.

Different commentators have made varying recommendations on how to better use the compulsory licensing regime to address the access imbroglio. For example, Amir Attaran has proposed making disputes arising out of the use of compulsory licensing non-justiciable provided the per capita income of the importing state is no more than $2,935, the importing country has an adult HIV prevalence of no less than one per cent and is experiencing a serious public health emergency.[23] This proposal may, however, result in arbitrary and autocratic outcomes and its compatibility with the idea of the rule of law is very suspect.

Frederick Abbott and Jerome Reichman have recommended a 'pooled' licensing scheme whereby different countries would be able to pool compulsory licences so as to enhance economies of scale in the manufacture of pharmaceuticals and procurement.[24] Robert Bird and Dan Cahoy have recommended a regional licensing scheme closely related to the pooled licence approach whereby regional trade bodies could issue licences and collectively determine the terms of such licences through their collective bargaining might.[25] It is, however, submitted that these latter recommendations will be more effective in a situation where there exists sufficient local manufacturing capacity to make the use of compulsory licensing attractive. Where, as in the case of most African countries, the country lacks the facilities to produce locally and can only import from outside the continent, the significant costs of importing under the system may be a real disincentive to the importing country.

3.2.2 The precautionary principle and compulsory licensing

The precautionary principle is a principle of law that allows the adoption of measures in pre-emption of a likely risk of harm to the public. According to Brent Blackwelder:

> The basic idea of the precautionary principle is that before imposing significant risks on others or society as a whole, we should have a solid grasp of what is being proposed. The principle embodies the wisdom of ancient adages such as "look before you leap" and "an ounce of prevention is worth a pound of cure".
>
> Thus the precautionary principle mandates that when there is a risk of significant health or environmental damage to others or to future generations, and when there is scientific uncertainty as to the nature of that damage or the likelihood of the risk, then decisions should be made so as to prevent

23 Attaran, above n 17, 760–764.

24 F M Abbott & J H Reichman, 'The Doha Round's Public Health Legacy: Strategies for the Production and Diffusion of Patented Medicines under the Amended TRIPS Provisions' (2007) 10 *Journal of International Economic Law* 921, 973–974.

25 R Bird & D R Cahoy, 'The Impact of Compulsory Licensing on Foreign Direct Investment: A Collective Bargaining Approach' (2008) 45 *American Business Law Journal* 283, 328.

> such activities from being conducted unless and until scientific evidence shows that the damage will not occur.[26]

In relation to compulsory licensing, there is the view that the 'better-safe-than-sorry' approach of the precautionary principle is supported by Article 31 of the TRIPS Agreement, which allows the issuance of compulsory licences without prior negotiations in cases of pandemic or urgent life-threatening public health crisis.[27] The argument is therefore that the precautionary principle should be more generally adopted in making use of the TRIPS compulsory licensing regime.[28] The precautionary principle is an ancient principle dating back to the days of Aristotle.[29] It however assumed significant notoriety in modern times through its incorporation in Paragraph 15 of the Rio Declaration which provides that:

> In order to protect the environment, the precautionary approach shall be widely applied by States according to their capabilities. Where there are threats of serious or irreversible damage, lack of full scientific certainty shall not be used as a reason for postponing cost-effective measures to prevent environmental degradation.

In extending this principle to the public health context, it has been argued that where there exists scientific proof that a particular practice is likely to have an uncertain health or environmental impact, policymakers ought to err on the side of caution by allowing the practice to be sufficiently curtailed so as to minimise its health and environmental hazards.[30] The compatibility of the precautionary principle with the TRIPS Agreement is very doubtful and its application in the context of the WTO IP regime may be unsupportable.

Jennifer Andrew has argued that the application of the precautionary principle to the TRIPS compulsory licensing regime is to be considered from two different perspectives.[31] The first issue to be considered is whether the principle has assumed the status of customary international law such that the WTO Dispute Settlement Board would have to take cognisance of it in interpreting the TRIPS Agreement. The second question is whether the provisions of TRIPS can be interpreted to have incorporated the precautionary principle.[32] Andrew

26 Testimony of Dr. Brent Blackwelder, President, Friends of the Earth, before the Senate Appropriate Committee, Subcommittee on Labor, Health and Human Services (24 January 2002).

27 J R Andrew, 'Swine Flu, Bird Flu, SARS, Oh My! Applying the Precautionary Principle to Compulsory Licensing of Pharmaceuticals under Article 31 of TRIPS' (2011) *Michigan State Law Review* 405, 408.

28 Ibid., 418.

29 Ibid.

30 M G Bloche, 'WTO Deference to National Health Policy: Toward and Interpretive Principle' (2002) 5 *Journal of International Economic Law* 825, 833.

31 Andrew, above n 27, 422.

32 Ibid.

opines that the principle's status as a rule of customary international law is largely unsettled[33] but nonetheless contends that there are sufficient provisions in TRIPS to support the use of precautionary measures.[34]

While Articles 7 and 8 of the TRIPS Agreement may have the effect of supporting the application of a precautionary principle, the provisions of both articles cannot override the express provisions of Article 31 of TRIPS. Article 31 only allows compulsory licences where there are real circumstances justifying their use and the language of Article 31 does not seem to support precautionary or pre-emptive measures. Article 31(b), it is submitted, requires the use of compulsory licensing to be based on some real circumstances and not just on anticipated outcomes without clear scientific or practical proof. Article 31(c) further provides that the scope and duration of the compulsory licence 'shall be limited to the purpose for which it was authorised'. It is therefore submitted that the scope of the TRIPS compulsory licensing scheme does not cover precautionary measures or pre-emptive circumstances.

3.3 Compulsory licensing and access to medicines

Although it is generally believed that the GATT/WTO system is more amenable to legal rather than political control,[35] the reality is that given the constant conflict of interest between major IP industries and developing countries requiring access to their products, the use of a power-based bargaining system is bound to be part of the legal order for international trade for a long time.[36] Compulsory licences are normally used by governments when it becomes impossible to get an acceptable price deal for pharmaceuticals. However, the use of compulsory licensing is bound to be heavily influenced by factors such as the anticipated net savings that would accrue from the issuance of the compulsory licence and the retaliatory measures that the patentees and their governments may foist on the country making use of the compulsory licence.[37] The net savings of a country issuing compulsory licences can be greatly increased where the country has sufficient manufacturing capacity in the pharmaceutical sector and this will enable such countries to make use of compulsory licenses when and if it becomes expedient.[38]

33 Ibid., 423.

34 Ibid., 440.

35 P M Gerhart & A S Kella, 'Power and Preferences: Developing Countries and the Role of the WTO Appellate Body' (2005) 30 *North Carolina Journal of International Law & Commercial Regulation* 515, 562–572.

36 See e.g. Joseph Straus, 'The Impact of the New World Order on Economic Development: The Role of the Intellectual Property Rights System' (2006) 6 *John Marshall Review of Intellectual Property Law* 1, 10.

37 D Benoliel & B Salama, 'Towards an Intellectual Property Bargaining Theory: The Post WTO-Era' (2010) 32 *University of Pennsylvania Journal of International Law* 265, 291–292.

38 Ibid., 293–301.

Although compulsory licensing remains a strong negotiation tool[39] the threat of compulsory licensing could only really be credible when emanating from a country with significant pharmaceutical manufacturing capacity.[40] In relation to retaliatory measures, the use of compulsory licences may result in a complaint being made to the WTO Dispute Settlement Board and where the issuance of the licence is found to be unsupportable, trade sanctions may be imposed on the erring country as a punitive measure. A state may also adopt a unilateral retaliatory measure such as is the case with the US Trade Representative Section 301 list. On the other hand, pharmaceutical companies that are affected by the compulsory licence or the threat of it may impose sanction costs such as reduced trade, unwillingness to encourage the offer of technical assistance or technology transfer and a general reluctance to promote foreign direct investment in the country making aggressive use of compulsory licensing.[41] In relation to the administrative costs, whilst the issuance of compulsory licences may reduce the overall costs of IP administration in the issuing country, such a country will have to consider the probability of undertaking very expensive litigation at the WTO level; a factor that may easily deter many least developed countries.[42]

The incorporation of TRIPS flexibilities into national laws can strengthen the bargaining power of developing countries in making deals with multinational pharmaceutical companies. However, many developing countries are yet to incorporate the TRIPS flexibilities in their domestic laws.[43] Daniel Benoliel and Bruno Salama have argued that the discouragement of foreign patenting may enable developing countries to benefit from the positive welfare effect of IP while also mitigating the cost to both consumers and entrepreneurs of compliance with the TRIPS Agreement.[44] Although incomes are much higher in developed countries, wholesale drug prices in developed countries are considerably the same as prices charged in developing countries.[45] The market power of most developing countries is therefore relatively low.[46] The point has therefore been made that WTO members having the highest economic wherewithal and highly

39 P K Yu, 'Access to Medicines, BRICS Alliances, and Collective Action' (2008) 34 *American Journal of Law and Medicine* 345, 358.

40 Benoliel & Salama, above n 37, 293–301.

41 Helpman, 'Innovation, Imitation, and Intellectual Property Rights' (1993) 61 *Econometrica* 1247, 1249.

42 Benoliel & Salama, above n 37, 300–301.

43 M A Oliveira et al., 'Has the Implementation of the TRIPS Agreement in Latin America and the Caribbean Produced Intellectual Property Legislation that Favors Public Health?' (2004) 82 *Bulletin of the World Health Organisation* 815, 818–819.

44 Benoliel and Salama, above n 37, 305–306.

45 F M Scherer & J Watal, Post-TRIPS Options for Access to Patented Medicines in Developing Countries 8-10 (World Health Org. Comm'n on Macroecon. & Health, Working Paper No. WG4: 1, 2001).

46 K E Maskus, 'Ensuring Access to Essential Medicines: Some Economic Considerations' (2002) 20 *Wisconsin International Law Journal* 563, 566.

diversified economies are in a much stronger bargaining power position in so far as negotiations for the issuance of compulsory licences are concerned.[47]

The issuance of compulsory licences is always a keenly contested issue in IP because it permeates the legal boundaries of the exclusivity of patent rights and the public interest in having reasonable access to the dividends of scientific progress.[48] Christopher Gibson has opined that a true patent system must contain nothing that restrains the power of the patent holder to act as a monopolist to the extent that he exercises his power within the patent system.[49] He further notes that for most countries, it can hardly be said that the grant of compulsory licences, which usually only occurs as an authorised act by a government due to exceptional circumstance, significantly undermines the effective working of the patent system such that the legitimate expectation of a foreign investor with respect to IP protection in entering a particular market would be largely unrealised.[50] Gibson argues that whether a compulsory licence would amount to indirect or regulatory expropriation in investment disputes would depend on the following three main considerations:

1 The impact of the compulsory licence on the investment;
2 The reasonableness of the expectations on the patent system in undertaking the investment; and
3 The nature of the government action including the regulatory objective behind the issuance of the compulsory licence.[51]

The greatest challenge in the use of compulsory licences, therefore, seems to be how to use the licence to achieve maximum drug access without attracting significant opposition or incurring trade sanctions for IP rights violation.[52] The grant of a compulsory licence can, apart from being likely to provide cheaper drugs, also come at an expensive price for the issuing country. For instance, when the Egyptian Ministry of Health, in response to pressure from local pharmaceutical industry, announced that it would issue compulsory licences to any local company willing to produce Pfizer's Viagra, Pfizer warned the Egyptian government that such an action would amount to a significant disincentive to foreign investors.[53] The Pharmaceutical Research and Manufacturers Associa-

47 See generally Benoliel & Salama, above n 37.

48 A Taubman, 'Rethinking TRIPS: "Adequate Remuneration" for Non-Voluntary Patent Licensing' (2008) 11 *Journal of International Economic Law* 927, 942.

49 C Gibson, 'A Look at the Compulsory License in Investment Arbitration: The Case of Indirect Expropriation' (2010) 25 *American Journal of International Law Review* 357, 388.

50 Ibid.

51 Ibid., 389.

52 See R C Bird, 'Developing Nations and the Compulsory License; Maximising Access to Essential Medicines While Minimizing Investment Side Effects' (2009) 37 *Journal of Law Medicines and Ethics* 209, 210.

53 R A Castellano, 'Patent Law for New Medical Uses of Known Compounds and Pfizer's Viagra Patent' (2006) 46 *The Intellectual Property Law Review* 283, 289.

tion of America (PhRMA) informed an Egyptian delegation that the absence of strong IP protection regime in the country discouraged pharmaceutical companies from investing over $300 million in Egypt's pharmaceutical industry.[54]

It has therefore been argued that when a government is sincerely interested in dealing with the access problems for life-saving drugs, any legislation enacted to meet the objective must be narrowly tailored for the purpose the law is meant to serve.[55] Otherwise, compulsory licensing might be viewed as an economic aggrandisement strategy that does little to advance the access to medicines cause.[56] Robert Bird further puts the argument that compulsory licensing may not be the solution to the access problem in the following terms:

> Many problems of transportation and health infrastructure are beyond the easy reach of developing nations to fix. Nations wishing to exploit a compulsory license require an established industrial sector that can reverse engineer the drug, produce it on a significant scale, and deliver it quickly to consumers. Even a country that manages to get another more developed country to manufacture the patented drug for it still needs an efficient network of roads, airports, seaports, and hospitals to transport and deliver the medicine in significant quantities.[57]

It is submitted, however that the relevance of compulsory licensing to the access to medicines conundrum cannot be disputed. While there are a number of other factors that have to be put in perspective in utilising compulsory licensing under the TRIPS Agreement, it nonetheless remains one of the most effective measures to ensure patent holders do not abuse their monopoly power. For Africa, compulsory licensing will work better, in the pharmaceutical context, in an environment that facilitates the local production of drugs and the free movement of goods within the continent.

3.3.1 Is compulsory licensing pivotal to access to medicines?

Compulsory licensing usually elicits political pressure from the right holder while also attracting economic pressure from the home government of the patent holder.[58] Thus, while compulsory licences may be available to countries seeking access to drugs at lower prices, the viability of pursuing that option is a factor that will have to be carefully considered. The country issuing the licence will have to be sure it is economically viable to pursue it, especially if it lacks the manufacturing capacity, which means it will have to pursue the option under the Doha Paragraph-6 System, which is a very rigorous and expensive procedure. In

54 Bird, above n 52, 212.
55 Ibid., 213.
56 Ibid., 214.
57 Ibid., 215.
58 Bird, above n 52, 216.

addition to that, the issuing country will have to be sure that it is politically wise to pursue the option in terms of its diplomatic ties, international relations and ability to withstand diplomatic pressures from strong nations that might find the use of the compulsory licence offensive. For instance, the Thai compulsory licences are criticised as lacking transparency and being incapable of advancing the access to medicines cause in a real sense.[59]

The use of compulsory licensing for cancer drugs and heart disease has also been condemned as running afoul of Article 31 of TRIPS and one that has a propensity to stifle innovation.[60]It is, however, incorrect to say that TRIPS has limited the use of compulsory licensing to particular diseases. Compulsory licences, it is submitted, can be issued for anticancer drugs and virtually any patented pharmaceutical provided they meet the requirements of TRIPS Article 31.

The problem of balancing IPRs with user interests has been addressed from different standpoints. Some argue that TRIPS flexibilities are good enough to address the access problem if properly used.[61] On the other hand, other commentators contend that there is real inequity in TRIPS and call for a pro-development interpretation of the Agreement.[62] Yet others argue that a trade-based strategy is a more effective way of addressing the problem.[63] There are also those who have challenged the legitimacy of TRIPS[64] and its significance for developing countries.[65] There is equally the argument that for the global IP regime to be successful, countries have to take cognisance of different societal objectives and values that underlie the protection of IP.[66] The pro-development interpretation and societal objectives issues are explored later in this work in the discussions on the human rights approach to the TRIPS Agreement.[67]

It is unrealistic to maintain the position that compulsory licensing is the only major solution to the global access to medicines problem. There is no gainsaying the fact that an effective use of compulsory licensing requires some level of technological sophistication that may not be readily available in most least developed and developing countries. Where there is no manufacturing capacity, the extent to which compulsory licensing or even the threat of it can benefit

59 Ibid.

60 K M Lybecker & E Fowler, 'Compulsory Licensing in Canada and Thailand: Comparing Regimes to Ensure Legitimate use of the WTO Rules' (2009) 37 *Journal of Law, Medicine & Ethics* 222, 236.

61 See e.g. J Nielsen & D Nicol, 'Pharmaceutical Patents and Developing Countries: the Conundrum of Access and Incentive' (2002) 13(1) *Australian Intellectual Property Journal* 289–308.

62 P K Yu, 'TRIPS and Its Discontents' (2006)10 *Marquette Intellectual Property Law Review* 369, 387–389.

63 R J Gutowski, Comment, 'The Marriage of Intellectual Property and International Trade in the TRIPs. Agreement: Strange Bedfellows or a Match Made in Heaven?' (1999) 47 *Buffalo Law Review* 713, 757–760.

64 See Harris, above n 3, 724–738.

65 Ibid., 736–737.

66 J J Osei-Tutu 'Value Divergence in Global Intellectual Property' (2012) 87 *Indiana Law Journal* 1639, 1646–1647.

67 See Chapters 6 and 7.

such countries is therefore suspect. Nonetheless, compulsory licensing is bound to remain one of the options countries seeking cheaper versions of drugs might want to consider in addressing the access to medicines problem. While its use may continue to generate controversies, especially from major IP exporters and industries, developing countries can rely on the available flexibilities in the international patent system to actually adopt an IPR regime that would best protect their national interests.

That said, it would be ill-advised to consider compulsory licensing as more than a mechanism to turn to as a last resort when all other options to salvage a public health crisis have failed. Compulsory licences for major products always come at significant costs for nations using the option and this is particularly so where the country concerned lacks the capacity to manufacture locally. For Africa, the economic and political viability of using compulsory licensing for pharmaceuticals will continue to be highly contentious until the continent is able to not only build significant manufacturing capacity in the pharmaceutical sector but also address a number of socio-economic problems confronting the continent.

3.4 Compulsory licensing in sub-Saharan Africa

Thus far, the legal framework for compulsory licensing in international patent law has been considered in significant detail, focusing particularly on the TRIPS Agreement and the implications for access to patented pharmaceuticals. The argument has also been made that compulsory licensing remains a viable option in addressing the access to medicines problem and steps should be taken to ensure the requirements for its invocation do not become more rigorous than those contained in the framework established by the TRIPS Agreement.

This section examines the existing legislative frameworks for compulsory licensing in selected sub-Saharan African jurisdictions with view to ascertaining the extent to which the laws in these jurisdictions comply with the TRIPS Agreement. The section also seeks to ascertain whether the current available frameworks are sufficient to encourage an effective use of compulsory licensing in the countries examined. The countries examined are Ghana, Kenya, Nigeria, Rwanda and South Africa, Malawi and Egypt. These countries represent different geopolitical zones in Africa and are illustrative of African countries at different levels of development. Ghana and Nigeria are located in West Africa, Kenya in East Africa; Rwanda is situated in the Central African region and the country is in the UN list of least developed countries. South Africa is in the Southern part of the continent. Malawi, a country currently ranked as a least developed country, is in Southeast Africa and Egypt is in North Africa.

3.4.1 Ghanaian law

The applicable law in Ghana is the Patents Act 2003. Section 13 of the Ghanaian Patents Act deals with the use of a patented invention by the government or persons authorised by the government. The law allows the government to authorise the use of a patented invention without the consent of the right owner where a judicial or administrative body has determined that the manner of exploitation of the invention by the right owner is anticompetitive and it is in the public interest for the government to authorise the use of the invention to remedy the anticompetitive practice.[68] The use of the invention is to be limited to the purpose for which it was authorised and subject to the payment of adequate remuneration to the right holder.[69] There must be prior negotiation with the right holder for a voluntary contractual licence and there must have been a failure to obtain the contractual licence on reasonable commercial terms before the government can authorise the exploitation of the invention without the patent holder's consent.[70] The prior negotiation requirement may however be dispensed with in cases of national emergency and extreme urgency.[71] Any exploitation pursuant to the provisions of the Section is required to be predominantly for the supply of the domestic market.[72] Particularly relevant to this discussion is Section 38 of the Ghanaian Patents Act which provides thus:

> The provisions of any international treaties in respect of industrial property to which the country is a party shall apply to matters dealt with by this Act and, in case of a conflict with this Act, the international treaty shall prevail over the Act.

The implication of this is that where any local law conflicts with the TRIPS Agreement, that local law will be null and void to the extent of its inconsistency.

The law in Ghana has limited the exploitation of patented inventions by the government to cases where 'public interest, in particular, national security, nutrition, health or the development of other vital sectors of the national economy so requires'[73] or where the patent holder is found to have engaged in anticompetitive practices. This is clearly a TRIPS-plus provision as TRIPS does not limit the availability of compulsory licensing to cases of anticompetitive practices, national security, nutrition or health. It is however pertinent to add that the Ghanaian law allows the court to authorise the issuance of a non-voluntary licence for failure to work the invention locally.[74] The Ghanaian Law is fully TRIPS compliant and has even gone a step further by allowing international IP law treaties to which the country is signatory to prevail over national law in the event of conflict.

68 Patents Act 2003 (Ghana) Section 13(1).
69 Patents Act 2003 (Ghana) Section 13(2).
70 Patents Act 2003 (Ghana) Section 13(9).
71 78Patents Act 2003 (Ghana) Section 13(10).
72 Patents Act 2003 (Ghana) Section 13(11).
73 Patents Act 2003 (Ghana) Section 13(1)(a).
74 Patents Act 2003 (Ghana) Section 14.

The Ghanaian government, pursuant to this legislation, issued a compulsory licence on 26 October 2005 for the supply of certain HIV/AIDS medicines, which at the time were not patented in Ghana, from India.[75] A compulsory licence will be required to use a patented product without the owner's authorisation even if it is not patented in the country of import where the product is patented in the country of export. Little detail is, however, available on the Ghanaian compulsory licence. The Ghanaian law is yet to incorporate the provisions of the Protocol Amending TRIPS and the limitation on the grounds for compulsory licensing under the law seems to be more burdensome than the standard imposed by TRIPS. Article 31 of the TRIPS Agreement provides that compulsory licence may be issued pursuant to a national legislation provided a voluntary licence cannot be obtained. Section 13 of the Ghanaian Patents Act has however limited its use to cases of anticompetitive practices, national security, nutrition, health or development of vital sectors of the national economy. The conditions under Section 13 of the Ghanaian Patents Act are thus much narrower than the conditions under Section 31 of the TRIPS Agreement.

3.4.2 Kenyan law

The Kenyan *Industrial Property Act 2001* provides for compulsory licensing. The Kenyan law provides that a person may apply to the Industrial Property Tribunal for a licence to exploit a patented invention on the ground that the invention is not available on reasonable terms in Kenya after four years from the filing date of an application or three years from the grant of the patent, whichever last expires.[76] However, the application for the non-voluntary licence will be refused if the patent owner satisfies the Tribunal that circumstances exist that justify the unavailability of the invention on reasonable terms in Kenya.[77] The law further provides that where a patented invention cannot be worked without infringing on an earlier patent, the owner of the latter patent may apply for a compulsory licence in respect of the earlier patent to an extent necessary for the working of its invention.[78]

The owner of the first patent is entitled to a cross-licence on reasonable terms to use the invention claimed in the second patent[79] and the use authorised in respect of the first patent shall be non-assignable except with the assignment of the second patent.[80] The person applying for a compulsory licence must satisfy the Tribunal that he or she has asked the owner of the patent for a contractual licence but has not obtained it on reasonable commercial terms within a

75 J Harper & M Gyansa-Lutherodt, *The Viability of Pharmaceutical Manufacturing in Ghana to Address Priority Endemic Diseases in the West Africa Sub-Region* (GTZ, Germany: 2007).
76 *Industrial Property Act 2001* (Kenya) Section 72(1).
77 *Industrial Property Act 2001* (Kenya) Section 72(2).
78 *Industrial Property Act 2001* (Kenya) Section 73(1).
79 *Industrial Property Act 2001* (Kenya) Section 73(2).
80 Ibid., Section 73(3).

reasonable period.[81] The applicant may however dispense with the requirement of prior negotiation with the patent holder in the event of national emergency or other circumstances of extreme urgency. In these circumstances, the patent holder must be notified as soon as it is reasonably practicable.[82] The applicant must also undertake to work the invention sufficiently to remedy the deficiencies which gave rise to the application.[83] The Kenyan Industrial Property Act 2001 substantially incorporates the provisions of the Kenyan Industrial Property Act 1989 which was enacted to replace the Patent Registration Act (a pre-independence colonial legislation) which was believed to favour foreign patents at the expense of local inventors.[84]

The Tribunal is required by law to ensure the compulsory licence meets the following requirements:

a is limited in scope and duration to the purpose for which it was issued and in the case of semiconductor technology shall only be for public non-commercial use or to remedy anticompetitive practices;
b is predominantly for the supply of the domestic market;
c is non-exclusive and non-assignable; and
d provides for the payment of equitable remuneration to the patent owner.[85]

A compulsory licence may be revoked for failure to comply with the terms of the licence or if the conditions which justified its issuance have ceased to exist and are unlikely to recur.[86]

Aside from the general compulsory licensing provisions enunciated above, Part XI of the Kenyan *Industrial Property Act* exclusively deals with the exploitation of patented inventions by the government or by third persons authorised by the government. The law provides that the Minister in charge of the Kenya Industrial Property Institute may order, subject to the payment of adequate compensation, that a patented invention be exploited in the public interest or to remedy a practice found by the Managing Director of the Kenya Industrial Property institute to be anticompetitive.[87] The Minister is also empowered to authorise by written order the importation, manufacture, supply or utilisation of any molecule or substance without notice to the patent holder or any other notifiable party with such order remaining in force until revoked by the Minister in writing after the provision of six months' notice of his intention to revoke.[88]

81 *Industrial Property Act 2001* (Kenya) Section 74(1)(a).
82 *Industrial Property Act 2001* (Kenya) Section 74(2).
83 *Industrial Property Act 2001* (Kenya) Section 74(1)(b).
84 P Kameri-Mbote, 'Intellectual Property Protection in Africa: An Appraisal of the Status of Laws, Research and Policy Analysis on Intellectual Property Rights in Kenya' (International Environmental Law Research Centre Working Paper, 2005).
85 *Industrial Property Act 2001* (Kenya) Section 75(2).
86 *Industrial Property Act 2001* (Kenya) Section 77(1).
87 *Industrial Property Act 2001* (Kenya) Section 80(1).
88 *Industrial Property Act 2001* (Kenya) Section 80(1A).

Such order must require the payment of compensation to the owner of the patent or licence holder or any other interested party.[89]

The Kenyan law is couched in such broad terms that it enables the government to grant compulsory licences for pharmaceutical patents without notifying the patentee or even meeting the prior notice requirements; a position that runs afoul of the TRIPS Agreement. The provision in the Kenyan law that authorises the state to issue a compulsory licence without fulfilling the remuneration requirement is obviously not TRIPS compliant and a derogation from Kenya's legal obligations under international law. The exploitation of an invention pursuant to the Minister's order must be primarily for the supply of the market in Kenya.[90] This is fully in line with the provision of TRIPS Article 31.

The other provisions of the law relating to exploitation of patented inventions by the government or third party authorised by government are very much the same as those that apply to the general provisions on compulsory licensing. The legal provisions for compulsory licensing under the Kenyan Industrial Property Act therefore discriminate between compulsory licences for pharmaceuticals and compulsory licences for other inventions. This is also inconsistent with Article 27.1 of the TRIPS Agreement. It is notable that the Kenyan law has not incorporated the WTO Implementation Decision. Kenya is, however, yet to issue a compulsory licence for patented pharmaceuticals. It came close to doing so in 2004 for HIV/AIDS treatment but voluntary licences were eventually agreed upon.[91]

3.4.3 Nigerian law

The applicable law in Nigeria is the *Patents and Designs Act 1990*. Under Nigerian law, the following are valid grounds for the grant of a compulsory licence:

- failure to work the patented invention in Nigeria;
- failure to meet on reasonable terms the demand for the product;
- failure to grant voluntary licences on reasonable terms.[92]

The law also provides that a compulsory licence may be granted to the patentee of a later patent in respect of an earlier patent where the later patent cannot be worked without infringing on the earlier patent.[93] The law further provides that where a Minister is satisfied that it is in the public interest to do so; he or she may authorise any person to exploit the invention.[94] Such authorisation shall have the effect of exempting the government or parties working under its authority

89 *Industrial Property Act 2001* (Kenya) Section 80(1B).

90 *Industrial Property Act 2001* (Kenya) Section 80(9).

91 See R Beall & R Khun, 'Trends in Compulsory Licensing of Pharmaceuticals Since the Doha Declaration: A Database Analysis' www.plosmedicine.org/article/info%3Adoi%2F10.1371%2Fjournal.pmed.1001154 accessed 25 January 2019.

92 *Patents and Designs Act 1990* (Nigeria) First Schedule, Paragraph 1.

93 *Patents and Designs Act 1990* (Nigeria) First Schedule, Paragraph 2.

94 *Patents and Designs Act 1990* (Nigeria) First Schedule, Paragraph 15.

from liability for the infringement of any patent relating to the relevant article or invention and from liability to make any payment to the patent holder by way of royalty or otherwise.[95]

Paragraph 20 of the First Schedule to the *Patents and Designs Act* further provides that during a period of emergency, the powers exercisable in relation to a patented article or invention on the authority of a minister shall include power to exploit the invention:

- a for the efficient prosecution of any war in which Nigeria is engaged; or
- b for the maintenance of supplies and services essential to the life of the community; or
- c for securing a sufficiency of supplies and services essential to the well-being of the community; or
- d for promoting the productivity of industry, commerce and agriculture; or
- e for fostering and directing exports and reducing imports (or any class or classes of imports) from all or any countries and fear redressing the balance of trade; or
- f generally for ensuring that the whole resources of the community are available for use, and are used, in a manner best calculated to serve the interests of the community.

The Nigerian law is not only outdated but is also manifestly inconsistent with the country's obligations under international law. The law is completely inconsistent with the TRIPS Agreement especially in relation to the grounds for the grant of compulsory licensing. The ability to grant compulsory licences without prior negotiations or payment of compensation are both provisions that run afoul of Nigeria's obligations as a member of the WTO.

3.4.4 Rwandan law

The Rwandan law recognises insufficient use of a patented invention, abuse of the exclusive rights conferred by patent and need to exploit a 'subsequent patent' which cannot be so exploited without infringing a 'previous patent' as valid grounds for obtaining a compulsory licence.[96] The conditions relating to the grant of compulsory licences under the Rwandan law are very much the same as those which apply under the law in Kenya. The Rwandan law also provides for the grant of an 'ex officio compulsory licence' for the use of a patented invention by the government or third parties authorised by the government, where it is necessary in the public interest. Situations where this provision might come into play include cases involving national security, public health, environmental protection or to remedy an anticompetitive practice.[97]

95 *Patents and Designs Act 1990* (Nigeria) First Schedule, Paragraph 17

96 *Law on the Protection of Intellectual Property 2009* (Rwanda) Article 47.

97 *Law on the Protection of Intellectual Property 2009* (Rwanda) Article 50.

The conditions guiding the grant of an 'ex officio compulsory licence' in Rwanda echo the conditions for the exploitation of patented inventions by the government under the Kenyan law, except there is no ground upon which the requirement for paying adequate remuneration or prior negotiations can be waived in Rwanda. In addition, the Rwanda law provides that the requirement of prior negotiations with the patent holder may be waived in a state of siege or other extremely urgent circumstances, the use of an invention for non-commercial public interest and for the correction of acts of unfair competition provided, the patent holder is notified of the government's decision to grant the licence within thirty days from the date it was made.[98] The Rwandan law does not recognise failure to work patents locally as a ground for compulsory licensing except where the failure to work has an anticompetitive effect. Finally, Article 290 of the Rwandan Law on the Protection of Intellectual Property provides as follows:

> The provisions of any international intellectual property treaty to which the Republic of Rwanda is party shall apply. In case of conflict with the provisions of this Law, the provisions of the international treaty shall prevail over the latter.

The Rwandan IP law is undoubtedly one of the most TRIPS compliant in Africa as it does not only directly incorporate the provisions of the TRIPS Agreement and the Paris Convention; it also unequivocally vests supremacy in the international conventions in the event of conflict with the municipal law. Whether it is desirable for a country ranked by the UN as a least developed country to have such high standards for IP protection is however a debatable issue. It is submitted that the highly protectionist IP regime in Rwanda may make it particularly difficult for the country to use flexibilities that may be expedient and in the national interest. It is nonetheless worth adding that despite this, Rwanda is the only country that has imported HIV/AID drugs from overseas under the Doha Paragraph-6 system.[99] The process of manufacturing and shipping the drugs to Rwanda was, however, as earlier noted, fraught with numerous challenges.

3.4.5 South African law

The grounds for obtaining a compulsory licence under the South African law are to enable the working of a dependent patent[100] or to remedy an abuse of patent rights.[101] A patent will be deemed to have been abused if any of the following circumstances exist:

98 *Law on the Protection of Intellectual Property* 2009 (Rwanda) Article 53.

99 See Section 1.3.

100 *Patents Act 1978* (as amended in 2002) (South Africa) Section 55.

101 *Patents Act 1978* (as amended in 2002) (South Africa) Section 56(1).

- the patent is not being worked;
- the demand for the patented invention is not being met on reasonable terms;
- the patentee's refusal to grant a voluntary license is prejudicial to trade; or
- the demand for the patented invention is being met by importation and the price charged by the patentee or his assignee is inordinate.[102]

It is also pertinent to note that under South African law, the patent rights on a medicine may not extend to any medicine that 'has been put onto the market by the owner of the medicine', or by another 'with his or her consent'.[103] The implication of this is that the South African government may legally not require a compulsory licence in respect of any medicine that has been put on the market anywhere in the world by the patent holder or by another with their consent.

The provision of the South African law in respect of pharmaceutical patents is couched in such broad terms that it actually elicited significant opposition from the pharmaceutical companies and the US, and it eventually paved the way for the Doha Declaration of 2001.[104] The framework for compulsory licensing in South Africa is also yet to be brought in line with the TRIPS Agreement. There is no requirement for adequate remuneration, prior negotiation or restriction of goods to the domestic market.

3.4.6 Malawian law

Malawi is a least developed landlocked country in Southeast Africa. The governing law in Malawi is the Patents Act (Chapter 49:02) (1986). Pursuant to Section 37 of the Act, any person may apply for a compulsory licence in relation to a patented invention in Malawi after three years from the date the paten is granted, provided they are able to demonstrate that the 'reasonable requirements of the public' in relation to the invention are not being met.[105] The 'reasonable requirements of the public' will not be satisfied where it is shown that the invention is not being worked on a commercial scale in Malawi, where the demand for the invention is not being met on reasonable terms, if the patent owner engages in anticompetitive practices or if the refusal to grant a voluntary licence is prejudicial to local industry or trade.[106]

The law also provides that compulsory licence must be issued in relation to patents for substances used for food or medicine or the process for manufacturing food or medicine except there are good reasons to refuse the application.[107] Compulsory licences are also to be available on demand for inventions used as

102 *Patents Act 1978* (as amended in 2002) (South Africa) Section 56(2).
103 *Medicines and Related Substances Control Act* (as amended in 2002) (South Africa) Section 15C(a).
104 See Section 1.2.2.
105 Patents Act (Chapter 49:02; 1986) (Malawi) Section 37(1).
106 Ibid., Section 37(6).
107 Ibid., Section 38(a) & (b).

part of a surgical or curative device.[108] Further, the law confers a wide power on the Government of Malawi to use any patented invention in Malawi in the following terms:

> Notwithstanding anything in this Act, any Government department or any person authorized in writing by the Minister may make, use or exercise any invention disclosed in any specification lodged at the Patent Office for the service of the Government...[109]

The framework for the grant of patents under Malawian law is very broad and does not satisfy the standards set by Article 31 of the TRIPS Agreement. For instance, where a compulsory licence is in relation to pharmaceutical products, public nutrition, therapeutic uses or methods or where it is to be used by the Government of Malawi, there is no requirement to enter into negotiations for a voluntary licence prior to applying for the compulsory licence. In all cases where a compulsory licence is to be granted, the law does not require the payment of compensation to the patent owner as a condition for the grant of the licence. The law is apparently not in accordance with the provisions of the TRIPS Agreement on compulsory licensing. However, Malawi is a least developed country and is covered by the exemption for least developed countries to exercise a right not to implement the substantive provisions of the TRIPS Agreement with the exemption of the non-discrimination principles until 2021.

3.4.7 Egyptian law

The governing law in Egypt is the Law No. 82 of 2002 on the Protection of Intellectual Property Rights. The law provides for seven different cases that may justify the grant of compulsory licences as follows:

1 Where the Minister finds that the compulsory licence will benefit public non-commercial interest including national security, nutrition, environment and health, emergency cases and to support national efforts in sectors of vital importance to the economy.[110]

2 Where the invention is in relation to pharmaceutical products. Article 23 (2) of the Egyptian Law provides that the Minister of Health may request the issuance of a compulsory licence:

> when the quantity of patented medicine, made available fail to adequately meet the national needs, due to their poor quality or if they are offered at a prohibitive price, or if the patent is related to medicines addressing critical cases, incurable or endemic diseases or products used

108 Ibid., Section 38(c).
109 Ibid., Section 40(1).
110 *Law No. 82 of 2002 on the Protection of Intellectual Property Rights* (Egypt) Article 23(1).

in the prevention of these diseases, or where the invention is related to the medicines, their manufacturing process, the raw materials necessary for their preparation or the process of manufacturing of those materials.[111]

The implication of the forgoing provision is that compulsory licence may be granted in Egypt in relation to patents for medicines generally irrespective of whether there exists a public health emergency or not.

3 Where following 'the offer of suitable terms' the patent owner refuses to grant a voluntary licence irrespective of the purpose for which the licence is sought.[112]
4 Where the patent owner fails to work or exploit the invention locally.[113]
5 Where it is determined that the patent owner has been involved in anticompetitive practices.[114]
6 Compulsory licence shall be available if it is necessary for the exploitation of another patented invention in which case the owner of the patent that is being compulsorily licensed will equally be entitled to a compulsory licence to use the other patented invention.[115]
7 With respect to inventions in the field of semiconductor technology, compulsory licences will be granted for public non-commercial purposes only.[116]

The law in Egypt has therefore provided a robust framework for the use of compulsory licences while still complying with the country's obligations under WTO law and the TRIPS Agreement. Article 24 of the Egyptian Law on the Protection of Intellectual Property Rights contains the general factors that must be taken into account when considering a request for the issuance of a compulsory licence. The law provides that where a compulsory licence is to be issued, each case is to be considered on its merits.[117] The party seeking a compulsory licence must have been unsuccessful in negotiating a voluntary licence on reasonable commercial terms.[118]

The patent owner has the right to seek a review of the decision to grant the compulsory licence.[119] The party seeking a compulsory licence is required by law to have the right to be able to exploit the invention in the country.[120] The licensee must abide by the terms of the compulsory licence[121] and the licence granted

111 *Law No. 82 of 2002 on the Protection of Intellectual Property Rights* (Egypt) Article 23(2).
112 *Law No. 82 of 2002 on the Protection of Intellectual Property Rights* (Egypt) Article 23(3).
113 *Law No. 82 of 2002 on the Protection of Intellectual Property Rights* (Egypt) Article 23(4).
114 *Law No. 82 of 2002 on the Protection of Intellectual Property Rights* (Egypt) Article 23(5).
115 *Law No. 82 of 2002 on the Protection of Intellectual Property Rights* (Egypt) Article 23(6).
116 *Law No. 82 of 2002 on the Protection of Intellectual Property Rights* (Egypt) Article 23(7).
117 *Law No. 82 of 2002 on the Protection of Intellectual Property Rights* (Egypt) Article 24(1).
118 Ibid., Article 24(2).
119 Ibid., Article 24(3).
120 Ibid., Article 24(4).
121 Ibid., Article 24(5).

must be non-assignable.[122] The patent owner is entitled to a fair compensation for the use of the patented invention.[123] The legal framework for compulsory licensing in Egypt, while apparently designed to make the use of compulsory licences available in every situation where the patent owner is unwilling to offer a voluntary licence, is substantially in line with the spirit and tenor of Article 31 of the TRIPS Agreement.

3.5 Utilising compulsory licensing in Africa

Table 3.1 briefly depicts the extent to which the applicable laws in the countries examined above comply with the TRIPS Agreement in terms of the prior negotiation requirement, the need to pay adequate remuneration and incorporation of the Doha Paragraph-6 system.

Table 3.1 IP laws in some sub-Saharan African countries and the degree of their consistency with the TRIPS Agreement

Legislation by Country	*Degree of compliance with the TRIPS Agreement*
Industrial Property Act 2001 (Kenya) S.80	Allows compulsory licences to be granted without meeting the prior negotiation requirement or paying remuneration to the patent holder (inconsistent with TRIPS Article 31). Does not incorporate the Paragraph-6 system
Patents Act 1990 (Nigeria) Para 15, Schedule 1	Same as Kenya, above
Medicines and Related Substances Control Act (as amended in 2002) (South Africa) Section 15C(a) Patents Act 1978 (as amended in 2002) (South Africa)	Provides that patent rights on a medicine may not extend to any medicine that has been put onto the market by the owner, or with their consent. May obviate the need for a compulsory licence in respect of any medicine that has been put on the market anywhere in the world by the owner or with their consent (inconsistent with TRIPS Articles 28 and 31). The Patents Act does not incorporate the Paragraph-6 system
Patents Act 2003 (Ghana)	Fully incorporates the provisions of TRIPS. Gives supremacy to international treaties over domestic laws where there is conflict between them (therefore fully TRIPS compliant) Does not incorporate the Paragraph-6 system
Law on the Protection of Intellectual Property 2009 (Rwanda)	Same as in Ghana above but the law incorporates the Paragraph-6 system.

122 Ibid., Article 24(6).
123 Ibid., Article 24(8).

Legislation by Country	*Degree of compliance with the TRIPS Agreement*
Law No. 82 of 2002 on the Protection of Intellectual Property Rights (Egypt)	The law is generally TRIPS compliant even though it provides a robust framework for compulsory licensing including licences for failure to work inventions locally. The law does not incorporate the Doha Paragraph-6 system as it was made prior to the Implementation Decision.
Patents Act (Chapter 49:02) 1986 (Malawi)	The law provides a broad framework for compulsory licensing without incorporating the TRIPS standards as it was made prior to the adoption of the TRIPS Agreement. As a least developed country, Malawi may choose not to implement the standard of protection required by the TRIPS Agreement until July 2021.

A look at the relevant provisions of the examined countries reveals there exists a relatively broad legal framework for compulsory licensing in some parts of Africa but its utilisation in the continent has not been so remarkable. A major reason for this is the fact that most African countries lack the necessary pharmaceutical manufacturing capacity for an effective utilisation of compulsory licensing.[124] It has been noted that no single country in the continent, whatever its size or economic development, is fully self-sufficient in the production of pharmaceuticals.[125] South Africa is the only sub-Saharan African country that has a limited primary manufacturing capacity (that is capable of producing Active Pharmaceutical Ingredients).[126] It is equally notable that the existing frameworks for compulsory licensing in most of these countries are not TRIPS compliant, with the exception of Rwanda and Ghana which have both made their laws fully subservient to the provisions of the Paris Convention, TRIPS and other international conventions on IP to which they are signatories. However, there has not been much opposition from the multinational pharmaceutical corporations in relation to the fact that the compulsory licensing provisions in some African countries fall short of TRIPS compliance. This is probably because the necessary structures for an aggressive use of compulsory licenses do not exist in Africa. Nonetheless, the TRIPS flexibilities should not be whittled down

124 See Tatum Anderson, 'Tide Turns for Drug Manufacturing in Africa' (2010) 375(9726) *The Lancet* 1597, 1598 to the effect that there is still inadequate pharmaceutical manufacturing capacity in Africa.

125 African Union, Draft Pharmaceutical Manufacturing Plan for Africa Doc. CAMH/MIN/7(III), 6 (10–13 April 2007).

126 See Council on Health Research for Development (COHRED) and New Partnership for Africa's Development (NEPAD), *Strengthening Pharmaceutical Innovation in Africa* (2009) 58–59.

through local implementation. African countries should make maximum use of the flexibilities currently available under the TRIPS Agreement. For countries like Rwanda and Ghana that have incorporated international IP law into their domestic legislation, amending their patent laws to incorporate all the flexibilities in the TRIPS Agreement will make it easier for them to use the existing flexibilities, and governments in these countries should take steps to make these amendments.

Compulsory licensing is very germane to the access to medicines debate, but its benefits are yet to be fully explored or utilised in Africa. For Africa to be able to benefit fully from the TRIPS compulsory licensing regime, a collaborative effort to boost local pharmaceutical manufacturing capacity is required.[127]

3.6 Conclusion

The access to medicines problem in Africa did not begin with the emergence of TRIPS. TRIPS only exacerbated the problem. The TRIPS Agreement has nonetheless provided certain safeguards for ensuring a balance of rights and obligations in the protection of IP. One of such measures is compulsory licensing. African countries must take the necessary steps to make maximum use of compulsory licensing and other TRIPS flexibilities whenever necessary. There is need to strongly resist TRIPS-plus provisions in free trade agreements that may have significant implications for countries in Africa. African nations must also not trade away the flexibilities available under the patent system by enacting laws that will impose higher obligations than necessary on them. More importantly, there is an urgent need for Africa to form a common front in addressing her access to medicines problem.

The starting point is to take the development of a strong pharmaceutical manufacturing capacity in the continent more seriously. Although it might be particularly difficult for a single country to do this, African countries can pool resources together under the auspices of an umbrella body like the African Union to develop a significant pharmaceutical manufacturing capacity that would be strong enough to provide medicines for the continent. The argument that the continent is too poor to have a strong pharmaceutical manufacturing capacity does not seem to be entirely correct.[128] Whilst it might still be difficult for a single country in the continent to muster the political will and financial strength required for such an undertaking, it is submitted that the African Union can play a cardinal role in bringing all member countries together to fund a project that will benefit the continent significantly not only by bringing about an enhanced healthcare delivery structure but also in spurring human development and economic growth in the long run. Africa can then as a continent

127 This is explored further in Chapter 9.

128 COHRED, 'COHRED Reiterates Its Backing for Africa's Pharmaceutical Manufacturing Plan' www.cohred.org/2012/02/cohred-reiterates-its-backing-for-africa%E2%80%99s-pharmaceutical-manufacturing-plan/ 25 January 2019.

benefit significantly from the current compulsory licensing scheme under the international patent system. It appears that access to medicines through the Doha Paragraph-6 system in particular can only offer immediate, short-term benefits. Thus, rather than relying solely on short-term waivers of patent rights to facilitate access to medicines, developing countries should be empowered to explore or develop their regional or domestic innovative capacity.

The benefits Africa stands to gain from developing a strong manufacturing capacity in the pharmaceutical sector at this point are quite immense having regards to the fact that 33 out of the current 54 fully recognised sovereign states in Africa are ranked as least developed countries by the United Nations.[129] Thus, up to 33 countries in Africa are eligible to refuse to grant patents for pharmaceuticals until January 2033.[130] If there exists a strong manufacturing capacity in the continent, this exemption will not only facilitate the production of generic drugs within Africa, it will also make the effective use of compulsory licences much easier and attractive. Until Africa develops this capacity, the effective use of compulsory licences is likely to remain highly invidious and somewhat illusory in Africa.

Bibliography

Abbott F M & Reichman J H, 'The Doha Round's Public Health Legacy: Strategies for the Production and Diffusion of Patented Medicines under the Amended TRIPS Provisions' (2007) 10 *Journal of International Economic Law* 921.

African Union, Draft Pharmaceutical Manufacturing Plan for Africa Doc. CAMH/MIN/7(III), 6 (10–13 April 2007).

Anderson H E (Jr.), 'We Can Work It Out: Co-operative Compulsory Licensing As the Way Forward in Improving Access to Anti-Retroviral Drugs' (2010) 16 *Boston University Journal of Science and Technology Law* 167.

Anderson T, 'Tide Turns for Drug Manufacturing in Africa' (2010) 375(9726) *The Lancet* 1597, 1598.

Andrew J R, 'Swine Flu, Bird Flu, SARS, Oh My! Applying the Precautionary Principle to Compulsory Licensing of Pharmaceuticals under Article 31 of TRIPS' (2011) *Michigan State Law Review* 405.

Ansari N, 'International Patent Rights in a Post-Doha World' (2002) 11 *International Trade Law Journal* 57.

Attaran A, 'Assessing and Answering Paragraph 6 of the Doha Declaration on the TRIPS Agreement and Public Health: The Case for Greater Flexibility and a Non-Justiciability Solution' (2003) 17 *Emory International Law Review* 743.

Bagley M A, 'The Morality of Compulsory Licensing as an Access to Medicines Tool' (2018) 102 *Minnesota Law Review* 2463.

129 See UN-OHRLLS, 'Least Developed Countries' http://unohrlls.org/custom-content/uploads/2018/12/list-of-least-developed-countries-rev1.pdf accessed 25 January 2019.

130 Council for TRIPS: Extension of the Transitional Period under Article 66.1 of the TRIPS Agreement for Least Developed Country Members for Certain Obligations with Respect to Pharmaceutical Products Ip/C/73 (6 November 2015).

Beall R & Khun R, 'Trends in Compulsory Licensing of Pharmaceuticals since the Doha Declaration: A Database Analysis' www.plosmedicine.org/article/info%3A doi%2F10.1371%2Fjournal.pmed.1001154 accessed 25 January 2019.

Beckerman-Rodau A, 'Balancing Profit Maximization and Public Access to Technology' (2002) 4 *Columbia Science and Technology Law Review* 1.

Benoliel D & Salama B, 'Towards an Intellectual Property Bargaining Theory: The Post WTO-Era' (2010) 32 *University of Pennsylvania Journal of International Law* 265, 291–292.

Bird R C, 'Developing Nations and the Compulsory License; Maximising Access to Essential Medicines While Minimizing Investment Side Effects' (2009) 37 *Journal of Law Medicines and Ethics* 209.

Bird R & Cahoy D R, 'The Impact of Compulsory Licensing on Foreign Direct Investment: A Collective Bargaining Approach' (2008) 45 *American Business Law Journal* 283, 328.

Blackwelder B, President, Friends of the Earth, Testimony before the Senate Appropriate Committee, Subcommittee on Labor, Health and Human Services (24 January 2002).

Bloche M G, 'WTO Deference to National Health Policy: Toward and Interpretive Principle' (2002) 5 *Journal of International Economic Law* 825.

Cahoy D R, 'Confronting Myths and Myopia on the Road from Doha' (2007) 42 *Georgia Law Review* 131.

Castellano R A, 'Patent Law for New Medical Uses of Known Compounds and Pfizer's Viagra Patent' (2006) 46 *The Intellectual Property Law Review* 283.

COHRED, 'COHRED Reiterates Its Backing for Africa's Pharmaceutical Manufacturing Plan' www.cohred.org/2012/02/cohred-reiterates-its-backing-for-africa%E2%80%99s-pharmaceutical-manufacturing-plan/ accessed 25 January 2019.

Council for TRIPS: Extension of the Transitional Period under Article 66.1 of the TRIPS Agreement for Least Developed Country Members for Certain Obligations with Respect to Pharmaceutical Products Ip/C/73 (6 November 2015).

Council on Health Research for Development (COHRED) and New Partnership for Africa's Development (NEPAD), *Strengthening Pharmaceutical Innovation in Africa* (2009).

Danzon P M & Furukawa M F, 'Prices and Availability of Pharmaceuticals: Evidence from Nine Countries' (2003) 22 *Health Affairs* W3-521.

Epstein R A & Kieff F S, 'The Licensing of Intellectual Property: Questioning the Frequency and Wisdom of Compulsory Licensing for Pharmaceutical Patents' (2011) 78 *University of Chicago Law Review* 71.

Gerhart P M & Kella A S, 'Power and Preferences: Developing Countries and the Role of the WTO Appellate Body' (2005) 30 *North Carolina Journal of International Law & Commercial Regulation* 515.

Gibson C, 'A Look at the Compulsory License in Investment Arbitration: The Case of Indirect Expropriation' (2010) 25 *American Journal of International Law Review* 357.

Gutowski R J, Comment, 'The Marriage of Intellectual Property and International Trade in the TRIPs. Agreement: Strange Bedfellows or a Match Made in Heaven?' (1999) 47 *Buffalo Law Review* 713.

Harper J & Gyansa-Lutherodt M, *The Viability of Pharmaceutical Manufacturing in Ghana to Address Priority Endemic Diseases in the West Africa Sub-Region* (GTZ, Germany, 2007).

Harris D P, 'Carrying a Good Joke Too Far: TRIPS and Treaties of Adhesion' (2006) 27 *University of Pennsylvania Journal of International Economic Law* 681.

Helpman, 'Innovation, Imitation, and Intellectual Property Rights' (1993) 61 *Econometrica* 1247.

Ho C M, 'Patent Breaking or Balancing?: Separating Strands of Fact from Fiction under TRIPS', (2009) 34 *North Carolina Journal of International Law & Commercial Regulation* 371.

Kameri-Mbote P, 'Intellectual Property Protection in Africa: An Appraisal of the Status of Laws, Research and Policy Analysis on Intellectual Property Rights in Kenya' (International Environmental Law Research Centre Working Paper, 2005).

Lucyk S, 'Patents, Politics and Public Health: Access to Essential Medicines under the TRIPS Agreement' (2006) 38 *Ottawa Law Review* 191.

Lybecker K M and Fowler E, 'Compulsory Licensing in Canada and Thailand: Comparing Regimes to Ensure Legitimate use of the WTO Rules' (2009) 37 *Journal of Law, Medicine & Ethics* 222.

Maskus K E, 'Ensuring Access to Essential Medicines: Some Economic Considerations' (2002) 20 *Wisconsin International Law Journal* 563.

Nielsen J & Nicol D, 'Pharmaceutical Patents and Developing Countries: the Conundrum of Access and Incentive' (2002) 13 (1) *Australian Intellectual Property Journal* 289.

Oliveira M A et al., 'Has the Implementation of the TRIPS Agreement in Latin America and the Caribbean Produced Intellectual Property Legislation that Favors Public Health?' (2004) 82 *Bulletin of the World Health Organisation* 815.

Osei-Tutu J J 'Value Divergence in Global Intellectual Property' (2012) 87 *Indiana Law Journal* 1639.

ReichmanJHwithHasenzahlC, *Non-voluntaryLicensingofPatentedInventions*(UNCTAD-ICTSD 2003). 143.

Scherer F M & Watal J, Post-TRIPS Options for Access to Patented Medicines in Developing Countries 8–10 (World Health Org. Comm'n on Macroecon. & Health, Working Paper No. WG4: 1, 2001).

Straus J, 'The Impact of the New World Order on Economic Development: The Role of the Intellectual Property Rights System' (2006) 6 *John Marshall Review of Intellectual Property Law* 1.

Subhan J, 'Scrutinized: The TRIPS Agreement and Public Health' (2006) 9(2) *McGill Journal of Medicine* 152.

Taubman A, 'Rethinking TRIPS: "Adequate Remuneration" for Non-Voluntary Patent Licensing' (2008) 11 *Journal of International Economic Law* 927.

UN-OHRLLS, 'Least Developed Countries' http://unohrlls.org/custom-content/uploads/2018/12/list-of-least-developed-countries-rev1.pdf accessed 25 January 2019.

World Trade Organization, Implementation of Paragraph 6 of the Doha Declaration on the TRIPS Agreement and Public Health WTO Doc WT/L/540 (2 September) (Decision of 30 August 2003).

Yu P K, Access to Medicines, BRICS Alliances, and Collective Action, (2008) 34 *American Journal of Law and Medicine* 345.

Yu P K, 'TRIPS and Its Discontents' (2006) 10 *Marquette Intellectual Property Law Review* 369.

4 The TRIPS regime for test data protection and access to medicines

4.1 Introduction

The Agreement on Trade Related Aspects of Intellectual Property Rights (the TRIPS Agreement) is the first international agreement to set certain minimum standards for the protection of test data submitted to national drug regulatory authorities for obtaining marketing approval for pharmaceuticals. This protection has created a sui generis proprietary right in undisclosed information very akin to a patent right. The TRIPS regime for test data protection is also popularly known as data exclusivity although, as will be seen later in the chapter, there is some controversy as to whether the TRIPS data protection provisions actually established a data exclusivity regime or not. There has been much concern on the effects that the TRIPS framework for test data protection may have on access to medicines, even though it has not attracted the same level of academic commentaries and analyses as the impact of the TRIPS patents regime. The standard of test data protection required by the TRIPS Agreement and the implications for access to medicines in developing countries are issues that are yet to be fully examined and understood. These points are explored in this chapter.

The chapter examines the legal framework for test data protection under the TRIPS Agreement and the obligations it creates for Member States in relation to data exclusivity. It investigates the extent to which the TRIPS test data protection requirements impose fetters on compulsory licensing and the question of whether the right to keep undisclosed information confidential can be dispensed with through the compulsory licensing mechanism. The chapter considers the connection between test data protection and the need to safeguard public health, with particular focus on the implication for access to medicines in Africa. It is posited that African countries and other developing countries are not likely to derive any real benefit from data exclusivity, other than as a possible boost to investment in the local pharmaceutical industry. However, they are still obliged to comply with their obligations under the TRIPS Agreement, including introducing data protection legislation, which could delay the availability of generic medicines.

The chapter argues that data exclusivity should not be a barrier to the use of compulsory licences and that it may be possible to rely on the grounds for compulsory licensing under the TRIPS Agreement to satisfy the exceptions to TRIPS data exclusivity requirements. The chapter considers TRIPS-plus test data protection in regional trade agreements and the potential impact on access to medicines in Africa and global public health. The chapter discusses the peculiar challenges raised by regulatory requirements for granting marketing approval for biologics. It takes the view that the promotion of free trade and development of pharmaceutical manufacturing capacity in Africa will go a long way in alleviating some of the challenges relating to access to medicines that may be caused by data exclusivity and intellectual property (IP) protection in the continent.

4.1.1 The nature of data exclusivity

Data exclusivity has to do with the protection offered to clinical test data submitted to a national regulatory body to prove the efficacy and safety of a new drug so that a generic manufacturer may not rely on the data to obtain marketing approval for its generic version.[1]

Data exclusivity has also been described as:

> a time-bound form of intellectual property protection that seeks to allow companies to recoup the cost of investment in producing data required by the regulatory authority. The effect of data exclusivity is to prevent the entry of generic competitors, independent of the patent status of the product in question.[2]

A data exclusivity regime is therefore concerned with the extent to which a national drug regulatory body may be prohibited from relying on originator's data in approving the products of prospective generic competitors. Test data normally contain information that enables the government to assess the risks and efficacy of a drug before granting it market authorisation.[3] Such information may include drug composition, factoring method and potential health risks on people thereby making the data of real commercial value.[4]

Generally, before marketing approval is granted for pharmaceuticals in any country, the relevant national drug regulatory authority must have been satisfied as to the safety, efficacy and quality of the drug. This is normally done through

1 G E Evans, 'Strategic Patent Licensing for Public Research Organizations: Deploying Restriction and Reservation Clauses to Promote Medical R&D in Developing Countries' (2008) 34 *American Journal of Law and Medicine* 175, 184.

2 C Clift, 'Data Protection and Data Exclusivity in Pharmaceuticals and Agrochemicals', in A Krattiger, R T Mahoney, L Nelsen, et al. (eds.), *Intellectual Property Management in Health and Agricultural Innovation: A Handbook of Best Practices* (MIHR and PIPRA: 2007) 435.

3 L Dwyer, 'Patent Protection and Access to Medicine: The Colombia and Peruvian Trade Promotion Agreements' (2007) 13 *Law & Business Review of the Americas* 825, 840.

4 Ibid.

reliance on the information that can be gleaned from the test data submitted by the manufacturing company, which would, amongst other things, include the chemical composition of the drugs and preclinical and clinical drug trials, as well as tests conducted in the manufacturing process. Such test data may subsequently be relied on to register generic substitutes on the ground of bioequivalence. The implication of this is that generic manufacturers are able to rely on proprietary information generated at considerable costs by the originator once the period of protection provided by the data exclusivity regime has expired. This allows generic manufacturers to enter the market without having to go through the financial burden of generating their own test data.

There are also ethical issues involved in allowing generic manufacturers to rely on the originator's test data. Clinical trials generally involve the use of both human and animal research subjects[5] and requiring generic manufacturers to duplicate clinical results will entail very onerous consequences for the research subjects. Paragraph 12 of the World Medical Association Declaration of Helsinki is particularly instructive in relation to the ethical issues involved in clinical trials. It provides:

> Medical research involving human subjects must conform to generally accepted scientific principles, be based on a thorough knowledge of the scientific literature, other relevant sources of information, and adequate laboratory and, as appropriate, animal experimentation. The welfare of animals used for research must be respected.

Paragraph 18 of the Helsinki Declaration further provides that any medical research involving the use of human subjects must be preceded by a careful assessment of the foreseeable risks and burdens to human subjects and communities affected by the investigation. The implication of these provisions is that where there is already sufficient knowledge in the field from previous clinical trials, there can hardly be a justified basis for repeating the same process. Precluding generic manufacturers from using submitted test data in order to gain access to a given market can pose a real barrier to access to medicines in developing countries.[6] It has thus been argued that the 'regulatory miasma' occasioned by the data exclusivity regime is a significant part of the global system that embargoes access to medicines in poor countries.[7]

The reason the data exclusivity regime is problematic in terms of access to medicines is that where test data is protected, generic manufacturers will not be able to rely on it for the purpose of seeking marketing approval until the

5 PhRMA, *Clinical Trials: The Phases of Drug Testing and Approval* (2006) www.phrma.org/innovation/clinical-trials accessed 26 January 2019.

6 M R Morgan, 'Medicines for the Developing World: Promoting Access and Innovation in the Post-TRIPS Environment' (2006) 64 *University of Toronto Faculty of Law Review* 45, 68.

7 B K Baker, 'Ending Drug Registration Apartheid: Taming Data Exclusivity and Patent/Registration Linkage' (2008) 34 *American Journal of Law and Medicine* 303, 344.

expiration of the protection offered. The implication is therefore that the rigorous, time-consuming and expensive process of generating test data will serve as a substantial disincentive to market entry by the generic industry and, as a consequence, access to cheaper medicines will be delayed.

Where a product is under patent, data exclusivity is unlikely to be of material effect as the patent has the same effect in preventing entry onto the market of generic versions of the product. However, where the product is not patentable or off patent, data exclusivity can act independently to prevent any generic companies wishing to enter the market from doing so until the data exclusivity regime ends.[8] Data exclusivity may on its own provide monopoly protection similar to a patent where the patent has expired before the pharmaceutical product enters the market due to prolonged delay in the drug development process.[9] For instance, it was reported that between 1998 and 2004, 137 new drugs were approved by the US Food and Drug Administration (FDA), of which 27 of the products were developed without patents.[10] Data exclusivity may offer a distinct protection in such cases. Data exclusivity may confer a stronger right than a patent as governments have limited ability to interfere with it. A government may interfere with the exclusive rights of a patent holder through compulsory licensing but a data exclusivity regime cannot be so easily truncated.[11]

Trade secrets have been recognised and protected under common law rules and unfair competition legislation in a number of countries for many years, long before the advent of TRIPS.[12] The TRIPS Agreement is, however, the first international convention to introduce an international regime for test data protection and this is generally considered one of its most significant features.[13] Prior to TRIPS, Article 10bis of the Paris Convention provided for protection against unfair competition in the following terms:

1 The countries of the Union are bound to assure to nationals of such countries effective protection against unfair competition.
2 Any act of competition contrary to honest practices in industrial or commercial matters constitutes an act of unfair competition.
3 The following in particular shall be prohibited:

   i all acts of such a nature as to create confusion by any means whatever with the establishment, the goods, or the industrial or commercial activities, of a competitor;

8 Clift, above n 2, 433.
9 See W Armoutia & M F A Nsoura 'Test Data Protection: Different Approaches and Implementation in Pharmaceuticals' (2016) 20 *Marquette Intellectual Property Law Review* 267, 280.
10 Ibid.
11 Clift, above n 2, 433.
12 UNCTAD-ICTSD, Resource Book on TRIPS and Development (Cambridge University Press, 2005) 522.
13 C M Correa, *Trade Related Aspects of Intellectual Property Rights: A Commentary on the TRIPS Agreement* (Oxford University Press, 2007) 367.

ii false allegations in the course of trade of such a nature as to discredit the establishment, the goods, or the industrial or commercial activities, of a competitor;

iii indications or allegations the use of which in the course of trade is liable to mislead the public as to the nature, the manufacturing process, the characteristics, the suitability for their purpose, or the quantity, of the goods.

A broad interpretation of Article 10bis of the Paris Convention may have the effect of protecting test data against unfair competition but does not offer anything akin to data exclusivity. However, as will be seen below, the TRIPS test data protection framework transcends the requirement of protecting products against unfair competition by establishing a data exclusivity framework that accords the status of an independent proprietary right on the party entitled to such protection.

4.1.2 Test data protection under TRIPS

The TRIPS Agreement imposes an obligation on all Member States to offer adequate protection for confidential information submitted as prerequisites for gaining market approvals for new drugs. Article 39 of the TRIPS Agreement addresses this issue in the following terms:

> In the course of ensuring effective protection against unfair competition as provided in Article 10bis of the Paris Convention (1967), Members shall protect undisclosed information in accordance with paragraph 2 and data submitted to governments or governmental agencies in accordance with paragraph 3.
>
> 1 Natural and legal persons shall have the possibility of preventing information lawfully within their control from being disclosed to, acquired by, or used by others without their consent in a manner contrary to honest commercial practices so long as such information:
>
> a is secret in the sense that it is not, as a body or in the precise configuration and assembly of its components, generally known among or readily accessible to persons within the circles that normally deal with the kind of information in question;
>
> b has commercial value because it is secret; and
>
> c has been subject to reasonable steps under the circumstances, by the person lawfully in control of the information, to keep it secret.
>
> 2 Members, when requiring, as a condition of approving the marketing of pharmaceutical or of agricultural chemical products which utilize new chemical entities, the submission of undisclosed test or other data, the origination of which involves a considerable effort, shall protect such data against unfair commercial use. In addition, Members shall protect such data against disclosure, except where necessary to protect the public, or unless steps are taken to ensure that the data are protected.

An argument has been made that the initial wording of Article 39.1, '*ensuring effective protection against unfair competition*', suggests that the protection afforded under Article 39 is founded on the rules relating to unfair competition as outlined in Article 10bis of the Paris Convention.[14] Such protection would therefore offer a safeguard against unfair commercial practices without giving rise to exclusive rights.[15] On this basis, Article 39 does not create proprietary rights but only gives a de facto control to the owner of the undisclosed information.[16]

Daniel Gervais has taken the view that the protection against unfair commercial use is enough to satisfy the protection against non-disclosure.[17] Carlos Correa also maintains the position that the text of Article 39 is 'unusually clear' in showing that the obligation under the provision does not go beyond the requirement of protection against unfair commercial practice recognised in the Paris Convention.[18] He further argues that not only does the language of Article 39 fall short of what could be recognised as data exclusivity or the creation of an independent proprietary right but also any interpretation of this Article requiring the establishment of exclusive rights (as constantly done by the US and the pharmaceutical industry) would be fundamentally at variance with the language of TRIPS.[19]

While the argument that Article 39 does not go beyond the requirement to protect against unfair commercial use (as provided for in the Paris Convention) does sound attractive, it is not necessarily compelling It is important to note that obligations under the Paris Convention are already incorporated in the TRIPS Agreement by virtue of Article 2, which provides:

> 1 In respect of Parts II, III and IV of this Agreement, Members shall comply with Articles 1 through 12, and Article 19, of the Paris Convention (1967).
> 2 Nothing in Parts I to IV of this Agreement shall derogate from existing obligations that Members may have to each other under the Paris Convention, the Berne Convention, the Rome Convention and the Treaty on Intellectual Property in Respect of Integrated Circuits.

Given the fact that obligations under the Paris Convention are already binding on parties, it would be unnecessary to reproduce Article 10bis of the Paris Convention in the text of the TRIPS Agreement. In addition, it is very obvious that Article 39 of TRIPS contains specific provisions that substantially differ from Article 10bis. Indeed, what the opening wording of Article 39 says is that

14 UNCTAD-ICTSD, above n 12, 527.
15 Ibid.
16 Ibid.
17 D Gervais, *The TRIPS Agreement: Drafting History and Analysis* (Sweet & Maxwell, Thomson Reuters 4th ed., 2012), 545.
18 Correa, above n 13, 367.
19 Ibid.

Members, in the course of ensuring adequate protection against unfair competition, must protect undisclosed information in line with the further standards imposed by the provision. It is therefore submitted that the protection required under Article 39 is not just confined to the protection against unfair commercial use, as a number of eminent scholars in the field have argued, but also requires standards significantly higher than those available under the Paris Convention. Writing in a similar vein, Nuno Pires de Carvalho argues:

> ...the purpose of Article 39 is not to oblige WTO Members to provide for effective protection against unfair competition, but rather to clarify two issues relating to the protection trade secrets that the legislation of many countries had failed to address appropriately....[20]

4.2 Is Article 39 about data exclusivity?

The drafting history of TRIPS shows that the US' attempt to introduce a ten-year data exclusivity standard was wholly rejected by the negotiators.[21] Correa has particularly argued that the language of TRIPS does not suggest that the mandated test data protection should be accorded through the grant of exclusive rights.[22] While a literal interpretation of TRIPS Article 39 does not disclose a data exclusivity requirement as such,[23] when interpreted against the backdrop of the fact that Article 39.3 is meant to restrain countries from acting in a way inconsistent with the trade secret status of test data, it would seem the reasonable inference to be drawn is that Article 39.3 is meant to operate as a data exclusivity standard.[24] Indeed, Lorna Dwyer has expressed the view that test data is fast becoming a new intellectual property (IP) right:

> It shifted from a mere trade secret to a separate right akin to a patent with a minimum protection of five years. It also shifted from a protection of undisclosed test information to a protection for even publicly available information. The impact has been to prevent generic pharmaceutical manufacturers from entering the market, thus preventing people in developing countries from receiving lifesaving medicines. No credible justification for such protection has been offered. The research and development costs have already been recovered by the patent holders, having been included in the price of the medications for over twenty years.[25]

20 N Pires de Carvalho, *The TRIPS Regime of Patent Rights* (Kluwer Law International 2nd ed. 2004), 388.

21 Gervais, above n 17.

22 Correa, above n 13.

23 A X Fellmeth, 'Secrecy, Monopoly, and Access to Pharmaceuticals in International Trade Law: Protection of Marketing Approval Data under the TRIPS Agreement' (2004) 45 *Harvard International Law Journal* 443, 459.

24 Ibid., 463.

25 Dwyer, 'Patent Protection and Access to Medicine: The Colombia and Peruvian Trade Promotion Agreements' (2007) 13 *Law & Business Review of the Americas* 825.

Aaron Fellmeth has argued that the public protection exception in Article 39.3 can only be justified in cases of real public emergency and that allowing a competitor to use the test data can hardly be justifiable even in an emergency except when it can be proven that the competitor had the only available facilities for testing the drug.[26] On the other hand *in dubiis benigniora praeferenda sunt* is a principle of statutory interpretation that says the imposition of onerous obligations should be discouraged where the language of a treaty is capable of different interpretations or admits of certain ambiguities.[27] Having regards to the fact that Article 39 allows the use of test data where such is necessary to protect the public, a literal interpretation of Article 39(3) does not support the view that such use can only be available where there is an emergency. It is submitted that all that is required to use test data under Article 39 is evidence that this use is clearly in the public interest and not for commercial considerations. To wait until there is a public health emergency before using it is to unnecessarily fetter the flexibility the TRIPS Agreement has allowed in that regard.

Data exclusivity has been the subject of much criticism for a number of reasons. It is viewed as conferring patent-like protection on test data through the creation of financial disincentives against generic manufacturers who may want to enter the market by requiring them either to wait for the data exclusivity to expire or to invest significantly in the production of a new set of test data. It also extends patent protection, which, it is believed, would have provided adequate compensation for the originator brand company.[28] It is therefore another factor that may have very serious implications for healthcare systems and access to affordable medicines in developing countries.

Whilst data protection tends to limit the ability of countries to derogate from the exclusive rights of originators by enhancing generic production, pharmaceutical companies continue to pursue greater protection for patents and test data and the reduction of price controls.[29] In the words of Fellmeth:

> ...economically developed countries have consistently pushed for an interpretation of the TRIPs Agreement that would confer on large pharmaceutical companies price-inflating monopolies over drugs that are neither patented nor patentable, through guarantees of exclusive rights to clinical testing data necessary to obtain marketing approval.[30]

Another significant consideration here is the effect of test data protection on patented products that are being compulsorily licensed. Given that the data exclusivity regime confers a right independent of the patent, the grant of a compulsory

26 Fellmet above n 23, 464.

27 B A Garner ed. *Black's Law Dictionary* (Thomson Reuters 9th ed. 2009) 1836.

28 T Lemmens & C Telfer, 'Access to Information and the Right to Health: The Human Rights Case for Clinical Trials Transparency' (2012) 38 *American Journal of Law & Medicine* 63, 85.

29 F M Abbott, 'The WTO Medicines Decision: World Pharmaceutical Trade and the Protection of Public Health' (2005) 99 *American Journal of International Law* 317, 357.

30 Fellmeth, above n 23, 445.

licence in relation to a pharmaceutical product is arguably without prejudice to the test data protection and the ability of the compulsory licensee to rely on the originator's clinical trials results for getting marketing approval on the basis of the compulsory licence alone may be debatable. This point is examined further below.

4.2.1 Elements of test data protection under the TRIPS Agreement

As already noted above, Article 39.3 provides for test data protection and encapsulates the TRIPS test data protection regime. This regime can be broken down into the following elements:

a the product must utilise new chemical entities (newness requirement);
b the origination of the undisclosed test data must involve considerable effort (origination requirement);
c the test data must be protected against unfair commercial use (protection against unfair competition requirement); and
d the test data must be undisclosed except where necessary to protect the public or where steps are taken against unfair commercial use (non-disclosure obligation and the exceptions).

4.2.1.1 Newness requirement

Article 39.3 provides that the pharmaceutical or agricultural chemical product for which protection is sought must utilise new chemical entities. It could be argued that the requirement that the chemical entity is 'new' is akin to the requirement for novelty in patent law. If this is the case, then the next question is what is the standard required to satisfy this newness requirement? Since this term is not defined by the TRIPS Agreement it is submitted that countries are at liberty to decide the standard of newness for test data protection that suits their local circumstances. This position is fully in consonance with the provision of Article 1.1 of the TRIPS Agreement which provides that members are under no obligation to provide more extensive protection than that required under the Agreement and that they shall be free to determine the suitable method of enforcing the provisions of the Agreement within their legal system and practice.

In the alternative, it has been argued that the concept of 'newness' in respect of chemical entities does not relate to the novelty or undisclosed nature of the data but the administrative act of registration.[31] In other words, the concept of 'new' under Article 39.3 has nothing to do with the patent standard of novelty but registration and the effects of registration of a chemical entity for purposes of its novelty are basically territorial.[32] Gervais has described this as the practical

31 Pires de Carvalho, above n 20, 397.
32 Ibid., 397–398.

approach to defining 'new' under Article 39.3.[33] He opines that provided that a chemical entity has not been previously submitted for regulatory approval in a given country, it should be considered new and the data generated on it should be eligible for protection.[34] To date, there has been no official guidance on which of these differing views should be adopted by Members as fulfilling the 'newness' requirement in Article 39.3. Section 201 of the US Food Drugs and Cosmetic Act for instance defines a new drug as:

> Any drug (except a new animal drug or an animal feed bearing or containing a new animal drug) the composition of which is such that such drug, as a result of investigations to determine its safety and effectiveness for use under such conditions, has become so recognized, but which has not, otherwise than in such investigations, been used to a material extent or for a material time under such conditions.

While using the act of registration as a benchmark for registration is defensible under Article 39, it is nonetheless submitted that the newness requirement in Article 39 should not be based on the act of registration but on the fact that the chemical composition is such that it had not been formerly recognised by people qualified by scientific training and experience to evaluate the drugs as safe and effective for the treatment it has been found to offer. There is also support for the view that Article 39.3 will not cover cases where approval is required for 'new dosage forms, combinations, new forms of administration, crystalline forms, isomers, etc. of existing product',[35] as they would not fall within the definition of new chemical entity. In sum, it is submitted that since TRIPS has not given a clear definition of the newness requirement, this is another flexibility and Members may rely on Article 1.1 of the TRIPS Agreement to interpret this in a way conducive to their socio-economic welfare.

4.2.1.2 Origination requirement

Article 39.3 provides that the origination of test data to be protected must involve considerable efforts. It is generally taken that for pharmaceuticals, the generation of test data in most cases would involve considerable efforts especially in conducting clinical trials.[36] It would appear that the reasonable inference to draw from this provision is that the 'effort' involved should not only be substantial economically but also in technical and scientific terms.[37] On the other hand, this part of the test data protection regime has been criticised as extending IP beyond its boundaries of rewarding the creators of original

33 Gervais, above n 17, 544–545.
34 Ibid.
35 Correa, above n 13, 379.
36 Gervais, above n 17, 545.
37 UNCTAD-ICTSD, 531.

ideas and new inventions to the protection of investment and not intellectual contribution.[38] The protection of investment, according to Correa, should be within the purview of competition law and not IP.[39] It is however doubtful if it can be rightly argued that the development of a new invention can be fully separated from the investment that inevitably goes with it. There is also no gainsaying the fact that test data generation involves substantial economic resources and scientific knowledge. It is thus submitted that the 'considerable effort' requirement will be easily met in virtually all cases of pharmaceutical test data generation.

4.2.1.3 Protection against unfair competition requirement

Article 39.3 requires national drug regulatory authorities to protect information submitted to them against unfair commercial use to the extent that such information remains undisclosed. It should be noted that the test data regime under Article 39.3 is essentially for regulatory approval for marketing pharmaceutical or agricultural products. It does not entail selling or offering data for sale.[40] To that extent, the point has been made that '*commercial use can only mean granting marketing approval to competing goods without the consent of the first registrant*'.[41] As Pires de Carvalho argues:

> The whole idea of Article 39.3 is to prohibit parasitic behaviour or free riding. Any measures, such as relying on bioequivalence tests or other abridged procedures that alleviate the second registrant from obligations that have been imposed to the first registrant should be deemed as such.

On the other hand, Correa has argued that the concept of 'unfair' is relative to the values of a particular community and varies among Members.[42] He posits that even though the use by government may have commercial implications, it still does not amount to a commercial activity but a defensible State practice.[43] He thus highlights the following as things countries may do without violating Article 39.3:

- a Require the second-entrant to produce its own testing data or to obtain an authorization of use from the 'originator' of the data;
- b Allow the second-entrant to rely on the 'originator's' data against payment of compensation;

38 Correa, above n 13, 380.
39 Ibid.
40 TRIPS Agreement Article 39.
41 Pires de Carvalho, above n 20, 393.
42 Correa, above n 11, 381.
43 Ibid., 383.

c Use the 'originator's' data in order to technically examine second-entry applications. In this case, the authority directly relies on the originator's data;
d Require the second-entrant to prove that his product is similar to an already registered product, without having to examine and rely upon the 'originator's' data.[44]

Hiroko Yamane also takes a similar view, positing that Article 39.3 only requires Members to prevent the disclosure of data submitted to regulatory bodies to competitors and does not entail more than the protection against unfair commercial use by competitors.[45] It is however submitted that use of test data under (c) and (d) above will be inconsistent with Article 39.3 as that will involve reliance on the originator's data which may also amount to an unfair commercial practice. Any use of the test data without the owner's consent will therefore be inconsistent with Article 39.

As mentioned earlier, one unsavoury effect of restraining drug regulatory authorities from granting marketing approval on the basis of bioequivalence is the problem of having to substantially repeat toxicological and clinical trials which will not only be profligate but also ethically problematic.[46] Nonetheless, it is very doubtful indeed that Article 39 can be construed as being limited to protection against unfair commercial use by competitors. It would appear that reliance on the first registrant's test data for the purposes of granting marketing approval to a generic company, whether state owned or not, would run afoul of the tenor of the provision.

4.2.1.4 Non-disclosure obligation and the public protection exception

Where generic companies rely on data that are publicly available, Article 39 will not apply, as the requirement is that the information must be undisclosed to qualify for protection. This provision is, however, subject to the public protection exception in Article 39.3.[47] The implication of this exception is that Members may disclose such information where necessary to protect public health or interest or where certain steps have been taken to adequately protect the disclosed data against unfair commercial use or competition. The TRIPS Agreement does not provide guidance on when it will be 'necessary to protect the public'. Professor Correa has opined that this provision is subject to a necessity test.[48] Deference may be given to Members in determining when such necessity arises but a Member invoking the provision may have to bear a very onerous burden of proof, should the measure taken be challenged.[49]

44 Ibid., 384.
45 H Yamane, *Interpreting TRIPS* (Hart Publishing, Oxford, 2011), 470–471.
46 UNCTAD-ICTSD, above n 12, 531.
47 Article 39.3, TRIPS Agreement.
48 Correa, above n 11, 380.
49 Ibid.

There is some support for the view that disclosure may be allowed to enable a compulsory licensee to acquire marketing approval, especially where the licence is issued to correct anticompetitive practices or to meet the demands of public health.[50] This is examined in Section 4.3.[51] It is important to note that Article 39 does not provide for a set duration of test data protection and it would seem such protection may continue indefinitely until the data can no longer be considered 'undisclosed'. The generally accepted term of protection, from the current practice amongst Members, is five to ten years.[52] It has been suggested that terms of protection should be decided on a case-by-case basis, taking into account the resources committed to the generation of the test data and its novelty, but subject to a maximum protection period to avoid abuses.[53]

4.3 Data exclusivity and compulsory licensing

A pertinent point to consider here is the likely implication of test data protection on the use of compulsory licensing. The potential problem that may arise is that even where a compulsory licence is issued, the generic manufacturer may still have to seek the approval of the patent holder to make use of the test data to obtain marketing approval.[54] Thus, where a compulsory licence is issued in respect of a drug, data exclusivity may still present a significant hurdle by making marketing authorisation for the drug more difficult.[55] This is because Article 39.3 establishes a quasi-proprietary, quasi-patent system that confers rights that are separate and distinct from a patent right.[56] It is thus submitted that the grant of a compulsory licence to produce generics does not, on its own, waive the protection available under Article 39.3.

The question that follows from this is whether a compulsory licensee may avoid gaining the data owner's authorisation for marketing approval. A case could be made for arguing that use by government pursuant to the grant of a compulsory licence is not unfair and should not be treated as such. This is because the compulsory licensing regime under Article 31 of the TRIPS Agreement requires the payment of adequate remuneration where a compulsory licence is to be issued. It is therefore presumed that the compensation paid to a patent holder for the compulsory licence would have taken the data exclusivity right into account and such use of the information should therefore no longer be considered unfair.

50 UNCTAD-ICSTD, above n 12, 532.
51 See Section 4.3.
52 IFPMA, *A Review of Existing Data Exclusivity Legislation in Selected Countries* (International Association of Pharmaceutical Manufacturers Association, 2002).
53 Pires de Carvalho, above n 20, 399.
54 Dwyer, above n 25, 843.
55 Clift, above n 2, 433.
56 Pires de Carvalho, above n 20, 390.

In a similar vein, use by a third party pursuant to a compulsory licence will not, it is submitted, be inconsistent with the provision of Article 39.3 provided the third party is required to pay adequate compensation to the patent holder who will also be owner of the test data. Article 31(h) of the TRIPS Agreement provides that '*the right holder shall be paid adequate compensation in the circumstances of each case, taking into account the economic value of the authorization*'. It is thus submitted that it will be an onerous burden indeed to expect a compulsory licensee to pay a separate remuneration for the patent right and another for data exclusivity. Since Article 31(h) already requires the compensation paid to the right holder to take cognisance of the economic value of the authorisation, this will be enough to compensate for the use of test data as well.

4.3.1 Can test data be compulsorily licensed?

Another issue that is necessary to consider is whether the government can grant a compulsory licence in relation to a test data right, especially in cases where there is no need to get a compulsory patent licence. A brief examination of the negotiation history of the TRIPS Agreement may be pertinent here. The Anell's draft (Chairman's draft) of July 23, 1990 provided as follows on this point:

> 2A(a). Parties shall not discourage or impede voluntary licensing of undisclosed information by imposing excessive or discriminatory conditions on such licences or conditions which dilute the value of such information.
>
> 2A(b). There shall be no compulsory licensing of proprietary information.[57]

The Brussels Draft of December, 1990 did not have the equivalent of Article 2A(b) in the Anell's draft but nonetheless provided thus:

> 3A. Parties shall not discourage or impede voluntary licensing of undisclosed information by imposing excessive or discriminatory conditions on such licences or conditions which dilute the value of such information.[58]

These provisions prohibiting or discouraging the compulsory licensing of proprietary information were not included in the final text of the TRIPS Agreement. Does this mean the TRIPS Agreement can now be interpreted as allowing the compulsory licensing of proprietary information? Pires de Carvalho argues that the fact that Article 39.3 does not mention compulsory licensing does not support the inference that it forbids it, as the Agreement does explicitly forbid

57 Chairman's Report to the GNG, Status of Work in the Negotiating Group, Negotiating Group on Trade-Related Aspects of Intellectual Property Rights, including Trade in Counterfeit Goods, WTO Doc MTN.GNG/NG11/W/76, (23 July 1990).

58 *Draft Final Act Embodying the Results of the Uruguay Round of Multilateral Trade Negotiations – Revision*, GATT Doc MTN.TNC/W/35/Rev.1 (December 3 1990).

compulsory licensing where such is deemed necessary. This is the case in respect of trademarks under Article 23, which provides thus:

> Parties may determine conditions on the licensing and assignment of trademarks, it being understood that the compulsory licensing of trademarks shall not be permitted and that the owner of a registered trademark shall have the right to assign his trademark with or without the transfer of the business to which the trademark belongs.

The argument therefore is that TRIPS has clearly and unequivocally made it known where compulsory licensing is not available, as in the case for trademarks, and in the absence of such express prohibition, it should be presumed that compulsory licensing will be available. While this argument is very compelling in principle, it is unlikely that compulsory licensing can be effectively pursued in practice under the provisions of Article 39.3 for a number of reasons. First, the earlier drafts of the Agreement shows there was a clear intention to prohibit compulsory licensing of undisclosed information,[59] though the removal of the prohibition may also indicate an intention to allow it. Secondly, no compulsory licence can be granted under Article 39.3 save to the extent necessary to protect public interest or unless adequate steps are taken to prevent unfair competition. It would therefore appear that compulsory licensing may be available under Article 39.3 where it is used as a measure for taking advantage of the exceptions recognised under that provision. Any step taken in excess of that will be afoul of the TRIPS Agreement.

4.4 Data exclusivity and biologics

The increasing significance of biologics to the data exclusivity debate raises special issues of concern for data exclusivity. Biologics are drugs that are made up of living material and are generally used to treat life-threatening conditions.[60] Biologics are large-molecule drugs that cannot be chemically synthesised and they include 'vaccines, cells, gene therapy agents, tissues, recombinant proteins, monoclonal antibodies, cytokines, and immunomodulators.'[61] While biologics offer great therapeutic promises, they are also very expensive. For instance, Brineura, a biologic produced by BioMarine Pharmaceutical as a therapy for Batten disease, a genetic walking disorder, is reported to cost $700,000 for a full-year treatment.[62]

59 See Section 4.3.1.

60 V Banthia, 'Biosimilars: Countering Shortages of Biotherapies in a Global And Local Context' (2017) 57 IDEA: *Journal of the Franklin Pierce for Intellectual Property* 359, 360.

61 M A Sanzo, 'The Promise and Problem of Biologics' (2017) *Santa Clara High Technology Law Journal* 78, 80.

62 I Haydon, 'Biologics: The Pricey Drugs Transforming Medicine', *The Conversation US*, 26 July 2017.

The Hatch Waxman Act was enacted by the US Congress in 1984 to regulate the entry of generic chemical drugs into the US market. The Hatch Waxman Act provides for a five-year data exclusivity period for a new chemical drug submitted to the FDA. Generic manufacturers will only be allowed into the market after the expiration of the data exclusivity period.[63] The Hatch Waxman Act does not, however, cover biologics, and generic drugs only require evidence of bioequivalence to the original brand which is generally unattainable in relation to follow on biologics or biosimilars.[64] Thus, the Biologics Price Competition and Innovation Act 2009 (BPCIA) was enacted to provide a legal framework for the marketing approval of biologics and biosimilars and it provides for a 12 years market exclusivity period for biologics.[65]

While there are a number of strict regulatory requirements for biologics and the high costs associated with them, the data exclusivity period associated with biologics in the US and Europe which clearly exceed the conventional exclusivity period for chemical drugs, can create additional access hurdles for follow-on biologics. A study found for instance that the total market exclusivity period for top-selling drugs in the US is 12.4 years taking into account monopoly conferred by patents and data exclusivity.[66] Writing on the study, Sanzo observed that should the current 12 years data exclusivity regime for biologics be extended:

> the importance of patents in maintaining exclusivity would be greatly diminished and litigation challenges to patents should decrease accordingly. A longer term would also have the effect of giving drug makers an extended period to recover production costs and potentially encourage them to reduce prices somewhat. However, extending exclusivity also means that the benefits of biosimilar entry on price reduction and innovation would be lost.[67]

Even though patents and data exclusivity are generally considered crucial to pharmaceutical innovation ecosystem, pharmaceuticals also benefit from other innovation incentives that are not connected to patents or the intellectual property framework.[68] Patents are generally used in tandem with trade secrets to protect pharmaceutical innovation portfolio and given the fact that trade secrets can continue for as long as the information is confidential, they may provide a more valuable protection than patents.[69] With respect to biologics, the complex-

63 Drug Price Competition and Patent Term Restoration Act 21 U.S.C. § 355(j)(5)(F)(ii) (2012).

64 See O Owoeye & O Owoeye, 'Biologics and Public Health: Prospects and Challenges (2018) *Journal of Law and Medicine* 170, 182–183.

65 Biologics Price Competition and Innovation Act of 2009, 42 U.S.C. § 262(k)(7)(A) (2012).

66 Bo Wang et al., 'Variations in Time of Market Exclusivity among Top-Selling Prescription Drugs in the United States', 175 *JAMA Internal Medicine* 635, 635 (Apr. 2015).

67 M A Sanzo, 'The Promise and Problem of Biologics' (2017) *Santa Clara High Technology Law Journal* 78, 103.

68 R E Sachs, 'The Uneasy Case for Patent Law' (2018) 117 *Michigan Law Review* 499, 500.

69 Ibid., 510.

ity of their manufacturing process will make it extremely difficult for biosimilars to enter the market where they are protected by trade secrets.[70] Data exclusivity can easily offer more protection in relation to biologics where patents may be unavailable or difficult to enforce as a result of the differences in the manufacturing process that may make it easier for the biosimilar to avoid patent infringement. Unlike patents, it is more difficult to challenge the validity of data exclusivity as they are automatically enforced by the relevant national regulatory body.[71] Microbiomes are biologics that may be protected by data exclusivity without a corresponding patent protection as they are unlikely to satisfy patentability criteria. The human microbiomes consist of the trillions of microorganisms that inhabit the human body from bacteria to viruses and fungi.[72] Microbiomes have been linked to a wide range of medical conditions.[73] Writing on microbiome, Nicola Davies observed thus:

> Over recent years the gut microbiome in particular has been linked to a plethora of diseases and conditions, from diabetes to autism and anxiety to obesity. The gut microbiome has also been linked to how individuals respond to certain drugs, including how cancer patients, and it has even, tentatively been suggested that it could be linked to how well we sleep.[74]

The pharmaceutical industry has shown tremendous interest in the field of microbiome in recent years with several small and larger pharmaceutical companies involved in the process of developing microbiome-based therapies for FDA approval.[75]

The US Supreme Court in *Association for Molecular Pathology v Myriad Genetics, Inc.*, held that the mere isolation of naturally occurring human genes that could be used in breast cancer therapy did not make the isolated genes patentable as 'Myriad did not create or alter any of the genetic information' in the genes.[76] In 2015, Myriad patents for BRCA (Breast Cancer susceptibility) genes were invalidated by the High Court of Australia on the ground that the patents were for naturally occurring genes that did not constitute a 'manner of manufacture' under Australian Patents Act.[77] The implication of these decisions is that microbiomes may not easily satisfy the requirements of patent protection except where some inventive modifications have been made on them. They can however still be protected by data exclusivity without patents and this may create

70 O Owoeye & O Owoeye, 'Biologics and Public Health: Prospects and Challenges (2018) *Journal of Law and Medicine* 170, 182.
71 R E Sachs, 'The Uneasy Case for Patent Law' (2018) 117 *Michigan Law Review* 499, 514.
72 J E Brody, 'Unlocking the Secrets of the Microbiome', *New York Times*, 6 November 2017.
73 Ibid.
74 N Davis, 'The Human Microbiome: Why Our Microbes Could Be Key to Our Health' *The Guardian*, 26 March 2018.
75 See R E Sachs, 'The Uneasy Case for Patent Law' (2018) 117 *Michigan Law Review* 499, 517.
76 In *Association for Molecular Pathology v Myriad Genetics, Inc.*, 569 US 576, 591 (2013).
77 D'Arcy v Myriad Genetics Inc. (2015) CLR 334, [94]; [2015] HCA 35.

special challenges for access. While data exclusivity and trade secrets may provide valuable protection and incentive for innovation in the field of microbiomes where patent protection may be unavailable, it is still important to consider policy options that will ensure such data exclusivity does not unreasonably inhibit access to the benefits of scientific progress.

4.5 The global move towards a universal standard for data exclusivity

Many countries have already legislated to provide for data exclusivity protection. In the US, the FDA (the national drug regulatory authority) is forbidden from accepting an application for marketing approval brand for a competitor for the first five years of registration without the consent of the initial registrant.[78] The same practice has been adopted by Health Canada.[79] In the European Community (EC), members are now required to grant six to ten years of data exclusivity to drugs that have been given marketing approval.[80] The EC has taken the position that the best way to protect test data against unfair commercial use is data exclusivity irrespective of whether the product is patented or not.[81] In Australia, test data registration is performed by the Therapeutic Goods Administration and protection is available for a period of five years from the date of registration.[82]

The justification for limiting the extent of the data exclusivity period, as already noted, is to avoid a situation whereby every generic manufacturer will have to undertake their own clinical trials which will not only entail significant waste of resources as well as ethical issues, but also make it substantially difficult for poor people in poor countries to have access to much needed drugs at affordable prices. The contrary argument put by the IP exporting countries is that there will be little incentive to market drugs in poor countries without a robust data exclusivity regime.[83] Test data protection offers another layer of protection to products that are not patented or where the patent term has expired or is close to expiration at the time of registration.

78 Drug Price Competition and Patent Term Restoration Act 21 U.S.C. § 355(j)(5)(F)(ii) (2012).

79 Food & Drugs Act (Canada) C.R.C. c. 870 (1985), amended by § C.08.004.1, 129 C. Gaz. 2494 (1995) (Can.).

80 Council Directive 2001/83, art. 10, 2001 O.J. (L 311) 75 (EC); I Dodds-Smith, 'Data Protection and Abridged Applications for Marketing Authorisations in the Pharmaceutical Industry', in R Goldberg & J Lonbay (eds.), *Pharmaceutical Medicine, Biotechnology and European Law* (Cambridge University Press, 2001) 93, 113.

81 *Communication from the European Communities and Their Member States to the Council on Trade-Related Aspects of Intellectual Property Rights*, WTO Doc 15 IP/C/W/280 (June 12, 2001) 6.

82 See Section 25A(2) (e)*Therapeutic Goods Act 1989* (Cth).

83 See C M Correa, *Protection of Data Submitted for the Registration of Pharmaceuticals: Implementing the Standards of the Trips Agreement* (South Centre, 2002) 6–7.

Since the emergence of the TRIPS Agreement, the US has developed the practice of including a five-year data exclusivity regime in its bilateral trade agreements.[84] The US has also been using more coercive measures under its 301 Watch List to enforce its interpretation of the TRIPS obligations. For instance, in 1996 a special 301 procedure was launched against Australia for failing to provide adequate protection to test data submitted for marketing approval.[85] This probably influenced Australia's adoption of its own five-year data exclusivity regime in 1998.[86] Other countries that have come under US trade sanctions or pressure for non-compliance with data exclusivity requirements include Argentina, Taiwan and Thailand.[87] In 2018, countries on the US 301 Priority watch list for non-compliance with test data obligations included Algeria; Argentina, Chile, China, India, Indonesia. Others on the watch list for inadequate test data protection were Brazil, Egypt, Saudi Arabia, Turkey and Vietnam.[88]

4.6 Free trade agreements and data protection

The various free trade agreements and bilateral trade agreements negotiated by the US contain provisions that impose a level of test data protection requirements going beyond those contained in TRIPS. For instance, the Peruvian Trade Promotion Agreement and the Colombia Trade Promotion Agreement both include provisions that prohibit the use of test data on safety and drug efficacy for obtaining governmental approval of generic drugs.

In a similar vein, the Dominican Republic-Central American Free Trade Agreement (CAFTA) requires signatories to provide test data protection for five years from the moment the product is granted market approval in their country.[89] This has been described as '*an effective five-year bar on compulsory licensing from the time of marketing approval*'.[90] The US-Morocco Free Trade Agreement (USMFTA) contains a similar provision.[91] It is very arguable that the standard of protection required by TRIPS is that test data must not be used for an unfair commercial purpose, and must not unduly restrict generic manufacturers seeking to use it for marketing approval. Data protection under TRIPS is only applicable to data relating to new chemical entities. However, under CAFTA, USMFTA and other US free trade agreements, it applies to new products with a chemical entity not

84 See Chapter 8.

85 US Trade Representative, *Fact Sheet: "Special 301" On Intellectual Property Rights* (1996) www.cptech.org/ip/health/ustr/301-96.htm accessed 26 January 2019.

86 Therapeutic Goods Legislation Amendment Act (Australia) 1998, No. 34.

87 US Trade Representative, above n 62.

88 US Trade Representative Special 301 List 2018.

89 *Dominican Republic-Central American Free Trade Agreement*, signed 5 August 2004 (entered into force 1 March 2006) art 15.10.1(b).

90 Cowley, 'The Right to Health: Guatemala's Conflicting Obligations under the Central American Free Trade Agreement and the International Covenant on Economic, Social and Cultural Rights' (2007) 11 *Michigan State University Journal of Medicine & Law* 227, 242.

91 US – Morocco Free Trade Agreement, 15.10(1).

formerly approved in the country irrespective of whether the chemical entity is new or not.[92]

4.7 Data exclusivity and the right to health

There is an emerging discourse on the need to recognise access to clinical trials information as a basic component of the right to health.[93] The connection between IP rights and the right to health are explored further in more detail in Chapter 4. The TRIPS data protection regime has been criticised as providing a de facto extension to patents, thereby preventing low-priced pharmaceuticals from entering the market and consequently affecting access to medicines in developing countries disproportionately.[94] While test data protection will normally expire before the patent, this will not be the case if the test data is introduced to a particular market for the first time long after the patent has been obtained and the data still meet the requirement for protection under Article 39.

It is important to note that the expiration of data exclusivity does not make the test data available to the public as such information still remains confidential even after the period of data exclusivity has expired. Arguably, there is, however, considerable public interest in making clinical trials results available to the public to safeguard public health. Access to early clinical trials, including Phase 1 exploratory trials, could provide helpful information about the health and safety issues that may attend the marketing of pharmaceutical products.[95] It is arguable therefore that there exists the need to develop appropriate knowledge systems and reliable regulatory structure around medical knowledge.[96] Hence, it is submitted that following the expiration of the data exclusivity period, such information should be readily available at least for the purposes of medical research and advancement of knowledge.

The controversy regarding research reporting and marketing practices of GlaxoSmithKline and the use of its drug Praxil for the treatment of depression in children illustrates the point that access to clinical trials information is in the public interest.[97] The company was prosecuted by the Attorney General of New York for failing to disclose negative data and lopsided publications to promote off-label prescriptions.[98] Another example was the controversy

92 Dominican Republic-Central American Free Trade Agreement, art 15.10.1(c).

93 See generally T Lemmens & C Telfer, 'Access to Information and the Right to Health: The Human Rights Case for Clinical Trials Transparency' (2012) 38 *American Journal of Law & Medicine* 63, 65.

94 Ibid., 85.

95 Ibid.

96 Ibid.

97 D Rennie, 'Trial Registration. A Great Idea Switches from Ignored to Irresistible' (2004) 292 *JAMA* 1359, 1359; J N Jureidini, L B McHenry & P R Mansfield, 'Clinical Trials and Drug Promotion: Selective Reporting of Study' (2008) 329, 20 *International Journal of Risk & Safety Medicine* 73.

98 See *New York v. GlaxoSmithKline*, No. 04-CV-5304 MGC (S.D.N.Y. Aug. 26, 2004).

surrounding Merck and its pain relief medication Vioxx estimated to have caused hundreds of thousands of severe myocardial infarctions and cardiac deaths.[99] These incidents provide a sound basis for the proposition that clinical trials data should be accessible where necessary to ascertain the safety and efficacy of pharmaceuticals.

The argument that access to test data is a fundamental part of the right to health is founded on the premise that test data are 'public goods'[100] and the ability to access test data information is seen as a major element of the right to the highest attainable standard of health.[101] As noted earlier in this chapter, the TRIPS Agreement does recognise the public interest in test data and thus provides an exception to the rule against disclosure where such is necessary to protect the public.[102] The right to health entails the actualisation of public goals such as availability, accessibility and quality,[103] particularly in the field of pharmaceuticals. Such goals can hardly be realised without some fair access to medical care that is substantially shown to be scientifically dependable and publicly accepted as effective. The European Court of Human Rights (ECHR) decision in *Sunday Times v United Kingdom* is somewhat pertinent to the topic.[104] An article in *The Sunday Times*, examining the history of the manufacturing and regulatory approval of thalidomide had been banned by an injunction because its publication would amount to contempt of court. The ECHR found that the injunction would amount to an unjustifiable infringement of Article 10 of the European Convention on Human Rights, which guarantees the freedom of expression. The ECHR particularly noted that in issues pertaining to public health, the public has a right to be 'properly informed'.[105]

The human right dimension to the data protection provision of the TRIPS Agreement may therefore be a powerful weapon in addressing the public health implications of the TRIPS data protection regime. There is definitely the possibility of public health issues arising from data protection and this is equally recognised in Article 39(3) of the TRIPS Agreement. Member States therefore reserve the right to use such information or allow an independent third party to use it where necessary to protect public health to the extent that the protection against unfair commercial use is not compromised. States in using

99 R Horton, 'Vioxx, the Implosion of Merck and Aftershocks at the FDA' (2004) 364 The Lancet 1595; E J Topol, 'Failing the Public Health – Rofecoxib, Merck, and the FDA' (2004) 351 *New England Journal of Medicine* 1707.

100 J H Reichman, 'Rethinking the Role of Clinical Trial Data in International Intellectual Property Law: The Case for a Public Goods Approach' (2009) 13 *Marquette* Intellectual Property *Law Review* 1.

101 Lemmens & Telfer above n 93, 99.

102 TRIPS Agreement art 39(3).

103 Special Rapporteur on the Right to Health, *Addendum to the Report of the Special Rapporteur*, U.N. Comm'n on Human Rights, Mission to the World Trade Organization, U.N. Doc. E/CN.4/2004/49/Add.1 (1 March 2004) 33–38.

104 *The Sunday Times v. The United Kingdom* (1979) 30 Eur. Ct. H.R. (ser. A), at 245.

105 Ibid., 66.

or allowing the use of such information can justify the use by relying on the right to health.

Apart from using originator test data for granting marketing approval to generic manufacturers either pursuant to a compulsory licence or following the expiration of the data exclusivity period, use or disclosure of such information can also be justified both under TRIPS and international human rights law for the purposes of ascertaining the efficacy or safety of the product provided adequate steps are taken to ensure the disclosure does not result in unfair commercial use of the data.

4.8 Test data and clinical trials reporting

In 2004, the Global Forum and Ministerial Summit on Health Research issued the *Statement on Health Research* which emphasised the need to promote access to reliable 'and up-to-date evidence on the effects of interventions' and called on the WHO to create a platform connecting 'a network of international clinical trials registers to ensure a single point of access and the unambiguous identification of trials'.[106] This was further reinforced by the fifty-eighth World Health Assembly in Resolution WHA58.34. As a result, the International Clinical Trial Registry Platform (ICTRP) was established by the WHO in 2005, with the aim of enhancing the WHO Trial Registration Data Set on all Clinical Trials and promoting public accessibility to the information.[107] The ICTRP search portal provides a one-stop point of access on information relating to current or completed clinical trials by using records submitted by data providers all over the world. The ICTRP is largely dependent on both national and regional regimes for implementation and enforcement.[108] Whilst the creation of the ICTRP is undoubtedly a significant step towards ensuring the accessibility of clinical trials data, a number of experts have taken the view that the ICTRP minimal data set was somewhat inadequate and more information would be required for any meaningful analysis of clinical trials to be possible.[109]

One major concern of the pharmaceutical industry is that clinical trial registration may offer competitors access to information that is substantially proprietary. Representatives of the industry have particularly expressed the objections of its members to the disclosure of five data items in the ICTRP system for being commercially sensitive, these being official scientific title, intervention name, target sample size, primary outcome and key secondary outcomes. The industry has argued that the disclosure of such information would deprive the originator

106 The Mexico Statement on Health Research from the Ministerial Summit on Health Research Mexico City, 16–20 November 2004.

107 WHO, *International Clinical Trials Registry: About the WHO ICTRP* (2013) www.who.int/ictrp/about/en/ accessed 26 January 2019.

108 Lemmens & Telfer, above n 93, 72.

109 C Haug, P Gatzsche & T Schoeder, 'Registries and Registration of Clinical Trials' (2005) 353 *New England Journal of Medicine* 2811, 2812.

company of the benefits of being the first to enter the market with a novel product.[110] It is, however, pertinent to note as stated earlier, that the obligation to protect test data under TRIPS is not unqualified. Disclosure is allowed where necessitated by overriding public interest and the implementation of registration and results reporting systems will fall within this exception.[111]

4.9 Data exclusivity in Africa

Data exclusivity is yet to be incorporated into the domestic laws of most African countries. Most countries in the continent do not have legislative frameworks for test data protection and where they exist, they usually offer protection against unfair commercial use.[112] However, the Ghanaian and Rwandan laws on test data protection seem to have fully incorporated the provisions of the TRIPS Agreement on data exclusivity. Section 5(4) of the Protection against Unfair Competition Act 2000 (Ghana) provides:

> 4 Any act or practice, in the course of industrial or commercial activities, shall be considered an act of unfair competition if it consists or results in –
>
> a an unfair commercial use of secret test or other data, the origin of which involves considerable effort and which have been submitted to a competent authority for the purposes of obtaining approval of the marketing of pharmaceutical or agricultural chemical products which utilise new chemical entities; or
>
> b the disclosure of such data, except where
>
> i it is necessary for the protection of the public; and
>
> ii steps are taken to ensure that the data are protected against unfair commercial use.

Section 6 of the Ghanaian *Competition Act* goes further to provide that any act or practice in the course of commercial activity that breaches Ghanaian law or international law (including the TRIPS Agreement) in a manner contrary to honest commercial practices constitutes an act of unfair commercial use. The provision of the Ghanaian law, it is submitted, is couched in such broad terms as to incorporate fully the TRIPS data exclusivity regime.

110 Letter from A Goldhammer, Associate Vice President, US Regulatory Affairs, to ICTRP, *RE: PhRMA's Second Round Comments on International Clinical Trials Registry Platform (ICTRP): Disclosure Timing* (World Health Organisation, 2006) www.who.int/ictrp/002-PhRMA_29March06.pdf accessed 26 January 2019.

111 Lemmens &Telfer, above n 93, 82.

112 P L Osewe, Y K Nkrumah & E K Sackey, *Improving Access to HIV/AIDS Medicines in Africa* (World Bank, 2008) 21 http://apps.who.int/medicinedocs/documents/s17514en/s17514en.pdf accessed 26 January 2019.

In Rwanda, Article 185 of the Law on the Protection of Intellectual Property deals with the protection of confidential information. The provision of Article 185 of the Law on Intellectual Property Protection, by itself, does no more than protect test data against unfair competition. However, the effect of Article 290 of the Law is to make the full provisions of the TRIPS Agreement and other international IP conventions binding on all persons and authorities in Rwanda. Article 290 of the Law provides:

> The provisions of any international intellectual property treaty to which the Republic of Rwanda is party shall apply. In case of conflict with the provisions of this Law, the provisions of the international treaty shall prevail over the latter.

In view of the fact the Rwanda is a least developed country, the TRIPS data exclusivity regime should ordinarily not apply to the country until least developed countries are bound to comply fully with the TRIPS patents regime and data exclusivity framework under WTO law. Thus, the current waivers the WTO has made for least developed countries in relation to compliance with Sections 5 and 7 of Part II of TRIPS should still be in force in Rwanda. It is also important to note that the WTO in 2013 extended the timeline for least developed countries to comply fully with the TRIPS Agreement to July 2021.[113] However, given the fact that the country has incorporated higher standards of protection in its national law, it is very doubtful if the country can still benefit from the waivers available to least developed countries under the TRIPS Agreement.

Nigeria and Kenya do not currently have legislations dealing with test data protection. Given the fact that the legal system in both countries follows the English common law tradition, the common law principles of confidential information and trade secrets protection will apply in these jurisdictions. However, the common law position can do no more than offer protection against unfair competition and cannot be extended to cover the data exclusivity standard required by TRIPS.

In sum, the legal framework for test data protection in a number of African countries is yet to fully incorporate the standard of the TRIPS Agreement although there are countries like Rwanda and Ghana that have legislated provisions that appear to give full force to their obligations in international law. The desirability of such full incorporation in developing countries that still need some significant flexibility in balancing IP rights with social policy goals, however, is debatable.

4.9.1 Data exclusivity and access to medicines in Africa

In general, the TRIPS Agreement seems to have imposed uniform standards that are likely to benefit major IP holders largely resident in developed countries at the

113 *Extension of the Transition Period under Article 66.1for Least Developed Country Members*, WTO Doc IP/C/64 (Decision of 11 June 2013).

expense of emerging and least developed economies which will have to pay more for the use of modern technology. This would also seem to be the case with regard to the specific provisions relating to data exclusivity. Indeed, for the vast majority of African countries and other developing countries without any significant manufacturing capacity in the pharmaceutical industry, data exclusivity offers no real benefits. Its contribution to boosting the investment climate in such countries is at best equivocal, given the fact that political stability, social security and economic viability are also important factors that inform investment decisions. Nonetheless, as succinctly noted by Michael Morgan, the TRIPS Agreement has become '*a reality that must be taken into account in any strategy to remedy the gaps in access and innovation in developing world pharmaceutical markets*'.[114]

The extent to which the TRIPS data protection requirements can be said to preclude the grant of marketing approval on the basis of bioequivalence may continue to elicit significant commentaries. It is nonetheless clear that the TRIPS negotiators directly rejected proposals to include provisions that might absolutely prohibit the use of originator test data in granting marketing approval to generic manufacturers. However, as Section 4.6 demonstrates, the flexibilities allowed under TRIPS are further circumscribed by the TRIPS-plus obligations contained in many free trade agreements pursued by the US and the EU. This point was noted by the African Union in the Cairo Declaration 2005 where the Ministers posited as follows:

> We note that the African Group initiated the discussion on the clarification of flexibilities in TRIPS, particularly in relation to patents and public health as well as biodiversity. We call on African countries to take appropriate measures at the national level to make full use of these flexibilities in line with the outcome of the AU Commission Workshop held in March 2005 in Addis Ababa. We call on the EU not to introduce in the EPA [Economic Partnership Agreement] negotiations any TRIPS plus proposals (which go beyond existing TRIPS obligations) which would compromise these flexibilities. If such proposals are advanced, they should be rejected.[115]

For Africa, it seems the need to build innovative capacity is not in any way enhanced by a data exclusivity regime, but the TRIPS Agreement contains certain safeguards to ensure IP protection does not become an impediment to free trade and development. It is unlikely that Africa and most developing countries really stand to benefit significantly from the global move towards a universal standard for data exclusivity and IP protection.

The WHO made known its perspective on the test data protection debate at a symposium in Geneva in 2010. The WHO affirmed its commitment to

114 M R Morgan, 'Medicines for the Developing World: Promoting Access and Innovation in the Post – TRIPS Environment' (2006) 64 *University of Toronto Faculty of Law Review* 45, 59.

115 African Union Conference of Ministers of Trade, 3rd Ordinary Session, AU's Ministerial Declaration on EPA Negotiations, AU/TI/MIN/DECL. (III) (2005).

> ...encourage and support the application and management of intellectual property in a manner that maximizes health-related innovation and promotes access to health products and that is consistent with the provisions in the TRIPS agreement and other WTO instruments related to that agreement and meets the specific R&D needs of developing countries.[116]

It is contended that it is critical for developing countries to form a common front in resisting bilateral or free trade agreements that tend to take away or circumscribe the flexibilities allowed in TRIPS. The TRIPS standard for data protection is that it must be protected against unfair commercial use. However, the obligation against disclosure does not preclude countries from acting in the national interests in the event of a public health emergency. It is submitted that developing countries need to ensure that these distinctions are captured in their national frameworks for data protection.

4.10 Conclusion

The impact of the TRIPS data exclusivity requirements on access to medicines is not without its controversies. It is incontrovertible that patents and obligations arising from their protection are not the only reasons for the access to medicines problems. A myriad of socio-economic factors are responsible for the access to medicines conundrum. That is why trade rules and IP protection should not be fashioned in a way that will exacerbate the problem.

It is beyond doubt that the regulatory purpose for drug marketing approval is more connected with efficacy and safety of drugs than lowering their prices. It appears data exclusivity will only be of real benefit to developing countries that have some substantial pharmaceutical manufacturing capacity.[117]

Article 39 of TRIPS should not be construed as making the use of compulsory patent licensing more onerous as the valid issuance of a compulsory licence under the TRIPS regime should adequately satisfy the requirements of Article 39.3. African countries are bound by their international obligations in relation to the protection of IP rights. However, the operation of the TRIPS Agreement is likely to make access to goods significantly difficult in regions that are yet to fully embrace the global move towards the promotion of free trade. The TRIPS Agreement was introduced to ensure the free flow of goods and services in international trade does not infringe on IP rights. Having a strong international IP framework without a corresponding removal of barriers to market entry is likely to make access to goods more difficult and expensive. An important way of addressing the access to medicines problem in Africa is through the stratagem

116 WHO, 'Test Data Protection: WHO Perspective' Symposium on the Evolution of the Regulatory Framework of Test Data – From the Property of the Intellect to the Intellect of Property, Geneva, February 8, 2010.

117 Yamane, above n 43, 478.

of free trade. The removal of barriers to trans-border movement of goods will further facilitate access to cheaper goods and even encourage manufacturers to invest more in the regions that are likely to be more commercially viable due to the absence of market barriers.

It is submitted that access to test data for the purposes of ensuring drug safety and efficacy is an integral part of the right to health and very germane to consumers' welfare and protection. The same argument applies to access to such products by market competitors especially where necessary to address a public health situation even if it is not an emergency. Data exclusivity, it is submitted, is not a barrier to the use of compulsory licences under TRIPS but neither is it of real significance where there is minimal pharmaceutical manufacturing capacity. Africa will therefore need to have a strong pharmaceutical manufacturing capacity to benefit from data exclusivity regimes.

Bibliography

African Union Conference of Ministers of Trade, 3rd Ordinary Session, *AU's Ministerial Declaration on EPA Negotiations*, AU/TI/MIN/DECL. (III) (2005).

Abbott F M, 'The WTO Medicines Decision: World Pharmaceutical Trade and the Protection of Public Health' (2005) 99 *American Journal of International Law* 317.

Armoutia W & Nsoura M F A 'Test Data Protection: Different Approaches and Implementation in Pharmaceuticals' (2016) 20 *Marquette Intellectual Property Law Review* 267.

Baker B K, 'Ending Drug Registration Apartheid: Taming Data Exclusivity and Patent/Registration Linkage' (2008) 34 *American Journal of Law and Medicine* 303.

Banthia V, 'Biosimilars: Countering Shortages of Biotherapies in a Global and Local Context' (2017) 57 *IDEA: Journal of the Franklin Pierce for Intellectual Property* 359.

Brody J E, 'Unlocking the Secrets of the Microbiome', *New York Times*, 6 November 2017.

Clift C, 'Data Protection and Data Exclusivity in Pharmaceuticals and Agrochemicals', in A Krattiger, R T Mahoney, L Nelsen, et al. (eds.) *Intellectual Property Management in Health and Agricultural Innovation: A Handbook of Best Practices* (MIHR and PIPRA: 2007).

Correa C M, *Trade Related Aspects of Intellectual Property Rights: A Commentary on the TRIPS Agreement* (Oxford University Press, 2007) 367.

Correa C M, *Protection of Data Submitted for the Registration of Pharmaceuticals: Implementing the Standards of the TRIPS Agreement* (South Centre, 2002).

Cowley, 'The Right to Health: Guatemala's Conflicting Obligations under the Central American Free Trade Agreement and the International Covenant on Economic, Social and Cultural Rights' (2007) 11 *Michigan State University Journal of Medicine & Law* 227.

Davis N, "The Human Microbiome: Why Our Microbes Could Be Key to Our Health" *The Guardian*, 26 March 2018.

Dodds-Smith, 'Data Protection and Abridged Applications for Marketing Authorisations in the Pharmaceutical Industry', in R Goldberg & J Lonbay (eds.), *Pharmaceutical Medicine, Biotechnology and European Law* (Cambridge University Press, 2001) 93.

Dwyer L, 'Patent Protection and Access to Medicine: The Colombia and Peruvian Trade Promotion Agreements' (2007) 13 *Law & Business Review of the Americas* 825.

Evans G E, 'Strategic Patent Licensing for Public Research Organizations: Deploying Restriction and Reservation Clauses to Promote Medical R&D in Developing Countries' (2008) 34 *American Journal of Law and Medicine* 175.

Fellmeth A X, 'Secrecy, Monopoly, and Access to Pharmaceuticals in International Trade Law: Protection of Marketing Approval Data under the TRIPS Agreement' (2004) 45 *Harvard International Law Journal* 443.

Garner B A ed. *Black's Law Dictionary* (Thomson Reuters 9th ed. 2009) 1836.

Gervais D, *The TRIPS Agreement: Drafting History and Analysis* (Sweet & Maxwell, Thomson Reuters 4th ed., 2012).

Goldhammer A, *Associate Vice President, U.S. Regulatory Affairs, Letter to ICTRP, RE: PhRMA's Second Round Comments on International Clinical Trials Registry Platform (ICTRP): Disclosure Timing* (World Health Organisation, 2006) www.who.int/ictrp/002-PhRMA_29March06.pdf accessed 26 January 2019.

Haug C, Gatzsche P & Schoeder T, 'Registries and Registration of Clinical Trials' (2005) 353 *New England Journal of Medicine* 2811.

Haydon I, 'Biologics: The Pricey Drugs Transforming Medicine', *The Conversation US*, 26 July 2017.

Horton R, 'Vioxx, the Implosion of Merck and Aftershocks at the FDA' (2004) 364 *The Lancet* 1595.

IFPMA, *A Review of Existing Data Exclusivity Legislation in Selected Countries* (International Association of Pharmaceutical Manufacturers Association, 2002).

Jureidini J N, McHenry L B &Mansfield P R, 'Clinical Trials and Drug Promotion: Selective Reporting of Study' (2008) 329, 20 *International Journal of Risk & Safety Medicine* 73.

Lemmens T & Telfer C, 'Access to Information and the Right to Health: The Human Rights Case for Clinical Trials Transparency' (2012) 38 *American Journal of Law & Medicine* 63, 85.

Mexico Statement on Health Research from the Ministerial Summit on Health Research Mexico City, 16–20 November 2004.

Morgan M R, 'Medicines for the Developing World: Promoting Access and Innovation in the Post – TRIPS Environment' (2006) 64 *University of Toronto Faculty of Law Review* 45.

Osewe P L, Nkrumah Y K & Sackey E K, *Improving Access to HIV/AIDS Medicines in Africa* (World Bank, 2008) 21 http://apps.who.int/medicinedocs/documents/s17514en/s17514en.pdf accessed 26 January 2019.

Owoeye O &Owoeye O, 'Biologics and Public Health: Prospects and Challenges' (2018) 26 *Journal of Law and Medicine* 170.

Pharmaceutical Patent Issues: Interpreting GATT: Hearings before the Senate Comm. on the Judiciary, 104th Cong. 35 (1997).

PhRMA, *Clinical Trials: The Phases of Drug Testing and Approval* (2006) www.phrma.org/innovation/clinical-trials accessed 26 January 2019.

Pires de Carvalho N, *The TRIPS Regime of Patent Rights* (Kluwer Law International, 2nd ed., 2004).

Reichman J H, 'Rethinking the Role of Clinical Trial Data in International Intellectual Property Law: The Case for a Public Goods Approach' (2009) 13 *Marquette Intellectual Property Law Review* 1.

Rennie D, 'Trial Registration. A Great Idea Switches from Ignored to Irresistible' (2004) 292 *JAMA* 1359.

Sachs R E, 'The Uneasy Case for Patent Law' (2018) 117 (3) *Michigan Law Review* 499.

Sanzo M A, 'The Promise and Problem of Biologics' (2017) 34 *Santa Clara High Technology Law Journal* 78.

Topol, 'Failing the Public Health -- Rofecoxib, Merck, and the FDA' (2004) 351 *New England Journal of Medicine* 1707.

UNCTAD-ICTSD, *Resource Book on TRIPS and Development* (Cambridge University Press, 2005) 522.

United Nations, Special Rapporteur on the Right to Health, *Addendum to the Report of the Special Rapporteur*, U.N. Comm'n on Human Rights, Mission to the World Trade Organization, U.N. Doc. E/CN.4/2004/49/Add.1 (Mar. 1, 2004).

U.S. Trade Representative, *Fact Sheet: "Special 301" On Intellectual Property Rights* (1996) www.cptech.org/ip/health/ustr/301-96.htm accessed 26 January 2019.

Wang Bo et al., 'Variations in Time of Market Exclusivity among Top-Selling Prescription Drugs in the United States' (2015) 175 *JAMA Internal Medicine* 635.

World Trade Organization, *Chairman's Report to the GNG, Status of Work in the Negotiating Group, World Trade Organization, Negotiating Group on Trade- Related Aspects of Intellectual Property Rights, including Trade in Counterfeit Goods*, WTO Doc MTN. GNG/NG11/W/76 (23 July 1990).

World Trade Organization, *Communication from the European Communities and Their Member States to the Council on Trade-Related Aspects of Intellectual Property Rights*, WTO Doc 15 IP/C/W/280 (12 June 2001).

World Trade Organization, *Draft Final Act Embodying the Results of the Uruguay Round of Multilateral Trade Negotiations – Revision*, GATT Doc MTN.TNC/W/35/Rev.1 (3 December 1990).

World Trade Organization, *Extension of the Transition Period under Article 66.1for Least Developed Country Members*, WTO Doc IP/C/64 (Decision of 11 June 2013).

World Health Organization, *International Clinical Trials Registry: About the WHO ICTRP* (2013) www.who.int/ictrp/about/en/ accessed 26 January 2019.

Yamane H, *Interpreting TRIPS* (Hart Publishing, Oxford, 2011).

5 The exhaustion doctrine, parallel trade and public health

5.1 Introduction

The Chapters 1–4 examined the significance of compulsory licensing in the access to medicines context and its connection with test data protection. In this chapter, the vexed issues of exhaustion of intellectual property rights (IPRs) and parallel importation are examined in the context of access to medicines in the developing world. It is a cardinal principle of intellectual property (IP) law that the right of IP holders to control the sale and movement of goods, in the ocean of trade, are exhausted once the IP protected products have been put on the market by the right holder, or with their consent. When the rights are exhausted, it becomes possible to import the products to high-price jurisdictions so as to make the products available at lower cost in the importing jurisdiction. Such importation is known as parallel importation. The Agreement on Trade Related Aspects of Intellectual Property Rights (TRIPS Agreement) explicitly recognises the right of countries to determine the type of exhaustion regime that suits them, subject to non-violation of the WTO non-discrimination principles. Exhaustion of rights and parallel importation are interrelated concepts as IP-protected products can only be parallel imported when the IPRs embodied in them have been exhausted. The TRIPS exhaustion regime is considered one of the major flexibilities of the TRIPS Agreement and it can, in certain circumstances, play a significant role in enhancing access to medicines at rates lower than the manufacturer's price. The relevance of the exhaustion principle in the access to medicines context is, however, bound to depend on a number of factors including the exhaustion regime available in the country using it, the manufacturer's differential pricing scheme, trade barriers and import duties, amongst others.

This chapter examines the legal framework for exhaustion of rights in public international law and how it relates to parallel importation (otherwise known as parallel trade). The chapter highlights the emerging conflicts between the concept of parallel importation and the differential pricing phenomenon as well as whether competition policy would be a more effective option than parallel trade. The significance of parallel trade in pharmaceutical products to the access to medicines challenge is considered with particular focus on the parallel importation of goods made pursuant to a compulsory licence. The chapter explores the significance of parallel trade to free trade in Africa.

5.2 The concept of parallel importation

The concept of parallel importation allows the importation of products manufactured and marketed by the patent owner in another country without the approval of the right holder usually with the objective of making the market for the goods more competitive in the importing country.[1] In other words, parallel imports are goods purchased in a foreign market by a third party and subsequently resold in the domestic market where their lower prices result in competition with those of authorised distributors.[2] Parallel importation allows for 'comparison shopping' by a third party where a patent holder sells their goods in different markets at different prices.[3] Parallel importation is, however, not the same thing as illegal trade in pirated goods.[4] The basic difference between parallel importation (also known as grey-market importation) and 'official' importation is that the parallel imports were produced originally for sale in a particular market and then were passed through an unauthorised dealer before reaching the consumers.[5] Parallel importation arises due to factors such as manufacturers' price discrimination, differential systems or price controls and vertical price setting (control of prices at retail) schemes in distribution systems.[6] Parallel trade can significantly limit manufacturers' profits through the substitution of sales in low-price markets for sales in high-price markets.[7] For instance, parallel trade in pharmaceuticals was reported to have cost the UK pharmaceutical industry not less than £1.3 billion in 2005.[8] The question that arises from this is whether the patent holder could restrain parallel importation of goods which they or their licensees have already

1 S Bartelt, 'Compulsory Licenses Pursuant to TRIPS Article 31 in the Light of the Doha Declaration on the TRIPS Agreement and Public Health' (2003) 6 (2) *Journal of World Intellectual Property* 284, 304.

2 T K Mirabile, 'Aids, Africa and Access to Medicines' (2002) 11 *Michigan State University-DCL Journal of International Law* 175, 212.

3 Ibid., 214.

4 See J R C Brown 'Exhaustion of Rights in the EEC: Some Special Cases, with Emphasis on Pharmaceuticals' (1990) 1 *Intellectual Property Journal* 139, 140; C Lawson, 'Flexibility in TRIPS: Using Patented Inventions without Authorisation of the Right Holder' (2004) 15 *Australian Intellectual Property Journal* 141, 14.

5 D Mathews & V Munoz-Tellez, 'Parallel Trade: A User's Guide' in A Krattiger et al. (eds.), *Intellectual Property Management in Health and Agricultural Innovation: A Handbook of Best Practices* (MIHR & PIPRA, 2007) 1429.

6 E Siew-Kwan Ng 'The Impact of the Bilateral US – Singapore Free Trade Agreement on Singapore's Post-TRIPS Patent Regime in the Pharmaceutical Context' (2010) 16 (5) *International Trade Law and Regulation* 121, 125.

7 C Stothers, 'State of the Art: Parallel Trade and Free Trade Agreements' (2006) 1(9) *Journal of Intellectual Property Law & Practice* 578, 578.

8 P Kanavos, D Gross & D Taylor, *Parallel Trading in Medicines: Europe's Experience and Its Implications for Commercial Drug Importation in the US* (AARP, 2005) 26 http://assets.aarp.org/rgcenter/health/2005_07_trade.pdf accessed 26 January 2019.

released into the market. This is where the doctrine of exhaustion of rights becomes relevant. Whether such goods can be parallel imported will depend on whether the IPRs embodied in them have been exhausted by previous sales.[9]

5.2.1 The exhaustion doctrine and its basis

The exhaustion of rights doctrine is seen as one of the most fundamental limitations on the exploitation of IPRs as it entails that once an article embodying IP is sold by the holder of the rights or with their consent, then the IPRs in that article are exhausted.[10] As succinctly put by Keith Maskus:

> Once rights are exhausted, it becomes legal for anyone to sell the goods he has purchased within the region of application. Because such transactions occur outside the distribution system of the original IPR owner, they are called 'gray market activities' (in the United States) or 'parallel imports'(in the EU and most of the world).[11]

IP holders constantly seek to maintain exclusivity in marketing of their goods and services through their authorised distribution channels. Parallel traders on the other hand enter the market by buying from low-price markets and reselling in high-price markets without going through the IP holder's authorised distribution channels. This creates competitive prices for genuine products in high-price markets.[12] Without the exhaustion doctrine, it would be possible for manufacturers to perpetually control the transfer or use of their IP-protected products even after those products have been released into the market.[13] The argument in support of the exhaustion doctrine is that once IP holders have been duly paid, they should not be able to restrain the resale of products in which their IPRs are embedded.[14]

The fundamental question in the protection of IP in relation to exhaustion is whether to give priority to free flow of goods (common market)[15] or IPRs.[16] The

9 D E Donelly, '(Comment) Parallel Trade and the International Harmonization of the Exhaustion of Rights Doctrine' (1997) 13 *Santa Clara Computer and High Technology Law Journal* 445, 447.

10 Ibid.

11 K E Maskus, 'The Curious Economics of Parallel Trade' (2010) 2 *World Intellectual Property Organisation Journal* 123.

12 I Avgoustis, 'Parallel Imports and Exhaustion of Trade Mark Rights: Should Steps Be Taken Towards an International Exhaustion Regime?' (2012) 34 *European Intellectual Property Review* 108.

13 E Bonadio, 'Parallel Imports in a Global Market: Should a Generalised International Exhaustion Be the Next Step?' (2011) 33 *European Intellectual Property Review* 153.

14 Ibid.

15 F M Abbott, 'First Report (Final) to the Committee on International Trade Law of the International Law Association on the Subject of Parallel Importation' (1998) 1 *Journal of International Economic Law* 607, 611.

16 L L Hicks & J R Holbein, 'Convergence of National Intellectual Property Norms in International Trading Agreements' (1997) 12 *American University Journal of International Law & Policy* 769, 770–771; D E Donnelly, 'Parallel Trade and International Harmonization of the

exhaustion doctrine intertwines the legal regimes of intellectual and tangible property. It provides the purchaser of patented goods with an absolute personal property in the goods such that their right to use and resell the goods are very much at large.[17]

The exhaustion doctrine does not absolutely take away all the rights of the IP holder in respect of an IP-protected product. The right to restrain third parties from the unauthorised imitation or production of their goods is still very much at large as the doctrine only restrains the prohibition on the sale of goods that have been appropriately acquired from legitimate channels.[18] The exhaustion doctrine does not therefore limit the exclusive right of the IP holder to manufacture the products. There are three basic types of exhaustion: national exhaustion, regional exhaustion and international exhaustion.[19] National exhaustion implies that the exclusive rights of an IP holder become exhausted once goods are put in the *national* market. Regional exhaustion regards the exclusive rights as exhausted with the first sale in a *regional* market, whilst the tenet of international exhaustion is that rights are exhausted with the first sale in any market.[20] Different countries have different exhaustion regimes.

Although the exhaustion of rights doctrine is one of those flexibilities allowed by the TRIPS Agreement, its use is limited both legally and practically as multinational manufacturers and distributors can, through their concerted efforts, restrict its use considerably.[21] The exhaustion of rights doctrine has its origin in national IP law as it is an essential constituent of each country's policy framework[22] and to this end countries are free to determine their legal framework for exhaustion and parallel trade in line with national interests.[23]

5.2.2 The history of the exhaustion doctrine in national law

In Europe, the origin of the exhaustion principle is traceable to the German jurist Joseph Kohler.[24] The word exhaustion ('Erschöpfung') was reportedly

Exhaustion of Rights Doctrine'(1997) 13 *Santa Clara Computer & High Technology Law Journal* 445, 447; K Ruping, 'Copyright and an Integrated European Market: Conflicts with Free Movement of Goods, Competition Law and National Discrimination' (1997) 11 *Temple International & Comparative Law Journal* 1, 5–12.

17 See M D Janis 'A Tale of the Apocryphal Axe: Repair, Reconstruction, and the Implied License in Intellectual Property Law' (1999) 58 *Maryland Law Review* 423, 434–435.

18 Bonadio, above n 13, 153.

19 Matthews & Tellez above n 5, 1432.

20 V Chiappetta, 'The Desirability of Agreeing to Disagree: The WTO, TRIPS, International IPR Exhaustion and a few Other Things' (2000) 21 *Michigan Journal of International Law* 333, 341.

21 See J D Blum 'The Role of Law in Global E-Health: A Tool for Development and Equity in a Digitally Divided World' (2002) 46 *Saint Louis University Law Journal* 85, 103.

22 K E Maskus, 'The Curious Economics of Parallel Trade' (2010) 2 *World Intellectual Property Organisation Journal* 123, 124.

23 See C Correa, *Trade Related Aspects of Intellectual Property Rights: A Commentary on the TRIPS Agreement* (Oxford University Press, 2007) 79.

24 J Kohler, *Deutsches Patentrecht* (J Bensheimer 1878) 100. See also D T Keeling, *Intellectual Property Rights in EU Law* (Oxford University Press, 2003) 75; I Avgoustis 'Parallel Imports and

used for the first time in the German case of *Kölnisch Wasser* on trademarks.[25] In the *Mariani* case, it was held that the exhaustion principle would apply where the goods are put in the market in a foreign country.[26] Both *Kolnisch Wasser* and *Mariani* favoured the international exhaustion doctrine.

In the US, the history of the exhaustion principle can be traced to litigation over William Woodworth's patent acquired on his planing machine in American 'Wooden Age',[27] when the cutting edge technology consisted of sawmills and planing machines.[28] In *Wilson v Rousseau*,[29] the exhaustion issue arose as a result of Woodworth's extension of his patent in December 1842 for a period of 7 years pursuant to the 1836 *Patent Act*.[30] Four years later, James Wilson (who had then acquired ownership of the Woodworth patent) sought to determine the legal effect of the extension before the US Supreme Court.[31] The question for determination before the court was whether the licensees for the original term were entitled to enjoy the use of the machine for the extended term.[32] The court held that since the patented articles had been purchased from the licensees and had gone into common use, the expiration of the original term of the licence would have no effect on the common use to which the patent had been put as that would leave the purchaser to the discretion or caprice of the patentee.[33] The court held that a construction 'fraught with such unmixed evil' was not contemplated by the Congress.[34] The court therefore held that whilst the patentee lost the right to control use exclusively upon first sale of the product, he still reserved the exclusive right to make the claimed invention.[35]

In *Bloomer v McQuewan*,[36] another case involving the Woodworth patent, the patent had again been extended for seven years pursuant to a law passed by the US Congress in 1845.[37] Bloomer, who had by then acquired ownership interest in the patent, claimed against parties who had constructed planing machines with the patent holder's authorisation during the original term.[38] The Court,

Exhaustion of Trade Mark Rights: Should Steps Be Taken towards an International Exhaustion Regime?' (2012) 34 *European Intellectual Property Review* 108, 110.

25 *Kölnisch Wasser* RG, February 28, 1902, 50 RGZ 229; I Avgoustis 'Parallel Imports and Exhaustion of Trade Mark Rights: Should Steps be taken towards an International Exhaustion Regime?' (2012) 34 *European Intellectual Property Review* 108, 111.

26 *Mariani* RG, May 2, 1902, 51 RGZ 263.

27 Janis above n 17, 430–431.

28 Ibid., at 430.

29 *Wilson v. Rousseau*, 45 U.S. (4 How.) 646, 687–688 (1846).

30 Ibid., 687.

31 Ibid., 673.

32 Ibid., 675.

33 Ibid., 684.

34 Ibid.

35 Ibid., 683.

36 *Bloomer v McQuewan*55 U.S. (14 How.) 539 (1852).

37 Ibid., 547.

38 Ibid.

relying on *Wilson v Rousseau* held that since the defendants had purchased the right to use the planing machine during the original term, they were entitled to continue its use during their extended term.[39] Of particular significance to the exhaustion doctrine is the statement of the court that:

> When the machine passes to the hands of the purchaser, it is no longer within the limits of the monopoly. It passes outside of it, and is no longer under the protection of the act of Congress....[40]

The law of exhaustion of rights has since been established in a long line of cases in US jurisprudence.[41] The underlying justification for the doctrine as established in the cases is that the essence of patent law is to serve as an incentive to innovate and that purpose is justified as soon as the patentee has received the sales price or royalty payment accruing from the initial sale of the patented article.[42] The idea behind the exhaustion of rights is therefore not to ensure the greatest possible financial return to the patent holder but to benefit the public, and extending the patent holder's right beyond the first sale would exceed what is necessary to provide an incentive to innovate, and constitute an undue interference with the free market.[43]

In English law, patent law used to be one field of IP law where the notion of exhaustion of rights was not applicable.[44] Thus, a patent holder, after putting their goods in the market, could still impose restrictions on further sale or use which would bind not only other contracting parties but all recipients of the products who had notice of the restriction.[45] The position in British law has, however, been altered by the *Resale Prices Act 1964* and the *Treaty of Rome* which enshrined the doctrine of free movement of goods and the rules of competition in Europe.[46]

Whilst national exhaustion of rights attempts to give an IP producer a larger rent, global or international exhaustion seeks to enhance trade and facilitate free flow of parallel imports.[47] One inherent disadvantage in the exhaustion of rights doctrine is that it can frustrate the efforts of IP holders to maintain differential

39 Ibid., 550.

40 Ibid., 549; Also quoted in Janis above n 17 at 434.

41 See *Adams v. Burke*, 84 U.S. (17 Wall.) 453, 456–457 (1873); *United States v. Univis Lens Co.*, 316 U.S. 241, 252 (1942).

42 M Barrett, 'The United States Doctrine of Exhaustion: Parallel Imports of Patented Goods' (2000) 27 *Northern Kentucky Law Review* 911, 921.

43 Ibid., at 922.

44 See W Cornish & D Llewelyn, *Intellectual Property: Patents, Copyright, Trade Marks and Allied Rights* (Thomson Sweet & Maxwell, 6th ed., 2007) 258.

45 See *Dunlop v Longlife* [1958] R.P.C. 473; *Goodyear v Lancashire Batteries* (1958) L.R. 1 R.P. 22 at 35, CA.

46 See Cornish & Llewelyn above n 44.

47 J H Barton 'Global Trade Issues in the New Millennium: The Economics of TRIPS: International Trade in Information Intensive Products' (2001) 33 George *Washington International Law Review* 473, 492.

pricing schemes across nations but non-recognition of the exhaustion of rights doctrine may also prejudice free trade in goods.[48]

5.2.3 Exhaustion of rights under TRIPS: a brief historical background

The emergence of the TRIPS Agreement has brought about some considerable harmonisation to the global IP system as all countries are bound to maintain the minimum standard of protection delineated by it.

The preamble to the *TRIPS Agreement* reads:

> Members, desiring to reduce distortions and impediments to international trade, and taking into account the need to promote effective and adequate protection of intellectual property rights, and to ensure that measures and procedures to enforce intellectual property rights do not themselves become barriers to legitimate trade….
>
> Hereby agree as follows…

This provision suggests that TRIPS seeks to address IP issues from three different standpoints: a desire to enhance unimpeded free trade in IP protected products, the need to safeguard ownership interest in IP products and the need to ensure such protection does not unduly restrain trade in related goods and services.[49] However, a careful evaluation of the substantive provisions of TRIPS does certainly reflect a clear preference for the protection of ownership interests in IPRs over free trade in similar goods and services.[50] Thus, it is pertinent to take a brief look at the circumstances that brought about the TRIPS exhaustion regime.

Intellectual property protection was traditionally considered to be within the exclusive preserves of national law[51] and consequently, early international IP agreements addressed it from the 'non-discrimination' perspectives rather than the substantive rights harmonisation standpoint.[52] As a result of this, differences in national economic conditions brought about different levels of IP protection in developed and developing countries.[53] Thus, developed countries

48 Donelly above n 9, 447.

49 Chiappetta, above n 20, 343.

50 Ibid.

51 Abbott, 'First Report (Final) to the Committee on International Trade Law of the International Law Association on the Subject of Parallel Importation' (n 15), 607.

52 D E Long, 'The Protection of Information Technology in a Culturally Diverse Marketplace' (1996) 15 *John Marshall Journal of Computer & Information Law* 129, 149–150; J H Reichman, 'Universal Minimum Standards of Intellectual Property Protection Under the TRIPS Component of the WTO Agreement', (1995) 29 *International Lawyer* 345, 347–348.

53 See F M Abbott, 'The WTO TRIPS Agreement and Global Economic Development' (1996) 72 Chicago-Kent Law Review 385, 387; J H Reichman, 'From Free Riders to Fair Followers: Global Competition Under the TRIPS Agreement' (1997) 29 *N.Y.U. Journal of International Law & Policy* 11, 12.

like the EU and US as net producers of IP products, favoured a high level of protection with strong enforcement mechanisms while developing countries as net importers of IP products supported easy access to IP to facilitate economic growth with the resultant effect of narrower IP protection and even more limited enforcement mechanisms.[54] With increasing growth in international trade, IP owners in developed countries began to fear that lack of adequate protection would not only impede access to a number of commercially viable markets but that the movement of goods from low-protection jurisdictions would have substantial negative effects on their returns from other markets.[55]

The issue of exhaustion was hotly debated during the TRIPS negotiations.[56] The non-exhaustion advocates maintained that allowing market divisions could have desirable effects on the creation and availability of IP products.[57] This, they believed, would curtail undue intrusion on the time-honoured principle of territorial sovereignty over IP issues.[58] The exhaustion proponents on the other hand posited that the free flow of parallel imports would facilitate the actualisation of market competition efficiencies desired by the General Agreement on Tariffs and Trade (GATT).[59] In the end, to borrow the words of Chiappetta, 'the exhaustion discussion exhausted the negotiators'.[60] What emerged was Article 6 of the TRIPS Agreement, which had the practical effect of leaving the issue of exhaustion to be determined in line with national law and practice.[61]

Towards the end of the TRIPS negotiations, it was argued that Article 6 was fundamental to a balanced agreement between rights and obligations of the patent owner, as well as to the benefits to societies in having access to goods in international markets under the best possible terms. Members were thus urged to leave it unchanged as it was necessary for securing an unrestricted flow of international trade.[62] According to Daniel Gervais, some WTO Members that supported national exhaustion during the TRIPS negotiations (including

54 V Chiappetta, 'The Desirability of Agreeing to Disagree: The WTO, TRIPS, International IPR Exhaustion and a few Other Things' (2000) 21 *Michigan Journal of International Law* 333, 343–344.

55 See F M Abbott, 'The WTO TRIPS Agreement and Global Economic Development' (1996) 72 *Chicago-Kent Law Review* 385, 388–389; M L. Doane, 'TRIPS and International Intellectual Property Protection in an Age of Advancing Technology', (19994) 9 *American University Journal of International Law & Policy* 465, 465–466; Chiappetta above n 18, 344.

56 F M Abbott, 'First Report (Final) to the Committee on International Trade Law of the International Law Association on the Subject of Parallel Importation' (n 15), 609.

57 Ibid., 622.

58 See C A Bradley, 'Territorial Intellectual Property Rights in an Age of Globalism' (1997) 37 *Vanderbilt Journal of International Law* 505, 584–585.

59 F M Abbott, 'First Report (Final) to the Committee on International Trade Law of the International Law Association on the Subject of Parallel Importation' (n 15), 609.

60 Chiappetta, above n 20, 346.

61 F M Abbott, 'First Report (Final) to the Committee on International Trade Law of the International Law Association on the Subject of Parallel Importation' (n 15), 609.

62 *Negotiation Group on Trade Related Aspects of Intellectual Property Rights, Including Trade in Counterfeit Goods, Meeting of Negotiating Group of 16 and 22 October 1991*, GATT/WTO Doc MTN.GNG/TRIPS/3 (18 November 1991) 3.

Switzerland and the United States) tried to enshrine the principle in the Agreement, while others (including Australia, Brazil, Hong Kong, India and New Zealand) defended so-called 'international exhaustion' or at least, the freedom for each WTO member to decide.[63]

5.3 Exhaustion of rights under the TRIPS agreement and the Paris Convention

It has been argued that a broad interpretation of TRIPS does not seem to support IP arbitrage as such arbitrage frustrates the objective of enabling innovators to recoup the cost of R&D investments on a global basis, but that a narrow interpretation of the same agreement seems to allow broad national discretion to allow nations to adopt rules that are most appropriate for their social and developmental goals.[64]

Article 6 of TRIPS states

> For the purposes of dispute settlement under this Agreement, subject to the provisions of Articles 3 and 4 nothing in this Agreement shall be used to address the issue of exhaustion of intellectual property rights.

The provision that nothing in the Agreement shall be required to address the issue of exhaustion of IPRs is subject to Articles 3 and 4 of the Agreement relating to the non-discrimination principles. Commenting on the nature of Article 6, Nuno Pires de Carvalho notes thus:

> Article 6 is undoubtedly one of the most contentious provisions of the TRIPS Agreement. It raises extremely complex legal and economic issues which have yet to be fully assessed and understood.[65]

He contends that given the high cost involved in producing test data, Article 39.3 of TRIPS requiring protection of test data against disclosure could ordinarily in practice constitute a serious barrier to parallel imports by generic manufacturers. He, however, opines that after the Doha Declaration on TRIPS and Public Health, no TRIPS provision other than Articles 3 and 4 should stand in the way of Members selecting the exhaustion regime that suits them.[66] He further contends that WTO Members that are Paris Union Members may not benefit from the freedom accorded with respect to exhaustion regimes as parallel imports are

63 D Gervais, *The TRIPS Patent Regime: Drafting History and Analysis* (Sweet & Maxwell, 3rd ed., 2008) 199.

64 P Samuelson 'Intellectual Property Arbitrage: How Foreign Rules Can Affect Domestic Protections' (2004) 71 *University of Chicago Law Review* 223, 238.

65 N Pires de Carvalho, *The TRIPS Regime of Patent Rights* (Kluwer Law International, 2005) 104.

66 Ibid., 107.

inconsistent with Article 4bis(1) of the Paris Convention.[67] Responding to this argument, Carlos Correa posits that it:

> ...overlooks, first, that Members are only obliged to comply with the Articles of the Paris Convention (including Article 4bis) with regard to Parts II, III, and IV of the TRIPS Agreement, and not with regard to Part 1 where Article 6 is included. Second, the argument incorrectly predicates that the exhaustion of rights in the importing countries are exclusively subject to domestic law and are unaffected by the legal status or changes in the legal status of foreign patents.... When parallel imports are admitted, it is because the domestic law of the importing country simply attributes certain effects to acts that have taken place in a foreign jurisdiction, independently of how such acts are qualified in the exporting country.[68]

The first point for consideration here is whether Correa was right in arguing although quite persuasively, that Paris Convention Members are not obliged to comply with Article 6 of *TRIPS*. It is submitted that this argument does not seem to be supportable. The argument of Correa is grounded on Article 2(1) of TRIPS. However, he does not consider the provision of Article 2.2 which provides that nothing in the TRIPS Agreement shall derogate from existing obligation under the Paris Convention.

The implication of this is that Members' obligations under the Paris Convention are still at large under Article 6 of the TRIPS Agreement. Besides, a combined reading of Articles 1.3, 3 and 6 of the TRIPS Agreement indicate that, contrary to the argument of Prof Correa, the Paris Convention has not been excluded from the ambit of Article 6 of TRIPS. Having thus argued that the Paris Convention applies to Article 6 of the TRIPS Agreement, the next point for consideration is whether indeed Article 4bis of the Paris Convention could be said to prohibit parallel importation. At this point, it is instructive to examine the tenor of Article 4bis of the Paris Convention. Article 4bis of the Paris Convention provides thus:

1 Patents applied for in the various countries of the Union by nationals of countries of the Union shall be independent of patents obtained for the same invention in other countries, whether members of the Union or not;
2 The foregoing provision is to be understood in an unrestricted sense, in particular, in the sense that patents applied for during the period of priority are independent, both as regards the grounds for nullity and forfeiture, and as regards their normal duration.

67 Ibid., 115–116.
68 Correa, above n 23, 81.

5.3.1 An analysis of exhaustion of patents rights under the TRIPS and the Paris Convention

The pertinent question here is whether TRIPS Members that are Paris Convention parties are prohibited from the use of regional or international exhaustion by reason of Article 4bis of the Paris Convention. A number of commentators hold the view that there is nothing in the earlier IP conventions, like the Paris Convention, dealing with the issue of exhaustion.[69] However, a critical evaluation of Article 4bis of the Paris Convention seems to suggest that the exhaustion of patent rights in one country does not exhaust them in other countries. This is because the provision states that patents applied for in one country shall be independent of patents in other countries in an unrestricted sense covering the grounds for nullity, forfeiture and duration. If the national independence of patents in terms of forfeiture and duration are interpreted to cover the exhaustion question, the implication of this would still be that countries have a right under the Paris Convention to determine that patent rights are exhausted by overseas sale. However, Article 6 of TRIPS has made it clear beyond doubt that the question of exhaustion is one that can be determined within national legal structures, and issues pertaining to it cannot come within the purview of the WTO dispute settlement framework.

It has also been posited that the patents rights conferred by TRIPS Article 28 are not absolute as they can be validly circumscribed by the exhaustion of IP doctrine pursuant to TRIPS Article 6 which makes the issue of exhaustion of rights non-justiciable in so far as dispute resolution within the WTO is concerned.[70]

> Article 28 of *TRIPS* provides thus
>
> 1 A patent shall confer on its owner the following exclusive rights:
>
> a Where the subject matter of a patent is a product, to prevent third parties not having the owner's consent from acts of: making, using, offering for sale, selling, or importing for these purposes that product;
>
> b Where the subject matter of a patent is a process, to prevent third parties not having the owner's consent from the acts of using the process, and from the acts of: using, offering for sale, selling, or importing for these purposes at least the product obtained directly by that process.
>
> 2 Patent owners shall also have the right to assign, or transfer by succession, the patent and to conclude licensing contracts.
>
> This right like all other rights conferred under this Agreement in respect of the use, sale, importation or other distribution of goods, is subject to the provisions of Article 6.

69 See D Gervais, *The TRIPS Agreement: Drafting History and Analysis* (Thomson Reuters, 3rd ed., 2008) 201; R K Rai, 'Should the WTO Harmonise Parallel Import Laws?' (2011) 6(12) *Journal of Intellectual Property Law and Practice* 898, 901.

70 See Mirabile, above n 2, 213.

It is, however, submitted that the ability to circumscribe a patent right by the exhaustion doctrine is largely limited as the exhaustion doctrine does not in any way derogate from the exclusive right of a manufacturer to regulate the production of the patented article. In any case, the non-justiciability of the exhaustion of rights doctrine under TRIPS is absolutely subject to the non-discrimination principle enshrined in the national treatment and most-favoured nation treatment provisions.[71] This therefore makes it very difficult indeed to argue that issues pertaining to exhaustion of rights are completely non-justiciable under the TRIPS Agreement. The national treatment principle provides that each Member shall accord to other Members no less favourable treatment than it accords to its own nationals in relation to the protection of IP.[72]

It is submitted that since the non-justiciability of TRIPS Article 6 is made subject to Article 3 which deals with national treatment, it follows that the issue of exhaustion can be a proper subject for dispute settlement where its application by a Member offends the national treatment principle. Thus, where country A does not recognise the first sale of a patented item as exhausting the patent for its nationals but considers patented products of country B as exhausted with the first sale of such products, then country A will be violating TRIPS Article 3 and can therefore be subject to dispute settlement procedure on that basis.

Another exception to the non-justiciability of the exhaustion of rights issue under TRIPS is where its application is inconsistent with the most-favoured-nation doctrine in Article 4. The most favoured nation's doctrine says that in relation to the protection of IP, '*any advantage, favour, privilege or immunity granted by a Member to the nationals of any other country shall be accorded immediately and unconditionally to the nationals of all other Members*'.[73] Thus, a country will run afoul of this principle and will consequently be subject to the TRIPS dispute settlement procedure if it allows parallel imports for some countries and does not allow them from some others. This will, however, not apply to practices based on the regional exhaustion principle as found in the EU as such practices are based on international agreements pertaining to matters that fall under the exemptions to the most favoured nation's principle pursuant to Article 4(a) & (d) of TRIPS.

5.3.2 TRIPS exhaustion regime and the GATT

Another point that is necessary to take into account is the argument that there exists a potential conflict between Article 6 of TRIPS delineating the framework for exhaustion of IPRs and Article XI of the GATT relating to the general elimination of quantitative restrictions.[74] The argument is that the TRIPS

71 See TRIPS Agreement, Article 6.

72 TRIPS Agreement, Article 3.

73 TRIPS Agreement, Article 4.

74 See C-F Lo, 'Potential Conflicts between TRIPS and GATT Concerning Parallel Importation of Drugs and Possible Solution to Prevent Undesirable Market Segmentation' (2011) 66 *Food and Drug Law Journal* 73, 76–83.

Agreement leaves the question of whether or not to prohibit parallel imports to the discretion of member countries whilst such prohibition runs afoul of Article XI of the GATT.[75] Article XI of the GATT provides:

> No prohibitions or restrictions other than duties, taxes or other charges, whether made effective through quotas, import or export licenses or other measures, shall be instituted or maintained by any contracting party on the importation of any product of the territory of any other contracting party or on the exportation or sale for export of any product destined for the territory of any other contracting party.

The argument is that the exception to this is found in Article XX(d) of the GATT which provides that nothing in the Agreement shall be construed to prevent the adoption or enforcement by any contracting party of measures:

> (d) necessary to secure compliance with laws or regulations which are not inconsistent with the provisions of this Agreement including those relating to customs enforcement, the enforcement of monopolies operated under paragraph 4 of Article II and Article XVII, the protection of patents, trademarks and copyrights, and the prevention of deceptive practices.

Article XX(d) of the GATT came up for interpretation in *United States – Imports of Certain Automotive Spring Assemblies* (26 May 1983) where the GATT Panel considered the legality of a US measure to restrain the importation from Canada of car parts that infringe US patents. The GATT Panel held that the US measure was in line with GATT Article XX(d) and noted that the measure could not be considered as a disguised restriction in international trade to the extent that the measure did not prevent the import into the US of original products made by the IP owner's licensee.

Frankel and Gervais have posited that the GATT has, arguably, not made all IP laws immune to GATT principles under the Article XX(d) exception and parallel importing may be one of the aspects of IP law that are not covered by the GATT exception mechanism.[76] They further contend that irrespective of the position under the GATT, the primary authority with respect to intellectual property in the WTO is the TRIPS Agreement and its provision on exhaustion remains the binding authority.[77] The fact however remains that there is no authority suggesting that some aspects of patents, trademark or copyright, including parallel importing, have been excluded from the ambit of GATT Article XX(d). While it is suggested, and rightly so, that TRIPS provides the overarching framework for

75 Ibid.

76 S Frankel & D J Gervais, 'International Intellectual Property Rules and Parallel Imports', in I Calboli & E Lee (eds.), *Research Handbook on Intellectual Property and Parallel Imports* (Cheltenham: Edward Elgar, 2016) 85–105 at 90.

77 Ibid.

intellectual property in the WTO system, it is important to note that the TRIPS Agreement has clearly excluded the issue of exhaustion of rights and parallel importation from the scope of the agreement and WTO Members reserve the right to adopt any exhaustion regime that suit them.

Chang-Fa Lo argues that although the prohibition of the parallel importation of pharmaceutical patents can fall under the protection of IP, such prohibition would nonetheless be inconsistent with the substantive provisions of the GATT and is therefore outside the exceptions mentioned in GATT Article XX.[78]

It is however difficult to agree with the argument that there exists a conflict between Article 6 of TRIPS and Article XI of the GATT. Lo in canvassing the argument on the conflict between the two agreements does not seem to take account of the provision of Article XI(2)(b) which provides that the provisions of Paragraph 1 of Article XI dealing with general elimination of quantitative restrictions shall not extend to '*import and export prohibitions or restrictions necessary to the application of standards or regulations for the classification, grading or marketing of commodities in international trade*'. In view of the fact that parallel importation of pharmaceutical products has the effect of frustrating market segmentation and differential pricing of pharmaceutical products, its prohibition conveniently falls under 'restrictions necessary to the application of standards or regulations for the classification, grading or marketing of commodities in international trade'. To that extent countries imposing such restrictions are not in violation of TRIPS Article 6 or the GATT. The implication of this is that irrespective of the exhaustion regime a country decides to follow, it cannot be inconsistent with Article 6 of TRIPS or the GATT. Members are therefore absolutely free to determine the exhaustion regime that suits them under both the GATT and the TRIPS Agreement. While some WTO Members may choose to adopt a more restrictive exhaustion regime such as the national exhaustion regime, the enforcement of the law will have to be confined to the territory of the Members favouring the restrictive approach. The implication of Article 6 of the TRIPS Agreement is that no question of law regarding the exhaustion of rights will be entertained by the WTO Dispute Settlement Body.

5.4 Parallel importation in international trade

Parallel importation may be active or passive. It is active when a foreign distributor or licensee of the IPR owner sells the products in countries other than the territory in which the licensee was allowed to produce the goods thereby competing with the authorised local distributor or licensee in the importing country.[79] Active parallel imports involve the circulation of goods outside the

78 See C-F Lo, 'Potential Conflicts Between TRIPS and GATT Concerning Parallel Importation of Drugs and Possible Solution to Prevent Undesirable Market Segmentation' (2011) 66 *Food and Drug Law Journal* 73, 80.

79 Bonadio, above n 13, 154.

official distribution channels authorised by the right owner and are therefore usually a consequence of the breach of a contractual obligation on the licensee or foreign distributor not to market the goods outside the authorised country of distribution.[80] On the other hand, passive parallel imports occur when arbitrageurs acquire goods in a foreign market and resell them in a domestic market.[81] Passive parallel imports are the most common form of parallel importation.[82] Both active and passive parallel imports are subject to the same border measures applicable to regular imports such as tariffs and technical standards as well as quantitative restrictions.[83]

The economic principle of comparative advantages is the bedrock of the WTO multilateral trade system.[84] The comparative advantage theory states that a country should export goods and services in areas where it possesses the highest comparative advantage and import those in which its comparative advantage is at the lowest ebb.[85] The prohibition of parallel trade will thus be contrary to the Ricardian theory of comparative advantage in that it would obstruct the free movement of goods and frustrate the efficient distribution of production resources globally.[86]

Another major concern about parallel trade is that it is likely to further impede the transfer of technology where patented technologies are licensed in countries with an international exhaustion regime. There is a possibility of local licensees in such countries competing with the IP holders on international markets by re-exporting the goods manufactured through knowledge acquired from technology transfer.[87] Allowing parallel trade in goods that are subject to government price control (such as pharmaceuticals) would amount to export subsidies and these are generally prohibited by the WTO Agreement on Subsidies and Countervailing Measures because such export would unduly distort international trade.[88]

While it is generally believed that parallel imports may affect the ability of manufacturers to recoup the cost of R&D investment, there doesn't seem to be much economics literature on this issue. In relation to pharmaceutical patents, national governments sometimes adopt price control policies that may encourage parallel importation.[89] Parallel trade therefore responds to these price

80 Ibid., 154–155.

81 C Fink, 'Entering the Jungle of Intellectual Property Rights Exhaustion and Parallel Trade' in C Fink & K E Maskus (eds.), *Intellectual Property and Development: Lessons from Recent Economic Research* (World Bank and Oxford University Press 2005) 172.

82 Ibid.

83 Ibid.

84 See T Widodo, 'Comparative Advantage: Theory Empirical Measures and Case Studies' (2009) 4 *Review of Economic and Business Studies* 57; Bonadio, above n 13, 155.

85 Widodo, above n 84, 59.

86 Bonadio, above n 13, 155.

87 C Fink, above n 80, 180.

88 M Bronckers, 'The Exhaustion of Patent Rights Under WTO Law' (1998) 32 *Journal of World Trade* 137; Bonadio, above n 13, 157.

89 Maskus, above n 11, 130.

differentials through the flow of pharmaceuticals from low-price market countries to countries having no price regulations or having higher price limits.[90]

A study has shown that parallel trade can drive down retail prices in unregulated markets thereby reducing the incentive to further invest in R&D.[91] International price discrimination usually reflects global variances in elasticity of demand[92] and Keith Maskus has thus opined that parallel trade may diminish economic well-being by frustrating efficient price-discrimination. Patrick Rey notes that in the absence of parallel imports, governments usually set the prices for pharmaceuticals after taking into consideration the link between price and R&D.[93] He thus argues that parallel trade does not result in 'market integration' but in uniform alignment on the lowest level of R&D which would have adverse effects on all countries.[94] There is support for the view that parallel trade helps in eliminating anticompetitive practices and improving consumer welfare.[95] It is however difficult to agree with Rey that parallel imports would result in uniform alignment as the cost of shipping products and trans-border tariffs would ultimately reduce if not obliterate any uniformity in price that parallel imports might seem to offer. In view of the fact that parallel trade allows importers to purchase goods from cheaper markets especially where manufacturers charge inordinate prices in certain countries, parallel trade can be a good competition measure.

Parallel imports are seen as the response to IP practice of international price discrimination, by charging according to the purchasing power of a given market.[96] It has nonetheless been noted that price differentials may not always arise as a result of price discrimination but a reflection of the higher cost incurred by the IP owner in putting the product in the market.[97] Price differentials are sometimes attributable to fluctuation in foreign exchange rates.[98] It has been suggested that parallel imports might sometimes be orchestrated by IP owners to enhance the bottom line of the foreign subsidiary that sells to those parallel importing.[99] Parallel importation may also be used to frustrate national distributors maximising profit margins in not allowing

90 Ibid.
91 P Rey, 'The Impact of Parallel Imports on Prescription Medicines' (2003) http://citeseerx.ist.psu.edu/viewdoc/download?doi=10.1.1.493.1937&rep=rep1&type=pdf accessed 26 January 2019.
92 P M Danzon, 'The Economics of Parallel Trade' (1998) 13 *Pharmacoeconomics* 293.
93 See Rey, above n 91, 18.
94 Ibid., 23.
95 Avgoustis, above n 12, 110.
96 See A J Stack, 'TRIPs, Patent Exhaustion and Parallel Imports' (1998) 1 *Journal of World Intellectual Property* 657, 682; J Hilke, 'Free Trading or Free-Riding: An Examination of the Theories and Available Empirical Evidence on Gray Market Imports' (1988) 32 *World Competition* 75, 78.
97 Barrett above n 42, 959.
98 See Hilke, above n 96, 81–82; S E Lipner, *The Legal and Economic Aspects of Gray Market Goods* (Quorum Books, 1990) 3.
99 Lipner, above n 98, 4–5.

consumers to benefit from their cost reductions,[100] or who are involved in industry-wide collusion.[101]

Developing countries are generally more supportive of liberal parallel trade regimes in all fields of IP than developed countries,[102] and this is a reflection of the stricter limitations on IPRs usually canvassed by developing countries and the widespread belief that the competitive market created by parallel importation can benefit low-income consumers.[103] There is also the argument that any attempt to restrain the free movement of original products legitimately acquired is inconsistent with the liberalisation of international trade which is the fundamental objective of the GATT/WTO.[104] However, as already argued above, the GATT does allow measures to be taken to protect IPRs and the prohibition of international exhaustion can qualify as one of such measures. Hence, it is not entirely correct to posit that the prohibition of parallel imports obstructs trade liberalisation.

5.4.1 Parallel importation and pharmaceuticals

Parallel importation of pharmaceutical products is viewed as more complex than the parallel imports of other products because it entails not only trade and IP issues, but also issues affecting the health policies of nations and consumer interests.[105] While manufacturers of goods are constantly pressing for more barriers to maintain price differences amongst different countries, most consumers find such differences unjustifiable in a world that is committed to obliterating impediments to international trade.[106] Parallel imports can have the effect of ensuring the maintenance of price competition in international markets[107] as pharmaceutical companies may be forced to lower the prices of drugs to compete with drugs made available through parallel importation.[108] Although strong arguments have been advanced against parallel importation of pharmaceuticals and international exhaustion, many of such arguments remain suspect.

A major argument for the prohibition of parallel importation of patented drugs is that it frustrates the ability of pharmaceutical companies to successfully maintain their differentiated prices in different markets.[109] This may not,

100 Hilke, above n 96, 80.
101 Ibid, 80–81
102 K E Maskus, 'Parallel Imports' (2000) 23 *The World Economy* 1269.
103 Maskus, above n 11, 125.
104 Avgoustis, above n 12, 118.
105 C-F Lo, 'Potential Conflicts Between TRIPS and GATT Concerning Parallel Importation of Drugs and Possible Solution to Prevent Undesirable Market Segmentation' (2011) 66 *Food and Drug Law Journal* 73.
106 See C Heath, 'Parallel Imports and International Trade' (1997) 28 *IIC* 623.
107 F M Abbott, 'First Report (Final) to the Committee on International Trade Law of the International Law Association on the Subject of Parallel Importation' (n 15), 622.
108 See Lo above n 105, 74.
109 Lo, above n 105, at 76.

however, be a significant problem in relation to developed economies as most developed countries do not favour the international exhaustion regime. Parallel imports from cheaper markets can therefore not be easily imported to countries that generally do not favour international exhaustion such as the EU. Another argument is that parallel importation undermines patent rights and may bring economic loss to both IP owners and consumers thereby resulting in anticompetitive effects.[110] It has been argued that parallel imports might make it impossible for drug manufacturers to recoup the cost of R&D research and other ancillary costs thereby stifling innovation, frustrating the differential pricing schemes of manufacturers and possibly also driving authorised distributors out of the market.[111] Again, this argument is at best theoretical and has no convincing empirical support. The gist of the matter is that parallel trade is still trade in original goods and the right holder must have released the product in the exporting country at a rate that would be clearly profitable in that country. Parallel trade may on the contrary increase substantially sales in the exporting country thereby increasing manufacturer's profit in general. It is therefore very unlikely that the movement of goods, originally released at a lower rate in a low-income country, to a high-income or another developing country would have the effect of creating any significant loss to the rights holder or even stifling innovation.

Another argument against international exhaustion of rights is that it can be to the disadvantage of consumers by whittling down the effectiveness of patents in protecting consumers by identifying the origin of products and ensuring that safety and technical standards are being maintained.[112] This argument however seems to lose sight of the point that parallel trade is not the same as trade in illicit or counterfeit goods and it doesn't always involve the repackaging of products. It is therefore hard to see how there can be problems with the identification of origin, or compromise in safety and technical standards.

The pharmaceutical industry has also argued that parallel importation of patented products is inconsistent with Article 28 of the TRIPS Agreement and that Article 6 only prevents Members from bringing actions against another Member before the WTO dispute settlement body for non-compliance with the rule.[113] Article 28 of TRIPS provides:

110 S A Singham, 'Competition Policy and the Stimulation of Innovation: TRIPS and the Interface between Competition and Patent Protection in the Pharmaceutical Industry' (2000) 26 *Brooklyn Journal of International Law* 363, 407.

111 Ibid.

112 See National Economic Research Associates, *The Economic Consequences of the Choice of Regime in the Area of Trademarks* (8 February 1999) Executive Summary at 6–7 www.eurasiancommission.org/ru/act/finpol/dobd/intelsobs/Documents/NERA%20study_TM_exhaustion%20(main).pdf accessed 26 January 2019); Singham, above n 113, 409.

113 See H E Bale, Jr., 'The Conflicts between Parallel Trade and Product Access and innovation: The Case of Pharmaceuticals' (1999) 1 *Journal of International Economic Law* 637, 641.

A patent shall confer on its owner the following exclusive rights:

a Where the subject matter of a patent is a product, to prevent third parties not having the owner's consent from the acts of: making, using, offering for sale, selling, or importing (see footnote 6) for these purposes that product.

[Footnote6: This right, like all other rights conferred under this Agreement in respect of the use, sale, importation or other distribution of goods is subject to the provisions of Article 6]

Whilst the tenor of Article 28 does empower patent holders to prohibit the importation of their products without their express consent, that power is made subject to the exhaustion doctrine which is exclusively within the ambit of national laws and policies and as such where a country adopts the regional or international exhaustion doctrine, a right holder can no longer rely on Article 28 to restrain the parallel importation of a product specifically placed on the market by himself or with his consent.

One must however hasten to add that TRIPS only sets minimum standards for IP protection and Members States are at liberty to impose higher standards than required by TRIPS. Thus Article 1 of the TRIPS Agreement provides inter alia:

> Members shall give effect to the provisions of this Agreement. Members may, but shall not be obliged to, implement in their law more extensive protection than is required by this Agreement, provided that such protection does not contravene the provisions of this Agreement.

In furtherance of this provision, the US has been vigorously pursuing bilateral free trade agreements with many countries all over the world and most such agreements contain provisions prohibiting the parallel importation of patented products. The argument has been made that negotiating TRIPS-plus agreements that seek to take away the liberty of countries to pursue an exhaustion regime that suits them, especially in relation to pharmaceutical products, offends the spirit of the Doha Declaration.[114] Such a bilateral approach is considered inconsistent with the multilateralism of the WTO and as such would be in contravention of international law obligations.[115] Whilst it is true that there are commentators who are very opposed to the proliferation of bilateral and plurilateral trade agreements in a multilateral trade setting, it is incontestable that such trade agreements are not only recognised but also encouraged by the WTO. It therefore seems that regional coalitions and free trade agreements have become an indispensable part of the WTO system. Such bilateral and plurilateral trade

114 UNCTAD/ICTSD, *TRIPS and Development Resource Book* (UNCTAD/ICTSD, 2005) 115–116.

115 M Ricolfi, 'Interface between Intellectual Property and International Trade: The TRIPS Agreement' (January 2002) *Italian Intellectual Property Law* 29, 41.

agreements do not however have to contain TRIPS-plus provisions and countries negotiating them, especially in the global south, can insist on this.

Another significant point for consideration is whether the adoption of a special or 'discriminatory' exhaustion of rights regime for pharmaceutical products would run afoul of Article 27(1) of TRIPS which states that patents shall be available and 'enjoyable without discrimination as to the place of invention, the field of technology and whether products are imported or locally produced'. A very good example of a law with special or 'discriminatory' provision for drug patents is Section 15C(a) of the South African *Medicines and Related Substances Amendment Acts 2002* which provides that the Minister may:

> notwithstanding anything to the contrary contained in the Patents Act, 1978 (Act 57 of 1978), determine that the rights with regard to any medicine under a patent granted in the Republic shall not extend to acts in respect of such medicine which has been put onto the market by the owner of the medicine or with his or her consent.

The question, then, is whether a provision such as this South African law runs afoul of the 'non-discriminatory' principle enshrined in TRIPS Article 27(1). The answer seems to be, prima facie, yes. However, the inconsistency is adequately cured by the combined effect of Articles 6 and 8 of the TRIPS Agreement. As previously noted, Article 6 states that nothing in the TRIPS Agreement shall be used to address the issue of exhaustion of rights for the purposes of dispute settlement. To this extent it can be argued that Article 27(1) has been effectively subsumed by Article 6 in so far as it relates to exhaustion of rights. Further, Article 8 allows Members to implement the provisions of TRIPS in a way conducive to their socio-economic welfare provided measures taken are consistent with the Agreement. Given that all patented pharmaceutical products are treated the same way irrespective of whether they are foreign or domestic, there can be no violation of the non-discriminatory principle.

It is however important to note that the argument that parallel trade promotes free trade has also been strongly challenged.[116] Georgios Tsouloufas argues that lower prices from exporting countries are achieved through price regulation, and this combined with low standard of IP protection and low per capita income pervasive in low-price markets, do not create efficiency gains.[117] On the other hand, functions ancillary to parallel trade like transportation, repackaging and quality control result in social costs that are not negligible.[118] He further argues that parallel trade results in temporary undersupply of pharmaceuticals in the country of export with an oversupply in the country of import and the citizens of the exporting country would be deprived of the fruits of pharmaceu-

116 G Tsouloufas, 'Limiting Pharmaceutical Parallel Trade in the European Union: Regulatory and Economic Justifications' (2011) 36 *European Law Review* 385, 393.

117 Ibid.

118 Ibid.

tical innovation because of manufacturers' unwillingness to supply medicines to states where parallel trade originates.[119] These factors, he argues, would result in 'allocative inefficiencies'.[120]

Again, this argument does not sound compelling. Allocative inefficiency is said to occur when economic resources are unable to satisfy economic wants.[121] If products are being purchased in great magnitude from a particular nation, the implication will be higher sales for the manufacturer at the prevailing price in that market, and the manufacturer is unlikely to want to leave that market undersupplied. Rather than reducing the supply in the country of export, the manufacturer may be constrained to adjust its differential pricing scheme and increase the level of supply in the exporting country. It is thus submitted that Tsouloufas' exposition of the 'allocative inefficiencies' associated with parallel importation is not without some degree of implausibility.

The relevance of parallel importation to the access to medicines debate remains a very topical issue.[122] One option is to allow parallel trade in IP-protected products which have been put on the market by the IP owner. The converse strategy would be to prohibit such trade while allowing manufacturers to use price discrimination to make drugs available to the developing world at lower costs.[123] It has been suggested that the international exhaustion principle would hardly enhance access to medicines in developing countries and that pharmaceutical companies should be allowed through IP law or otherwise to prevent the importation of low-price pharmaceuticals from developing countries to high-price markets.[124] The problem with this argument, however, is that such countries would have to depend substantially on the benevolence of multinational pharmaceutical companies to meet the health needs of their nationals. This is not a very dependable way of addressing health crises in countries in dire need of affordable drugs. Mathias Ganslandt et al have opined that there is an important need to draw a dividing line between incentive to innovate and distribution needs.[125] Thus, where the technical and financial resources are made available to develop drugs for diseases afflicting people in poor countries, steps may need to be taken to ensure drugs specially made for people in such countries do not find their way to high-price markets.[126]

119 Ibid.

120 Ibid.

121 See W C Spaulding, 'Allocative Efficiency and the Production Possibilities Frontier' http://thismatter.com/economics/allocative-efficiency.htm accessed 26 January 2019.

122 See generally R K Rai, 'Should the WTO Harmonise Parallel Import Laws? An Analysis of the Exhaustion Doctrine' (2011) 6(12) *Journal of Intellectual Property Law and Practice* 898.

123 J Atik & H H Lidgard, 'Embracing Price Discrimination: TRIPS and the Suppression of Parallel Trade in Pharmaceuticals' (2006) 27 *University of Pennsylvania Journal of International Economic Law*, 1043, 1059–1060.

124 Ibid., at 60.

125 M Ganslandt, K E Maskus & E V Wong, 'Developing and Distributing Essential Drugs to Poor Countries: The DEFEND Proposal' (2001) 24 *The World Economy* 779.

126 D K Brown & G Norman, 'Optimal Intellectual Property Rights and Humanitarian Assistance During a National Health Emergency' Tufts University Working Paper (2003).

5.4.2 *Differential pricing*

Differential pricing – otherwise known as price discrimination – of patented products or processes can take different forms: varying licence fees according to licensee's willingness or ability to pay; licensing patented technology at a reduced price whilst requiring licensees to purchase supplies for use with the patented product only from the patentee; and restricting the use to which purchasers of products sold at discounted price may put them, otherwise known as geographic price discrimination.[127] For the present purposes, differential pricing will be examined in relation to geographic price discrimination. Parallel imports are usually used to take advantage of the differential pricing phenomenon.[128]

The strategy deployed for geographic differential pricing is to divide the world into different zones and to adjust prices within each zone to maximise the firm's profit.[129] To this end, differential pricing seeks to adapt prices charged by sellers to the purchasing power of governments and citizens in different countries.[130] It is said to be perhaps the most recognised mechanism for global financing of novel technologies in developing countries.[131] Geographic differential pricing of informational goods (goods deriving value from the information embedded in them) is probably most notorious in relation to pharmaceutical patents,[132] as pharmaceutical companies are generally believed to sell their product at different prices in different countries.[133] For instance, a drug manufacturer would be willing to sell pharmaceutical products at a more reduced price in poor countries than in rich countries to the extent that the lower prices cover marginal costs.[134] Differential pricing is very important for the successful development and sale of IP products and developing countries stand to benefit from the lower prices appropriate market segmentation will offer.[135]

For a viable differential pricing scheme to exist, there must be fixed costs of production, sufficient market power and safeguards to forestall market leakage to high-cost markets.[136] 'Ramsey pricing' is a concept of differential pricing which recognises the need for patented goods with significant public and social

127 W W Fisher III, 'When Should We Permit Differential Pricing of Information' (2007) 55 *UCLA Law Review* 1, 6.

128 Rai, above n 125, 904.

129 Ibid.

130 See J Watal, *Workshop on Differential Pricing and Financing of Essential Drug* (World Trade Organization and World Health Organization 2001) 11 www.wto.org/english/tratop_e/trips_e/wto_background_e.pdf accessed 26 October 2019.

131 Blum, above n 21, 105.

132 See Fisher III above n 127, 19.

133 P M Danzon & M F Furukawa, 'Prices and Availability of Pharmaceuticals: Evidence from Nine Countries', *Health Affairs*, 29 October 2003 at W3-521, www.healthaffairs.org/doi/full/10.1377/hlthaff.W3.521 accessed 26 January 2019.

134 Maskus, above n 11, 124.

135 Barton above n 47, 493.

136 See Watal, above n 130, 13–14.

benefits such as life-saving drugs, to be specially priced or discounted in poor countries.[137] A market-based differential pricing scheme will require an open and free market, which is not always present in developing countries.[138] Another approach is to have bilateral negotiated discounts whereby the supplying company decides what discount to be given on the basis of cost and profitability.[139] Other approaches are voluntary and non-voluntary licences, regional and global bulk purchasing, and public/private partnership in which prices are country specific.[140] A number of these approaches require a solid public law foundation,[141] and there is not yet an adequate international legal foundation to support diverse approaches to global differential pricing schemes.[142]

Whilst differential pricing for HIV drugs was common in the 1990s, there were few variations in the costs of AIDS drugs in different countries by 2000.[143] Despite the fact that many manufacturers have significantly reduced the prices charged in certain developing countries,[144] many people infected with HIV still do not have access to cheap versions of the best drugs.[145] Barton has argued that differential pricing should be encouraged but global exhaustion should be prohibited in relation to goods that are genuinely information intensive such as goods protected by patents and copyright, whilst global exhaustion should be encouraged in relation to goods with little information content when compared to the other content of the product.[146]

It has been posited that in relation to pharmaceuticals there is a good case for differential pricing to allow for two or three global prices (as between developed nations, middle-income nations and low-income countries) such that grey markets (parallel imports) would be open within each of the tiers, but the price differences between the tiers would be protected.[147] It is submitted that whilst differential pricing can be a very good way of taking local circumstances into account in regulating the prices of goods, that should not be used to prohibit the use of parallel trade. It is further submitted that parallel trade will not pose any threat to the economic interest of the manufacturer if indeed its differential pricing scheme is an accurate reflection of the local circumstances in the relevant markets, as the cost of importing the products in such cases would most likely make it unattractive to the parallel traders.

137 Ibid., at 12.
138 Blum, above n 21, 106.
139 Ibid.
140 See Watal above n 130.
141 Blum, above n 21, 106.
142 See Watal, above n 130.
143 Ibid., 12.
144 Ibid., at 7; Atik & Lidgard, above n 123, 1043; P J Hammer, 'Differential Pricing of Essential AIDS Drugs: Markets, Politics, and Public Health' (2002) 5 *Journal of International Economic Law* 883, 896.
145 See Fisher III, above n 130, 9.
146 See Barton, above n 47, 494.
147 Ibid., at 495.

The differential pricing phenomenon is particularly relevant to the access to medicines debate as it can enhance access to essential medicines in low-income countries whilst still allowing producers to recoup the costs of R&D through sales made at much higher rates in high-income nations.[148] Despite this, price discrimination might not be a good solution to the global access to medicines problem for reasons such as cross-border internet sales and 'pharmaceutical tourism' (a situation whereby people travel to neighbouring countries to buy cheaper drugs for personal use).[149] Parallel importation can make the maintenance of differential pricing very difficult and is thus seen as a form of arbitrage with a tendency to obliterate differences in prices across different markets.[150] However, as mentioned above, there are other costs involved in parallel trade across borders that will still make it hard to achieve price uniformity. The argument that parallel imports will eventually abolish differences in prices across markets is therefore not entirely correct.

Manufacturers' differential pricing schemes can be a good way of taking local circumstances into account in regulating prices. However, it is submitted that it should be without prejudice to the right of countries to use parallel trade to meet the needs of the local market where that can make some significant difference. The argument that parallel trade can drive local industries out of the market seems to have been exaggerated, as there are legal measures available in international trade law to address such situations.[151] For developing countries, it will appear that the best option is to allow differential pricing to be complementary to parallel trade. This is permissible under Article 6 of TRIPS.

5.4.3 Parallel importation and competition policy

Intellectual property and competition law are two interdependent fields with seemingly conflicting roles.[152] While IP protects creativity, innovative progress, business reputation and information or ideas capable of industrial application with utility value so as to reward creativity and inventive activities, competition law seeks to safeguard the healthy operation of markets by putting a check on any anticompetitive use of IP monopoly rights.[153] A strong competition policy is needed to get the lowest possible price for pharmaceuticals, as competition will encourage trade liberalisation and foreign direct investment (FDI) whilst

148 J J Darrow, (Column) 'Recent Developments in Health Law: Why International Price Discrimination May Increasingly Be the Wrong Solution to a Global Drug Problem' (2011) 39 *Journal of Law, Medicine and Ethics* 291.

149 Ibid.

150 E Siew-Kwan Ng, 'The Impact of the Bilateral US–Singapore Free Trade Agreement on the Singapore's Post-TRIPS Patent Regime in the Pharmaceutical Context' (2010) 16 (5) *International Trade Law and Regulation* 121, 125.

151 The WTO Agreement on Safeguards Article 2 allows countries to take measures against the importation of foreign products where such importation is injurious to the local industry.

152 Avgoustis above n 12, 108.

153 Ibid.

creating a regulatory framework to prevent monopolisation and the exploitation of market power.[154]

There is an argument that without a strong competition policy, the exhaustion doctrine would have negative effects, as domestic brands may be part of a single alliance that would conspire to maintain high prices through exclusive distributorship agreements.[155] On the other hand, parallel trade may equally promote free trade by removing potential anticompetitive practices. An example of anticompetitive practices is manufacturers' vertical restraint through exclusive distribution channels which may enable the control of the availability of products both nationally and internationally.[156] National exhaustion is seen as permissible, as is regional exhaustion (as in the case of the EU which operates a single European Market).[157] The argument is that regional exhaustion should not cover free trade areas or countries where market conditions differ substantially.[158] Another argument is that parallel trading is anticompetitive because it would ultimately erode all IPRs whereas IPRs are not only tolerated by competition law but also encouraged by it.[159] Again, however, the problem with this line of argument is that it seems to undermine the fact that parallel imports are not the same as trade in counterfeit or illegal goods and to that extent IPRs are still very much at large and enforceable provided the parallel trade has not gone beyond the confines of sale or resale of legitimate goods. As succinctly stated by Carlos Correa:

> ...it is important to emphasize that the issue of parallel imports is completely distinct from the issue of counterfeit pharmaceutical products. Parallel imports, by definition, relate to products which have been legitimately put on the market, not to imitations of original products. Parallel imports would be subject, in principle, to the same import and other regulations applicable to any other imported medicine.[160]

The TRIPS Agreement does recognise that the use of IPRs should not have anticompetitive effects. The objectives and principles of the TRIPS Agreement, as stated in Articles 7 and 8 accentuate the need to balance IP law with competition policies. Thus Article 7 of TRIPS provides:

> The protection and enforcement of intellectual property should contribute to the promotion of technological innovation and to the transfer and dissemination of technology, to the mutual advantage of producers and users of

154 Singham, above n 110, 408.
155 Singham above n 110, 409.
156 Avgoustis above n 12, 117.
157 Ibid., 410.
158 Ibid.
159 Ibid.
160 C Correa, 'Public Health and Patent Legislation in Developing Countries' (2001) 3 *Tulane Journal of Technology & Intellectual Property* 1, 41.

> technological knowledge and in a manner conducive to social and economic welfare, and to a balance of rights and obligations.

Article 8(2) further provides

> Appropriate measures, provided that they are consistent with the provisions of this Agreement, may be needed to prevent the abuse of intellectual property rights by right holders or the resort to practices which unreasonably restrain trade or adversely affect the international transfer of technology.

The foregoing provisions, it is submitted, are wide enough to empower countries to adopt a strong competition law framework to ensure a balance of rights and obligations. The interpretation of these provisions has not been without some controversy.[161] In *Canada – Patent Protection of Pharmaceutical Products*,[162] the European Communities (EC) contended that the regulatory review and stockpiling exceptions in the patent law in Canada run afoul of the TRIPS Agreement.[163] In response, Canada maintained that governments are sufficiently empowered by Articles 7 and 8 of TRIPS to adjust patent rights to strike a convenient balance with other essential national policies.[164] The EC in response to Canada's reliance on Articles 7 and 8 argued that the provisions merely describe the balancing of goals that had already been concluded in negotiating the TRIPS Agreement and that to view the flexibility allowed by TRIPS Article 30 (dealing with the right to provide limited exceptions to patents) as an opportunity to 'renegotiate' the overall balance of the Agreement would not be in line with its spirit and purport.[165] The Panel observed that whilst 'basic balance' had indeed been achieved in the Agreement, patent rights might require certain adjustments without renegotiating the balance achieved in the Agreement.[166] According to the Panel:

> Article 30's very existence amounts to a recognition that the definition of patent rights contained in Article 28 would need certain adjustments. On the other hand, the three limiting conditions attached to Article 30 testify strongly that the negotiators of the Agreement did not intend Article 30 to bring about what would be equivalent to a renegotiation of the basic balance of the Agreement. Obviously, the exact scope of Article 30's authority will depend on the specific meaning given to its limiting conditions. The words of those conditions must be examined with particular care on this point. Both the goals and the limitations stated in Articles 7

161 See P K Yu, 'The Objectives and Principles of the TRIPS Agreement' (2009) 46 *Houston Law Review* 979, 992.
162 Panel Report, Canada – Patent Protection of Pharmaceutical Products, WTO Doc WT/DS114/R (17 March 2000).
163 Ibid.
164 Ibid.
165 Ibid.
166 Ibid.

and 8.1 must obviously be borne in mind when doing so as well as those of other provisions of the TRIPS Agreement which indicate its object and purposes.[167]

Daniel Gervais posits that Article 8 is '*essentially a policy statement that explains the rationale for measures taken under arts 30, 31 and 40*'.[168] Nevertheless, he concedes that it may serve an interpretative function. Article 8.2 has particularly been described as a redundant provision as all the public policy objectives mentioned therein have already been addressed in other parts of the Agreement.[169] Peter Yu has further described both Articles 7 and 8 as not only providing a balance that makes the TRIPS Agreement a legitimate bargain between developed and less developed countries but as also sowing the seeds for the development of new international norms within and without the TRIPS Agreement.[170] It is therefore relatively well-settled that Articles 7 and 8 of the TRIPS Agreement are largely hortatory provisions. Despite this, it is contended that they still provide some leeway for giving some force to local exigencies in the interpretation of TRIPS. This is well accentuated in the recent decision of the WTO Panel in *DS467: Australia — Certain Measures Concerning Trademarks, Geographical Indications and Other Plain Packaging Requirements Applicable to Tobacco Products and Packaging*.[171]

Whilst competition laws and policies are generally acknowledged as desirable for the well-being of an economy and the protection of consumer interests, the plethora of socio-economic problems in many developing countries may make it difficult to view the development of competition rules as a priority.[172] The potential for anticompetitive practices on the part of pharmaceutical companies can be well addressed by utilising the existing flexibilities in the TRIPS Agreement. Although it is correct that the myriad economic problems in developing countries may make it difficult to view the implementation of effective competition policy structures as a matter of much significance in a number of such countries, competition policies remain very important to the developmental goals of many developing countries[173] especially in the African continent. It is submitted that rather than refusing to adopt a competition regime, the option should be to devise effective means of adopting competition strategies that would take account of the peculiar needs of the country concerned and fashioning the competition law regime to serve their national interests. A detailed discussion of the competition law dimension to the discussion is, however, not within the scope of this work.

167 Ibid.

168 D Gervais, *The TRIPS Agreement: Drafting History and Analysis* (Sweet & Maxwell, 3rd ed., 2008) 209.

169 See Yu above n 164, 1017.

170 Ibid., 1046.

171 This is discussed in Chapter 8.

172 U Ewelukwa, 'Patent Wars in the Valley of the Shadow of Death: The Pharmaceutical Industry, Ethics and Global Trade' (2005) 59 *University of Miami Law Review* 203, 286.

173 T Nguyen, *Competition Law, Technology Transfer and the TRIPS Agreement: Implication for Developing Countries* (Edward Elgar, 2010) 254–255.

5.4.4 Parallel importation of goods made under compulsory licensing

One point that remains largely unsettled is the extent to which goods made under compulsory licences can be parallel imported under the TRIPS patent regime. This point arose for consideration by the European Court of Justice in *Pharmon v Hoechst*.[174] The facts of the case were that Hoechst held patents for the drug frusemide in Germany, Holland and the UK. A compulsory licence which prohibited export was obtained for the drug pursuant to the *British Patents Act 1949*. The licensee sold a considerable amount to Pharmon for marketing in the Netherlands. The ECJ held that marketing in a Member State pursuant to rights acquired by a compulsory licence was not a consensual sale that exhausted the patent right.[175]

Since Article 31(f) allows a compulsory licence to be granted 'predominantly' for the domestic market; it therefore permits at least part of the production under licence to be 'parallel imported'. Arguably, such exports are permissible even when they are to countries where there is patent protection, as there is no basis to assume that Article 31(f) would only apply when the product produced under the compulsory licence is not protected in the importing country.[176] In the words of Carlos Correa:

> If parallel imports were outlawed in cases where there is remuneration of, but no consent by the patent owner (as in the case of compulsory licences), the usefulness of parallel imports as a pro-competitive mechanism would be seriously curtailed, since in most instances the patent owner may attach sale limitations on his licenses not to export without patent owner's authorization.[177]

Gervais observes that whilst some believe that only goods made with the consent of the right holder may be subject to parallel importation, some would also include goods made under a compulsory licence.[178] He posits that, given the wording of Article 6 and the Doha Declaration which seems to favour a liberal interpretation of the TRIPS flexibilities, WTO Members are relatively free to determine what constitutes legitimate goods, and that Article 31(f) seems to allow some export in relation to goods made under compulsory licence.[179] In contrast, Maskus has opined that a major exception to the exhaustion doctrine is that products placed on the market in furtherance of a compulsory licensing order may not be parallel imported.[180]

Although both Correa and Gervais favour the view that goods made under a compulsory license can be parallel imported, they seem to ignore the import

174 Case 19/84, *Pharmon BV v. Hoechst AG*, 3 CMLR 775 (1985).
175 Ibid.
176 Correa above n 23, 86.
177 Ibid.
178 Gervais above n 63, 198–201.
179 Ibid.
180 Maskus, above 11, 124.

of Paragraph 5 of the Doha Paragraph-6 Implementation Decision which provides:

> Members shall ensure that the availability of effective legal means to prevent the importation into, and sale in, their territories of products produced under the system set out in this Decision and diverted to their markets inconsistently with its provisions, using the means already required to be available under the TRIPS Agreement. If any Member considers that such measures are proving insufficient for this purpose, the matter may be reviewed in the Council for TRIPS at the request of that Member.[181]

In the light of the foregoing provision, it is submitted that the parallel importation of goods made under the special compulsory licensing regime established by the Doha Implementation Decision cannot be considered legitimate. It is also doubtful whether the parallel importation of goods made pursuant to compulsory licences generally can be considered legitimate. This is because the exhaustion doctrine entails the voluntary placement of goods in the market by the right holder. Goods made available pursuant to a compulsory licence cannot be said to have been released by the IP holder and it will in that case be arguably an aberration to argue that the patent holder has exhausted its rights where non-voluntary licences are involved.

5.5 Parallel trade as a mechanism for accessing medicines in Africa

In Africa, most countries do not have provisions on exhaustion of rights and parallel importation. The South African law, however, particularly recognises international exhaustion with respect to pharmaceutical patents.[182] The law in Ghana also provides that rights conferred on patents shall not extend to articles released in the market in any country by the right holder or with his consent.[183] This is also the position favoured by the Kenyan law.[184] In Rwanda, the law allows national exhaustion of patent rights generally.[185] The Rwandan Law however allows the Minister to allow international exhaustion in the following circumstances where the patent:

1. is not available in the territory of the Republic of Rwanda;
2. is available on the territory of the Republic of Rwanda with quality levels unreasonably low;

181 *Implementation of Paragraph 6 of the Doha Declaration on the TRIPS Agreement and Public Health WTO*, Doc WT/L/540 (2 September) (Decision of 30 August 2003); Section 2.3.2 discusses the Doha Paragraph-6 Implementation Decision in detail.

182 *Medicines and Related Substances Control Act* (as amended in 2002) (South Africa) Section 15C(a).

183 Patents Act 2003 (Ghana) Section 11(4)(a).

184 Industrial Property Act 2001 (Kenya) Section 58(2).

185 Law on Protection of Intellectual Property 2009 (Rwanda) Article 40.

3 amount is not sufficient to satisfy domestic demand;
4 is a price that the Minister considers improper;
5 for any public purpose, including anticompetitive practices.

The Patents Act of Nigeria however contains no provision whatsoever on exhaustion of rights. While South Africa, Kenya and Ghana clearly provide for international exhaustion of rights in their patents law, the Rwandan law explicitly provides for a national exhaustion regime subject to certain exceptions. The standard of IP protection established by the Rwandan law seems to be quite high for a country that is still on the UN list of least developed countries.

Africa can benefit immensely from the TRIPS parallel trade flexibility by adopting an international exhaustion regime that would allow African countries to import IP products from the cheapest market available. The type of regional exhaustion available in Europe will not be particularly suitable in Africa as Africa, unlike Europe, is a net IP importer and not a producer. Given the fact that over 50% of the countries in Africa are currently in the UN list of least developed countries[186] and all the others are still in the OECD list of developing countries,[187] the best exhaustion regime that would suit Africa at her current level of development is an unrestricted international exhaustion regime. This will enable African countries to import products from the cheapest market available anywhere in the world to meet the needs of her populace.

5.6 Conclusion

Despite the significant controversy that the use of parallel trade usually generates, it is still one of the major flexibilities allowed by TRIPS in the access to medicines context. International exhaustion is likely to frustrate the move towards differential pricing, which can be of immense benefit to low-income countries in their quest to meet the global access to medicines challenge. However, if developing countries adopt a regional exhaustion regime, this will enable them to benefit from parallel trade as well as differential pricing. Developing a good competition framework can also help in ensuring access to medicines in many poor countries. Developing countries should stop viewing competition policy as a cosmetic remedy that does little to address their pressing economic problems. On the contrary, they can actually fashion their competition law in a way that will not only improve the options available to them in having access to affordable medicines but also boost their economy through trade liberalisation and FDI. Most African countries are yet to enact provisions that incorporate the

186 UN Office of the High Representative for the Least Developed Countries, Landlocked Developing Countries and Small Island Developing States(UN-OHRLLS), 'Least Developed Countries' http://unohrlls.org/custom-content/uploads/2018/12/list-of-least-developed-countries-rev1.pdf accessed 26 January 2019.

187 OECD, 'The DAC List of ODA Recipients: Factsheet – January 2012' (2012). www.oecd.org/dac/stats/49483614.pdf accessed 26 January 2019.

TRIPS flexibilities in their patent laws. Whilst some commentators have advocated for more flexible standards in the international patent system to adequately address the access to medicines problem, the myriad of free trade agreements incorporating TRIPS-plus standards currently being pursued by the US are a clear indication to developing countries that they should be more interested in protecting the existing flexibilities than in advocating for more. It would appear the problem with TRIPS is not about insufficient flexibilities. Rather, it is more about the underutilisation of the existing ones. It is therefore very important for Africa to fully embrace the existing flexibilities under TRIPS and strongly resist every attempt to be made subject to TRIPS-plus standards.

More importantly, it is becoming increasingly expedient for African countries to form a common front to address the access to medicines problem in the continent. The need for alliances and collaborative efforts in addressing the challenges posed by access to medicines is being recognised all over the world. The African access to medicines problem is making the need for an African regional trade area more compelling. With the current proliferation of Regional Trade Agreements (RTAs) in the WTO multilateral trade system, it is in Africa's interest to establish its own RTA to be able to compete favourably in the global governance of trade. Trade barriers and absence of free trade within the continent is a significant part of the access to medicines problem. The use of parallel importation and the other flexibilities available in TRIPS are likely to be significantly enhanced in Africa through the stratagem of an RTA. Such an economic alliance will not only enable Africa to adopt a common front in addressing the access to medicines problem, it will also put Africa in a position of power to jointly resist unfair trade rules in multilateral and plurilateral trade negotiations.

Bibliography

Abbott F M, 'First Report (Final) to the Committee on International Trade Law of the International Law Association on the Subject of Parallel Importation' (1998) 1 *Journal of International Economic Law* 607.

Abbott F M, 'The WTO TRIPS Agreement and Global Economic Development' (1996) 72 *Chicago-Kent Law Review* 385.

Atik J & Lidgard H H, 'Embracing Price Discrimination: TRIPS and the Suppression of Parallel Trade in Pharmaceuticals' (2006) 27 *University of Pennsylvania Journal of International Economic Law* 1043.

Avgoustis I, 'Parallel Imports and Exhaustion of Trade Mark Rights: Should Steps Be Taken Towards an International Exhaustion Regime?' (2012) 34 *European Intellectual Property Review* 108.

Bale H E Jr., 'The Conflicts Between Parallel Trade and Product Access and innovation: The Case of Pharmaceuticals' (1999) 1 *Journal of International Economic Law* 637.

Barrett M, 'The United States Doctrine of Exhaustion: Parallel Imports of Patented Goods' (2000) 27 *Northern Kentucky Law Review* 911.

Bartelt S, 'Compulsory Licenses Pursuant to TRIPS Article 31 in the Light of the Doha Declaration on the TRIPS Agreement and Public Health'(2003) 6(2) *Journal of World Intellectual Property* 284.

Barton J H, 'Global Trade Issues in the New Millennium: The Economics of TRIPS: International Trade in Information Intensive Products' (2001) 33 *George Washington International Law Review* 473.

Blum J D, 'The Role of Law in Global E-Health: A Tool for Development and Equity in a Digitally Divided World' (2002) 46 *Saint Louis University Law Journal* 85.

Bonadio E, 'Parallel Imports in a Global Market: Should a Generalised International Exhaustion Be the Next Step?' (2011) 33 *European Intellectual Property Review* 153.

Bradley C A, 'Territorial Intellectual Property Rights in an Age of Globalism' (1997) 37 *Vanderbilt Journal of International Law* 505.

Bronckers M, 'The Exhaustion of Patent Rights Under WTO Law' (1998) 32 *Journal of World Trade* 137.

Brown D K & Norman G, 'Optimal Intellectual Property Rights and Humanitarian Assistance During a National Health Emergency' Tufts University Working Paper (2003).

Brown J R C, 'Exhaustion of Rights in the EEC: Some Special Cases, with Emphasis on Pharmaceuticals' (1990) 1 *Intellectual Property Journal* 139.

Chiappetta V, 'The Desirability of Agreeing to Disagree: The WTO, TRIPS, International IPR Exhaustion and a few Other Things' (2000) 21 *Michigan Journal of International Law* 333, 341.

Cornish W & Llewelyn D, *Intellectual Property: Patents, Copyright, Trade Marks and Allied Rights* (Thomson Sweet & Maxwell, 6th ed., 2007).

Correa C, 'Public Health and Patent Legislation in Developing Countries' (2001) 3 *Tulane Journal of Technology & Intellectual Property* 1.

Correa C M, *Trade Related Aspects of Intellectual Property Rights: A Commentary on the TRIPS Agreement* (Oxford University Press, 2007) 79.

Danzon P M, 'The Economics of Parallel Trade' (1998) 13 *Pharmacoeconomics* 293.

Danzon P M & Furukawa M F, 'Prices and Availability of Pharmaceuticals: Evidence from Nine Countries', *Health Affairs*, Oct 29 2003 at W3–521, www.healthaffairs.org/doi/full/10.1377/hlthaff.W3.521 accessed 26 January 2019.

Darrow J, (Column) 'Recent Developments in Health Law: Why International Price Discrimination May Increasingly Be the Wrong Solution to a Global Drug Problem' (2011) 39 *Journal of Law, Medicine and Ethics* 291.

Doane M L, 'TRIPS and International Intellectual Property Protection in an Age of Advancing Technology', (19994) 9 *American University Journal of International Law & Policy* 465.

Donelly D E, '(Comment) Parallel Trade and the International Harmonization of the Exhaustion of Rights Doctrine' (1997) 13 *Santa Clara Computer and High Technology Law Journal* 445.

Ewelukwa U, 'Patent Wars in the Valley of the Shadow of Death: The Pharmaceutical Industry, Ethics and Global Trade (2005) 59 *University of Miami Law Review* 203.

Fink C, 'Entering the Jungle of Intellectual Property Rights Exhaustion and Parallel Trade' in C Fink & K E Maskus, *Intellectual Property and Development: Lessons from Recent Economic Research* (World Bank and Oxford University Press 2005) 172 available at http://siteresources.worldbank.org/INTRANETTRADE/Resources/Pubs/IPRs-book.pdf (accessed 23 March 2019).

Fisher W W III 'When Should We Permit Differential Pricing of Information' (2007) 55 *UCLA Law Review* 1.

Ganslandt M, Maskus K E & Wong E V, 'Developing and Distributing Essential Drugs to Poor Countries: The DEFEND Proposal' (2001) 24 *The World Economy* 779.

Gervais D, *The TRIPS Patent Regime: Drafting History and Analysis* (Sweet & Maxwell, 3rd ed., 2008).

Hammer P J, 'Differential Pricing of Essential AIDS Drugs: Markets, Politics, and Public Health' (2002) 5 *Journal of International Economic Law* 883.

Heath C, 'Parallel Imports and International Trade' (1997) 28 *IIC* 623.

Hicks L L & Holbein J R, 'Convergence of National Intellectual Property Norms in International Trading Agreements' (1997) 12 *American University Journal of International Law & Policy* 769.

Hilke J, 'Free Trading or Free-Riding: An Examination of the Theories and Available Empirical Evidence on Gray Market Imports' (1988) 32 *World Competition* 75.

Janis M D, 'A Tale of the Apocryphal Axe: Repair, Reconstruction, and the Implied License in Intellectual Property Law' (1999) 58 *Maryland Law Review* 423.

Kanavos P, Gross D & Taylor D, *Parallel Trading in Medicines: Europe's Experience and Its Implications for Commercial Drug Importation in the US* (AARP, 2005) 26 http://assets.aarp.org/rgcenter/health/2005_07_trade.pdf accessed 26 January 2019.

Keeling D T, *Intellectual Property Rights in EU Law* (Oxford University Press, 2003).

Lawson C, 'Flexibility in TRIPS: Using Patented Inventions without Authorisation of the Right Holder' (2004) 15 *Australian Intellectual Property Journal* 141.

Lipner S E, *The Legal and Economic Aspects of Gray Market Goods* (Quorum Books, 1990).

Lo C-F, 'Potential Conflicts between TRIPS and GATT Concerning Parallel Importation of Drugs and Possible Solution to Prevent Undesirable Market Segmentation' (2011) 66 *Food and Drug Law Journal* 73.

Long D E, 'The Protection of Information Technology in a Culturally Diverse Marketplace' (1996) 15 *John Marshall Journal of Computer & Information Law* 129.

Maskus K E, 'The Curious Economics of Parallel Trade' (2010) 2 *World Intellectual Property Organisation Journal* 123.

Maskus K E, *Intellectual Property and Development: Lessons from Recent Economic Research* (World Bank and Oxford University Press 2005).

Maskus K E, 'Parallel Imports' (2000) 23 *The World Economy* 1269.

Mathews D & Munoz-Tellez V, 'Parallel Trade: A User's Guide' in A Krattiger et al. (eds.) *Intellectual Property Management in Health and Agricultural Innovation: A Handbook of Best Practices* (MIHR & PIPRA, 2007) 1429.

Mirabile T K, 'Aids, Africa and Access to Medicines' (2002) 11 *Michigan State University-DCL Journal of International Law* 175.

National Economic Research Associates, *The Economic Consequences of the Choice of Regime in the Area of Trademarks* (Feb. 8, 1999) Executive Summary at 6–7 www.eurasiancommission.org/ru/act/finpol/dobd/intelsobs/Documents/NERA%20study_TM_exhaustion%20(main).pdf accessed 26 January 2019.

Ng E S, 'The Impact of the Bilateral US – Singapore Free Trade Agreement on Singapore's Post – TRIPS Patent Regime in the Pharmaceutical Context' (2010) 16 (5) *International Trade Law and Regulation* 121.

Nguyen T, *Competition Law, Technology Transfer and the TRIPS Agreement: Implication for Developing Countries* (Edward Elgar, 2010).

OECD, 'The DAC List of ODA Recipients: Factsheet – January 2012' (2012). www.oecd.org/dac/stats/49483614.pdf accessed 26 January 2019.

Pires de Carvalho N, *The TRIPS Regime of Patent Rights* (Kluwer Law International 2005).

Rai R K, 'Should the WTO Harmonise Parallel Import Laws? An Analysis of the Exhaustion Doctrine' (2011) 6(12) *Journal of Intellectual Property Law and Practice* 898.

Reichman J H, 'From Free Riders to Fair Followers: Global Competition Under the TRIPS Agreement' (1997) 29 *N.Y.U. Journal of International Law & Policy* 11.

Reichman J H, 'Universal Minimum Standards of Intellectual Property Protection Under the TRIPS Component of the WTO Agreement', (1995) 29 *International Lawyer* 345.

Rey P, 'The Impact of Parallel Imports on Prescription Medicines'(2003) http://citeseerx.ist.psu.edu/viewdoc/download?doi=10.1.1.493.1937&rep=rep1&type=pdf accessed 26 January 2019.

Ricolfi M, 'Interface between Intellectual Property and International Trade: The TRIPS Agreement' (January 2002) *Italian Intellectual Property Law* 29.

Ruping K, 'Copyright and an Integrated European Market: Conflicts with Free Movement of Goods, Competition Law and National Discrimination' (1997) 11 *Temple International & Comparative Law Journal* 1.

Samuelson P, 'Intellectual Property Arbitrage: How Foreign Rules Can Affect Domestic Protections' (2004) 71 *University of Chicago Law Review* 223.

Singham S A, 'Competition Policy and the Stimulation of Innovation: TRIPS and the Interface between Competition and Patent Protection in the Pharmaceutical Industry' (2000) 26 *Brooklyn Journal of International Law* 363.

Spaulding W C, 'Allocative Efficiency and the Production Possibilities Frontier' http://thismatter.com/economics/allocative-efficiency.htm accessed 26 January 2019.

Stack A J, 'TRIPs, Patent Exhaustion and Parallel Imports' (1998) 1 *Journal of World Intellectual Property* 657.

Stothers C, 'State of the Art: Parallel Trade and Free Trade Agreements' (2006) 1(9) *Journal of Intellectual Property Law & Practice* 578.

Frankel S & Gervais D J, 'International Intellectual Property Rules and Parallel Imports', in I Calboli & E Lee (eds.), *Research Handbook on Intellectual Property and Parallel Imports* (Cheltenham: Edward Elgar, 2016).

Tsouloufas G, 'Limiting Pharmaceutical Parallel Trade in the European Union: Regulatory and Economic Justifications' (2011) 36 *European Law Review* 385.

UN Office of the High Representative for the Least Developed Countries, Landlocked Developing Countries and Small Island Developing States(UN-OHRLLS), 'Least Developed Countries' http://unohrlls.org/custom-content/uploads/2018/12/list-of-least-developed-countries-rev1.pdf accessed 26 January 2019.

UNCTAD/ICTSD, *TRIPS and Development Resource Book*, (UNCTAD/ICTSD, 2005) 115–116.

Watal J, *Workshop on Differential Pricing and Financing of Essential Drug* (World Trade Organization and World Health Organization 2001) 11 www.wto.org/english/tratop_e/trips_e/wto_background_e.pdf.

Widodo T, 'Comparative Advantage: Theory Empirical Measures and Case Studies' (2009) 4 *Review of Economic and Business Studies* 57.

World Trade Organization, *Implementation of Paragraph 6 of the Doha Declaration on the TRIPS Agreement and Public Health*, WTO Doc WT/L/540 (2 September) (Decision of 30 August 2003).

World Trade Organization, *Negotiation Group on Trade Related Aspects of Intellectual Property Rights, Including Trade in Counterfeit Goods, Meeting of Negotiating Group of 16 and 22 October 1991*, GATT/WTO Doc MTN.GNG/TRIPS/3 (18 November 1991).

Yu P K, 'The Objectives and Principles of the TRIPS Agreement' (2009) 46 *Houston Law Review* 979.

6 Pharmaceutical patents and the obligation to protect health

6.1 Introduction

Global health has been defined as embracing the 'consideration of the health needs of the people of the whole planet above the concerns of particular nations'.[1] The determinants of health, such as pathogens, food, water and air, cut across borders, thereby making threats to health a global concern.[2] Protecting the health of the world's population therefore requires significant international cooperation and global governance.[3] The future of global health looks quite dismal in view of the fact that countries mostly affected by scourges of diseases are insufficiently economically buoyant to resolve the problem internally, and countries with the wherewithal are hardly willing to commit significant resources to improving the standard of health outside their borders save where overwhelming humanitarian considerations exist.[4] Development assistance is usually driven by natural disasters or major emergencies evoking public compassion.[5]

Health inequity entails health discrepancies that are unfair because they are unnecessary and avoidable.[6] Populations in developed countries are mainly susceptible to chronic non-communicable diseases because the available technologies are sufficiently effective to substantially control the communicable ones.[7] Inhabitants of poor countries, conversely, are significantly affected by all forms of contagious, avoidable and curable diseases, whilst also being susceptible to

1 M Merritt, 'Bioethics, Philosophy, and Global Health' (2007) 7 *Yale Journal of Health Policy, Law & Ethics* 273, 274.

2 L O Gostin, 'Meeting Basic Survival Needs of the World's Least Healthy People: Towards a Framework on Global Health' (2008) 96 *George Town Law Journal* 331, 333.

3 *See* D P Fidler, 'The Globalization of Public Health: Emerging Infectious Diseases and International Relations' (1997) 5 *Indiana Journal of Global Legal Studies* 11, 17–18, 30–31.

4 Gostin, above n 2, 333–334.

5 Ibid., 334.

6 J N Erdman, 'Human Rights in Health Equity: Cervical Cancer and HPV Vaccines' (2009) 35 *American Journal of Law & Medicine* 365, 367.

7 See A Daar, H Thorsteinsdóttir, D K Martin, A C Smith, S Nast & P A Singer, 'Top Ten Biotechnologies for Improving Health in Developing Countries' (2002) 32 *Nature Genetics* 229, 229–232.

a higher degree of chronic non-communicable diseases at the same time.[8] To a large extent, there exists a general consensus that global health disparities based on wealth are unethical.[9] Social and environmental circumstances are usually responsible for the degree to which people may be capable of living healthy lives.[10]

The incongruence in the ability of people to achieve the best attainable health standards prompts a significant social justice question: does society owe a moral obligation to reduce as much as possible the inequalities engendered by variables such as socio-economic factors, gender, race, education or even geographical location? Montesquieu has argued that society takes away the equality all men share at birth and that equality may best be recovered through the protection of the law.[11] On this reasoning, there is a compelling moral obligation on society to strive to ameliorate, where possible, the disparities in the attainment of good health. This obligation, it would seem, is best discharged through the instrumentality of the law. Intellectual property (IP) law seeks to protect the economic interest in goods directly accruing from human ingenuity or creativity. With respect to pharmaceuticals, IP protection encourages innovation, but may sometimes have the unsavoury effect of limiting the availability of goods to those with the financial wherewithal. This raises concerns on how best to strike a good balance between the protection of IPRs and respect for human rights.

This chapter discusses the human right to health in the context of patent protection and access to medicines. It examines the extent to which human rights considerations are relevant in the domestic implementation of trade and IP instruments and whether a country can rely on its human rights obligations in exploring the flexibilities in the Agreement on Trade Related Aspects of Intellectual Property Rights (TRIPS) discussed in Chapters 1–5. It considers the limitations in international human rights law especially in relation to socio-economic rights that make it difficult for the right to health to be a potent justification for derogation from trade or IPRs. The potential for conflicts between IP, international trade law and human rights is examined. The chapter discusses access to medicines as an integral part of the Sustainable Development Goals and the extent to which the human right to access to medicines may be justiciable in Africa under national and regional instruments. It is argued that trade and IP agreements must be interpreted in ways that resolve any apparent inconsistency with the right to health in favour of the latter. It is also argued that even where international

8 O Adeyi, O Smith & S Robles, *Public Policy and the Challenge of Chronic Noncommunicable Diseases* (World Bank, 2007).

9 J Ruger, 'Rethinking Equal Access: Agency, Quality, and Norms' (2007) *2 Global Public Health* 78, 88; P Hunt, *Neglected Diseases: A Human Rights Analysis* (WHO, 2007).

10 E W Parento, 'Health Equity, Health People 2020, and Coercive Legal Mechanisms as Necessary for the Achievement of Both' (2012) 58 *Loyola Law Review* 655, 656.

11 C de Montesquieu, The Spirit of Laws, bk. VIII, § 3 (1750) www.constitution.org/cm/sol_08.htm accessed 26 January 2019.

human rights obligations are not directly enforceable by national courts, such courts are nonetheless obliged to apply their national laws, as much as possible, in a way that gives effect to their international human rights obligations.

6.1.1 Theoretical foundation of human rights

It is pertinent, at this point, to briefly examine the theoretical basis for human rights in terms of the nature and rationale for their existence to further understand their significance. The theoretical foundation for human rights has a history spanning thousands of years.[12] It has indeed been said that 'human rights have always existed with the human being'.[13] The history of the human rights movement began with ancient religions and societies and dates as far back as the 3rd century B.C.E.[14] This was later formalised in significant legal language in Europe with the adoption of the Magna Carta, the Treaty of Westphalia, the Napoleonic Code and a number of other instruments.[15] The international protection of human rights is one of the ultimate objectives of modern international law.[16] Human rights governance is based on the concept that a government's treatment of its citizens is an issue of international concern.[17] Thus Article 1(3) of the United Nations (UN) Charter[18] identifies as one of the purposes of the UN the promotion and encouragement of 'respect for human rights and for fundamental freedoms for all without distinction as to race, sex, language, or religion'.[19] Article 1(4) adds that the UN shall be a centre 'for harmonizing the actions of states in the attainment of these ends'.[20]

Human rights can be understood philosophically as the rights accruing to human beings by reason of common humanity.[21] On this basis, the fact that the rights are not respected or adequately enforced would not ipso facto render

12 See C Bettinger-Lopez et al., 'Redefining Human Rights Lawyering Through the Lens of Critical Theory: Lessons for Pedagogy and Practice' (2011) 18 *Georgetown Journal of Poverty Law and Policy* 337, 340; G P Smith, 'Human Rights and Bioethics: Formulating a Universal Right to Health, Health Care, or Health Protection' (2005) 38 *Vanderbilt Journal of Transnational Law*, 1295.

13 F S Nariman, 'The Universality of Human Rights', (1993) 50 *The Review/International Commission of Jurists* 8, 17 (quoting Judge Tanaka of the International Court of Justice).

14 S P Marks, 'The Evolving Field of Health and Human Rights: Issues and Methods' (2002) 30 *Journal of Law, Medicines & Ethics*, 739.

15 See J F Jones, 'Human Security and Social Development' (2004) 33 *Denver Journal of International Law and Policy* 92, 96.

16 D Shelton, 'International Human Rights Law: Principled, Double or Absent Standards?' (2007) 25 *Law & Inequality* 467, 472.

17 Shelton, above n 16, 490–491.

18 United Nations Charter, Article 1(3).

19 Ibid.

20 Ibid., Article 1(4).

21 R D Sloane, 'Outrelativizing Relativism: A Liberal Defense of the Universality of International Human Rights' (2001) 34 *Vanderbilt Journal of Transnational Law* 527, 538.

otiose their universal possession by all human beings.[22] On the other hand, human rights can also be understood in strict legal sense to represent the bundle of legal claims that individuals and sometimes communities may rely upon such that the existence of adequate enforcement mechanisms would be sine qua non to the legal validity of the rights.[23] Human rights may thus be defined as those fundamental, inviolable and sublime principles upon which the political, social and legal structures of the modern society are founded.[24]

Moral theories, founded on the inalienability of human rights derivable from the basic hypothesis of equal human dignity, have been advanced to justify the significance of human rights.[25] Some scholars take the contractarian approach to the moral theory by positing that persons ignorant of their real nationality can count on international institutions which are committed to safeguarding the rights of all human beings.[26] Others take the welfarist position on the basic postulate that human rights enhance the welfare of the world population.[27] These moral theories have proved to be controversial and the resulting dissatisfaction with them led to the emergence of political theories founded on the argument that States or groups within States have an interest in respecting human rights.[28] Human rights are thus founded on universal ideals that are difficult to resist because of their universal approbation and the apparent legitimacy derivable from democracy.[29] In the words of Erick Engle,

> the idea of human rights is, in fact, so attractive, that it is literally impossible for all but the most tyrannical of states to deny their existence and retain credibility as legitimate expressions of popular will.[30]

Apart from the use of human rights for legitimation purposes, States also observe human rights for the purposes of power politics, using compliance with them as a strong weapon of international diplomacy.[31]

22 Ibid., 538–539.
23 Ibid., 539.
24 See D Kindley, 'Human Rights Fundamentalisms' (2007) 29 *The Sydney Law Review* 545, 546.
25 See generally A Buchanan & D Golove, 'Philosophy of International Law', in J Coleman & Scott Shapiro (eds.), *Oxford Handbook of Jurisprudence and Philosophy of Law* (Oxford University Press, 2002) 808.
26 C R Beitz, *Political Theory and International Relations* (Princeton University Press, 1979) 139; T W Pogge, *Realizing Rawls* (Cornell University Press, 1989) 53.
27 P Singer, *One World: The Ethics of Globalization* (Yale University Press, 2004) 98–99.
28 See C R Beitz, 'Human Rights as a Common Concern' (2001) 95 *American Political Science Review* 269, 279–281; J Donnelly, 'The Relative Universality of Human Rights', (2007) 29 *Human Rights Quarterly* 281, 292–293; C R Beitz, 'What Human Rights Mean' (2003) 132(1) *Daedalus* 36, 44–46.
29 E Engle, 'Universal Human Rights: A Generational History' (2006) 12 *Annual Survey of International and Comparative Law*, 219, 229.
30 Ibid., 230.
31 Ibid., 231.

A distinction has been drawn between legal rights and human rights.[32] Legal rights are rights created by the relevant lawmaking body of a given government and thus constitute the law that citizens must obey. Human rights also translate into the legal duties that government officials are enjoined to obey.[33] Human rights in this sense will, however, assume the status of legal rights binding on both citizens and the State once they are incorporated into domestic law. To take human rights seriously necessitates recognition of the fact that every human being has inherent and equal dignity and possesses all the inalienable rights of all members of the human family.[34]

6.1.2 Human rights in international law

The current configuration of human rights norms is traceable to the revolutions of freedom and fairness that swept across Europe and North America in the 18th century.[35] This also played a crucial role in the liberation of subjugated people across the globe in the 19th and 20th centuries.[36] The modern conception, however, can be traced to the UN's adoption of the Universal Declaration of Human Rights (UDHR) at the end of World War II.[37] The UDHR was originally conceived as a 'common standard of achievement for all people and all nations'[38] rather than as creating legally enforceable obligations.[39] It nonetheless set in motion several progressive initiatives that have since seen the application of human rights as the yardstick for gauging national behaviour or even challenging governmental legitimacy.[40] As aptly noted by George Smith, it has provided '*a framework for expanding and recreating the very boundaries of human rights*'.[41]

The UN General Assembly followed the UDHR by dividing human rights into civil and political rights and economic, social and cultural rights.[42] The UDHR, the International Covenant for Civil and Political Rights (ICCPR) and

32 See E L Rubin, 'Rethinking Human Rights' (2003) 9 *International Legal Theory* 5, 9.
33 Ibid.
34 W P Quigley, 'Revolutionary Lawyering: Addressing the Root Causes of Poverty and Wealth' (2006) 20 *Washington University Journal of Law and Policy* 101, 117.
35 Marks, above n 14, 740.
36 Marks, above n 14, 740.
37 See C Bettinger-Lopez et al., 'Redefining Human Rights Lawyering through the Lens of Critical Theory: Lessons for Pedagogy and Practice' (2011) 18 *Georgetown Journal of Poverty Law and Policy* 337, 340.
38 *Universal Declaration of Human Rights*, GA Res 217(III) A, U.N. Doc A/810 at 71 (adopted 10 December 1948) Preamble.
39 See S P Marks & B H Weston, 'International Human Rights at Fifty: A Foreword' (1998) 8 *Transnational Law and Contemporary Problems* 113.
40 Ibid.
41 G P Smith, 'Human Rights and Bioethics: Formulating a Universal Right to Health, Health Care, or Health Protection' (2005) 38 *Vanderbilt Journal of Transnational Law*, 1295.
42 S R Harris, 'Recent Development: Asian Human Rights: Forming A Regional Covenant' (2000) 1 *University of Hawaii Asian-Pacific Law & Policy Journal* 17.

the International Covenant for Economic, Social and Cultural Rights (ICESCR) have been described as the International Bill of Rights which seek to regulate the behaviour of States.[43]

Human rights jurisprudence imposes an obligation on States to respect, protect and fulfil the rights of their nationals.[44] Given that the international law of human rights originally emerged from the obligations assumed by States in international instruments, and notwithstanding the fact that these instruments provide for individual rights, a State's responsibility and the rights of the citizens do not always exist in parallel legal order.[45] Smith has identified three perspectives with which to appraise the integrity of international human rights instruments, which can be summarised as follows:

1 Human rights are largely seen as an interstate matter whereby a State undertakes to act as promised with other States having a corresponding right to have the promise kept.[46]
2 International human rights law does not only create rights and duties between States but also confers rights against the States upon individuals that are directly enforceable by interState remedies, governments or international organisations acting on behalf of the individual.[47]
3 Governments have an obligation to implement human rights and provide a private legal remedy for enforcement in domestic courts because party States to human rights conventions have legislated human rights into international law and have accordingly given those rights affirmative independent values.[48]

The ICCPR is often referred to as specifying 'first generation rights' whilst the ICESCR is seen as embodying 'second generation rights' suggesting a lower degree of importance or priority.[49] The ICCPR has also been described as a charter of negative rights while the ICESCR is seen as a charter of positive rights.[50] Negative rights are rights to be free from interference from the government and others whilst positive rights are rights to receive benefits from the government.[51] The appropriateness of social rights embodied in the ICESCR continues to be a controversial point as some believe that the judicial enforcement of these rights

43 Engle, above n 29, 227.
44 Z Lazzarini, 'Access to HIV Drugs: Are We Changing the Two World Paradigm?' (2002) 17 *Connecticut Journal of International Law* 281, 288.
45 Smith, above n 41, 1301.
46 Ibid.
47 Ibid., 1303.
48 Ibid., 1304.
49 See C Soohoo & J Goldberg, 'The Full Realization of Our Rights: The Right to Health in State Constitutions' (2010) 60 *Case Western Reserve Law Review* 997, 1004.
50 E A Posner, 'Human Welfare, Not Human Rights' (2008) 108 *Columbia Law Review* 1758, 1764.
51 Ibid., 1765.

would produce undesirable outcomes.[52] Judges, they argue, lack the democratic legitimacy to be involved in the subtle policymaking required in the enforcement of social rights as such a power will be beyond the institutional capacity of the judiciary.[53] As Frank Cross puts it, '*It is futile to rely on the judiciary to provide basic welfare for the disadvantaged, if the political branches are unwilling to do so*'.[54]

It is noteworthy that even negative rights (rights that do not necessarily require a positive action from the State) such as the right to dignity of the human person, the right to be left alone and freedom of expression, still require the government to do something positive, for instance, to maintain a police court and independent judiciary.[55] Governments must, however, expend more resources to fulfil positive rights such as the right to food, basic healthcare and basic education.[56] Nonetheless, the propriety of drawing a distinction between positive and negative rights remains debatable.[57] Whilst not all governments can easily fulfil economic rights, international law requires States to progressively work towards the realisation of these rights within the confines of their resources.[58] Although the legal enforcement of economic rights may not be a realistic objective in all cases, it is submitted that the whole essence of modern governance is the progressive realisation of such rights. States therefore have an obligation to ensure the welfare of the disadvantaged is given sufficient consideration in the polity.

The 'negative rights' enshrined in the ICCPR have in recent years been used to encourage the rule of law in countries with democratic forms of government, whilst the 'aspirational rights' of the ICESCR are now being used to formulate development policies and serve as a basis for discussing the need to invest in the social sector of developing countries.[59] The field of human rights has therefore become a prominent arm of international law and all States seek to respect these universal rights to enhance their diplomatic relations with other nations and protect their legitimacy in the comity of nations.

6.2 The right to health in international law

The preamble to the WHO Constitution defines health as '*a state of complete physical, mental and social well-being and not merely the absence of disease or*

52 D Landau, 'The Reality of Social Rights Enforcement' (2012) 53 *Harvard International Law Journal* 189, 194.

53 Ibid.

54 See F B Cross, 'The Error of Positive Rights' (2001) 48 *UCLA Law Review* 857, 888.

55 See G J Annas, 'Bioethics: American Bioethics and Human Rights: The End of All Our Exploring' (2004) 32 *Journal of Law & Medicine* 658, 660.

56 Ibid.

57 See S R Keener & J Vasquez, 'A Life Worth Living: Enforcement of the Right to Health through the Right to Life in the Inter American Court of Human Rights' (2009) 40 *Columbia Human Rights Law Review* 595.

58 Ibid.

59 R S Lawrence, I Chan & E Goodman, 'Poverty, Food Security and the Right to Health' (2008) 15 *Georgetown Journal on Poverty Law & Policy* 583, 592.

infirmity'.[60] There is a significant connection between health and human rights which can be understood in terms of the influence of health policies on human rights and the effect of human rights violation on health.[61] It follows that health is intricately connected to human rights, meaning that the abuse of human rights in any form might have some significant implications for the health of the victim. In this regard, it has been argued that the effects of human rights abuses on health are underappreciated and that health can be affected by most if not all human rights violations.[62]

While the concept of health as a human right has gained significant prominence over time, the agitation for the universal recognition and implementation of human rights continues to be a contemporary issue. Former judge of the High Court of Australia, the Honourable Michael Kirby, has noted that in line with the current trend towards globalism, judges should utilise human rights law to fill the gaps in the legislation when ambiguities are to be resolved.[63]

Nonetheless, there remain a number of questions regarding conceptualisations of the right to health as well as evaluation of its observance and general enforcement measures. Alicia Yamin notes that it is difficult to contend that the right to health is too vague for enforcement legislations or that it simply embodies a set of political aspirations.[64] The Economic, Social and Cultural Rights Committee, in its General Comment No 14 on the Right to the Highest Attainable Standard of Health, Stated that all healthcare facilities including medicines should be available, accessible and of good quality.[65]

Indeed, the right to life, a time-honoured, non-derogable human right can be interpreted to cover the right to health and access to medicines. Access to medications also has significant implications for other human rights as well as the right to health, such as the right to the benefits of scientific progress, the right to education, work and an adequate standard of living. In addition, the right to health entails economic accessibility in the sense that health facilities, medicines and services should be accessible and affordable to all without discrimination.

6.2.1 *The right to health in international conventions*

The preamble to the Constitution of the World Health Organization (WHO) declares that the 'enjoyment of highest attainable standard of health is one of the

60 The Constitution of the World Health Organisation, Preamble.

61 E M Walker, 'The HIV AIDS Pandemic and Human Rights: A Continuum Approach' (2007) 19 *Florida Journal of International Law* 335, 379.

62 Ibid.

63 M Kirby, *Judicial Activism: Authority, Principle and Policy in the Judicial Method*, Fifty-Fifth Hamlyn Lecture 74 (2003) www.hcourt.gov.au/assets/publications/speeches/former-justices/kirbyj/kirbyj_19nov.html accessed 26 January 2019.

64 A E Yamin, 'Not Just a Tragedy: Access to Medications as a Right under International Law' (2003) *Boston University International Law Journal*, 325, 336.

65 UNCESCR, General Comment No 14 on the Right to the Highest Attainable Standard of Health.

fundamental rights of every human being without distinction of race, religion, political belief, economic or social condition'.[66] The UDHR States that 'everyone has the right to a standard of living adequate for the well-being of himself and of his family, including food, clothing, housing and medical care and necessary social services'.[67] In a similar vein, the ICESCR requires States to recognise the right of everyone to the enjoyment of the highest attainable standard of physical and mental health.[68] Article 12.2(D) of the ICESCR provides that States should ensure '*creation of conditions which would assure to all medical service and medical attention in the event of sickness*'. This, it has been argued, raises a policy objective that imposes on governments an obligation to provide access to health facilities.[69] It also requires States to ensure the equitable distribution of such facilities for all without discrimination, particularly in relation to vulnerable and marginalised populations.[70]

The right to health is recognised in many regional instruments and in not less than 115 national constitutions.[71] The entrenchment of human rights in the domestic laws of countries makes such rights directly enforceable in the respective national courts of such countries. The African Charter on Human and Peoples' Rights also recognises the right of every individual to attain the highest State of physical and mental health and all States parties to the Convention are enjoined to protect the health of their people and to ensure they receive medical attention when they are sick.[72] The Protocol of San Salvador requires States to recognise health as a public good and adopt necessary measures to safeguard the right to health.[73]

66 *Constitution of the World Health Organization* opened for signature 22 July 1946 (entered into force 7 April 1948).

67 *Universal Declaration of Human Rights*, UN Doc A/810 (1948) Article 25.

68 *International Covenant on Economic, Social and Cultural Rights*, opened for signature 16 December 1966, 993 UNTS 3 (entered into force 3 November 1976) art. 12(1). Other international conventions recognising the right to health are:

- a The *International Convention on the Elimination of All Forms of Racial Discrimination* opened for signature 21 December 1965 (entered into force 4 January 1969) Article 5(e)(iv);
- b *The Convention on the Elimination of All Forms of Racial Discrimination against Women*, opened for signature 1 March 1980 (entered into force 3 September 1981) Articles. 11(1)(f), 12 and 14(2)(b);
- c *The Convention on the Rights of the Child*, opened for signature 20 November 1989, (entered into force 2 September 1990) Article 24;
- d *The International Convention on the Protection of Rights of All Migrant Workers and Members of their Families*, opened for signature 18 December 1990 (entered into force 1 July 2003) Articles. 28, 43(e) and 45(c);
- e *The Convention on the Right of Persons with Disabilities* (2006); Article 25.

69 J N Erdman, 'Human Rights in Health Equity: Cervical Cancer and HPV Vaccines' (2009) 35 *American Journal of Law & Medicine* 365, 379.

70 Ibid.

71 See *The Right to Health*, Fact Sheet No 31, Geneva, OHCHR June 2008, p. 10.

72 *African (Banjul) Charter on Human and Peoples' Rights*, opened for signature 27 June 1981 OAU Doc. CAB/LEG/67/3 rev. (entered into force in 21 October 1986) art. 16.

73 *Additional Protocol to the American Convention on Human Rights in the Area of Economic, Social and Cultural Rights 'Protocol of San Salvador', opened for signature 17 November 1988 (entered into force 16 November 1999) Article 10.*

Article 24 of the Children's Convention explicitly provides for the right to health. The International Convention on the Elimination of All Forms of Racial Discrimination 1965 and the Convention on the Elimination of All Forms of Discrimination against Women both require signatories to eradicate race and gender-based discrimination in the provision of health services and public health facilities.[74]

The right to health is therefore well recognised as a human right in myriad international conventions and States that fail to respect and fulfil it are in breach of their obligations in international law. The recognition accorded health in international agreements and instruments also demonstrate that the right to health permeates the legal boundaries of socio-economic and civil rights and it should therefore not be completely relegated to the status of economic rights that are only subject to fiscal realities.

6.2.2 Bioethics Declaration

UNESCO established the International Bioethics Committee (IBC) in 1993 with the mandate of discharging the obligations of UNESCO to consider bioethical issues of international concern.[75] The Universal Declaration on Bioethics and Human Rights (the Bioethics Declaration) prepared by the IBC was adopted at the UNESCO General Conference on 19 October 2005.[76] The Bioethics Declaration focuses on the 'ethical issues relating to medicine, life sciences and associated technologies as applied to human beings, taking into account their social, legal and environmental dimensions'.[77] The Bioethics Declaration seeks to provide a global framework of principles and procedures that would not only guide States in developing legislations,[78] policies and other instruments in the field of bioethics[79] but also serves as a guide for individuals, groups, corporate bodies and various institutions.[80] According to the Honourable Michael Kirby, the innovative features of the Declaration include:[81]

74 International Convention on the Elimination of All Forms of Racial Discrimination 1965; Convention on the Elimination of All Forms of Discrimination against Women.

75 UNESCO, 'International Bioethics Committee (IBC)' www.unesco.org/new/en/social-and-human-sciences/themes/bioethics/international-bioethics-committee/ accessed 26 January 2019.

76 See UNESCO Press Release, *UNESCO General Conference adopts Universal Declaration on Bioethics and Human Rights* (October 19, 2008).

77 *Bioethics Declaration*, Article 1(1).

78 Ibid., Article 2(a).

79 Ibid.

80 Ibid., Art. 2(b).

81 The Hon. M Kirby 'Human Rights and Bioethics: The Universal Declaration of Human Rights and the UNESCO Declaration on Bioethics and Human Rights' (2009) 25 *Journal of Contemporary Health Law & Policy* 309, 323; Hon Kirby was a member of the International Bioethics Committee that prepared the Bioethics Declaration.

- the expansion of the concept of bioethics from the individual to the human community, the environment and humanity in general;
- the attempted amalgamation of matters traditionally within the purview of medical bioethics and the concepts derived from international human rights law; and
- the introduction of significant novel ideas especially those relating to universal access to healthcare and social responsibility.

In the Honourable Michael Kirby's words:

> The principle focuses attention on access to healthcare and essential medicines; access to adequate nutrition and water; and the reduction of poverty and illiteracy as well as improvement of living conditions and of the environment.[82]

The universal access to medicines and healthcare principle enunciated in the Bioethics Declaration is therefore one designed to apply to inhabitants of both developing and developed nations.

The Bioethics Declaration clearly recognises the need for progress in science and inventive activities to enhance access to quality healthcare and essential medicines. Whilst the Bioethics Declaration is incontestably a non-binding declaration of a United Nations agency, it can nonetheless influence the interpretation of national laws in domestic courts and municipal law is increasingly operating in the context of international law[83] as national laws are being substantially influenced by international policies. Additionally, a non-binding resolution of a United Nations agency containing legal principles and policy can influence further international discourse on the topic and ultimately evolve into customary international law.[84] As such, the Bioethics Declaration may have relevance in the interpretation of the economic and social rights, like the right to health in international law, and both domestic and international courts can take it into account in determining the scope of such rights.

6.2.3 Access to medicines and the right to health

Access to medicines is germane for people to be able to work, secure good education and enjoy a good standard of living as well as social security.[85] Article 15 of the ICESCR expressly recognises the right of everyone 'to enjoy the benefits of scientific progress and its applications'.

The UN Economic and Social Cultural Rights (ESCR) Committee General Statement on 'Human Rights and Intellectual Property' States that both national

82 Ibid.
83 Ibid., 328.
84 Ibid.
85 Declaration of Alma-Ata, International Conference on Primary Health Care, Alma-Ata, USSR, 6–12 September 1978 Article II.

and international rules and policies on IP, including the TRIPS Agreement, must comply with international human rights law.[86] The ESCR Committee goes further to State that 'any intellectual property regime that makes it more difficult for a State party to comply with its core obligations in relation to health, food, education, especially or with any other right set out in the Covenant is inconsistent with the legally binding obligations of the state party'.[87]

The UN Human Rights Committee has interpreted the role of governments in protecting the right to health as including obligations to lessen infant mortality, to improve life expectancy and to eradicate malnutrition and epidemics.[88] The American Convention on Human Rights[89] provides particularly for the recognition and enforcement of civil and political rights. It contains no explicit provision for the implementation of the right to health and other socio-economic rights but it does provide in Article 26 that States should adopt measures:

> ...with view to achieving progressively by legislation or other appropriate means the full realization of the rights implicit in the economic, social, educational, scientific, and cultural standards set forth in the Charter of the Organization of American States as amended by the Protocol of Buenos Aires.

It is therefore defensible to posit that there exists in international law a recognised right to health. While this right may be cognisable, its enforceability seems to be somewhat suspect and inchoate as the Section 6.3 reveals.

6.3 Access to medicines and the Sustainable Development Goals (SDGs)

In September 2000, the United Nations General Assembly adopted the United Nations Millennium Declaration.[90] Through the United Nations Millennium Declaration (UNMD), world leaders made a firm commitment to address a number of challenges relating to extreme poverty, development, health and environmental protection with clear targets to be achieved by 2015.[91] The UNMD thus set out the framework for the United Nations Millennium Development Goals (MDG). Access to medicines was particularly addressed in the UNMD as Paragraph 20 of the UNMD explicitly expressed the resolve of the UN General Assembly to 'encourage the pharmaceutical industry to make essential drugs more

86 See, *Human Rights and Intellectual Property, United Nations Committee on Economic Social and Cultural Rights*, 27th Sess., P 3, U.N Doc. E/C.12/2001/15 (2001).

87 See, *Human Rights and Intellectual Property, United Nations Committee on Economic Social and Cultural Rights*, 27th Sess., P 3, U.N Doc. E/C.12/2001/15 (2001).

88 *The Right to Life*, U.N. GAOR Human Rights Comm., 37th Sess., Supp. No. 40, at Gen. Comment No. 6, P 5, U.N. Doc. A/37/40 (1982).

89 The Inter-American Convention on Human Rights.

90 *UN General Assembly, United Nations Millennium Declaration*, UN Doc. No. (A/55/L.2) 8 September 2000. Available at: www.un.org/millennium/declaration/ares552e.htm.

91 Ibid.

widely available and affordable by all who need them in developing countries'.[92] Another major health related MDG was to halt and begin to reverse 'the spread of HIV/AIDS, the scourge of malaria and other major diseases that afflict humanity' by the year 2015.[93] The MDG brought about some profound achievement in the access to medicines context. There was 40% reduction in new HIV infections between 2000 and 2013, 6.2 million malaria deaths were averted between 2000 and 2015 and an estimated 37 million lives were saved from tuberculosis during the same period.[94] Despite the significant achievements made with the MDG targets, extreme poverty continued to impede access to basic services, including medicines, in many parts of the world in 2015.[95] Thus, in September 2015, the UN General Assembly adopted the UN Sustainable Development Goals (SDGs), a new global development agenda that 'builds on the Millennium Development Goals and seeks to complete what they did not achieve, particularly in reaching the most vulnerable'.[96] The SDGs set out 17 major goals that are to be achieved by 2030.[97] Goal 3 of the SDGs is to 'Ensure healthy lives and promote well-being for all at all ages'. Of particular significance to access to medicines is the following trenchant declaration of the UN General Assembly:

> We are committed to ensuring universal access to sexual and reproductive health-care services, including for family planning, information and education. We will equally accelerate the pace of progress made in fighting malaria, HIV/AIDS, tuberculosis, hepatitis, Ebola and other communicable diseases and epidemics, including by addressing growing anti-microbial resistance and the problem of unattended diseases affecting developing countries. We are committed to the prevention and treatment of non-communicable diseases, including behavioural, developmental and neurological disorders, which constitute a major challenge for sustainable development.[98]

Access to medicines is essential for Goal 3 of the UN SDGs to be actualised as the prevention and treatment of communicable, non-communicable and neglected diseases ravaging third world countries will be impossible without access to affordable medicines. Thus, Target 3b of SDG 3 underscores the role of access to medicines in the realisation of the SDGs by enjoining nations of the world to collectively support the research development of pharmaceutical products for treating and preventing both communicable and non-communicable

92 Ibid., Paragraph 20.

93 Ibid., Paragraph 19.

94 UN, Millennium Development Goals Report 2015 (UN: New York,2015) p 6.

95 Ibid., p8–p9.

96 *UN General Assembly, Transforming our World: the 2030 Agenda for Sustainable Development*, UN Resolution No. A/RES/70/1, Paragraph 16.

97 See *Preamble to Transforming our World: the 2030 Agenda for Sustainable Development*, UN Resolution No. A/RES/70/1.

98 *UN General Assembly, Transforming our World: the 2030 Agenda for Sustainable Development*, UN Resolution No. A/RES/70/1, Paragraph 26.

diseases affecting developing countries so as to promote access to medicines for vulnerable populations.[99]

In June 2017, the United Nations Human Rights Council adopted a resolution calling upon the international community to continue to assist developing countries in promoting the actualisation of the right to health and the SDGs 'through access to medicines, in particular essential medicines, vaccines, diagnostics and medical devices that are affordable, safe, efficacious and of quality'.[100] The UN SDGs, as noted in its preamble, are a set of development-oriented objectives that are considered exigent to put the world on a 'sustainable and resilient path'.[101] They are goals that encompass the human rights principles that are needed to promote equity and sustainable development in all nations of the world including developed and developing countries. The right to health is an essential component of the SDGs and access to affordable medicines is one of its major objectives. The SDGs have also accentuated the need to promote access to medicines through the use of the TRIPS flexibilities in line with the spirit of the Doha Declaration on the TRIPS Agreement and Public Health. Promoting access to medicines is therefore a goal that requires the cooperation and commitment of the international community to ensure the continuing growth of an increasingly globalised world in a manner that is sustainable.

6.4 Domestic implementation of the right to health

A fundamental right to health ordinarily entails something that cannot be guaranteed in a real sense – perfect health.[102] This is because perfect health is relative from person to person and nation to nation and is therefore, in real terms, an indeterminate variable.[103] Critics maintain that an argument for the right to health is either misconceived or incapable of resulting in specific policy regulation beyond the minimal acknowledgement of the right in question.[104] While it would be misleading to refer to a governmental responsibility to guarantee an individual's good health, a case could be made for a right to health protection which would consist of a right to healthcare and a right to live under healthy circumstances.[105] There is, however, still a large divide between the rights contained in the human rights instruments and their implementation especially in relation to social and economic rights.[106]

99 Ibid., 16–17.

100 UN Human Rights Council, *The Right of Everyone to the Enjoyment of the Highest Attainable Standard of Physical and Mental Health in the Implementation of the 2030 Agenda for Sustainable Development*, UN Resolution A/HRC/35/L.18/Rev.1, (21 June 2017) p 6.

101 UN General Assembly, *Transforming our World: the 2030 Agenda for Sustainable Development*, UN Resolution No. A/RES/70/1, preamble.

102 Smith, above n 41, 1315.

103 Ibid.

104 Merritt, above n 1, 276.

105 Smith, above n 41, 1317.

106 O Schachter, 'The Genesis of the Declaration: A Fresh Examination' (1999) 11 *Pace International Law Review* 51, 57.

The ESCR Committee in its review of the enjoyment of economic, social and cultural rights in Zambia, noted its alarm:

> about the devastating impact of the HIV/AIDS pandemic on the enjoyment of economic, social and cultural rights by the people of Zambia. The Committee is also concerned that people afflicted with HIV/AIDS seldom have adequate access to the necessary health-care services, including antiretroviral drugs, appropriate facilities and food.[107]

The UK has equally been criticised by the Committee for the prevalence of HIV in some of its Caribbean territories and the unavailability of access to HIV treatment for migrant workers and AIDS orphans.[108]

Given that treatment of life-threatening diseases forestalls death and morbidity, access to medicines is considered an essential component of the right to life, the right to health and the right to live in dignity.[109] Rights to health are seen as a bundle of claims demanding positive actions on the part of a government.[110] However, since States are required by the ICESCR to promote the enforcement of the right to health by 'using the maximum available resources', it is possible to take advantage of the flexible language of the treaty to avoid any real obligation. The right to health is made subject to fiscal and political realities in many countries and is therefore not justiciable.[111] Thus, judges, especially in the US, have refused to provide remedies for alleged violations of the ICESCR on the basis that the indeterminacy of its principles makes it difficult for it to be capable of being judicially applied.[112]

It has been argued that the right to health in international law does not suggest that the failure to provide medical care due to resource constraints would constitute 'a human rights failure'.[113] Implementing laws that are obviously inconsistent with the realisation of the right to health would amount to a violation of international law.[114] In addition, failure to formulate health policies or to implement laws that are connected to health would also be an omission that is inconsistent with the right to health under international law.[115] These arguments

107 ESCOR, *Committee on Economic Social and Cultural Rights, Concluding Observation of the Committee on Zambia*, UN. Doc. E/C/12/1/Add.106 (23 June 2005).

108 ESCOR, *Committee on Economic Social and Cultural Rights, Concluding Observations of the Committee on the United Kingdom*, U.N. Doc E/C.12/1/Add.79 (5 June 2009).

109 N Novogrodsky, 'The Duty of Treatment: Human Rights and the HIV/AIDS Pandemic' (2009) 12 *Yale Human Rights and Development Law Journal* 1, 17.

110 Ibid., 19.

111 Examples of such countries are Nigeria, South Africa and India.

112 *Flores v. S. Peru Copper Corp.*, 414 F.3d 233, 255 (2d Cir. 2003). The United States has not ratified the ICESCR. *Cf. San Antonio Indep. Sch. Dist. v. Rodriguez*, 411 U.S. 1 (1973).

113 Stephen P Marks, 'Normative Expansion of the Right to Health and the Proliferation of Human Rights' (2016) 49 *George Washington International Law Review* 97, 138.

114 E George, 'South Africa and South-South Cooperation to Reframe Global Intellectual Property Principles and Promote Access to Essential Medicines' (2011) 18 *Indiana Journal of Global Legal Studies* 167, 179.

115 U.N. Econ. & Soc. Council [ECOSOC], *Committee on Economic Social and Cultural Rights, The Right to the Highest Attainable Standard of Health, P 49*, U.N. Doc. E/C.12/2000/4 (11 August 2000).

may lend credence to the position taken by Benjamin Meier and Alicia Yamin, that international human rights provide a strong basis for advancing justice in health. They contend that viewing

> threats to public health as "rights violations" offers international standards by which to frame responsibilities and evaluate health policies and outcomes under law, shifting the debate from political aspiration to legal responsibility.[116]

Professor Justice Modibo Ocran of the Supreme Court of Ghana has postulated the following in a seminal paper on the enforcement of socio-economic rights in Africa[117]:

- socio-economic rights should be seen as rights in the legal sense if they are enshrined in the national constitution or incorporated in the municipal legal system; and
- actions based on socio-economic rights could be enforceable in the courts even if all the resources for their implementation are not immediately available as the notion of progressive realisation of such rights puts a mandate on the government to implement the rights to the extent allowed by the available resources.

The view has been expressed that for the right to health to be obligatory on governments, it must possess conditions that are realistic for most States, irrespective of their level of development and such conditions must not be unnecessarily onerous on poor countries.[118]

The justiciability of human rights has been undermined by the absence of strong enforcement mechanisms.[119] Rights are certainly of no significance unless they are enforceable.[120] Most human rights conventions usually provide for some form of enforcement mechanisms. Such mechanisms include an expert monitoring body with power to consider petitions on human rights violation and present reports to a committee, a right of States against States and in some cases an individual right of action may lie.[121] These mechanisms, however, are not of significant practical utility when compared with the highly organised enforcement procedure for the TRIPS Agreement under the WTO system.

116 B M Meier & A E Yamin, 'Emerging Topics in Public Health law and Policy: Right to Health Law Litigation and HIV/AIDS Policy' (2011) 39 *Journal of Law, Medicine and Ethics* 81.

117 Justice Professor M Ocran, 'Socio-Economic Rights in the African Context: Problems with Concept and Enforcement' (2007) 5 *Loyola University Chicago International Law Review* 1, 13.

118 Ibid., 735–736.

119 E M Hafner-Burton, Trading Human Rights: How Preferential Trade Agreements Influence Government Repression, (2005)59(3) *International Organization* 593, 603.

120 See J F Jones, 'Human Security and Social Development' (2004) 33 *Denver Journal of International Law and Policy* 92, 97.

121 Engle, above n 29, 226.

For example, although the ESCR Committee is the body established to monitor the implementation of the ICESCR, it has no power to sanction States that fail to meet the obligations imposed on them by the treaty. As such, it lacks the power to compel the implementation of the right to health.[122] Multiple international investigative or adjudicatory bodies have been identified as relevant to the enforcement of human rights.[123] For instance, Article 18 of the ICESCR provides:

> Pursuant to its responsibilities under the Charter of the United Nations in the field of human rights and fundamental freedoms, the Economic and Social Council may make arrangements with the specialized agencies in respect of their reporting to it on the progress made in achieving the observance of the provisions of the present Covenant falling within the scope of their activities. These reports may include particulars of decisions and recommendations on such implementation adopted by their competent organs.

In the absence of effective international framework for the enforcement of the right to health, scholars have recommended the use of national adjudication[124] and strong advocacy for compliance with the right by non-governmental organisations.[125] Except where the right to health is expressly provided for in domestic laws, individuals and communities cannot, generally speaking, enforce the right to health in international law as they lack the *locus standi* to so do.

There is need for States, irrespective of the level of development, to put in place strong structures for the enforcement of health rights as the progressive realisation of socio-economic rights required in international law must also be subject to some form of assessment. States must therefore provide a means of enforcing health rights even if such enforcement is to be made subject to the availability of resources. A number of reasons have however been advanced for the unwillingness to enforce health rights. Some of the reasons are explored in Section 6.4.1.

6.4.1 Reasons for the reluctance to enforce social, economic and cultural rights

As human rights are universal and interdependent, some believe that their enforcement should be brought under a single uniform mechanism.[126] There is

122 M A Torres, 'The Human Right to Health, National Courts, and Access to HIV/AIDS Treatment: A Case Study from Venezuela' (2002) 3 *Chicago Journal of International Law* 105, 108.

123 Smith, above n 41, 1304.

124 Yamin, above n 64, 1156.

125 See B M Meier, 'Employing Health Rights for Global Justice: The Promise of Public Health in Response to the Insalubrious Ramifications of Globalization' (2006) 39 *Cornell International Law Journal* 711, 737.

126 Ibid.

equally the view that social and cultural rights, including the right to health, are unsuitable for judicial review because of their indeterminacy.[127] While some argue that human rights should be prioritised with varying moral weight attached to them, others hold the view that some rights cannot be considered superior to others.[128]

Another major problem with the implementation of the right to health is the fact that along with other rights in the ICESCR, it is subject to 'progressive realization',[129] which takes into account the resources at a country's disposal to provide the necessary facilities for basic healthcare. Paucity of funds is always a good justification for not meeting human rights obligations in view of the treaty's language.[130] There is also the problem of ascertaining the exact contours of the right to health and this may make it difficult to establish, in clear-cut terms, an infringement of the right.[131] It has been argued that international human rights law appears to lack the framework for creating incentives, legally binding obligations and funding or services to protect the world's vulnerable population.[132] This has thus resulted in a situation whereby the global health problem remains a particularly intractable one.[133]

The challenge in enforcement of human rights is accentuated by the fact that the human rights conventions generally allow reservations and that enforcement protocols are usually not mandatory.[134] The flexibility of the conditions for accession to the conventions is, however, defensible in that it makes it easier for many States to ratify the convention.[135]

In 2008, the General Assembly adopted the Optional Protocol to the ICESCR, which allows the ESCR Committee to consider complaints by individuals or on their behalf.[136] It would therefore appear that individuals and NGOs acting on behalf of individuals who have suffered a violation of a right under the ICESCR can now make special reports to the Committee to ensure rights guaranteed under the Covenant are not violated with impunity. Thus, people denied the

127 Ibid.
128 Ibid., at 1308.
129 ICESCR, supra, Article 2(1) ('Each State Party to the present Covenant undertakes to take steps ... to the maximum of its available resources, with a view to achieving progressively the full realization of the rights recognized in the present Covenant ... .'); Children's Convention, supra, Article 24(4) ('States Parties undertake to promote and encourage international co-operation with a view to achieving progressively the full realization of the right recognized in the present article. In this regard, particular account shall be taken of the needs of developing countries').
130 S R Keener & J Vasquez, 'A Life Worth Living: Enforcement of the Right to Health through the Right to Life in the Inter American Court of Human Rights' (2009) 40 *Columbia Human Rights Law Review* 595, 599.
131 Ibid.
132 Ibid.
133 Ibid.
134 See Engle above n 29, 228.
135 Ibid., at 228–229.
136 Optional Protocol to the ICESCR, GA resolution A/RES/63/117.

right to health may now by themselves or through NGOs make a case for the Committee to intervene to give them succour. Countries receiving recommendations to act in the interest of their citizens may rely on such recommendations in defending any trade dispute that may arise out of the measures taken.

In sum, States are expected to take all reasonable steps to ensure their activities and policies are not inconsistent with their human rights obligations. The argument has been advanced that, in so far as an action has been properly brought before the court, there is a duty on that court to develop a manageable standard for the enforcement of human rights. The court is therefore bound to resolve the action through a consideration of all the available authorities and resources at its disposal.[137] Accordingly, even though international conventions are not directly enforceable in most national courts, such courts nonetheless are expected by the rules of statutory interpretation to apply national laws, as much as possible, in a way that is consistent with their international obligations. The duty of national courts to adopt purposive interpretative rules where possible to give effect to human rights is explored in Section 6.4.2.

6.4.2 Enforcement in national courts

Some national courts are beginning to find the right to health justiciable in relation to access to medicines. In the South African case of *Minister of Health v Treatment Action Campaign*,[138] the Constitutional Court rejected the government's contention that it lacked jurisdiction to adjudicate on social-economic rights claims and found the right to health as fully justiciable. The applicants in the case were a number of organisations and civil societies involved in the treatment of HIV/AIDS. The application was brought against the South African government at the Pretoria High Court to compel the government to make HIV drugs available to pregnant women and develop a national policy for the prevention of mother-to-child transmission. The High Court ordered the government to provide nevirapine (an HIV/AIDS drug capable of preventing mother-to-child transmission) to pregnant women and new born babies. It further mandated the government to develop a policy to make the drug available at public hospitals and clinics. On appeal to the Constitutional Court, the final appellate court for constitutional matters, the Court ordered the government to without delay permit and facilitate the use of nevirapine. The court further held that the government had a duty under the constitution to devise and implement within its available resources a comprehensive programme to realise progressively the

137 See C Soohoo & J Goldberg, 'The Full Realization of Our Rights: The Right to Health in State Constitutions' (2010) 60 *Case Western Reserve Law Review* 997, 1009–1010.

138 M Heywood, 'Current Developments: Preventing Mother-to-Child Transmission in South Africa: Background, Strategies and Outcomes of the Treatment Action Campaign Case Against the Minister of Health' (2003) 19 *South African Journal of Human Rights* 278, 285–286; *Minister of Health v Treatment Action Campaign & Others* (2002) BCLR 1033 (CC) at P 115.

right of pregnant women to have access to health services to reduce mother-to-child transmission.

The Indian Supreme Court, the highest court in India, has similarly held that the right to life includes the right to live with dignity and to possess basic necessities such as adequate nutrition, shelter and clothing.[139] According to the court, any act that impairs human dignity would amount to a violation of the right to life.[140]

In *Luis Guillermo Murillo Rodriguez v. Caja Constarricense de Seguro Social*[141] and *William Garcia Alvarez v. Caja Constarricense de Seguro Social*,[142] the Constitutional Chambers of the Costa Rican Supreme Court, the highest court in Costa Rica, held that the State is bound to provide AIDS treatment.[143] The Venezuelan Supreme Court reached a similar decision in *Cruz Bermudez v. Ministerio de Sanidad v Asistencia Social*.[144]

Although the right to health is not specifically protected under the US Constitution, the US courts have upheld the right of HIV-positive prisoners to access medicines and healthcare facilities in a number of cases.[145] Thus in *Montgomery v Pinchak*, the US Court of Appeals, Third Circuit, had to determine an appeal from a summary judgment of the District Court against Montgomery, an inmate of the New Jersey State correctional system. Montgomery had alleged amongst other things that he was denied access to his HIV drugs and the right to a counsel in pursuing his case against the defendants. The Court of Appeal in vacating the District Court summary judgment noted that Montgomery's allegations established a prima facie case of nonchalance to a serious medical need and it was held that he was entitled to the appointment of counsel.

In a similar vein, in *Brown v Johnson*, the US Court of Appeals of the 11th Circuit, in overruling the lower court, held that a prisoner who suffered from HIV and hepatitis and alleged 'the withdrawal of treatment in deliberate indifference to his serious medical needs' would meet the threshold of 'imminent danger of serious physical injury'.[146]

Thus, even where access to medicines or the right to health is not a recognised right in the national law of a given country, it is submitted that health and access

139 *Mullen v. Union Territory of Delhi*, 2 S.C.R. 516 (1981).

140 Ibid.

141 *Luis Guillermo Murillo Rodriguez v. Caja Constarricense de Seguro Social*, Constitutional Chamber of the Supreme Court of Justice, Decision No. 6096–6097 (1997) (Costa Rica).

142 *William Garcia Alvarez v. Caja Costarricense de Seguro Social*, Constitutional Chamber of the Supreme Court of Justice, Decision No. 5934–5997 (1997) (Costa Rica).

143 See R Elliott (ed.), *Courting Rights: Case Studies in Litigating the Human Rights of People Living with Aids* (Canadian HIV/AIDS Legal Network and UNAIDS, 2006) 54.

144 *Cruz Bermudez v. Ministerio de Sanidad y Asistencia Social*, Supreme Court of Justice of Venezuela, Case No. 15.789, Decision No. 916 (1999) (Venez).

145 See *Montgomery v. Pinchak* 294 Fed 492 (3d Cir. 2002); *Smith v. Carpenter* 316 F.3d 178 (2d Cir.2003); *Brown v. Johnson* 387 F.3d 1344, 1352 (11th Cir.2004).

146 Brown v Johnson, United States Court of Appeals Eleventh Circuit, No. 03-14158 (18 October 2004).

to medicines can be interpreted as germane to giving effect to the fundamental right to life and dignity of the human person. Where no human rights whatsoever exist in the domestic framework of a given country, the court may nonetheless apply the fundamental rights to life and dignity of human person to give effect to the right to life. This is because the right to life and the dignity of human person are cognisable rights in customary international law and they can be enforced by national courts on the basis that parliament, except where a definite contrary intention is disclosed, does not intend to contravene international law.

6.4.3 Enforcement in regional courts

What follows is a discussion of the extent to which the right to health is being enforced in regional courts in Africa, the Americas and Europe.

6.4.3.1 The Inter-American court experience

The Inter-American Court of Human Rights, an independent judicial body of the Organisation of American States, has developed a jurisprudence that allows the enforcement of the right to health through the right to life. Whilst the Court has held that individual claims are not justiciable by their own force under Article 26 of the American Convention on Human Rights,[147] the Court has relied on Article 4 guaranteeing the right to life, in order to secure health. Thus, in *'Street Children' (Villagran-Morales et al.) v. Guatemala*[148] where the police murdered five young men in an attempt to counter juvenile delinquency, the court held as follows:

> In essence, the fundamental right to life includes not only the right of every human being not to be deprived of his life arbitrarily, but also the right that he will not be prevented from having access to the conditions that guarantee a dignified existence. States have the obligation to guarantee the creation of the conditions required in order that violations of this basic right do not occur.[149]

Of further relevance to this discourse are the two cases of *Yakye Axa*[150] and *Sawhoyamaxa*.[151] In both cases, indigenous groups were displaced through the acquisition of their land by non-indigenous populations.[152]This resulted in a

147 See *'Five Pensioners' v Peru*2003 Inter-Am. Ct. H.R. (ser. C) No. 98, p 88 (28 February 2003).

148 1999 Inter-Am. Ct. H.R. (ser. C) No. 63 (19 November 1999).

149 Ibid., 144. Also quoted in S R Keener & J Vasquez, 'A Life Worth Living: Enforcement of the Right to Health through the Right to Life in the Inter American Court of Human Rights' (2009) 40 *Columbia Human Rights Law Review* 595, 606.

150 *Yakye Axa Indigenous Community v. Paraguay*, 2005 Inter-Am. Ct. H.R. (ser. C) No. 125, 33 (17 June 2005).

151 See *Sawhoyamaxa Indigenous Community v. Paraguay*, 2006 Inter-Am. Ct. H.R. (ser. C) No. 146, 69 (29 March 2006).

152 Ibid., 73(1)–(4); *Yakye Axa*, 2005 Inter-Am. Ct. H.R. (ser. C) No. 125, 50.1–50.11.

decline in their standard of living, as a result of which the communities brought legal action to reclaim their territories.[153] Whilst waiting for the outcome of the legal action, the condition of the people deteriorated significantly resulting in malnutrition, diseases and high infant deaths.[154] In both cases, the Inter-American Court adopted a liberal interpretation of the right to life enshrined in Article 4 the American Convention.[155] In the *Yakye Axa* case in particular, the court noted:

> One of the obligations that the State must inescapably undertake as guarantor, to protect and ensure the right to life, is that of generating minimum living conditions that are compatible with the dignity of the human person and of not creating conditions that hinder or impede it. In this regard, the State has the duty to take positive, concrete measures geared toward fulfillment of the right to a [dignified life], especially in the case of persons who are vulnerable and at risk, whose care becomes a high priority.[156]

Hence, the Inter-American Court ordered that the State must inter alia provide potable water in sufficient quantity for the ousted group, provide medical care and appropriate medicines to the community and adequate treatment for worming of the people. The incorporation of a positive duty of providing necessary facilities to live a dignified life into the right to life – traditionally considered a negative right – is in line with the right to health and a means of securing health in the Inter-American system.[157] These decisions have adopted a liberal interpretation of the right to life. The jurisprudence being developed can be very helpful in safeguarding the health of people in developing countries through the enforcement of the right to life, which is generally considered an enforceable right.

The right to life is arguably wide enough to cover not only the right to health but also access to medicines. This is because life can hardly be secure without good health and access to essential health facilities. The nexus between the right to health and the right to life is another good illustration of the interdependence and indivisibility of human rights.

6.4.3.2 The African human rights court

The African Charter on Human and Peoples' Rights (ACHPR)[158] provides for the establishment of an African Commission on Human and Peoples' Rights.[159] If a State party to the ACHPR reasonably believes there has been a violation of the

153 *Sawhoyamaxa*, 2006 Inter-Am. Ct. H.R. (ser. C) No. 146, PP 73(6)–(7), 73(17)–(61); *Yakye Axa*, 2005 Inter-Am. Ct. H.R. (ser. C) No. 125, 50.12–50.90.

154 *Sawhoyamaxa*, 2006 Inter-Am. Ct. H.R. (ser. C) No. 146, 73(67)–(74); *Yakye Axa*, 2005 Inter-Am. Ct. H.R. (ser. C) No. 125, 50.93–50.98.

155 *Sawhoyamaxa*, 2006 Inter-Am. Ct. H.R. (ser. C) No. 146, 153.

156 *Yakye Axa*, 2005 Inter-Am. Ct. H.R. (ser. C) No. 125, 161–162. 154*Yakye Axa*, 2005 Inter-Am. Ct. H.R. (ser. C) No. 125, 221.

157 Keener & Vasquez, above n 124, 618–619.

158 African Charter on Human and Peoples' Rights.

159 Article 30 of the ACHPR.

provisions of the Charter by another Member State, it may notify that Member State of the violation.[160] If the issue is not resolved within three months, the matter may be taken before the Commission which can then launch an investigation and make findings thereon.[161] The findings will be submitted to the Assembly of Heads of State and Government with recommendations on the appropriate action to be taken.[162] Public interest groups may also report cases of human rights violation.[163] The paradigm delineated for human rights enforcement under the African Charter has been described as basically 'an intergovernmental arrangement for the invocation of the remedial process' with its attendant high level of politicisation.[164] The ACHPR is particularly relevant to this discourse because apart from the fact that it does provide that everyone 'shall have the right to enjoy the best attainable State of physical and mental health',[165] it provides for a number of health-related rights including non-consensual treatment and medical experimentation.[166]

The Commission has found that the right to health guaranteed under the Charter obliges States to provide medical care to prisoners.[167] Also, failure to provide prisoners with adequate food, blankets and clothing have all been found to be in violation of the right to health as well as the right to dignity.[168] In a similar vein, the Commission found that Nigeria violated the right to health through oil exploration that led to significant environmental degradation and health deterioration amongst its native Ogoni people.[169]

The African Union (then Organization for African Unity) adopted the Protocol to the African Charter on Human and Peoples' Rights on the Establishment of an African Court on Human and Peoples' Rights on 9 June 1998.[170] The Protocol entered into force on 1 January 2004. Article 5(3) of the Protocol provides for the ability of individuals to have access to the African Human Rights Court in the following terms:

> The Court may entitle relevant Non Governmental Organizations (NGOs) with observer status before the Commission, and individuals to institute cases directly before it, in accordance with Article 34 (6) of this Protocol.

160 Articles 47 through 53.
161 Ibid., Article 48.
162 Articles 52–53.
163 Article 55.
164 Ocran, above n 109, 10.
165 Article 16(1).
166 Article 5.
167 *Media Rights Agenda & Others v Nigeria*, 14th Annual Activity Report of the African Court for Human and Peoples' Rights (2000–2001).
168 See 13th Annual Activity Report of the African Court on Human and Peoples' Rights (1999–2000).
169 See *The Social and Economic Rights Action Center and the Center for Economic and Social Rights v. Nigeria*, African Commission on Human and Peoples' Rights, Comm. No. 155/96 (2001).
170 Organization of African Unity, Protocol to the African Charter on Human and Peoples' Rights on the Establishment of an African Court on Human and Peoples' Rights, opened for signature 9 June 1998 (entered into force 25 January 2005).

However, by virtue of Article 34(6) of the Protocol, this provision is only operative where a State Party has deposited an instrument of declaration accepting the jurisdiction of the court to receive cases under Article 5(3). In *Femi Falana v African Union*,[171] the applicant having failed to successfully persuade his government to make a declaration accepting the jurisdiction of the court over claims brought pursuant to Article 5(3) approached the African Court with an application urging it to declare Article 34(6) void for being inconsistent with the fair hearing and non-discrimination provisions of the African Charter. The applicant sought this declaratory relief against the African Union as the representative body for its 53 Member States. The African Court however declined jurisdiction to consider the claim on the basis that the jurisdiction of the court is defined by the Protocol and as the African Union is not a party to the Protocol, it cannot be sued under it. It therefore follows that the court cannot exercise jurisdiction over individual claims emanating from a State that has made no declaration to accept the jurisdiction of the court over cases brought by individuals.

In sum, regional courts in Africa and the Americas are giving force to the right to health through other rights such as the right to life and the right to the dignity of the human person. The right to health is therefore becoming more intertwined with civil and political rights and there currently exists a stronger foundation for its enforceability. Access to medicines as an integral part of the right to health may therefore be enforced through civil rights such as the right to life and the right not to be subjected to degrading treatment. Whilst access to medicines is fundamental to safeguarding health as a human right, it is important to bear in mind that patent and other IP rights are also human rights. Section 6.5 explores the concept of property rights as human rights.

6.5 Economic and property rights as human rights

The discussion in the preceding sections focused on the significance of the right to health and access to medicines from the human rights perspective. It is, however, germane to note that the IP and human rights debate is not only about reconciling IP with human rights, as IPRs are also human rights. The debate equally covers the question whether property rights are as important or fundamental as the right to access to medicines.

Intellectual property rights are well recognised as human rights in a number of international conventions, including the UDHR and the ICESCR. Article 27 of the UDHR provides that everyone has the right to the protection of the moral and material interests resulting from any scientific, literary and artistic production of which he is the author. A similar provision exists in Article 15 of the ICESCR, which provides that States contracted to respect the right of everyone to benefit from the protection of the moral and material interests resulting from

171 *Femi Falana v African Union, African Court on Human and Peoples' Rights* Application No 001/2011.

any scientific, literary and artistic production of which he is the author. Articles 21(1) of the American Convention on Human Rights, Article 14 of the ACHPR and Article 1 of Protocol 1 to the European Convention on Human Rights all recognise the right to property.

These provisions demonstrate that property rights are recognised as human rights in international law. The question that arises is whether certain human rights are superior to others, or, putting it in more specific terms, whether the right to health is superior to the right to protect IP? It has been eloquently argued that the right to health is a basic right vital to a minimally adequate standard of living, and therefore should assume eminence over rights that are based on wants or desires.[172] Henry Schermers in particular has argued that property rights cannot be rightly described as fundamental rights except to the extent that they are needs-based property rights that are essential to the exercise of rights that are really fundamental such as the right to life.[173] However, it is equally arguable that property rights are fundamental and vital to an adequate standard of existence although it is not easy to reach a consensus on this point.[174] Writing on the subject, Peter Drahos notes as follows:

> Thinking about the right of property in the context of human rights reveals nicely the "paradox of property". At one level it is inconceivable that the development of human personality and the protection of individual interests within a group can take place in the absence of property rules that guarantee the stability of individual possession. Yet within the context of the social group no other rules require the continuous adjustments that the rules of property do... It is for this reason that, when a general right of property is recognised in a human rights instrument, it is made subject to some sweeping public interest qualification.[175]

It stands to reason that IPRs as private rights ought to give deference to public rights and public interest qualifications in the event of conflict, as to do otherwise would be to challenge the very basis upon which all modern legal institutions are founded: that public interest should always take precedence over private interests that run contrary to it. It is, therefore, submitted that reliance can be

172 R Chandra, 'The Role of National Laws in Reconciling Constitutional Right to Health with TRIPS Obligations: An Examination of the Glivec Patent Case in India' in T Pogge, M Rimmer & K Rubenstein (eds.), *Incentives for Global Public Health: Patents Law and Access to Essential Medicines* (Cambridge University Press, 2010), 381.

173 H G Schermers, 'The International Protection of the Right of Property', in F Matscher & H Petzold (eds.), *Protecting Human Rights: The European Dimension* (Carl Heymanns Verlag KG, Köln, 1988), 565–580.

174 See P Cullet, 'Human Rights and Intellectual Property Protection in the TRIPS Era' (2007) 29 *Human Rights Quarterly* 403, 405.

175 P Drahos, 'Intellectual Property and Human Rights' (1999) 3 *Intellectual Property Quarterly* 349, 360.

placed on the right to health in facilitating access to medicines through the use of the TRIPS flexibilities.

The UN Sub-Commission on the Promotion and Protection of Human Rights noted in 2000 that the Human Development Reports 1999 and 2000 identify circumstances occasioned by TRIPS that constitute contraventions of international human rights law.[176] It further notes that:

> actual or potential conflicts exist between the implementation of the TRIPS Agreement and the realization of economic, social and cultural rights in relation to, inter alia, ... access to patented pharmaceuticals and the implications for the enjoyment of the right to health.[177]

The ESCR Committee, in its authoritative interpretive comment on Article 15(1)(c) of the ICESCR, which provides for the right to benefit from the protection of any scientific, literary or artistic work of which one is an author, also notes that IP is a social product with a social function. It further recognises the broad right of States to safeguard human rights by preventing unreasonably high costs of medicines and ensuring the benefits of scientific and technical progress are not used to put the right to life and the right to health in jeopardy.[178]

There is therefore good support for the proposition that States should refrain from using IP rights, including patents, in a way that derogates from the right of people to good health in international law. It is also submitted that advancement in technology should be used to promote the public interest in enjoying better standards of living. While the right of inventors to enjoy the fruits of their labour is not to be discountenanced, there must also be a fine balance between the economic rights of inventors and the public interest in scientific progress. Considerable public funds are equally invested in scientific research and it is very germane to ensure patents do not become a major impediment to the public interest in ensuring people all over the world enjoy the highest attainable standard of health. Measures taken to ensure patents do not render the right to health ineffectual can hardly be considered unlawful to the extent that such measures are adequately within the confines of international human rights law.

The significance of access to medicines to the right to health cannot be overemphasised. Hans Morten Haugen notes that laying claim to social human rights '*such as the right to food or the right to health, is about the accessibility to important*

176 The Sub-Commission on the Promotion and Protection of Human Rights, *Intellectual Property Rights and Human Rights*, Sub-Comm'n on Human Rights Res. 2000/7, 2, U.N. Doc. E/CN.4/Sub.2/RES/2000/7 (Aug. 17, 2000).

177 Ibid.

178 *Committee on Economic Social and Cultural Rights*, General Comment No. 17: The Right of Everyone to Benefit from the Protection of the Moral and Material Interests Resulting from Any Scientific, Literary or Artistic Production of Which He Is the Author (Article 15, Paragraph 1(c), of the Covenant) 35, U.N. Doc. E/C.12/GC/17 (12 January 2006.

goods and resources'.[179] Thus, given the paramount contribution of health to the capabilities of people, health deserves a special moral significance that must be given utmost priority by every government.[180]

6.5.1 International trade law and human rights: is there a conflict?

Trade in high-priced pharmaceuticals may have the effect of denying poorer countries any affordable means of obtaining essential medicines for pressing health problems.[181] There also seems to be some documentary evidence to suggest that the drafters of international human rights documents intended them to take precedence over other international agreements including those related to trade. This documentary evidence can be found in the UN Charter, which accentuates the primacy of the need to respect human rights and dignity. The Agreement Establishing the WTO and the TRIPS Agreement also expressly recognise the need for trade arrangements to promote human rights and general well-being. Thus, parties to the Agreement Establishing the WTO expressly recognise 'that their relations in the field of trade and economic endeavour should be conducted with a view to raising standards of living', and in a way that will facilitate economic development.[182]

Article XX of the General Agreement on Tariffs and Trade (GATT) allows States to adopt measures for the protection human life or health. However, the fact that human rights obligations are not expressly integrated into the WTO Agreements has resulted in a situation whereby human rights are seen as subordinate to trade agreements.[183] There is some support for the view that States can use the human rights argument to justify the use of TRIPS flexibilities as provided for in Article 31 of TRIPS.[184] It has also been argued that the human rights debate may be used to justify the creation of additional grounds for compulsory licensing having regards to the provision in Paragraph 5 of the Doha Declaration on the TRIPS Agreement and Public Health.[185] The need for compliance with human rights obligations is therefore part of the hierarchy of norms to which WTO Agreements and trade agreements belong[186] as the whole

179 H M Haugen 'Patents Rights and Human Rights: Exploring their Relationship' (2007) 10 *Journal of World Intellectual Property* 97, 98.

180 R V V Puymbroeck, 'Coming to Grips with TRIPS: Conversion + Calculation' (2010) 38 *Journal of Law, Medicines and Ethics* 520, 527.

181 Lazzarini, above n 44, 287.

182 Marrakesh Agreement Establishing the WTO, Preamble.

183 See A R Chapman, *Approaching Intellectual Property as a Human Right: Obligations Related to Article 15 (1) (c)*, U.N. Doc. E/C.12/2000/12 (3 October 2000).

184 See discussion on compulsory licensing in Chapter 1.

185 E M Walker, 'The HIV AIDS Pandemic and Human Rights: A Continuum Approach' (2007) 19 *Florida Journal of International Law* 335, 361.

186 Ibid., 367; see also F M Abbott, The WTO Medicines Decision: World Pharmaceutical Trade and the Protection of Public Health' (2005) 99 *American Journal of International Law* 317, 356–357.

body of WTO law is no more than an integral part of the general body of public international law and to that extent, it is not superior to any other specialised area of law.[187]

In implementing trade agreements, States should incorporate all available safeguards and flexibilities to ensure prevention, treatment and access to medicines.[188] On this basis, it is right to posit that international trade and IP protection must be pursued in a way that does not impede the general standard of living of the world's citizens. Trade laws, with real likelihood of further widening the north-south divide, are in principle inconsistent with not only international human rights laws but also the fundamental objectives of the WTO and the TRIPS Agreement. The WTO Appellate Body, the highest dispute settlement organ of the WTO has explicitly noted that WTO law is not to be interpreted in clinical isolation from the general field of public international law.[189] The protection of human rights should therefore not be considered as inconsistent with the tenets and principles of the WTO. Where there exists a potential or real conflict between the WTO Agreement and the right of people to reasonable healthcare, the interpretation which best resolves the inconsistency in favour of the protection of peoples' health should be adopted. Given the fact that the objective of the WTO is not to act at variance with international human rights, it is submitted that where there exists an irreconcilable conflict between IP or trade obligation and the right to health, then the conflict should be resolved in so far as possible in favour of the right to health and life as any contrary approach will not only be immoral but will also amount to a grave affront to the fundamental principles and objectives of the international legal order.

Specifically, there seems to be some conflict between the obligation to protect patents on pharmaceuticals and the duty to safeguard public health especially in the global south.[190] While it is true that TRIPS may have a significant negative effect on the domestic cost of pharmaceutical products and healthcare in developing countries, there is also some evidence that a weak IP system will reduce inventive activities.[191] Patents may however have the undesirable effect of stifling innovation, especially where a developer of healthcare products has to make use of different levels of innovation which are already protected by a range

187 See P Lamy, Director-General, World Trade Organization, *The Place and Role of the WTO (WTO Law) in the International Legal Order* (Address at the European Society of International Law in Sorbonne, Paris May 19, 2006) www.wto.org/english/news_e/sppl_e/sppl26_e.htm accessed 26 January 2019.

188 Walker, above n 185, 373.

189 United States – Standards for Reformulated and Conventional Gasoline, WTO Doc WT/DS2/AB/R Appellate Body Report (29 April 1996) 17.

190 E George, 'South Africa and South-South Cooperation to Reframe Global Intellectual Property Principles and Promote Access to Essential Medicines' (2011) 18 *Indiana Journal of Global Legal Studies* 167, 181.

191 See, S Chaudhuri, P K Golberg & P Jia, 'Estimating the Effects of Global Patent Protection in Pharmaceuticals: A Case Study of Quinolones in India' (2006) 96 *American Economic Review* 1477, 1480–1481; J O Lanjouw & I M Cockburn, 'New Pills for Poor People? Empirical Evidence after GATT' (2001) 29 *World Development* 265.

of patents.[192] This conflict between patents and public health can be resolved by striking a fine balance between the private right of inventors to the dividends of their invention and the public right of citizens to have reasonable access to essential medicines. This balance is struck when patent protection does not become an impediment to the reasonable and legitimate exercise of measures in the interest of public health.

It is thus submitted that where countries have taken reasonable measures that are legitimate either under a WTO Agreement or the general body of public international law, for the purposes of safeguarding public health, then such measures should always take precedence over any trade agreement to the contrary.

6.6 Access to medicines, the right to health and pharmaceutical patents

Against the backdrop of the legal framework for the right to health in international law and the human rights interest in the protection of IPRs examined thus far, what follows targets the connection between pharmaceutical patents and the right to health in the access to medicines context.

The right to health is wide enough to cover obligations to promote medical research and to ensure the distribution of the benefits of medical research especially in relation to medicines.[193] The view that patents are indispensable in relation to the promotion of medical research has been challenged on a number of grounds. First, it has been argued that pharmaceutical companies only invest in products that would attract a viable market as not even patents create a market where none exists.[194] Secondly, granting broad patents over a wide range of drugs to certain companies may result in market dominance and anticompetitive practices that may stifle innovation.[195] Thirdly, many pharmaceutical patents are only for what are termed 'me-too drugs' which only possess some slight inventive step over the existing similar drugs and are not significantly innovative or novel in the real sense.[196] Access to medicines is a significant component of the right to health[197] and about two billion people have been reported to lack access to essential medicines all over the world.[198] The 2005 Montreal Statement on the Human Right

192 See J Reichman, 'Of Green Tulips and Legal Kudzu: Repackaging Rights in Subpatentable Innovation' (2000) 53 *Vandebilt Law Review* 1743; *Madey v. Duke University*, US Court of Appeal for the Federal Circuit, 3 October 2002, 307 F 3d 1351 where the court refused an experimental use defence in a legal action against Duke University for patents infringement.

193 V Vadi, 'Sapere Audi! Access to Knowledge as a Human Right and a Key Instrument of Development' (2008) 12 *International Journal of Communications Law and Policy* 345, 358.

194 Ibid., 359.

195 A K Rai, 'Fostering Cumulative Innovation in the Biopharmaceutical Industry: The Role of Patents and Antitrust' (2001) 16 *Berkeley Technology Law Journal* 813.

196 Vadi, above n 193, 359.

197 See George above n 190, 168.

198 A Grover, *Report of the Special Rapporteur on the Right of Everyone to the Enjoyment of the Highest Attainable Standard of Physical and Mental Health*, 11th Sess., P 14, U.N. Doc. A/HRC/11/12 (31 March 2009).

to Essential Medicines was drawn by a group of stakeholders from civil society organisations, academic institutions, governments and international agencies following a workshop on human rights and access to medicines. Although the Montreal Statement cannot be regarded as a legal text in international law, a brief discussion of its provisions can be instructive as it offers some guidance on how to resolve the conflict between trade agreements and the right of people to have access to medicines. According to the Montreal Statement, people lack access to medicines either as a result of the fact that research and development do not focus on the ailments afflicting them or due to inadequate health systems and the unaffordable costs of existing medicines.[199] The Montreal Statement notes that existing rules and institutions are causing significant deprivations on an alarming scale and it recommends urgent reforms that will ensure trade agreements, international institutions, IP laws and national laws and policies are designed in a way that will protect the right to essential medicines.[200] It emphasises the need for international assistance and cooperation in human rights fulfilment and affluent States are enjoined to ensure fairer trade and investment whilst contributing equitably to international cooperation geared towards the complete realisation of the right to essential medicines.[201]

6.6.1 Human rights, human security and public health

Human rights are closely aligned with human security, which has been expressed in terms of the right to protection and the right to provision.[202] The former relates to the right to protection by the State and, in some cases, from the State, while the latter relates to the right to services or resources such as education, healthcare or employment which the government must provide.[203] Thus, for people in low-income countries and for disadvantaged people worldwide, health and safety are of paramount importance to their security.[204] Security has thus assumed a broader ambit, which includes sustainable development and social welfare in addition to the protection of human rights.[205] The safety and well-being of people are therefore very germane to the attainment of global peace and security.[206] Health insecurity might arise from the non-existence or inadequacy

199 For a full commentary on the Montreal Statement, see T Pogge, 'Montreal Statement on the Human Right to Essential Medicines' (2007) 16 *Cambridge Quarterly Healthcare Ethics* 97, 104.
200 Ibid.
201 Ibid., 106.
202 See J F Jones, 'Human Security and Social Development' (2004) 33 *Denver Journal of International Law and Policy* 92, 95.
203 Ibid., 96.
204 Ibid., 99.
205 Ibid., 100.
206 See C D Cowger, Dilemmas of Peace and Justice, in D S Sanders & J K Matsuoka (eds.), *Peace and Development: An Interdisciplinary Perspective* (University of Hawaii, School of Social Work, 1989) 79–88.

of health services, both of which account for the death of millions of people annually in developing countries.[207] It has thus been observed that the various threats to human security are closely intertwined and there can be no weakness in one category without significant corresponding effects on others.[208] It therefore follows that access to medicines is also a means of ensuring human security.

The fields of bioethics, health law and human rights are all part of the broad human rights community as the boundaries between them are permeable.[209] Bioethics and health law are very fundamental to the protection of public health and the human right to health. Public health can be used to denote the responsibility of government to create and maintain conditions that will keep its people healthy, while medicine is more about therapeutic treatment in clinical settings.[210] A viable public health system is therefore dependent on the facilities that advance the health interests of the populace. The public health movement has a history that corresponds to the human rights movement, the real intersection between both streams is to a large extent a current development.[211] The promotion and safeguard of the health and welfare of citizens is generally regarded as one of the most important obligations of the modern State.[212]

Gerald Oppenheimer, Ronald Bayer and James Colgrove have argued that the application of human rights to public health is like putting old wine in new bottles because the agitation for the promotion of public health has its foundation in an agenda for social justice with implications that are more radical than those flowing from a human rights perspective.[213] On the other hand, it has been noted that the refusal of the US to ratify the ICESCR and its opposition to the right to health resolution may be a pointer to the fact that human rights seek to challenge the structures that protect inequalities.[214] Human rights policy will inevitably involve conflict between rights and when there are conflicts they should be resolved by the hierarchy of values.[215] In the words of William Quigley:

> In a new justice-based value system, people must be valued more than property. Human rights must be valued more than property rights. Minimum standards of living must be valued more than the privileges that come from

207 United Nations Development Programme, *Human Development Report 1994* (1994) 27.

208 See Jones, above n 17, 103.

209 See G J Annas, 'Bioethics: American Bioethics and Human Rights: The End of All Our Exploring' (2004) 32 *Journal of Law & Medicine* 658.

210 See B M Meier, 'Employing Health Rights for Global Justice: The Promise of Public Health in Response to the Insalubrious Ramifications of Globalization' (2006) 39 *Cornell International Law Journal* 711, 739.

211 See S P Marks above n 14, 741.

212 G Rosen, *A History of Public Health*, expanded edition (Baltimore: Johns Hopkins University Press, 1998) lxxxix.

213 G M Oppenheimer, R Bayer, & J Colgrove, 'Health and Human Rights: Old Wine in NewBottles?' (2002) 30 *Journal of Law, Medicine & Ethics*, 522–532.

214 See Marks above n 14, 741–742.

215 Quigley, above n 34, 124.

> being well-off. Basic freedom for all must be valued more than the privileged liberty of accumulated political, social and economic power. Finally, the goal of increasing the political, social, and economic power of those who are left out of current arrangements must be valued more than the preservation of the existing order that created and maintains unjust privileges.[216]

Prioritising human rights will, however, attract fierce resistance from those who profit from the current order of things as well as inequalities.[217] It is nonetheless important that human rights that are essential for survival, like health rights, prevail over property rights or a system that promotes inordinate acquisition of wealth by a privileged few[218] even though the current legal order does not really operate that way. The interface between human rights and health can also be seen in the connection between international humanitarian law (otherwise known as the law of armed conflict) and the reduction of avoidable mortality and morbidity in times of crisis.[219] The right to health entails the provisions of healthcare services necessary to save lives such as the treatment of prevalent ailments, access to essential medicines and protection against environmental health hazards.[220]

In sum, access to medicines is very germane to human security, as people cannot enjoy any significant sense of safety or security where there is high morbidity without the appropriate treatment and healthcare delivery structure to address the problem. The connection between public health and human security is subtle but powerful. Inadequate public health facilities can create a great feeling of insecurity in the populace and there can be no real security where the public is constantly denied reasonable access to life-saving medications. Access to affordable medicines is therefore an essential component of human welfare and security.

6.6.2 The interface between trade, intellectual property and access to medicines

Having discussed in preceding sections the significance of safeguarding the right to health in the protection of property by patents and the connection between health and human security, it is now necessary to consider how international trade and IP affect access to medicines. The non-existence of a Global State to enforce the myriad of international laws has brought about the need to create or strengthen institutions that would have the power to enforce norms to enhance the globalisation of trade and finance.[221] These institutions are the WTO, the World Bank

216 Ibid., 124.

217 P G Lauren, *The Evolution of International Human Rights* (University of Pennsylvania Press 2d ed., 2003) 283.

218 Quigley above n 34, 127.

219 See Marks above n 14, 742.

220 B M Meier, 'Employing Health Rights for Global Justice: The Promise of Public Health in Response to the Insalubrious Ramifications of Globalization' (2006) 39 *Cornell International Law Journal* 711, 735.

221 B S Chimni, 'A Just World under Law: A View from the South' (2007) 22 *American University International Law Review* 199, 207.

and the International Monetary Fund (IMF), which have all been described as the 'principal building blocks of an emerging Global State'.[222] The influence and policies of these organisations may also have some effect on the ability of developing countries to implement socio-economic human rights. The IMF and World Bank have significant influence in many developing countries because of their ability to determine the terms of loans, which may be the only major source of finance for many poor countries. For instance, where the IMF and World Bank require a particular country to enforce structural adjustment policies as a condition precedent to obtaining financial assistance, the short-term effect of this may be drastic cuts in social services such as healthcare facilities and social support.[223] The WTO treaties, including the TRIPS Agreement, also have very significant impacts on measures a country may wish to explore to facilitate access to medicines.[224]

There was a time when the connection between international trade and human rights was a very controversial issue.[225] There currently exists, however, a widely held view that trade and human rights are well connected in ways that require some critical investigation.[226] As noted by Eleanor Kinney:

> In more recent years, the WTO has become more aware of the clash of trade policy and health policy and has worked with the WHO to mitigate these problem areas.[227]

The UN human rights institutions and the civil society (particularly NGOs) have played very significant roles in identifying the nexus between trade and human rights as well as enhancing conversation between the two.[228] Thus, the UN Human Rights Commission has noted that 'achieving fair and equitable trade liberalization by adopting human rights approaches to WTO rules will be an important step in establishing a just international and social order'.[229] The UN High Commissioner for Human Rights has made a case for the assessment of the impacts of rules on human rights before they are finalised.[230] The UN ESCR Committee has equally emphasised the point that WTO Members are required to comply with human rights obligations in multilateral trade negotiations.[231]

222 Ibid., 207–208.

223 Lazzarini, above n 44, 287.

224 Ibid., 286–287.

225 A T F Lang, 'Re-thinking Trade and Human Rights' (2007) *Tulane Journal of International and Comparative Law* 335, 336.

226 Ibid., 336.

227 E Kinney, 'Realization of the International Human Right to Health in an Economically Integrated North America' (2009) 37 *Journal of Law, Medicine and Ethics* 807, 808.

228 Lang, above n 225, 339.

229 See *Globalization and Its Impact on the Full Enjoyment of Human Rights*, U.N. Doc. E/CN.4/2002/54 9.

230 Ibid., 46.

231 *Substantive Issues Arising from the Implementation of the International Covenant on Economic, Social and Cultural Rights* – General Comment No. 15, U.N. Doc. E/C.12/2002/11 (20 January 2003) 35.

Trade and investment liberalisation have opened up developing country markets to highly processed nutrient-deprived food and tobacco products thereby increasing the prevalence of chronic non-communicable diseases such as diabetes, stroke, but there has been no corresponding liberalisation of the options available to tackle public health problems in these countries.[232]

There are, however, those who hold the view that international trade and IP both serve the common purpose of promoting human rights. The argument is that the protection of IP in the world trade regime would further enhance trade liberalisation,[233] which is considered as very germane to wealth maximisation.[234] The corollary to this, as already pointed out by the WTO Consultative Board, is that the WTO trade regime will have effects that would traverse the field of commerce to the extent of yielding outcomes that promote and enhance the human rights movement.[235] This seems to reinforce the prescient observation of B S Chimni that international human rights law and international economic law would in the course of time 'complement each other to create a global law of welfare'.[236] He goes further, however, to note that human rights law is not currently delivering on its promise because the world economy is driven by States and forces who do not give pride of place to the travail and language of rights particularly in relation to implementing economic, social and cultural rights.[237] There is therefore a compelling need for the rules governing international trade to take full cognisance of human right obligations and the public interest in safeguarding the health of people who need access to life-saving medications.

6.6.3 Public interest measures in the TRIPS Agreement

Article 7 of the TRIPS Agreement provides that the protection and enforcement of IP rights should be done in '*a manner conducive to social and economic rights and to a balance of rights and obligations*'. In a similar vein, Article 8.1 of the TRIPS Agreement reads:

> Members may, in formulating or amending their laws and regulations, adopt measures necessary to protect public health and nutrition, and to promote the public interest in sectors of vital importance to their socio-economic and technological development, provided that such measures are consistent with the provisions of this Agreement.

232 K Yelpaala, 'Quo Vadis WTO? The Threat of TRIPS and the Biodiversity Convention Human Health and Food Security' (2012) 30 *Boston University International Law Journal* 55, 85–86.

233 A Narlikar, *The World Trade Organization: A Very Short Introduction* (Oxford University Press 2005) 28–29.

234 Ibid., 2.

235 P Sutherland et al., *The Future of the WTO: Addressing Institutional Challenges in the New Millennium* (World Trade Organization, 2004) 10.

236 Chimni, above n 221, 206.

237 Ibid., 206–207.

It has been argued that Article 8 does not empower Members to adopt measures they consider useful in the protection of public health and nutrition but only to adopt measures that are necessary to achieve such ends.[238] It is also argued that the use of the word 'necessary' rather than 'it considers necessary' in Article 73 suggests that the adoption of such measures is not at the absolute discretion of the Member invoking the provision, but is subject to potential review by the WTO in terms of validity.[239] The experience of a number of developing countries over the years has shown that the flexibilities allowed by the TRIPS Agreement are not really as flexible as one might assume. The position is quite succinctly put by Zita Lazzarini who notes that in practice, '*trade negotiations and applications have often been characterised by widespread disregard for human rights and the welfare of the poorest and most vulnerable groups*'.[240]

It is submitted on this point that the fact that Article 8 contains a proviso to the effect that the measures adopted must be '*consistent with the provisions of this Agreement*' seems to eliminate any power to adopt measures in a nation's national interest that might otherwise have been conferred by this provision. The proviso may be interpreted as suggesting that the public interest benefit in the Agreement is subject to the protection of the rights guaranteed in it and that the protection of IP rights should take precedence in the event of a conflict. It would appear the various qualifications and ambiguities in the language of the TRIPS Agreement are a reflection of the highly rigorous debates and deliberations that took place amongst the negotiators in the process of drafting the treaty.

Indeed, one cannot but wonder whether Article 8 should be considered an example of 'TRIPS flexibility' or 'TRIPS contradiction' in view of the fact that it does seem to mitigate in its proviso any flexibility it would appear to have contained.[241] Peter Yu however argues that a combined reading of Articles 7 and 8 may help remove any potential inconsistency inherent in the TRIPS Agreement, thereby giving effect to the objectives.[242] In a similar vein, Carlos Correa has noted that Article 7 should be understood in the context of the preamble of TRIPS Agreement, such that the balance of IP obligations and socio-economic welfare need be taken into account.[243]

The fact however remains that the flexibilities available under TRIPS are more restrictive than the safeguard measures under Article XX of the GATT. Whilst

238 P K Yu, 'The Objectives and Principles of the TRIPS Agreement' (2009) 46 *Houston Law Review* 979, 1013.

239 W A Cann, Jr., 'On the Relationship Between Intellectual Property Rights and the Need of Less-Developed Countries for Access to Pharmaceuticals: Creating a Legal Duty to Supply under a Theory of Progressive Global Constitutionalism' (2004) 25 *University of Pennsylvania Journal of International Economic Law* 755, 808.

240 Lazzarini, above n 44, 289–290.

241 See also Yu, above n 240, 1014 (describing the constraint as 'eroding the pro-development aspect of Article 8').

242 Ibid.

243 C M Correa, *Trade Related Aspects of Intellectual Property Rights: A Commentary on the TRIPS Agreement* (2007) 104.

in the case of the GATT, the need to protect human life or health may prevail over the general rules of the agreement subject to the non-discrimination principle, the TRIPS flexibilities '*are circumscribed by various procedural and compensatory encumbrances*'[244] that make their use very daunting. Given the fact that both the GATT and the TRIPS Agreement are part of the multilateral trade agreements under the Agreement Establishing the WTO, both are subject to the WTO Agreement in the event of any inconsistency.[245] However, the GATT and TRIPS Agreement are coordinate agreements in the WTO hierarchy and to that extent neither can be binding on the other.[246]

Although the Doha Declaration on the TRIPS Agreement and Public Health and the Implementation Decision on Paragraph 6 of Doha Declaration on TRIPS and Public Health tend to address some of the problems of access to medicines under the TRIPS regime, a number of issues still remain unresolved. The WTO Appellate Body has expressed the view that 'WTO Members have a right to determine the level of protection of health that they consider appropriate in a given situation'.[247] The Global Commission on HIV and the Law (an independent UN-led group) in its landmark report released in July 2012 noted as follows:

> In spite of their potential benefits, TRIPS flexibilities have proved insufficient in obviating the shortages of affordable medicines that TRIPS itself has contributed to creating. The TRIPS Agreement on paper affords flexibility as to how its obligations are implemented by national governments. Nevertheless, in practice, the attempts by low and middle-income countries to use measures to promote access to affordable medicines have been fraught with difficulty and met with retaliation and opposition from some high-income countries and corporations.

However, a recent WTO Decision reinforces the view that legitimate measures taken to protect public health will not infringe on multilateral trade obligations under the WTO system.

In *Australia – Certain Measures Concerning Trademarks, Geographical Indications and Other Plain Packaging Requirements Applicable to Tobacco Products and Packaging*, Australia was challenged for adopting certain measures imposing restrictions on the use of trademarks and geographical indications with respect to tobacco packaging. It was alleged that the Australian tobacco plain packaging measures were inconsistent with Article 2.2 of the Technical Barriers to Trade (TBT) Agreement, Article 20 of the TRIPS Agreement and other trademark-related rights conferred

244 UNCTAD-ICTSD, Resource Book on TRIPS and Development (UNCTAD-ICTSD, 2005) 132.

245 The Agreement Establishing the WTO Article XVI (3).

246 Ibid., Articles II(2) and III(1).

247 Appellate Body Report, *European Communities – Measures Affecting Asbestos and Asbestos-Containing Products*, 168, WT/DS135/AB/R (5 April 2001).

by the TRIPS Agreement.[248] Article 2.2 of the TBT Agreement allows the use of technical regulations in international trade provided they are not more restrictive than is necessary to achieve a legitimate objective. Such legitimate objectives include 'national security requirements; the prevention of deceptive practices; protection of human health or safety, animal or plant life or health, or the environment'.[249] The WTO Panel in holding that the measure taken by Australia was a valid and legitimate measure under Article 2.2 of the TBT noted thus:

> We have determined above that the objective pursued by Australia through the TPP measures is the protection of human health, and more precisely the improvement of public health by reducing the use of, and exposure to, tobacco products.
>
> The "protection of human health or safety" is one of the "legitimate objectives" explicitly identified in Article 2.2. We note in this respect that, in the context of Article XX(b) of the GATT 1994, the preservation of human life and health through the elimination or reduction of well-known and life-threatening health risks (in that instance, as caused by asbestos fibers) was considered to be a value "both vital and important in the highest degree".[250]

The WTO Panel, thus held 'that the improvement of public health by reducing the use of, and exposure to, tobacco products is a "legitimate objective" within the meaning of Article 2.2 of the TBT Agreement'.[251]Article 20 of the TRIPS Agreement provides that the 'use of a trademark in the course of trade shall not be unjustifiably encumbered by special requirements'. In response to the argument that the Australian tobacco packaging measures were in violation of Article 20 of TRIPS, the WTO panel found that

> special requirements that involve a high degree of encumbrance, such as those in the TPP measures that prohibit the use of stylized word marks, composite marks, and figurative marks, are not per se unjustifiable.

In coming to this conclusion, the WTO Panel underscored the importance of the principles and objectives of the TRIPS Agreement to the interpretation of the Agreement by noting thus:

> Articles 7 and 8, together with the preamble of the TRIPS Agreement, set out general goals and principles underlying the TRIPS Agreement, which

248 Panel Report, Australia – Certain Measures Concerning Trademarks, Geographical Indications and Other Plain Packaging Requirements Applicable to Tobacco Products and Packaging, WT/DS435/R, WT/DS441/R; WT/DS458/R, WT/DS467/R (28 June 2018).

249 Article 2.2 TBT Agreement.

250 Panel Report, Australia – Certain Measures Concerning Trademarks, Geographical Indications and Other Plain Packaging Requirements Applicable to Tobacco Products and Packaging, 195.

251 Ibid., 196.

> are to be borne in mind when specific provisions of the Agreement are being interpreted in their context and in light of the object and purpose of the Agreement. As the panel in Canada – Pharmaceutical Patents observed in interpreting the terms of Article 30 of the TRIPS Agreement, "[b]oth the goals and the limitations stated in Articles 7 and 8.1 must obviously be borne in mind when doing so as well as those of other provisions of the TRIPS Agreement which indicate its object and purposes".[252]

With this decision, the WTO Dispute Settlement Body has clearly demonstrated that the protection of public health exception enshrined in the TRIPS Agreement and other WTO Agreements are not merely hortatory provisions. Thus, legitimate measures taken to safeguard public health will not be inconsistent with the intellectual property obligations covered by the TRIPS Agreement. To this end, all the flexibilities available under the TRIPS Agreement may be legitimately used to promote public health objectives and access to medicines for populations lacking access to medicines in Africa and vulnerable populations all over the world.

At a domestic level, the essence of the TRIPS public interest provision became a particularly pertinent issue in the India case of *Novartis AG v Union of India*.[253] Novartis obtained a US patent for its anticancer drug, Gleevec (imatinib), on 28 May 1996. At that time, as a result of the fact that there was no product patent for pharmaceuticals under Indian law, no application was filed in India. However, with the Exclusive Marketing Rights (EMR) which came with the TRIPS regime,[254] Novartis was able to file an application for the beta crystalline form of imatinib mestylate in India on 17 July 1998 and was able to obtain an EMR for imatinib mestylate. On 25 January 2006, the Controller of Patents declined the patent application for this drug consequent upon opposition initiated by the competitors who were ready to make generic version of the drug available at significantly lower rates. Novartis challenged the Controller's decision at the Madras High Court, alleging non-compliance with the TRIPS Agreement. The court upheld the constitutionality of Section 3(d) of the India Patents Act and transferred the petition questioning the order of the Controller to the Intellectual Property Appellate Board. The Intellectual Property Appellate Board upheld the decision of Patents Controller and Novartis further appealed to the Supreme Court.

252 Ibid., 725.

253 *Novartis AG v Union of India*, IPAB Order No 100/2009; SC CIVIL APPEAL Nos. 2706-2716 OF 2013.

254 Article 70(8) & (9) of the TRIPS Agreement provide that countries that are yet to have a legal structure for pharmaceutical patent protection after the entry into force of the Agreement must have an arrangement for granting exclusive marketing rights to owners of pharmaceutical or agricultural products that satisfy the criteria for patentability pending the determination of the patent applications for such products under the patent regime required by the TRIPS Agreement.

On first April 2013, the Indian Supreme Court in a landmark decision held that Glivec failed to meet the patentability criteria for pharmaceutical products under Indian law.[255] However in coming to that conclusion, the Supreme Court made reference to a number of fundamental issues that the court had to take into account in interpreting the Indian Patents Act. One such issue is the human rights obligation of the Government under the Indian Constitution. The Indian Supreme Court, like the Intellectual Property Appellate Board (IPAB), referred in its judgment to the following trenchant observation of the Madras High Court:

> We have borne in mind the object which the amending Act wanted to achieve namely, to prevent evergreening; to provide easy access to the citizens of the country to life saving drugs and to discharge their constitutional obligation of providing good health care to its citizens.[256]

The Supreme Court of India also noted the provision in Article 8 of TRIPS and other flexibilities in that Agreement that allow countries to implement it in a way that take the exigencies of local circumstances into account.

The decision demonstrates that national courts can adopt a functional principle of interpretation that will give effect to human rights. Even where access to medicines or the right to health is not a recognised right in the national law of a given country, it is submitted that health and access to medicines can be interpreted as germane to giving effect to the fundamental right to life and dignity of the human person. Where no human rights whatsoever exist in the domestic framework of a given country, the court may nonetheless apply the fundamental rights to life and dignity of human person which are rights in customary international law to give effect to health on the basis that parliament, except where a definite contrary intention is disclosed, does not intend to contravene international law.

The WTO Appellate body has equally expressed the view that 'WTO Members have a right to determine the level of protection of health that they consider appropriate in a given situation'.[257]

6.6.4 The right to health and the duty of multinational pharmaceutical companies

Following the emergence of the WTO in 1994, the global trends towards trade liberalisation, privatisation and foreign investment have all made it increasingly difficult for States to meet their human rights obligations in international law.[258] The

255 *Novartis AG v Union of India* (SC), n 248.

256 Ibid., 11.

257 Appellate Body Report, *European Communities -- Measures Affecting Asbestos and Asbestos-Containing Products*, 168, WT/DS135/AB/R (5 April 2001).

258 I Halpern, 'Tracing the Contours of Transnational Corporations' Human Rights Obligations in the Twenty-First Century' (2008) 14 *Buffalo Human Rights Review* 129, 143.

human rights most susceptible to abuse by transnational corporations are the so-called economic, social and cultural rights which in most cases are not actionable.[259] Multinational companies are critical of any measure taken to derogate from their IP rights and are ever ready to use their intimidating presence in the global market to resist any act that fails to give primacy to the protection of their IP interests. Even the legitimate use of TRIPS flexibilities is constantly being challenged.by these companies, as experiences in Brazil, Thailand, India and South Africa have shown.[260] Decrying the welfare losses occasioned by pharmaceutical companies' trade in antiretroviral medicines, Michele Boldrine and David Levine observe as follows:

> Drugs for AIDS are relatively inexpensive to produce. They are sufficiently inexpensive to produce that the benefits to Africa in lives saved exceed the costs of producing the drugs by orders of magnitude. But the large pharmaceutical companies charge such a large premium over the cost of producing the drugs – to reap profits from sales in Western countries where those drugs are affordable – that African nations and individuals cannot afford them. They create artificial scarcity – excluding Africa from AIDS drugs – to garner a higher price for their product in the United States and Europe. Through 'intellectual property' and international 'free' trade agreements, they also prevent potential competitors (read: imitators) from entering the African or Latin American markets for such drugs. The welfare triangle – the net loss to society – from this policy is real and enormous. That is IP – inefficiency at work on a global scale.[261]

So far, the major mode of censuring transnational corporations or imposing obligations on them has been through market-based influence such as public campaigns, competitive practices, well-informed investment tactics and other strategies that are not legal in nature.[262] There is need for multinational companies especially in the pharmaceutical sector to look beyond economic consideration and be more tolerant of measures taken to address public health at domestic levels. The use of flexibilities allowed by the TRIPS Agreement should not always result in patent litigations at the instance of pharmaceutical companies as occurred in the pre-Doha South African HIV case[263] and the Indian Novartis

259 See D Kinley & J Tadaki, 'From Talk to Walk: The Emergence of Human Rights Responsibilities for Corporations at International Law' (2004) 44 *Virginia Journal of International Law* 931, 935.

260 See Sections 2.2.2 and 2.3.4.

261 M Boldrin & D K Levine, *Against Intellectual Monopoly* 68 (New York: Cambridge University Press, 2008) 69–70; also quoted in R V V Puymbroeck, 'Coming to Grips with TRIPS: Conversion + Calculation' (2010) 38 *Journal of Law, Medicines and Ethics* 520, 529.

262 See F Fortanier & M Maher, *Foreign Direct Investment and Sustainable Development* (OECD, 2001) 5; R G Steinhardt, 'Corporate Responsibility and the International Law of Human Rights: The New Lex Mercatoria' in P Alston (ed.), *Non-State Actors and Human Rights* (Oxford University Press, 2005) 177, 180–187.

263 See Section 6.6.3.

Glivec case.[264] Such flexibilities are legitimate measures expressly allowed by the TRIPS Agreement. Pharmaceutical companies have a moral and even a legal duty to respect human rights and the use of TRIPS flexibilities to foster access to medicines is in line with the duty to respect and fulfil these rights. There is therefore the need for pharmaceutical companies to ensure their property rights are not being used in a way that substantially impedes the ability of countries, especially in the global south, to fulfil their human rights obligations in the access to medicines context.

6.7 Conclusion

The right to health is well recognised in the international human rights system but there currently exists no potent mechanism for its enforceability in international law. Many countries have come to recognise the right to health in their municipal laws even though it is hardly justiciable as a right on its own because of the significant political considerations that its enforcement entails. However, there is an emerging jurisprudence in regional and national courts all over the world that is beginning to give force to the right to health indirectly through enforceable rights like the right to life and the right to dignity. It is submitted that countries, in exploring the derogations and flexibilities in the international IP system may still rely on their obligation to make adequate provisions for the public health needs of their people under international law. While the right to health may not be directly enforceable in international law, it is nonetheless a well-recognised right in the international legal system.

Human rights obligations of States should also be taken into account in interpreting trade agreements in the WTO system. There is emerging jurisprudence that supports the view that international trade law is part of the general body of public international law. It therefore follows that the human rights obligations of parties under public international law are to be taken into account in interpreting the TRIPS Agreement and other trade agreements that may tend to frustrate the ability of people to legitimately exercise their rights to health. It is thus submitted that where there is an apparent conflict between a trade agreement or an international IP regime and international human rights law, the relevant adjudicating body must proceed on the presumption that States do not intend to act in violation of their obligations under international human rights law. To that extent, an interpretation that tends to be consistent with international human rights obligation must be considered.

In Africa, the Protocol to the African Charter on Human and People's Rights on the Establishment of an African Court on Human and People's Rights has made it possible for NGOs acting on behalf of individuals and individuals whose rights have been violated or are likely to be violated to approach the court for

264 *Novartis AG v Union of India*, IPAB Order No 100/2009; SC CIVIL APPEAL Nos. 2706-2716 OF 2013.

relief. This is a significant development in the human rights and social justice advocacy. It is now possible for individuals whose rights to health are in jeopardy to seek personal remedies through the regional court provided their countries have accepted the jurisdiction of the court in that regard. The human rights jurisprudence is therefore very important to individuals who are being denied reasonable access to life-saving drugs. Human rights may also provide a good defence where trade sanctions and even legal actions are being used to restrain a State from legitimately pursuing goals that may advance the socio-economic rights of its citizens and their right to have access to affordable drugs.

Bibliography

Abbott F M, 'The WTO Medicines Decision: World Pharmaceutical Trade and the Protection of Public Health' (2005) 99 *American Journal of International Law* 317.

Adeyi O, Smith O & Robles S, *Public Policy and the Challenge of Chronic Noncommunicable Diseases* (World Bank, 2007).

Annas G J, 'Bioethics: American Bioethics and Human Rights: The End of All Our Exploring' (2004) 32 *Journal of Law & Medicine* 658.

Beitz C R, 'Human Rights as a Common Concern', (2001) 95 *American Political Science Review* 269.

Beitz C R, *Political Theory and International Relations* (Princeton University Press, 1979) 139.

Beitz C R, 'What Human Rights Mean' (2003) 132(1) *Daedalus* 36.

Bettinger-Lopez C et al., 'Redefining Human Rights Lawyering Through the Lens of Critical Theory: Lessons for Pedagogy and Practice' (2011) 18 *Georgetown Journal of Poverty Law and Policy* 337.

Boldrin M & Levine D K, *Against Intellectual Monopoly* 68 (New York: Cambridge University Press, 2008).

Buchanan A & Golove D, 'Philosophy of International Law', in J Coleman & S Shapiro (eds.), *Oxford Handbook of Jurisprudence and Philosophy of Law* (Oxford University Press, 2002) 808.

Cann, W A Jr., 'On the Relationship between Intellectual Property Rights and the Need of Less-Developed Countries for Access to Pharmaceuticals: Creating a Legal Duty to Supply Under a Theory of Progressive Global Constitutionalism' (2004) 25 *University of Pennsylvania Journal of International Economic Law* 755.

Chandra R, 'The Role of National Laws in Reconciling Constitutional Right to Health with TRIPS Obligations: An Examination of the Glivec Patent Case in India' in T Pogge, M Rimmer & K Rubenstein (eds.), *Incentives for Global Public Health: Patents Law and Access to Essential Medicines* (Cambridge University Press, 2010).

Chapman A R, *Approaching Intellectual Property as a Human Right: Obligations Related to Article 15(1)(c)*, U.N. Doc. E/C.12/2000/12 (3 October 2000).

Chaudhuri S, Golberg P K & Jia P, 'Estimating the Effects of Global Patent Protection in Pharmaceuticals: A Case Study of Quinolones in India' (2006) 96 *American Economic Review* 1477.

Chimni B S, 'A Just World under Law: A View from the South' (2007) 22 *American University International Law Review* 199.

Correa C M, *Trade Related Aspects of Intellectual Property Rights: A Commentary on the TRIPS Agreement* (Oxford University Press, 2007).

Cowger C D, 'Dilemmas of Peace and Justice', in D S Sanders & J K Matsuoka (eds.), *Peace and Development: An Interdisciplinary Perspective* (University of Hawaii, School of Social Work, 1989).

Cross F B, 'The Error of Positive Rights' (2001) 48 *UCLA Law Rev*iew 857.

Cullet P, 'Human Rights and Intellectual Property Protection in the TRIPS Era' (2007) 29 *Human Rights Quarterly* 403.

Daar A, Thorsteinsdóttir H, Martin D K, Smith A C, Nast S & Singer P A, 'Top Ten Biotechnologies for Improving Health in Developing Countries' (2002) 32 *Nature Genetics* 229.

Donnelly J, 'The Relative Universality of Human Rights', (2007) 29 *Human Rights Quarterly* 281.

Drahos P, 'Intellectual Property and Human Rights' (1999) 3 *Intellectual Property Quarterly* 349.

Elliott R (ed.), *Courting Rights: Case Studies in Litigating the Human Rights of People Living with Aids* (Canadian HIV/AIDS Legal Network and UNAIDS, 2006).

Engle E, 'Universal Human Rights: A Generational History' (2006) 12 *Annual Survey of International and Comparative Law* 219.

Erdman J N, 'Human Rights in Health Equity: Cervical Cancer and HPV Vaccines' (2009) 35 *American Journal of Law & Medicine* 365.

Fidler D P, 'The Globalization of Public Health: Emerging Infectious Diseases and International Relations' (1997) 5 *Indiana Journal of Global Legal Studies* 11.

Fortanier F & Maher M, *Foreign Direct Investment and Sustainable Development* (OECD, 2001).

George E, 'South Africa and South-South Cooperation to Reframe Global Intellectual Property Principles and Promote Access to Essential Medicines' (2011) 18 *Indiana Journal of Global Legal Studies* 167.

Gostin L O, 'Meeting Basic Survival Needs of the World's Least Healthy People: Towards a Framework on Global Health' (2008) 96 *George Town Law Journal* 331.

Grover A, *Report of the Special Rapporteur on the Right of Everyone to the Enjoyment of the Highest Attainable Standard of Physical and Mental Health*, 11th Sess., P 14, U.N. Doc. A/HRC/11/12 (31 March 2009).

Hafner-Burton E M, 'Trading Human Rights: How Preferential Trade Agreements Influence Government Repression' (2005) 59(3) *International Organization* 593.

Halpern I, 'Tracing the Contours of Transnational Corporations' Human Rights Obligations in the Twenty-First Century' (2008) 14 *Buffalo Human Rights Review* 129.

Harris S R, 'Recent Development: Asian Human Rights: Forming A Regional Covenant' (2000) 1 *University of Hawaii Asian-Pacific Law & Policy Journal* 17.

Haugen H M, 'Patents Rights and Human Rights: Exploring their Relationship' (2007) 10 *Journal of World Intellectual Property* 97.

Heywood M, 'Current Developments: Preventing Mother-to-Child Transmission in South Africa: Background, Strategies and Outcomes of the Treatment Action Campaign Case Against the Minister of Health' (2003) 19 *South African Journal of Human Rights* 278.

Hunt P, *Neglected Diseases: A Human Rights Analysis* (WHO, 2007).

Jones J F, 'Human Security and Social Development' (2004) 33 *Denver Journal of International Law and Policy* 92.

Keener S R & Vasquez J, 'A Life Worth Living: Enforcement of the Right to Health through the Right to Life in the Inter American Court of Human Rights' (2009) 40 *Columbia Human Rights Law Review* 595.

Kindley D, 'Human Rights Fundamentalisms' (2007) 29 *The Sydney Law Review* 545.
Kinley D & Tadaki J, 'From Talk to Walk: The Emergence of Human Rights Responsibilities for Corporations at International Law' (2004) 44*Virginia Journal of International Law* 931.
Kinney E, 'Realization of the International Human Right to Health in an Economically Integrated North America' (2009) 37 *Journal of Law, Medicine and Ethics* 807.
Kirby M, 'Human Rights and Bioethics: The Universal Declaration of Human Rights and the UNESCO Declaration on Bioethics and Human Rights' (2009) 25 *Journal of Contemporary Health Law & Policy* 309.
Kirby M, *Judicial Activism: Authority, Principle and Policy in the Judicial Method*, Fifty-Fifth Hamlyn Lecture 74 (2003) www.hcourt.gov.au/assets/publications/speeches/former-justices/kirbyj/kirbyj_19nov.html accessed 26 January 2019.
Lamy P, Director-General, World Trade Organization, *The Place and Role of the WTO (WTO Law) in the International Legal Order* (Address at the European Society of International Law in Sorbonne, Paris May 19, 2006) www.wto.org/english/news_e/sppl_e/sppl26_e.htm accessed 26 January 2019.
Landau D, 'The Reality of Social Rights Enforcement' (2012) 53 *Harvard International Law Journal* 189.
Lang A T F, 'Re-thinking Trade and Human Rights' (2007) *Tulane Journal of International and Comparative Law* 335, 336.
Lanjouw J O & Cockburn I M, 'New Pills for Poor People? Empirical Evidence after GATT' (2001) 29 *World Development* 265.
Lauren P G, *The Evolution of International Human Rights* (University of Pennsylvania Press, 2d ed., 2003).
Lawrence R S, Chan I & Goodman E, 'Poverty, Food Security and the Right to Health' (2008) *Georgetown Journal on Poverty Law & Policy* 583.
Lazzarini Z, 'Access to HIV Drugs: Are We Changing the Two World Paradigm?' (2002) 17 *Connecticut Journal of International Law* 281.
Marks S P, 'Normative Expansion of the Right to Health and the Proliferation of Human Rights' (2016) 49 *George Washington International Law Review* 97.
Marks S P, 'The Evolving Field of Health and Human Rights: Issues and Methods' (2002) 30 *Journal of Law, Medicines & Ethics* 739.
Marks S P & Weston B H, 'International Human Rights at Fifty: A Foreword' (1998) 8 *Transnational Law and Contemporary Problems* 113.
Meier B M, 'Employing Health Rights for Global Justice: The Promise of Public Health in Response to the Insalubrious Ramifications of Globalization' (2006) 39 *Cornell International Law Journal* 711.
Meier B M & Yamin A E, 'Emerging Topics in Public Health law and Policy: Right to Health Law Litigation and HIV/AIDS Policy' (2011) 39 *Journal of Law, Medicine and Ethics* 81.
Merritt M, 'Bioethics, Philosophy, and Global Health' (2007) 7 *Yale Journal of Health Policy, Law & Ethics* 273.
de Montesquieu C, The Spirit of Laws, bk. VIII, § 3 (1750) www.constitution.org/cm/sol_08.htm accessed 26 January 2019.
Nariman F S, 'The Universality of Human Rights', (1993) 50 *The Review/International Commission of Jurists* 8.
Narlikar A, *The World Trade Organization: A Very Short Introduction* (Oxford University Press 2005).
Novogrodsky N, 'The Duty of Treatment: Human Rights and the HIV/AIDS Pandemic' (2009) 12 *Yale Human Rights and Development Law Journal* 1.

Ocran M, 'Socio-Economic Rights in the African Context: Problems with Concept and Enforcement' (2007) 5 *Loyola University Chicago International Law Review* 1.

OHCHR, *The Right to Health*, Fact Sheet No 31, Geneva, OHCHR June 2008.

Oppenheimer G M, Bayer R, & Colgrove J, 'Health and Human Rights: Old Wine in New Bottles?' (2002) 30 *Journal of Law, Medicine & Ethics* 522.

Parento E W, 'Health Equity, Health People 2020, and Coercive Legal Mechanisms as Necessary for the Achievement of Both' (2012) 58 *Loyola Law Review* 655.

Pogge T, 'Montreal Statement on the Human Right to Essential Medicines' (2007) 16 *Cambridge Quarterly Healthcare Ethics* 97.

Pogge T W, *Realizing Rawls* (Cornell University Press, 1989).

Posner E A, 'Human Welfare, Not Human Rights' (2008) 108 *Columbia Law Review* 1758.

Puymbroeck R V, 'Coming to Grips with TRIPS: Conversion + Calculation' (2010) 38 *Journal of Law, Medicines and Ethics* 520.

Quigley W P, 'Revolutionary Lawyering: Addressing the Root Causes of Poverty and Wealth' (2006) 20 *Washington University Journal of Law and Policy* 101.

Rai A K, 'Fostering Cumulative Innovation in the Biopharmaceutical Industry: The Role of Patents and Antitrust' (2001) 16 *Berkeley Technology Law Journal* 813.

Reichman J, 'Of Green Tulips and Legal Kudzu: Repackaging Rights in Subpatentable Innovation' (2000) 53 *Vandebilt Law Review* 1743.

Rosen G, *A History of Public Health*, expanded edition (Johns Hopkins University Press, 1998).

Rubin E L, 'Rethinking Human Rights' (2003) 9 *International Legal Theory* 5.

Ruger J, 'Rethinking Equal Access: Agency, Quality, and Norms' (2007) 2 *Global Public Health* 78.

Schachter O, 'The Genesis of the Declaration: A Fresh Examination' (1999) 11 *Pace International Law Review* 51.

Schermers H G, 'The International Protection of the Right of Property', in F Matscher & H Petzold (eds.), *Protecting Human Rights: The European Dimension* (Carl Heymanns Verlag KG, Köln, 1988).

Shelton D, 'International Human Rights Law: Principled, Double or Absent Standards?' (2007) 25 *Law & Inequality* 467.

Singer P, *One World: The Ethics of Globalization* (Yale University Press, 2004).

Sloane R D, 'Outrelativizing Relativism: A Liberal Defense of the Universality of International Human Rights' (2001) 34 *Vanderbilt Journal of Transnational Law* 527.

Smith G P, 'Human Rights and Bioethics: Formulating a Universal Right to Health, Health Care, or Health Protection' (2005) 38 *Vanderbilt Journal of Transnational Law* 1295.

Soohoo C & Goldberg J, 'The Full Realization of Our Rights: The Right to Health in State Constitutions' (2010) 60 *Case Western Reserve Law Review* 997.

Steinhardt R G, 'Corporate Responsibility and the International Law of Human Rights: The New Lex Mercatoria' in P Alston (ed.), *Non-State Actors and Human Rights* (Oxford University Press, 2005) 177.

Sutherland P et al., *The Future of the WTO: Addressing Institutional Challenges in the New Millennium* (World Trade Organization, 2004).

Torres M A, 'The Human Right to Health, National Courts, and Access to HIV/AIDS Treatment: A Case Study from Venezuela' (2002) 3 *Chicago Journal of International Law* 105.

UNCESCR, General Comment No 14 on the Right to the Highest Attainable Standard of Health.

UNCTAD-ICTSD, *Resource Book on TRIPS and Development* (UNCTAD-ICTSD, 2005).

UNESCO, 'International Bioethics Committee (IBC)' www.unesco.org/new/en/social-and- human-sciences/themes/bioethics/international-bioethics-committee/ accessed 26 January 2019.

UNESCO Press Release, UNESCO General Conference adopts Universal Declaration on Bioethics and Human Rights (19 October 2008).

United Nations, *Committee on Economic, Social, and Cultural Rights, Concluding Observations of the Committee on the United Kingdom*, U.N. Doc E/C.12/1/Add.79 (5 June 2009).

United Nations, *Committee on Economic Social and Cultural Rights*, Concluding Observation of the Committee on Zambia, UN. Doc. E/C/12/1/Add.106 (23 June 2005).

United Nations, *Committee on Economic Social and Cultural Rights*, General Comment No. 17: The Right of Everyone to Benefit from the Protection of the Moral and Material Interests Resulting from Any Scientific, Literary or Artistic Production of Which He Is the Author (Article 15, Paragraph 1 (c), of the Covenant) U.N. Doc. E/C.12/GC/17 (12 January 2006).

United Nations, *Committee on Economic Social and Cultural Rights*, The Right to the Highest Attainable Standard of Health, U.N. Doc. E/C.12/2000/4 (11 August 2000).

United Nations, *General Assembly, Transforming our World: The 2030 Agenda for Sustainable Development*, UN Resolution No. A/RES/70/1.

United Nations, *Globalization and Its Impact on the Full Enjoyment of Human Rights*, U.N. Doc. E/CN.4/2002/54.

United Nations, *Human Rights Council, The Right of Everyone to the Enjoyment of the Highest Attainable Standard of Physical and Mental Health in the Implementation of the 2030 Agenda for Sustainable Development*, UN Resolution A/HRC/35/L.18/Rev.1, (21 June 2017).

United Nations, *Human Rights and Intellectual Property, United Nations Committee on Economic Social and Cultural Rights*, 27th Sess., U.N Doc. E/C.12/2001/15 (2001).

United Nations, *Substantive Issues Arising from the Implementation of the International Covenant on Economic, Social and Cultural Rights - General Comment No. 15*, U.N. Doc. E/C.12/2002/11 (20 January 2003).

United Nations, *The Right to Life*, U.N. GAOR Human Rights Comm., 37th Sess., Supp. No. 40, at Gen. Comment No. 6, U.N. Doc. A/37/40 (1982).

United Nations, *The Sub-Commission on the Promotion and Protection of Human Rights, Intellectual Property Rights and Human Rights, Sub-Comm'n on Human Rights Res.* 2000/7, U.N. Doc. E/CN.4/Sub.2/RES/2000/7 (17 August 2000).

United Nations, *UN General Assembly, United Nations Millennium Declaration*, UN Doc. No. (A/55/L.2) (8 September 2000).

United Nations Development Programme, *Human Development Report 1994* (1994).

Vadi V, 'Sapere Audi! Access to Knowledge as a Human Right and a Key Instrument of Development' (2008) 12 *International Journal of Communications Law and Policy* 345, 358.

Walker E M, 'The HIV AIDS Pandemic and Human Rights: A Continuum Approach' (2007) 19 *Florida Journal of International Law* 335.

Yamin A E, 'Not Just a Tragedy: Access to Medications as a Right under International Law' (2003) 21(2) *Boston University International Law Journal* 325.

Yelpaala K, 'Quo Vadis WTO? The Threat of TRIPS and the Biodiversity Convention Human Health and Food Security' (2012) 30 *Boston University International Law Journal* 55.

Yu P k, 'The Objectives and Principles of the TRIPS Agreement' (2009) 46 *Houston Law Review* 979, 1013.

7 Patents, access to medicines and the human right to development

This chapter explores the connection of health to socio-economic development and the protection of pharmaceutical patents. The chapter examines access to medicines as a right to development issue under the UN framework and under the African Charter. The chapter discusses the concept of development in international law and the right to development as a human right. The provisions of the General Agreement on Tariffs and Trade (GATT) and the Agreement on Trade Related aspects of Intellectual Property Rights (TRIPS Agreement) that are significant to the pursuit of development are addressed. It also discusses the technology transfer provisions in the TRIPS Agreement and how technical cooperation arrangement may be used to foster human development in Africa.

7.1 Introduction

Whilst there was a time when health was considered a consequence and not necessarily a determining factor for development,[1] modern theories of development do recognise the significance of human capital, of which health is an essential component.[2] The creation of wealth requires, inter alia, a healthy labour force and to that extent, an international agreement with the cardinal objective of fostering socio-economic development through trade in goods and services should not impose conditions likely to constitute real impediments to the ability of states to improve health.[3]

The problem with viewing development solely in the context of economic growth is that it fails to take cognisance of the fact that a majority of a country's citizens could be living in impoverished circumstances without access to

1 See generally P A Yotopoulos & J B Nugent, *Economics of Development: Empirical Investigations* (Harper & Row, 1976); L Taylor, *Macro Models for Developing Countries* (McGraw-Hill, 1979); A C Kelly, J G Williamson & R J Cheetham, *Dualistic Economic Development: Theory and History* (University of Chicago Press, 1972); T Morgan, *Economic Development: Concept and Strategy* (Harper & Row, 1975) 167.

2 L J Currat, A A Hyder, T C Nchinda & E Carey-Bumgarner, *10/90 Report on Health Research 1999* (Global Forum for Health Research, 1999).

3 K Yelpaala, 'Quo Vadis WTO? The Threat of TRIPS and the Biodiversity Convention Human Health and Food Security' (2012) 30 *Boston University International Law Journal* 55, 85.

essential goods while only a negligible proportion of the population captures a significant part of the nation's overall wealth.[4] The human development approach, based on the postulate that a society cannot experience real development without providing its people with the essential needs of life, is yet to receive the recognition it deserves in intellectual property (IP) globalisation.[5] IP may place a lopsided emphasis on wealth or utility maximisation while placing overall global social welfare and the world's most vulnerable people at a disadvantage.[6] The relation between IP and development is significant for both the developed and developing nations. Given that IP protection essentially imposes monopoly rights that may have significant implications for social welfare and access to knowledge as well as goods essential for human resource development, there is a need to situate the protection of IP within the concept of national development.

In the context of access to medicines, food security, technological innovations and human rights, it has been argued that the relations between IP and global governance do not produce fair distributional outcomes.[7] While current developments may suggest that many developed countries are not dissatisfied with the level of protection offered by existing IP multilateral treaties, developing and least developed countries continue to deprecate IP protection that tends to limit access to medicines, knowledge and other significant development resources.[8] Some developing countries have however made laws that provide for strong IP protection because they expect it to encourage foreign direct investment. Pharmaceutical patents have significant implications for access to medicines and by extension human development. This is because access to affordable medicines is critical to the attainment of good standard of living which is fundamental to the realisation of a high level of human development. IP protection in the access to medicines context should not as a result negatively impact the achievement of the highest attainable standard of health.

This chapter explores the connection of health to socio-economic development and the protection of pharmaceutical patents. The chapter examines access to medicines as a right to development issue under the UN framework and under the African Charter. The chapter discusses the concept of development in international law and the right to development as a human right. The provisions of the GATT and the TRIPS Agreement) that are significant to the pursuit of development are addressed. It also discusses the technology transfer provisions in the TRIPS Agreement and how technical cooperation arrangement may be used to foster human development in Africa.

4 M Chon, 'Intellectual Property and the Development Divide' (2006) 27 *Cardozo Law Review* 2821, 2832.
5 Ibid.
6 Ibid., 2834.
7 C Oguamanam 'IP in Global Governance: A Venture in Critical Reflection' (2011) 2(2) *WIPO Journal* 196, 199.
8 P K Yu, 'The Global Intellectual Property Order and Its Undetermined Future' (2009) 1(1) *WIPO Journal* 1.

7.1.1 The concept of development

The term 'development' should not be taken in isolation but must be placed in the appropriate context to be capable of any meaningful interpretation.[9] Development has always been one of the essential criteria for defining countries and peoples.[10] The development of countries, traditionally, is defined against the backdrop of their economic growth and the standard of living of their citizens.[11] Overtime, the concept has, however, been expanded to cover the social development of people as well as economic development. The position is put succinctly by Amartya Sen in the following terms:

> The end means of development require examination and scrutiny for a fuller understanding of the development process; it is simply not adequate to take as our basic objective just the maximization of income or wealth, which is, as Aristotle noted, "merely useful for the sake of something else". For the same reason economic growth cannot sensibly be treated as an end in itself. Development has to be more concerned with enhancing the lives we live and the freedom we enjoy.[12]

Writing in a similar vein, Peter Drahos defines development as being concerned with 'achieving a group of objectives for poor people including better educational and job opportunities, greater gendered equality, better health and nutrition, protection of the environment, natural resources and biodiversity'.[13] Richard Peet and Elaine Hartwick reject the idea of viewing economic growth as a metric of development. They maintain that development differs from economic growth because it is connected with circumstances surrounding production as well as social consequences such as income distribution and human welfare.[14]

Viewing national economic growth as a metric of development may not necessarily present an accurate picture of the standard of living of the populace. A nation may be recording substantial economic growth without ensuring an even circulation of the wealth amongst her populace. Economic growth does not necessarily translate to human development and there can hardly be real human development without economic growth. Accordingly, development for the

9 M Chemillier-Gendreau, 'Relations between the Ideology of Development and Development Law' in F Synder & P Slinn (eds.), *International Law of Development: Comparative Perspectives* (Professional Books, 1987) 57, 59.

10 R Gordon & J H Sylvester, 'Deconstructing Development' (2004) 22 *Wisconsin. International Law Journal* 1, 2.

11 A Allot, 'The Law of Development and the Development of Law' in F Synder & P Slinn (eds.), *International Law of Development: Comparative Perspectives* (Professional Books, 1987) 69, 70.

12 A Sen, *Development as Freedom* (Oxford University Press, 1999) 14; also cited in M Chon, 'Intellectual Property and the Development Divide' (2006) 27 *Cardozo Law Review* 2821.

13 P Drahos & R Mayne, *Global Intellectual Property Rights: Knowledge, Access and Development* (Palgrave MacMillan, 2002) 3.

14 R Peet with E Hartwick, *Theories of Development: Contentions, Arguments, Alternatives* (The Guilford Press, 2009) 1–2.

purposes of this discourse is to be understood in the contexts of both economic growth and human development as they both have considerable implications in relation to peoples' ability to achieve the highest attainable living standard.

7.1.2 The legal order for international economic law

The Bretton Woods Agreements were signed in 1944 by 44 countries to reduce national trade barriers and guard against economic repression which was recognised as one of the factors that instigated World War II.[15] The Agreements culminated in the emergence of the International Monetary Fund and the World Bank.[16] In 1947, 23 countries adopted the GATT to liberalise international trade. The GATT was originally concerned with trade in goods. But since the 1984 Uruguay Round of trade negotiations, which saw the establishment of the World Trade Organisation (WTO), the GATT now covers broader themes such as trade in services, investment and intellectual property (IP) rights. Today, the impact of the WTO and the suite of associated international trade agreements on socio-economic development on world's populations continue to be an issue of significant interest.[17]

Article XVIII.1 of the GATT states that the Contracting Parties recognise that the attainment of the objectives of this Agreement will be facilitated by the progressive development of their economies, particularly of those Contracting Parties the economies of which can only support low standards of living and are in the early stages of development.

Thus, whilst participation in international trade is capable of promoting economic growth, it is premised on a requirement that a country must already have attained a degree of economic development.[18]

A cardinal objective of the WTO in liberalising international trade is to promote sustainable development in Member countries. Whilst less developed countries may find it more difficult to benefit from the international economic system, the GATT contains some provisions to ease their participation in international trade. For instance, Article XXXVI.8 of the GATT provides that developed Contracting Parties should not expect reciprocity in relation to commitments made by them in trade negotiations to reduce or eliminate tariffs and should not create other hindrances to the trade of less developed Member countries.

The word 'development' in the original GATT 1947 context related mainly to the exploitation of resources towards the achievement of economic growth

15 E Kinney, 'Health Care Financing and Delivery in the US, Mexico and Canada: Finding and Establishing Intentional Principles for Sound Integration' (2009) 26(3) *Wisconsin International Law Journal* 935–965.

16 Ibid.

17 E D Kinney, 'Realization of the International Human Right to Health in an Economically Integrated North America' (2009) 37 *Journal of Law, Medicine and Ethics* 807, 808.

18 N Pires de Carvalho, *The TRIPS Regime of Patent Rights* (Kluwer Law International, 2nd ed., 2004) 434.

and not necessarily to advance the cause of underprivileged people or peoples.[19] Over time, though, the advancement of developing economies was accepted as a natural consequence of trade expansion. Today, development is portrayed as the all-embracing objective of international trade with the interest of developing countries now considered as requiring careful consideration in trade negotiations.[20] The current emphasis on development in the WTO has been described as the 'developmentification' of the WTO, which is considered as being done in furtherance of the WTO's quest for legitimacy.[21] This is unsurprising in view of the complaints arising from the asymmetrical rules of the WTO, especially in relation to IP protection, and problems they cause for countries striving to achieve developmental goals bearing in mind that most WTO Members are developing countries.[22]

Developing countries face these problems largely due to their weak bargaining positions, particularly in relation to the negotiation of bilateral free trade agreements under the WTO system. The current emphasis on development in the WTO system is seen as not only moving beyond influencing the aspirations associated with the organisation and its traditional mandate, but as signifying the potential recognition of development as a 'right' in global economic policymaking in general and the WTO in particular.[23] The expectation is that developing countries in particular and the international community in general can reasonably demand that the policies agreed upon in the WTO should be implemented to serve the right to development which must be understood to entail an obligation to reduce penury and enhance human capabilities all over the world.[24] The 'developmentification' of the WTO thus suggests that development is becoming a benchmark for assessing the success or otherwise of multilateral trade rules[25] and perhaps the international economic system.

7.2 The right to development as a human right

Whilst the right to development can now be said to be cognisable in international law, its status in terms of legal force remains debatable. Some hail it as a significant breakthrough in the history of human rights while others have described it

19 T Broude, 'The Rules(s) of Trade and the Rhetos of Development: Reflections on the Functional and Aspirational Legitimacy of the WTO' (2006) 45 *Columbia Journal of Transnational Law* 221, 223.

20 Word Trade Org. [WTO], Ministerial Declaration of 14 November 2001, WT/MIN(01)/DEC/1.

21 Ibid., 224.

22 See R Ricupero, 'Rebuilding Confidence in the Multilateral Trading System: Closing the "Legitimacy Gap"', in G P Sampson (ed.), *Role of the World Trade Organization in Global Governance* (United Nations University Press, 2001) 37, 49–50.

23 Broude, above n 19, 244.

24 Ibid., 245.

25 Sub-Comm. on Promotion and Protection of Human Rights, *Mainstreaming the Right to Development into International Trade Law and Policy at the World Trade Organization*, U.N. ESCOR, 56th Sess. Agenda Item 4, UN Doc. E/CN.4/Sub.2/2004/17 (9 June 2004) 15.

as nothing more than a distracting ideological initiative.[26] The United Nations (UN) adopted the Declaration on the Right to Development in 1986. The preamble to the Declaration recognises development as:

> ...a comprehensive economic, social, cultural, and political process, which aims at the constant improvement of the well-being of the entire population and of all individuals on the basis of their active, free and meaningful participation in development and in the fair distribution of benefits resulting therefrom.[27]

Article 8.1 addresses the issue of access to medicines by providing thus:

> States should undertake, at the national level, all necessary measures for the realization of the right to development and shall ensure, inter alia, equality of opportunity for all in their access to basic resources, education, health services, food, housing, employment and the fair distribution of income.

The Right to Development Declaration may have the long-term effect of removing the existing boundary between economic and non-economic development, but it has so far not been a significant means of legal change.[28] Despite this, the right to development, like the right to health, has assumed the status of a human right in international law. The right to development entails the continual improvement of the living standard of individuals and so has significant implications for public health. Accordingly, it stands to reason that trade and IP rights should not be employed in such a way as to obfuscate the ability of people to enjoy this right.

The UN Intergovernmental Working Group on the Right to Development was created to oversee the implementation of the right to development. The Working Group[29] in its recommendations for the period 1998–2010, by consensus concluded that IP protection should not undermine the enjoyment of human right to health or limit access to essential medicines.[30] It also stressed the importance of undertaking social impacts assessments in the areas of trade and development, and to strengthen human rights standards and principles in pursuing impact assessment of trade and development at both national and international levels.[31]

26 I D Bunn, 'The Right to Development: Implications for International Economic Law' (2000) 15 *American University Law Review* 1425, 1426.

27 UN Declaration on the Right to Development, GA Res 41/128, 97th plen mtg, UN Doc A/RES/41/128 (4 December 1986).

28 M Chon, 'Intellectual Property and the Development Divide' (2006) 27 *Cardozo Law Review* 2821, 2870.

29 The Working Group was created by the Commission on Human Rights resolution 1998/72 and endorsed by Economic and Social Council decision 1998/269, with the mandate to monitor and review the progress made in the enforcement and implementation of the right to development.

30 See *The Right to Development Report of the Secretary General* (UN Doc A/66/216) August 2011, 15–16.

31 Ibid.

It is pertinent to note that the TRIPS Agreement recognises the right of states to legitimately pursue their public interests and developmental goals, as stated Chapter 6.[32]

7.2.1 The right to development under the African Charter

Apart from the UN Declaration on the Right to Development, the right to development is well recognised in Africa through its entrenchment in the African Charter on Human and Peoples' Rights. Article 22 of the African Charter provides thus in relation to the right to development:

1 All peoples shall have the right to their economic, social and cultural development with due regard to their freedom and identity and in the equal enjoyment of the common heritage of mankind.
2 States shall have the duty, individually or collectively, to ensure the exercise of the right to development.

While the right to development in international law may not be justiciable as a human right, the right conferred under the African Charter is fully justiciable in the African human rights system through the operation of the Protocol to the African Charter on Human and Peoples' Rights on the Establishment of the African Court on Human and Peoples' Rights. While the right to development incorporates some of the elements in other human rights, it has also attained the status of a distinct and independent right that is owned by people collectively.[33] The all-encompassing nature of the right to development was well adumbrated in the following trenchant observation of the African Commission on Human and Peoples' Rights in *Sudan Human Rights Organisation & Centre on Housing Rights and Evictions (COHRE) v Sudan*:

> The attacks and forced displacement of Darfurian people denied them the opportunity to engage in economic, social and cultural activities. The displacement interfered with the right to education for their children and pursuit of other activities. Instead of deploying its resources to address the marginalisation in the Darfur, which was the main cause of the conflict, the Respondent State instead unleashed a punitive military campaign which constituted a massive violation of not only the economic social and cultural rights, but other individual rights of the Darfurian people. Based on the analysis hereinabove, concerning the nature and magnitude of the violations, the Commission finds that the Respondent State is in violation of 22 of the Africa Charter.[34]

32 See Section 6.6.3.

33 O Owoeye & J Oduwole, 'Development, Access to Medicines and the Ebola Virus Epidemic in West Africa' (2017) 24 *Journal of Law and Medicine* 722, 727.

34 Commission on Human and People's Rights, *Communication Nos 279/03-296/05*, 45th sess (27 May 2009).

Thus, the right to development under the African Charter can be viewed as broad enough to incorporate all the elements of the human rights covered by the International Covenant on Economic, Social and Cultural Rights and distinct enough to be an independent right. The right to development under the African Charter is also collectively and individually enforceable against the state and individuals and groups may pursue legal actions against their governments under the African Charter before the African Court on Human and Peoples' rights provided their countries have acceded to the Protocol Establishing the African Court.[35]

7.2.2 TRIPS and development

What is examined below is the concept of development in relation to the TRIPS Agreement. The major challenge with the right to development is that, like other social, economic and cultural rights, its status seems to be considered as more of a political declaration than a legal right. While every state seeks to pursue interests that promote sustainable development, the right to development in international law is yet to assume a level of legal recognition that would make it a powerful defence for derogating from obligations directly arising from international conventions such as the WTO Agreements. This however does not mean the right to development is of no significance in taking advantage of all available flexibilities in the international IP regime. Whilst development as a human right may not have an overwhelming presence, the pursuit of development is still arguably the most powerful justification for IP flexibilities.

Due to the fact that the WTO is mostly concerned with trade, IP is viewed as more or less a commodity. The WTO regime does not seem to take sufficient cognisance of the fact that IP not only encompasses cultural values, it equally protects goods that are essential to social welfare.[36] The protection of IP should therefore strike a balance between access and proprietary interests.[37] In this regard, the TRIPS Agreement lacks robust exceptions for the protection of national interests.[38]

The preamble to the TRIPS Agreement expressly recognises developmental and technological objectives as part of the underlying public policy objectives of national systems of IP. It also acknowledges the need for utmost flexibility in the enforcement of IP laws and regulations especially for least developed countries so that they can develop a sound and sustainable technological base. The objectives and principles of the TRIPS Agreement enunciated in Articles 7 and 8 are particularly relevant to the link between IP and development.

35 See Article 5 of the Protocol to the African Charter on Human and Peoples' Rights on the Establishment of the African Court on Human and Peoples' Rights.

36 G B Dinwoodie & R C Dreyfuss 'Designing a Global Intellectual Property System Responsive to Change: The WTO, WIPO and Beyond' (2009) 46 *Houston Law Review* 1187, 1194–1195.

37 Ibid.

38 See Section 6.5.3.

The emphasis in Article 8 on development can be said to have incorporated a substantive equality principle into the TRIPS Agreement.[39] A problem with the weight to be attached to Article 8 however stems largely from the fact that the proviso contained in Article 8 stipulates that measures taken to enhance socio-economic and developmental goals must be consistent with the TRIPS Agreement. Thus, any measure taken must be expressly or implicitly allowed by the TRIPS Agreement and no measure that is at variance with the provisions of the Agreement can be valid. The implication of this is that the promotion of socio-economic interests of a nation must not jeopardise the protection of the rights guaranteed in TRIPS.

The conflict between TRIPS and development has been described as resulting from the need to strike a balance between social desirability of unrestrained dissemination of available know-how and the need for society to create economic incentives for creators of new information.[40] The conflict seems to have been resolved in favour of rewarding the creators of new information.[41]

Ruth Gana opines that although IPRs might also have the status of human rights, the right to development nonetheless is a more compelling interest that overrides rights in inventions.[42] She suggests that strong protection of IPRs possessed by foreign corporations might have negative economic effects on developing countries because of the ability of right holders to determine the availability or otherwise of certain goods in a given market.[43] IP is undeniably significant for industrial progress given the protection it offers inventive activities and while it may not be the sole prescription for development, it remains an essential part of a development plan.[44] But the IP component of any national development plan must make allowance for the peculiarities of the society for which it is fashioned. IP protection must not be so rigid or excessive as to become a barrier to access or even a more subtle but real impediment to human development.

In sum, whilst TRIPS does recognise the need for countries to take developmental interests into account in the protection of IPRs, its language does not really allow countries to adopt measures that are not directly sanctioned by it, even if these are unequivocally in the public or national interest. Nonetheless, since a fundamental objective of the IP system is to promote socio-economic and technological advancement,[45] it is arguable that measures that are clearly geared towards that end should be presumed to be in consonance with the provisions

39 M Chon, 'Intellectual Property and the Development Divide' (2006) 27 *Cardozo Law Review* 2821, 2836; see also Section 6.1.2.

40 R J Gutowski, 'The Marriage of Intellectual Property and International Trade in the TRIPS Agreement: Strange Bedfellows or a Match Made in Heaven?' (1999) *Buffalo Law Review* 713, 746.

41 Ibid., 746–747.

42 R L Gana (Okediji), 'The Myth of Development, The Progress of Rights: Human Rights to Intellectual Property and Development' (1996) 18 *Law & Policy* 315, 326.

43 Ibid.

44 Gutowski, above n 40, 760.

45 See Section 2.1.2.

of TRIPS. A purposive interpretation should therefore be adopted to give effect to such measures, except where they are completely inconsistent or irreconcilable with the provisions of the TRIPS Agreement.

7.3 Intellectual property, economic growth and development

As noted earlier,[46] the focus of this Chapter and the context in which the right to development is used encompasses both economic growth and human development. There are many scholars who favour the concept of development as a measure of economic growth. What follows considers the extent to which IP can be rightly said to foster economic growth.

Development is progressively becoming one of the cardinal objectives of the international legal regime within which IP functions.[47] Barbosa et al have recommended following interpreting Articles 7 and 8 of the TRIPS Agreement to promote national interests while positioning 'development' as quality principle the implementation of intellectual property and trade agreements.[48]

Intellectual property laws limit the options for liberalising knowledge goods to enhance domestic capacity building for human development.[49] This is the 'development as freedom' model.[50] The UN Development Programme (UNDP) and the World Health Organization increasingly rely on the human development index as a development metric.[51] IP and trade institutions on the other hand, adopt the 'development as growth' model.[52] The latter, propounded by the IMF and the World Bank,[53] considers IP as enhancing economic growth through greater access to international trade, foreign direct investment (FDI) and technology transfer.[54] Ruth Okediji has advocated the need for resource allocation, including IPRs allocation, to take the promotion of domestic welfare into account as globalisation does not connote a total loss of sovereignty.[55] In another article, she further argues that the international system should only pierce the sovereignty veil when states fail in their mandate, either by

46 See Section 7.1.
47 See D B Barbosa, M Chon & M von Hase, 'Slouching Towards Development in International Intellectual Property Law' (2007) *Michigan State Law Review* 71, 72.
48 Ibid., 73–74.
49 Ibid., 75.
50 Ibid., 76.
51 See UNDP, Human Development Report 1991; World Health Organization, Guiding Principles for Strategic Resource Allocation, RC/ 2005/1 (1 June 2005).
52 See D B Barbosa, M Chon & M von Hase, 'Slouching Towards Development in International Intellectual Property Law' (2007) *Michigan State Law Review* 71, 77.
53 J E Stigliz, *Globalisation and its Discontents* (W W Norton & Company 2002).
54 D J Gervais, 'Intellectual Property, Trade & Development: The State of Play' (2005) 74 *Fordham Law Review* 505, 516–520.
55 R G Okediji, 'Copyright and Public Welfare in Global Perspective' (1999)7 *Indiana Journal of Global Legal Studies* 125.

offering inordinate IP protection or by having a patently inadequate system of IP protection.[56]

Intellectual property is seen as having the potential of facilitating development by encouraging FDI,[57] which is believed to be capable of increasing knowledge capacity, inventive activity and economic growth in developing countries.[58] Margaret Chon observes that policy debates over development concerns such as access to medicines have not been addressed under either IP law or trade generally but within human rights and public health paradigms.[59]

Intellectual property seems to promise economic growth to nations through FDI. This innovation-driven growth may, nonetheless, be more of a mirage. This is especially so in least developed countries as multinational companies are unlikely to enter the poorest countries, however strong their IP regime, because consumers would be too poor to pay for the goods.[60] Besides, many developing countries hold the view that a harmonised system that seeks to establish a stronger IP regime would only benefit some developed countries at the detriment of many developing countries.[61] For instance, it was revealed in a particular study that the major beneficiary of the TRIPS Agreement is the US with developing nations being the major contributors.[62] This is because the US is the biggest producer and exporter of IP products in the world and the developing countries are the major importers of such products.

The role of IP in economic growth inevitably varies from country to country.[63] Whilst IP has played a significant role in the economic advancement of the US over the last three decades, it is also true that until 1982, the US had one of the world's least protective patent laws. It also had weak copyright law until 1978 and its competition law was largely interventionist with a strong doctrine of patent misuse until the 1980s.[64] Countries like Brazil, China, India, Japan, Korea and Malaysia were all able to record significant economic growth without strong IP

56 R L Okediji, 'The Institutions of Intellectual Property: New Trends in an Old Debate' (2004) 98 *American Society of International Law Proceedings* 219, 221.

57 K E Maskus & J H Reichman, 'The Globalization of Private Knowledge Goods and the Privatization of Global Public Goods' in K E. Maskus & J H. Reichman (eds.), *International Public Goods and Transfer of Technology Under a Globalized Intellectual Property Regime* (Cambridge University Press, 2005) 3, 11–15.

58 Gervais, above n 54, 508–509.

59 M Chon, 'Intellectual Property and the Development Divide' (2006) 27 *Cardozo Law Review* 2821, 2863.

60 Commission on Intellectual Property Rights, *Integrating Intellectual Property Rights and Development Policy* (2002) 40–46 www.iprcommission.org/papers/pdfs/final_report/ciprfullfinal.pdf accessed 27 January 2019.

61 D Chun, 'Patent Law Harmonization in the Age of Globalisation: The Necessity and Strategy for a Pragmatic Outcome' (2011) 93 *Journal of Patent and Trademark Office Society* 127, 129.

62 P McCalman, *Reaping What You Sow: An Empirical Analysis of International Patent Harmonization* (Working papers in Economics and Econometrics, June 1999) 30.

63 J H Reichman, 'Intellectual Property in the Twenty-First Century: Will the Developing Countries Lead or Follow? (2009) *Houston Law Review* 1115, 1116.

64 Ibid., 1117.

protection.[65] India developed a very strong generic pharmaceutical industry because of its restriction on the patentability of pharmaceuticals.[66] It is nonetheless true that emerging economies like China, Brazil and Korea may not attain significant levels of economic growth in the future without the appropriate structures for IP protection[67] as they may be unable to convert their indigenous intangibles into commercial knowledge goods without the suitable IP laws and policies.[68]

Intellectual property rights are, however, just one component of overall economic growth and, as Reichman puts it, for countries at the early stage of development:

> A sound agricultural policy or a sound pro-competitive industrial policy with a supportive political and legal infrastructure are more likely to stimulate economic growth than intellectual property laws.[69]

Reichman further notes that the experience in a number of OECD countries is beginning to show that excessively protectionist IP regimes can stifle innovation by making it too expensive and cumbersome to achieve while properly designed IP laws protect small and medium-size firms from the anticompetitive practices of larger corporations.[70]

7.3.1 Patent harmonisation and development

The agitation for a harmonised patent system is in response to the overwhelming challenges posed by globalisation and internationalisation.[71] The limited capability of patent offices and the growing number of patent backlogs are some of the reasons for seeking a harmonised framework.[72] The patenting of emerging

65 R C Dreyfuss, 'The Role of India, China, Brazil and Other Emerging Economies in Establishing Access Norms for Intellectual Property and Intellectual Property Lawmaking' (Int'l Law & Justice Working Paper 2009/5, 2009) 2–4, 11.

66 A Kapczynski, 'Harmonization and Its Discontents: A Case Study of TRIPS Implementation in India's Pharmaceutical Sector' (2009) 97 *California Law Review* 1571.

67 R C Dreyfuss, 'The Role of India, China, Brazil and Other Emerging Economies in Establishing Access Norms for Intellectual Property and Intellectual Property Lawmaking' (Int'l Law & Justice Working Paper 2009/5, 2009) 2–4, 11.

68 D Gervais, 'TRIPS and Development', in D J Gervais (ed.), *Intellectual Property, Trade and Development: Strategies to Optimise Economic Development in a TRIPS Plus Era* (Oxford University Press, 2007) 3; P Yu, 'Intellectual Property, Economic Development, and the China Puzzle' in D J Gervais (ed.), *Intellectual Property, Trade and Development: Strategies to Optimise Economic Development in a TRIPS Plus Era* (Oxford University Press, 2007)173, 195.

69 J H Reichman, 'Intellectual Property in the Twenty-First Century: Will the Developing Countries Lead or Follow?' (2009) *Houston Law Review* 1115, 1117.

70 Ibid., 1121.

71 D Chun, 'Patent Law Harmonization in the Age of Globalisation: The Necessity and Strategy for a Pragmatic Outcome' (2011) 93 *Journal of Patent and Trademark Office Society* 127, 142–147.

72 E R Kazenske, *Patent Offices: Strategies For Work Sharing* (Fordham IP Conference 2009) http://fordhamipconference.com/wp-content/uploads/2010/08/Kaz_Kazenske_Patent_Offices_Strategy_for_Work_Sharing.pdf accessed 27 January 2019.

advanced technologies requires highly specialised knowledge that makes it expedient for patent offices to cooperate internationally in issuing timely patentability criteria.[73] The quest for harmonisation therefore has arisen as a result of the need to devise a practical and effective solution to the problem of increasing number of patent applications and haphazard validity criteria in a globalised world.[74]

The 'one size fits all' approach to IP may, on a global scale, aggravate the difficult and significant inequalities of access and information that are the current features of development in regional and national terms.[75] It is doubtful whether the current exceptions and limitations to patent rights suffice to give force to domestic welfare values as global IP policymakers continue to view patents in property rights terms.[76] The substantive legal harmonisation of patent law may be viewed with circumspection in countries with no competitive framework for patent protection.[77] This is because implementing a harmonised system would involve making alterations to existing legislation, strengthening IP administration and providing effective administrative framework for enforcement, all of which would certainly entail a huge financial cost particularly in developing countries.[78]

The harmonised system established by the TRIPS Agreement may also impede state's freedom to use their discretion in fashioning a system that suits their peculiar needs. Given that most developing countries are far from being in the frontline of innovative activities, they would ordinarily prefer a patent system that would be flexible enough as not to constitute a potential or real threat to national development. The harmonised system enshrined in TRIPS has, conversely, restricted to a large extent the ability of developing countries to use patents as a tool for fashioning national economic and industrial policies that would bring about sustainable development.[79] Jerome Reichman and Rochelle Dreyfuss put the position succinctly when they opine that it would be ill advised to adopt deep substantive harmonisation as that would further impede technological advancement in developing countries.[80]

Although TRIPS prohibits 'free riding' that would impede the recovery of costs invested in research and development, it is capable in its own right of impeding development by reducing the spread of technology, stifling innovation and hampering the ability of developing countries to compete in markets

73 D Chun, 'Patent Law Harmonization in the Age of Globalisation: The Necessity and Strategy for a Pragmatic Outcome' (2011) 93 *Journal of Patent and Trademark Office Society* 127, 142–147.

74 Ibid.

75 K Aoki, 'Notes Toward a Cultural Geography of Authorship' (1996) 48 *Stanford Law Review* 1293, 1344–1345.

76 Ibid., 1345–1347.

77 D Chun, 'Patent Law Harmonization in the Age of Globalisation: The Necessity and Strategy for a Pragmatic Outcome' (2011) 93 *Journal of Patent and Trademark Office Society* 127, 142–147.

78 Ibid.

79 Getachew Mengistie, *The Impact of the International Patent System on Developing Countries* (World Intellectual Property Organization, 2003) 33 www.wipo.int/edocs/mdocs/govbody/en/a_39/a_39_13_add_1.pdf accessed 27 January 2019.

80 J Reichman & R C Dreyfuss, 'Harmonisation Without Consensus: Critical Reflections on Drafting a Substantive Patent Law Treaty' (2007) 57 *Duke Law Journal* 85, 91.

currently being controlled by the industrial world.[81] It is therefore expedient to interpret TRIPS in a way that recognises the potential hindrances that rigid IP standards may pose to human development.[82] Dongwook Chun has argued that since substantive legal harmonisation of the patent system is difficult to achieve, substantive administrative measures might be a more realistic alternative as they do not require changing existing laws or concluding international conventions.[83] The substantive administrative measures could avoid heavy financial costs or need to pass through the rigorous process of obtaining parliamentary approval.[84] Chun argues that the substantive administrative harmonisation would be implemented through the cooperation of interested patent offices and it would focus on the patent prosecution process rather than the enforcement or infringement, which would require some legal foundation.[85] The basic goal of the substantive administrative measure is work sharing[86] which, it is believed, will give patent offices a better understanding of each other's work method.[87]

Whilst administrative harmonisation will undoubtedly make it easier for countries to offer IP protection that is not adverse to their national interest, the drafters of the TRIPS Agreement desired more than mere administrative harmonisation. The need for a global framework for IP protection necessitated not just administrative but substantive harmonisation. The substantive harmonisation process has reached a level where it would be futile to recommend its abrogation. The preferred option is to work with a substantive harmonisation framework that makes allowance for countries to differ on points of detail where socio-economic and technological development interests so require. If all states act in good faith in pursuing substantive harmonisation without fostering the interest of well-developed economies at the expense of those struggling to develop, it could hold long-term benefits for all nations irrespective of their current level of development.

7.3.2 The WTO and WIPO development agendas

The concerns of the developing world over the shortcomings of the TRIPS Agreement[88] and international framework for patent protection led to a concerted push for the establishment of a developmental agenda at the beginning of the new millennium.[89] This has also brought about a more IP conscious

81 J H Barton, J L Goldstein, T E Josling & R H Steinberg, *The Evolution of the Trade Regime: Politics, Law and Economics of the GATT and WTO* (Princeton University Press, 2006) 142.

82 Barbosa et al., above n 39, 91.

83 Chun, above n 77, 147–148.

84 Ibid.

85 Ibid.

86 Ibid.

87 Ibid.

88 See Section 2.2.2.

89 P K Yu, 'The Global Intellectual Property Order and Its Undetermined Future' (2009) 1(1) *WIPO Journal* 1, 11.

public.[90] The WTO Doha Round was launched following the September 11 attacks to nurture public confidence in the WTO and give greater weight to the interests of less developed nations.[91] Of particular significance in the field of IP was the adoption of the Doha Ministerial Declaration and the Doha Declaration on TRIPS and Public Health.[92] Paragraph 19 of the Doha Ministerial Declaration deals with the work conducted by the TRIPS Council, and reads:

> We instruct the Council for TRIPS, in pursuing its work programme including under the review of Article 27.3(b), the review of the implementation of the TRIPS Agreement under Article 71.1 and the work foreseen pursuant to paragraph 12 of this declaration, to examine, inter alia, the relationship between the TRIPS Agreement and the Convention on Biological Diversity, the protection of traditional knowledge and folklore, and other relevant new developments raised by members pursuant to Article 71.1. In undertaking this work, the TRIPS Council shall be guided by the objectives and principles set out in Articles 7 and 8 of the TRIPS Agreement and shall take fully into account the development dimension.[93]

Whilst the Doha Round focused largely on access to medicines in developing countries, it also considered issues such as the connection between TRIPS and the Biodiversity Convention and the protection of folklore and traditional knowledge.[94]

In parallel, Argentina and Brazil introduced a proposal to establish a World Intellectual Property Organization (WIPO) Development Agenda to the WIPO General Assembly in October 2004. The WIPO Development Agenda was formally adopted by the WIPO General Assembly in October 2007.[95] Paragraph 9 of the Development Agenda provides that WIPO should promote the use of IP and technical cooperation in a manner supportive of public interest flexibilities and technological development.[96]

It emphasises the need for IP agreements and minimum standards to be fashioned in a way responsive to the different levels of development and social needs

90 See P K Yu, 'A Tale of Two Development Agendas' (2009) 35 *Ohio Northern University Law Review* 465, 540–573.

91 L Amoore et al., Series Preface to Amrita Narlikar, *International Trade and Developing Countries: Bargaining Coalitions in the GATT & WTO* (Routledge 2003) xiii; see also Section 1.2.2.

92 P K Yu, 'A Tale of Two Development Agendas' (2009) 35 *Ohio Northern University Law Review* 465, 512–513.

93 Word Trade Org. [WTO], Ministerial Declaration of 14 November 2001, WT/MIN(01)/DEC/1, 41 I.L.M. 746 (2002).

94 P K Yu, 'A Tale of Two Development Agendas' (2009) 35 *Ohio Northern University Law Review* 465, 515.

95 WIPO Press Release, *Member States Adopt a Development Agenda for WIPO* (1 October 2007), www.wipo.int/pressroom/en/articles/2007/article_0071.html accessed 22 October 2013.

96 WIPO, Proposal to Establish a Development Agenda for WIPO: An Elaboration of Issues Raised in Document WO/GA/31/11, IIM/1/4 (6 April 2005).

and industrial challenges of Member countries.[97] Sisule Musungu and Graham Dutfield have argued that WIPO should pursue broad development measures that would ensure developing countries are not deprived of the benefits of the modern scientific and technological advancements in health, communication technology, food and nutrition amongst others.[98]

According to Neil Netanel, the WIPO Development Agenda favours the position that strong IP protection does not necessarily promote creativity, technology transfer or development.[99] He notes that the Agenda has firmly placed the advantages of national flexibilities in the implementation of IP treaty provisions, access to knowledge and UN development objectives within WIPO's mandate.[100] Whilst it is easy to focus on the concerns emanating from the TRIPS Agreement and efforts to address them in the Doha Round,[101] it is also important not to ignore current developments in WIPO that may equally play a profound role in resolving some of the major concerns in the global IP regime.

The concept of development has not been given a particular definition in the WTO jurisprudence. The WTO Appellate Body tacitly avoided a functional definition of development in the *Generalized System of Preferences (GSP) case* but it noted that different countries may have different development needs.[102] India had alleged in the GSP case that the European Communities (EC) scheme of generalised tariff preferences (GSP scheme) would affect India's export of pharmaceuticals to the EC and was therefore inconsistent with the most-favoured-nation principle and the Decision on Differential and More Favourable Treatment, Reciprocity, and Fuller Participation of Developing Countries (the 'Enabling Clause').[103] The Appellate Body, while acknowledging that the development needs of countries are bound to differ, found that the EC was bound to accord the same treatment to similarly-situated GSP beneficiaries and that the EC had failed to justify the challenged measure under the Enabling Clause. The Panel similarly noted in *Brazil – Export Financing Programme for Aircraft* that the question of what the development needs of a nation are is one within the exclusive preserve of the developing country in question.[104] Canada had argued in that case that the use of export subsidies by Brazil under the WTO Agreement on Subsidies and Countervailing

97 Ibid.

98 S F Musungu & G Dutfield, *Multilateral Agreements and a TRIPS-plus World: The World Intellectual Property Organisation (WIPO)* (Quaker United Nations Office, TRIPS Issues Paper No. 3, 2003) 18.

99 N W Netanel ed., *The WIPO Development Agenda and Its Development Policy Context* (Oxford University Press, 2009) 1, 2.

100 Ibid.

101 See P K Yu, 'A Tale of Two Development Agendas' (2009) 35 *Ohio Northern University Law Review* 465, 521.

102 Appellate Body Report, European Communities – Conditions for the Granting of Tariff Preferences to Developing Countries, WT/DS246/AB/R (7 April 2004) 157–174.

103 GATT/WTO Decision on Differential and More Favourable Treatment, Reciprocity, and Fuller Participation of Developing Countries.

104 Panel Report, Brazil – Export Financing Programme for Aircraft, ¶ 7.89, WT/DS46/R (14 April 1999).

Measures was inconsistent with Brazil's development needs. The Panel noted that the question of development needs was of a peculiarly economic and political nature and one that the Panel was not competent to review. The Panel held the view that Canada had failed to present sufficient evidence to raise a presumption that Brazil's use of export subsidies was inconsistent with her development needs. The sense of restraint exercised by the WTO judicial body in introducing development concerns into the WTO jurisprudence is understandable in view of the fact that doing so might disrupt the heritage of trade rules.[105] It will also be very difficult to decipher the legal confines of the concept of development from the myriad of largely directory legal texts making reference to it.[106] The WTO trade regime is built on the foundational Most Favoured Nations (MFN) principle which is a firmly established norm. However, the pursuit of development requires some relativity and divisibility which would require the WTO functional principle of MFN to give way to new aspirations.[107] The MFN reciprocity principle may however be largely unsuitable for an institutional system that seeks to promote development goals in poor countries rather than obliterating trade barriers.[108]

It is noteworthy that the WTO MFN principle does not apply to regional trade agreements (RTAs) within the WTO multilateral trade system. RTAs can be used by developing countries to foster their national interest and development goals. The proliferation of free trade agreements and RTAs in the WTO system is raising concerns as to the continuing relevance of the MFN principle. RTAs have nonetheless become an integral and indispensable part of the WTO system and developing countries that do not take full advantage of them are likely to lose out on a number of benefits that others enjoy.[109]

In sum, there seems to be a general trend within WIPO and the WTO towards ensuring that the IP system takes development concerns into account. This will require a degree of relativity which, prima facie, may appear incompatible with the WTO MFN principle, but arguably is still capable of being accommodated within the WTO system through the use of free trade agreements. WIPO seems to have been more responsive so far to the development concerns of poor countries than the WTO and there is need for the WTO to take the concept of development beyond a mere inchoate recognition to a more cognisable obligation in its institutional framework.

7.4 The TRIPS technology transfer regime and implications for development

This section examines the technology transfer provisions embedded in Articles 66 and 67 of TRIPS. Technology transfer plays a significant role as a catalyst

105 Broude, above n 19, 254.
106 Ibid.
107 Ibid.
108 Ibid.
109 This issue is fully explored in Chapter 9.

for economic growth and development.[110] Given that new technologies are overwhelmingly based in developed countries, developing countries must rely largely on access to foreign inventions to be able to incorporate new technologies into their local production structures.[111] Local production will create more employment opportunities, boost industrial policy and development goals, diminish procurement and distribution problems, enhance the local tax base and reduce the demand for foreign currency reserves as well as import financing.[112]

The Preamble of the TRIPS Agreement explicitly recognises the special need of developing countries in relation to technological advancement by providing thus:

> Recognizing the underlying policy objectives of national systems for the protection of intellectual property, including developmental and technological objectives: Recognizing also the needs of the least-developed country Members in respect of maximum flexibility in the domestic implementation of laws and regulations in order to enable them to create a sound and viable technological base....

Another provision of TRIPS with particular relevance to development is Article 66(2), which enjoins developed country Members to encourage technology transfer to least developed countries. It reads:

> Developed country Members shall provide incentives to enterprises and institutions in their territories for the purpose of promoting and encouraging technology transfer to least-developed country Members in order to enable them to create a sound and viable technological base.

Article 66(2) recognises that the protection of many areas of IP is only relevant in countries where some degree of technological base exists.[113] The abject poverty in least developed countries makes it difficult for them to participate fully in international trade or even benefit from the rewards international trade in goods and services offers.[114] Article 66(2) therefore imposes an obligation on developed country Members to provide incentives to enterprises and institutions in their countries to promote technology transfer to least developed countries. It is noteworthy that the obligation on developed countries to provide incentives to encourage technology transfer only applies to least developed countries and not

110 K E Maskus, 'Using the International Trading System to Foster Technology Transfer for Economic Development' (2005) *Michigan State Law Review* 219.

111 Ibid., 220.

112 B K Baker, 'Arthritic Flexibilities for Accessing Medicines: Analysis of WTO Action Regarding Paragraph 6 of the Doha Declaration on the TRIPS Agreement and Public Health' (2004) 14 *Indiana International and Comparative Law Review*, 613, 644.

113 N Pires de Carvalho, above n 18, 434.

114 Ibid.

developing countries in general. Further, the implementation of this provision remains quite nebulous due largely to the generality of the text.[115]

Nevertheless, this provision was reinforced in Paragraph 7 of the Doha Declaration on TRIPS and Public Health where the WTO Ministers reaffirmed

> …the commitment of developed-country members to provide incentives to their enterprises and institutions to promote and encourage technology transfer to least-developed country members pursuant to Article 66.2.

The WTO Ministerial Conference has confirmed that Article 66.2 is not merely directory but mandatory. This is evident in the Decision on Implementation-Related Issues and Concerns adopted in Doha on 14 November 2001. Subparagraph 112 of the Decision on Implementation states:

> Reaffirming that the provisions of Article 66.2 of the TRIPS Agreement are mandatory, it is agreed that the TRIPS Council shall put in place a mechanism for ensuring the monitoring and full implementation of the obligations in question.

Indeed, the existence or creation of a 'technological base' is sine qua non to building an advanced and industrial economy.[116] The Council for TRIPS adopted the Implementation of Article 66.2 of the TRIPS Agreement: Decision of the Council for TRIPS in February 2003. The Article 66.2 Implementation Decision established mechanisms for ensuring the full implementation of the obligations in Article 66.2 including an obligation to submit annual reports on actions taken pursuant to the commitment.

The obligation of developed country WTO Members, however, ends at providing incentives. There is no obligation to intervene directly in the transfer of technology.[117] Their role is therefore no more than encouraging private holders of IPRs to engage in business partnerships with local firms in least developed countries.[118] Daniel Gervais has noted that the ability of developed state governments to foster technology transfer is usually limited by two factors: that governments do not own the vast majority of the available technologies; and that they cannot compel the private sector to transfer the technologies.[119] Thus, the incentives provided by developed country governments can only serve the purpose of promoting, encouraging and facilitating technology transfer projects

115 C M Correa, *Trade Related Aspects of Intellectual Property Rights: A Commentary on the TRIPS Agreement* (Oxford University Press 2007) 501.

116 See D Gervais, *The TRIPS Agreement: Drafting History and Analysis* (Sweet & Maxwell 3rd ed., 2008) 522.

117 Pires de Carvalho, above n 18, 435–436.

118 Ibid., 436.

119 D Gervais, *The TRIPS Agreement: Drafting History and Analysis* (Sweet & Maxwell, 3rd ed., 2008) 525.

in least developed countries.[120] To this may be added another challenge highlighted by Maskus, namely that even where governments in developed countries are willing to offer substantial incentives, they are likely to encounter stiff domestic political opposition in doing so.[121] He further argues that Article 66.2 should be expanded to include all developing countries especially those with no significant science and technology base as the current designation of 'least developed countries' deprives many truly underdeveloped countries of the benefit of Article 66.2 for no legitimate reason.[122]

In a similar vein, Article 67 enjoins developed countries to provide technical and financial cooperation to developing and least developed countries in the implementation of the TRIPS Agreement.

The technical cooperation envisaged in Article 67 deals essentially with the preparation of laws and regulations that are TRIPS-compliant, the establishment or restructuring of national offices and the training of personnel.[123] The technical cooperation is also subject to 'mutually agreed terms' which means that although it is obligatory on developed country Members to provide technical and financial support, its supply rests on the willingness of developed countries and the resources they choose to allocate for that purpose.[124] While Article 67 does not mention international transfer of technology, its scope is arguably wide enough to cover means of making Article 66 effective. The technical assistance would include programmes aimed at enhancing the ability of least developed countries to increase the inflow of technology transfer.[125]

In 2001, the WTO constituted a Working Group on Trade and Technology Transfer to examine the interface between trade and technology transfer and available options to bring about enhanced international technology transfer in developing countries.[126] Correa views TRIPS as a mechanism for protecting the market power of global information developers that may eventually make the transfer of technology to poor countries more arduous.[127] However, Maskus has argued that whether international technology transfer would increase or diminish because of TRIPS would depend on local factors such as investment climate, market competition, availability of skilled workforce and governance policies.[128] Maskus therefore posits that while IPRs might be a crucial factor in determining

120 Ibid.
121 Maskus, above n 110, 236.
122 Ibid., 239.
123 Gervais, above n 122, 528.
124 C M Correa, *Trade Related Aspects of Intellectual Property Rights: A Commentary on the TRIPS Agreement* (Oxford University Press 2007), 502.
125 Maskus, above 110, 226.
126 Ibid., 221.
127 C M Correa, 'Can the TRIPS Agreement Foster Technology Transfer to Developing Countries?' in K E Maskus & J H Reichman (eds.), *International Public Goods and the Transfer of Technology under a Globalized Intellectual Property Regime* (Cambridge University Press, 2005) 227–256.
128 Maskus, above n 110, 222.

the volume and quality of technology transfer, it is neither necessary nor sufficient to establish significant inflows of technology.[129]

Paragraph 7 of the Doha Paragraph-6 Implementation Decision makes reference to the need for technology transfer in the pharmaceutical sector. Pharmaceutical manufacturing capacity appeared to have abated with the advent of TRIPS as many major manufacturers chose to shut down the local 'finishing factories' that were originally established to meet the pre-TRIPS local working requirements.[130] It remains to be seen if TRIPS has really been instrumental in facilitating technology transfer in developing countries since its emergence over eighteen years ago.

Though there are technology transfer obligations in TRIPS, these are relevant only to the extent that they encourage innovators and companies in developed countries to transfer their technical skills to developing countries. There is no obligation on developed countries to become directly involved in technology transfer under the TRIPS Agreement. Additionally, developing countries cannot count on TRIPS to enhance foreign technology transfer in their countries and instead must direct their energies into creating suitable investment climate for the transfer of technology as well as the development of IP laws capable of promoting the transfer of technology without making the process of doing so unnecessarily onerous. Developing countries therefore have a greater obligation to create conducive investment climate for the TRIPS technology transfer provisions to be of any real significance to them.

7.5 Pharmaceutical patents, health and development

It has been argued that the TRIPS Agreement holds more benefits for developed countries and that IP protection has not been shown to result in any significant development for developing countries.[131] There exists a real nexus between health and development and the access to medicines problem consequently has significant implications for human capacity building and development. As discussed in Chapter 4, human rights activists in particular have been pursuing human rights advocacy to enhance access to medicines especially with respect to the HIV/AIDS epidemic.[132] In Chapter 4, it was highlighted that in Latin America, advocates have been able to successfully rely on human rights provisions in national constitutions to compel governments to provide HIV treatment for people living with the disease.[133] The efforts of activists also resulted in the establishment of a scheme to procure and make available drugs for those in need through the public health system in Brazil.[134] The significance of health to the

129 Ibid., 223.

130 Baker, above n 112, 644.

131 See Gutowski, above n 40, 746.

132 Z Lazzarini, 'Access to HIV Drugs: Are we Changing the Two World Paradigm?' (2002) 17 *Connecticut Journal of International Law* 281, 289.

133 Ibid.

134 Ibid.

empowerment of populations and their socio-economic development is well reflected in the following trenchant observation of Gostin:

> Without minimum levels of health, people cannot fully engage in social interactions, participate in the political process, exercise rights of citizenship, generate wealth, create art, and provide for the common security.... Population health becomes a transcendent value because a certain level of human functioning is a prerequisite for activities that are critical to the public's welfare—social, political, and economic.[135]

The issue here is whether stronger or weaker IP protection better enhances the development of developing countries. This cannot be theoretically ascertained but requires empirical analysis.[136] Some empirical research suggests that stronger IP protection is positively connected to some aspects of development, such as foreign technology licensing, foreign investment and higher degree of trade.[137] However, significant variability amongst countries and sectors prompts the conclusion that the effects of stronger IP protection will be largely informed by the underlying conditions in each country.[138] In a similar vein, the World Bank has recommended that countries should adopt an IP strategy suitable to their level of development and then meticulously determine if any IP provision ought to be included in their various trade agreements.[139]

It has also been argued that strong IP protection is not always in the best interest of industrialised states as it not only results in short-term welfare loss but may also stifle innovation in the long run due to the barriers built around the free flow of knowledge.[140] The access to medicines debate has focused largely on the use of compulsory licensing and parallel importation in addressing the problem without the same level of focus on capacity building in developing countries. There is a real need to fashion IPRs in a way that will serve development interests.[141] The pursuit of development is accordingly germane in establishing a strategic and sustainable framework for access to medicines. IPRs must promote capacity building and technology transfer, especially in relation to pharmaceutical manufacturing capacity in order to provide a durable solution to the access to medicines problem.

135 L O Gostin, 'Meeting Basic Survival Needs of the World's Least Healthy People: Towards a Framework on Global Health' (2008) 96 *George Town Law Journal* 331, 344.

136 See C Fink and K E Maskus, eds., *Intellectual Property and Development: Lessons from Recent Economic Research* (Oxford University Press and World Bank, 2005) 2–3.

137 Ibid.

138 Ibid., 2.

139 K E Maskus, *Intellectual Property Rights in the Global Economy* (Institute for International Economics, 2000) 235–241.

140 J E Stiglitz, *Making Globalization Work* (W.W. Norton & Company, 2007) 105–117.

141 G E Evans, 'Strategic Patent Licensing for Public Research Organizations: Deploying Restriction and Reservation Clauses to Promote Medical R&D in Developing Countries' (2008) 34 *American Journal of Law and Medicine* 175, 178.

Some studies report that the distributive effects of pharmaceutical patents are of significant economic benefits to industrialised states whilst the potential of benefits to developing nations remains uncertain.[142] Patent protection must therefore be put in the context of national strategic and fundamental goals such as the protection of public health and national industrial development.[143] The access to medicines concern is not only a public health conundrum, it also raises serious issues in relation to a country's ability to foster job creations and achieve sustainable development.[144] Sadly, even laws formulated as concessions to developing countries, such as the technical cooperation provision of TRIPS, may not work to the advantage of these countries.[145] Peter Drahos put the situation quite aptly when he notes that '*underneath the development ideology of intellectual property there lies an agenda of underdevelopment. It is all about protecting the knowledge and skills of the leaders of the pack*'.[146]

In sum, it is submitted that while the flexibilities in TRIPS might be effective in addressing public health emergencies in developing countries, a durable solution lies in having a framework within the IP system that will facilitate capacity building, technology transfer and human development. The development objective of the IP system should assume something much stronger than its current inchoate form such that IP protection must not be incompatible with measures taken in good faith to enhance human development in poor countries.

7.6 Conclusion

The interface between IP and development will continue to remain controversial because of the vagaries of intricate economic issues involved. Whilst IP might, in certain contexts, be a real impetus for economic growth, its contribution to the development as freedom concept is suspect. The pursuit of development is a legitimate goal recognised in international law and is arguably a non-derogatory norm of international law. While it may be conceded that the right to development in international law has not attained a status that can be considered to carry a significant legal weight, the concept of development seems to be an essential and fundamental part of the current international legal order such that it can be argued that it is something close to a peremptory norm of international law. To this extent, developing countries may resist efforts to erode the current

142 K E Maskus & J H Reichman, 'The Globalization of Private Knowledge Goods and the Privatization of Global Public Goods', in K E Maskus & J H Reichman (eds.), *International Public Goods and Transfer of Technology Under a Globalized Intellectual Property Regime* (Cambridge University Press, 2005) 65, 65–66.

143 R V V Puymbroeck, 'Coming to Grips with TRIPS: Conversion + Calculation' (2010) 38 *Journal of Law, Medicines and Ethics* 520, 527.

144 Ibid., 542.

145 See K M Koepsel, 'How Do Developed Countries Meet Their Obligations Under Article 67 of the TRIPS Agreement?' (2004) 44 *IDEA* 167.

146 See P Drahos with J Braithwaite, *Information Feudalism: Who Owns the Knowledge Economy?* 12 (Earthscan Publications Limited, 2002).

flexibilities in the TRIPS Agreement by relying on the international law of development or the concept of development in international law. It is certainly impossible to reconcile a 'one size fits all' or a highly harmonised IP regime with the varying needs of developing countries and this is why even the significant harmonisation achieved in the TRIPS Agreement still leaves room for some flexibilities.

The problem, however, lies in the fact that the effective utilisation of these flexibilities is increasingly being undermined by the myriad free trade agreements being pursued especially by the US worldwide. There is a compelling need for trade and IP agreements to foster rather than impede the developmental objectives of the world's nations. While compulsory licensing and parallel importation may address public health emergencies in developing countries, the effectual recognition of development in the global IP system can provide a more durable solution to the access to medicines crisis in developing countries.

It is submitted that developing countries can vigorously rely on the concept of development as a fundamental principle of international law in their resistance of TRIPS-plus agreements and utilisation of the TRIPS flexibilities. In doing this, developing countries will need a coalition strategy. For Africa, that can come in the form of a regional economic community that will enable countries in the continent to maintain a common front in protecting their economic and developmental interests. The significance of an African RTA to this issue is explored further in Chapter 9.

Bibliography

Allot A, 'The Law of Development and the Development of Law' in F Synder & P Slinn (eds.), *International Law of Development: Comparative Perspectives* (Professional Books, 1987).

Amoore L et al., *Series Preface to Amrita Narlikar, International Trade and Developing Countries: Bargaining Coalitions in the GATT & WTO* (Routledge, 2003).

Aoki K, 'Notes Toward a Cultural Geography of Authorship' (1996) 48 *Stanford Law Review* 1293.

Baker B K, 'Arthritic Flexibilities for Accessing Medicines: Analysis of WTO Action Regarding Paragraph 6 of the Doha Declaration on the TRIPS Agreement and Public Health' (2004) 14 *Indiana International and Comparative Law Review* 613.

Barbosa D B, Chon M & von Hase A M, 'Slouching Towards Development in International Intellectual Property Law' (2007) *Michigan State Law Review* 71, 72.

Barton J H, Goldstein J L, Josling T E, Steinberg R H, *The Evolution of the Trade Regime: Politics, Law and Economics of the GATT and WTO* (Princeton University Press, 2006).

Broude T, 'The Rules(s) of Trade and the Rhetos of Development: Reflections on the Functional and Aspirational Legitimacy of the WTO' (2006) 45 *Columbia Journal of Transnational Law* 221, 223.

Bunn I D, 'The Right to Development: Implications for International Economic Law' (2000) 15 *American University Law Review* 1425, 1426.

Chemillier-Gendreau M, 'Relations between the Ideology of Development and Development Law' in F Synder & Slinn P (eds.), *International Law of Development: Comparative Perspectives* (Professional Books, 1987).

Chon M, 'Intellectual Property and the Development Divide' (2006) 27 *Cardozo Law Review* 2821, 2832.

Chun D, 'Patent Law Harmonization in the Age of Globalisation: The Necessity and Strategy for a Pragmatic Outcome' (2011) 93 *Journal of Patent and Trademark Office Society* 127.

Commission on Intellectual Property Rights, *Integrating Intellectual Property Rights and Development Policy* (2002) 40-at www.iprcommission.org/papers/pdfs/final_report/ciprfullfinal.pdf accessed 27 January 2019.

Correa C M, 'Can the TRIPS Agreement Foster Technology Transfer to Developing Countries?' in K E Maskus & J Reichman J H (eds.), *International Public Goods and the Transfer of Technology under a Globalized Intellectual Property Regime* (Cambridge University Press, 2005).

Correa C M, *Trade Related Aspects of Intellectual Property Rights: A Commentary on the TRIPS Agreement* (Oxford University Press, 2007).

Currat L J, Hyder A A, Nchinda T C & Carey-Bumgarner E, *10/90 Report on Health Research 1999* (Global Forum for Health Research, 1999).

Dinwoodie G B & Dreyfuss R C, 'Designing a Global Intellectual Property System Responsive to Change: The WTO, WIPO and Beyond' (2009) 46 *Houston Law Review* 1187.

Drahos P with Braithwaite J, *Information Feudalism: Who Owns the Knowledge Economy?* 12 (Earthscan Publications Limited, 2002).

Drahos P & Mayne R, *Global Intellectual Property Rights: Knowledge, Access and Development* (Palgrave MacMillan, 2002).

Dreyfuss R C, 'The Role of India, China, Brazil and Other Emerging Economies in Establishing Access Norms for Intellectual Property and Intellectual Property Lawmaking' (Int'l Law & Justice Working Paper 2009/5, 2009).

Evans G E, 'Strategic Patent Licensing for Public Research Organizations: Deploying Restriction and Reservation Clauses to Promote Medical R&D in Developing Countries' (2008) 34 *American Journal of Law and Medicine* 175, 178.

Fink C and Maskus K E, eds., *Intellectual Property and Development: Lessons from Recent Economic Research* (Oxford University Press and World Bank, 2005).

Gana (Okediji) R L, 'The Myth of Development, The Progress of Rights: Human Rights to Intellectual Property and Development' (1996) 18 *Law & Policy* 315.

Gervais D J, 'Intellectual Property, Trade & Development: The State of Play' (2005) 74 *Fordham Law Review* 505.

Gervais D J, *The TRIPS Agreement: Drafting History and Analysis* (Sweet & Maxwell, 3rd ed., 2008).

Gervais D J, 'TRIPS and Development', in D J Gervais (ed.), *Intellectual Property, Trade and Development: Strategies to Optimise Economic Development in a TRIPS Plus Era* (Oxford University Press, 2007).

Getachew Mengistie, *The Impact of the International Patent System on Developing Countries* (World Intellectual Property Organization, 2003) 33 www.wipo.int/edocs/mdocs/govbody/en/a_39/a_39_13_add_1.pdf accessed 27 January 2019.

Gordon R & Sylvester J H, 'Deconstructing Development' (2004) 22 *Wisconsin. International Law Journal* 1.

Gostin L O, 'Meeting Basic Survival Needs of the World's Least Healthy People: Towards a Framework on Global Health' (2008) 96 *George Town Law Journal* 331, 344.

Gutowski R J, 'The Marriage of Intellectual Property and International Trade in the TRIPS Agreement: Strange Bedfellows or a Match Made in Heaven?' (1999) *Buffalo Law Review* 713.

Kapczynski A, 'Harmonization and Its Discontents: A Case Study of TRIPS Implementation in India's Pharmaceutical Sector' (2009) 97 *California Law Review* 1571.

Kazenske E R, *Patent Offices: Strategies for Work Sharing* (Fordham IP Conference 2009) http://fordhamipconference.com/wp-content/uploads/2010/08/Kaz_Kazenske_Patent_Offices_Strategy_for_Work_Sharing.pdf accessed 27 January 2019.

Kelly A C, Williamson J G & Cheetham R J, *Dualistic Economic Development: Theory and History* (University of Chicago Press, 1972).

Kinney E, 'Health Care Financing and Delivery in the US, Mexico and Canada: Finding and Establishing Intentional Principles for Sound Integration' (2009) 26(3) *Wisconsin International Law Journal* 935–965.

Kinney E, 'Realization of the International Human Right to Health in an Economically Integrated North America' (2009) 37 *Journal of Law, Medicine and Ethics* 807.

Koepsel K M, 'How Do Developed Countries Meet Their Obligations Under Article 67 of the TRIPS Agreement?' (2004) 44 *IDEA* 167.

Lazzarini Z, 'Access to HIV Drugs: Are we Changing the Two World Paradigm?' (2002) 17 *Connecticut Journal of International Law* 281.

Maskus K E, *Intellectual Property Rights in the Global Economy* (Institute for International Economics, 2000).

Maskus K E, 'Using the International Trading System to Foster Technology Transfer for Economic Development' (2005) *Michigan State Law Review* 219.

Maskus K E & Reichman J H, 'The Globalization of Private Knowledge Goods and the Privatization of Global Public Goods' in K E Maskus & J H Reichman (eds.), *International Public Goods and Transfer of Technology Under a Globalized Intellectual Property Regime* (Cambridge University Press, 2005).

McCalman P, *Reaping What You Sow: An Empirical Analysis of International Patent Harmonization* (Working papers in Economics and Econometrics, June 1999).

Morgan T, *Economic Development: Concept and Strategy* (Harper & Row, 1975).

Musungu S F & Dutfield G, *Multilateral Agreements and a TRIPS-plus World: The World Intellectual Property Organisation (WIPO)* (Quaker United Nations Office, TRIPS Issues Paper No. 3, 2003).

Netanel N W ed., *The WIPO Development Agenda and Its Development Policy Context*, (Oxford University Press, 2009).

Oguamanam C, 'IP in Global Governance: A Venture in Critical Reflection' (2011) 2(2) *WIPO Journal* 196, 199.

Okediji R, 'Copyright and Public Welfare in Global Perspective' (1999)7 *Indiana Journal of Global Legal Studies* 125.

Okediji R, 'The Institutions of Intellectual Property: New Trends in an Old Debate' (2004) 98 *American Society of International Law Proceedings* 219, 221.

Owoeye O & Oduwole J, 'Development, Access to Medicines and the Ebola Virus Epidemic in West Africa' (2017) 24 *Journal of Law and Medicine* 722.

Peet R with Hartwick E, *Theories of Development: Contentions, Arguments, Alternatives* (The Guilford Press, 2009).

Pires de Carvalho N, *The TRIPS Regime of Patent Rights* (Kluwer Law International, 2nd ed., 2004).

Puymbroeck R V, 'Coming to Grips with TRIPS: Conversion + Calculation' (2010) 38 *Journal of Law, Medicines and Ethics* 520.

Reichman J H, 'Intellectual Property in the Twenty-First Century: Will the Developing Countries Lead or Follow? (2009) *Houston Law Review* 1115.

Reichman J H and Dreyfuss R C, 'Harmonisation Without Consensus: Critical Reflections on Drafting a Substantive Patent Law Treaty' (2007) 57 *Duke Law Journal* 85.

Ricupero R, 'Rebuilding Confidence in the Multilateral Trading System: Closing the "Legitimacy Gap"', in G P Sampson (ed.), *Role of the World Trade Organization in Global Governance* (United Nations University Press, 2001).

Sen A, *Development as Freedom* (Oxford University Press, 1999).

Stigliz J E, *Globalisation and its Discontents* (W W Norton & Company, 2002).

Stiglitz J E, *Making Globalization Work* (New York: W.W. Norton & Company, 2007).

Taylor L, *Macro Models for Developing Countries* (McGraw-Hill, 1979).

United Nations, Commission on Human and People's Rights, *Communication Nos 279/03–296/05*, 45th sess (27 May 2009).

United Nations, *Sub-Comm. on Promotion and Protection of Human Rights, Mainstreaming the Right to Development into International Trade Law and Policy at the World Trade Organization*, U.N. ESCOR, 56th Sess. Agenda Item 4, UN Doc. E/CN.4/Sub.2/2004/17 (9 June 2004) 15.

United Nations, *The Right to Development Report of the Secretary General* (UN Doc A/66/216) August 2011.

United Nations Development Programme, Human Development Report 1991.

World Health Organization, *Guiding Principles for Strategic Resource Allocation*, RC/2005/1 (1 June 2005).

World Intellectual Property Organization, Press Release, *Member States Adopt a Development Agenda for WIPO* (Oct. 1, 2007), www.wipo.int/pressroom/en/articles/2007/article_0071.html accessed 27 January 2019.

World Intellectual Property Organization, *Proposal to Establish a Development Agenda for WIPO: An Elaboration of Issues Raised in Document*, WO/GA/31/11, IIM/1/4 (6 April 2005).

World Trade Organization, Ministerial Declaration of 14 November 2001, WT/MIN(01)/DEC/1, 41 I.L.M. 746 (2002).

Yelpaala K, 'Quo Vadis WTO? The Threat of TRIPS and the Biodiversity Convention Human Health and Food Security' (2012) 30 *Boston University International Law Journal* 55.

Yotopoulos P A & Nugent J B, *Economics of Development: Empirical Investigations* (Harper & Row, 1976).

Yu P K, 'A Tale of Two Development Agendas' (2009) 35 *Ohio Northern University Law Review* 465, 540–573.

Yu P, 'Intellectual Property, Economic Development, and the China Puzzle' in D J Gervais (ed.), *Intellectual Property, Trade and Development: Strategies to Optimise Economic Development in a TRIPS Plus Era* (Oxford University Press, 2007).

Yu P K, 'The Global Intellectual Property Order and Its Undetermined Future' (2009) 1(1) *WIPO Journal* 1.

8 Regional trade agreements, TRIPS-plus provisions and the African access to medicines conundrum

8.1 Introduction

The World Trade Organization (WTO) was established in 1995 to provide an institutional structure for the regulation of international trade among its Members.[1] The WTO provides a multilateral framework for trade governance among Member States and all the agreements and instruments included as Annexes 1 to 3 of the Marrakesh Agreement Establishing the WTO are generally known as 'Multilateral Trade Agreements' and are binding on all WTO Members.[2] The agreement that are only binding on Members that have accepted them and not on all Members are the 'Plurilateral Trade Agreements'.[3]

The General Agreement on Tariffs and Trade (GATT) 1994 is one of the Multilateral Trade Agreements under the WTO framework and it sets out the foundational non-discrimination principles of the WTO. Article I of the GATT provides that with respect to any customs duties, charges, rules and formalities applied in relation to the importation or exportation of products, 'any advantage, favour, privilege or immunity granted by any contracting party to any product originating in or destined for any other country shall be accorded immediately and unconditionally to the like product originating in or destined for the territories of all other contracting parties'.[4] This is generally known as the most-favoured-nation principle. The implication of the most-favoured-nation principle is that any benefit or special treatment offered to a WTO Member must be accorded without delay to all other Members.

The other fundamental non-discrimination principle is the national treatment principle. Article III of the GATT provides that national taxes, charges, laws and regulations affecting products in the course of trade must 'not be applied to imported or domestic products so as to afford protection to domestic production'.[5] The national treatment principle prohibits any attempt to offer special treatment

1 Marrakesh Agreement Establishing the World Trade Organization, 15 April 1994, 1867 U.N.T.S. 154, Article II(1).

2 Ibid., Article II(2).

3 Ibid., Article II(3).

4 General Agreement on Tariffs and Trade 1994 Article I(1).

5 Ibid., Art. III(1).

to local products in a way that would put imported products at a disadvantage in the course of trade.

These non-discrimination principles are also enshrined in Articles 3 and 4 of the Agreement on Trade Related Aspects of Intellectual Property Rights (the TRIPS Agreement). Apart from the minimum standards of protection available under the TRIPS Agreement, the proliferation of regional trade agreements (RTAs) has brought about higher standards of intellectual property (IP) protection that may have the effect of eroding the flexibilities that currently exist under the WTO framework for IP governance.[6]

The chapter highlights the challenges posed by the proliferation of RTAs to access to affordable medicines. It places a spotlight on TRIPS-plus provisions in free trade agreements negotiated by the US with Australia, Morocco, Mexico and Canada. It highlights how TRIPS-plus standards contained in US RTAs may affect access to medicines in Africa and globally. It also highlights how investor-state dispute settlement clauses in trade or investment agreements may whittle down the available flexibilities in the TRIPS Agreement. The chapter provides possible policy options that may be explored by African countries to address these issues.

8.2 RTAs and the WTO

As of May 2018, and the date of writing, there had been not less than 459 RTA notifications from WTO Members counting agreements dealing with goods and services separately, with up to 287 RTAs in force.[7] While RTAs may by their nature derogate from the WTO non-discrimination principles, they are, nonetheless, considered to be beneficial to the global trade liberalisation objectives of the WTO. Although the WTO is founded on the principles of trade liberalisation and non-discrimination, RTAs are encouraged within the WTO system. Thus Article XXIV of the GATT creates a special exception for free trade agreements under the WTO framework in the following terms:

> Accordingly, the provisions of this Agreement shall not prevent, as between the territories of contracting parties, the formation of a customs union or of a free-trade area or the adoption of an interim agreement necessary for the formation of a customs union or of a free trade area.[8]

Regional trade agreements may be defined as preferential and reciprocal trade agreements between two or more contracting nations to form a free-trade accord,

6 O Owoeye, O Olatunji & B Faturoti, 'Patents and the Trans-Pacific Partnership: How TPP-Style Intellectual Property Standards May Exacerbate the Access to Medicines Problem in the East African Community'. (2017) *International Trade Journal* 1 – 22 doi:10.1080/08853908.2017.1386143 accessed 27 January 2019.

7 WTO, Regional trade agreements www.wto.org/english/tratop_e/region_e/region_e.htm accessed 27 January 2019.

8 GATT Art. XXIV(5).

a customs union or a common market.[9] A free-trade area is normally created between Parties to a regional or free trade agreement. An RTA is therefore generally an agreement providing for the elimination of duties and other restrictive trade regulations with respect to substantially all the trade between the contracting parties.[10] An RTA may also create a customs union. The GATT provides a detailed definition of a customs union. Article 8(a) of the GATT provide that a customs union is created where the Parties to an RTA have agreed to eliminate duties and other restrictive trade regulations in relation to substantially all the trade between the contracting parties and the contracting parties have decided to adopt substantially the same trade duties and regulations to countries that are not in the customs union.

The GATT sums up the importance of RTAs thus:

> The contracting parties recognize the desirability of increasing freedom of trade by the development, through voluntary agreements, of closer integration between the economies of the countries parties to such agreements. They also recognize that the purpose of a customs union or of a free-trade area should be to facilitate trade between the constituent territories and not to raise barriers to the trade of other contracting parties with such territories.[11]

Thus, RTAs are desirable on the basis that they build regional blocs to enhance economic competitiveness for a more open and integrated global economy.[12]

8.3 Regional trade agreement, TRIPS-plus provisions and access to medicines

The TRIPS Agreement is one of the Multilateral Trade Agreements included in Annex 1 of the Marrakesh Agreement Establishing the WTO and is as such binding on all WTO Members. While the TRIPS Agreement contains some flexibilities that are intended to ensure its implementation does not inflict undue hardship on vulnerable populations across the world in relation to their ability to have access to affordable drugs, the use of these flexibilities, especially in relation to the compulsory licensing provisions, has been controversial. The proliferation of RTAs has also brought about a range of free trade agreements that have covered IP protection with provisions that exceed the standards negotiated under the TRIPS Agreement.[13] The higher standards of IP protection imposed by RTAs are generally known as TRIPS-plus provisions.

9 See O Owoeye, 'Regionalism and WTO Multilateralism: The Case for an African Continental Free Trade Area' (2016) 50(6) *Journal of World Trade* 1085, 1086.

10 GATT Art. XXIV (8)(b).

11 GATT Art. XXIV(4).

12 See O Owoeye, 'Regionalism and WTO Multilateralism: The Case for an African Continental Free Trade Area' (2016) 50(6) *Journal of World Trade* 1085, 1090.

13 A K Sanders, 'Intellectual Property, Free Trade Agreements and Economic Development' (2007) 23 *Georgia State University Law Review* 893, 897.

It has in fact been argued that the proliferation of free trade agreements has more to do with promoting corporate power through the codification of anti-competitive rights than creating fair trade rules that boost trade liberalisation and the economic competitiveness of contracting parties.[14] While the Doha Declaration on the TRIPS Agreement and Public Health underscores the right of WTO Members to make maximum use of the TRIPS flexibilities to promote access to medicines for all, the US has gone on to negotiate a plethora of free trade agreements with different countries of the world with provisions that impose standards higher than the minimum standards of protection required under the TRIPS Agreement. It is pertinent to note that the TRIPS Agreement only requires a minimum standard of protection from WTO Members while preserving their rights to negotiate and implement extensive protection that exceed the minimum standards available under the Agreement.[15] The right of WTO Members to implement higher standards of IP protection is however subject to the condition that the more extensive protection does not contravene the provisions of the TRIPS Agreement.[16] The US presently has free trade agreements with 20 countries[17] with most of these agreements containing IP provisions with TRIPS-plus standards. US free trade agreements with Australia, Morocco and the US-Mexico-Canada Agreement are discussed next to illustrate how the patent-related provisions in US RTAs may impact on access to medicines.

8.3.1 US-Australia Free Trade Agreement

The United States-Australia Free Trade Agreement was signed on 18 May 2004 and it entered into force on 1 January 2005. The Australia-US Free Trade Agreement (AUSFTA) contains the following patent-related TRIPS-plus provisions with special implications for access to medicines.

AUSFTA provides that 'patents shall be available for any new uses or methods of using a known product'.[18] The TRIPS Agreement only requires patents to be new and to possess inventive steps. The TRIPS Agreement does not define novelty, and this is generally recognised as one of the existing flexibilities under TRIPS. The provision of AUSFTA that patents shall extend to 'any new uses or methods of using a known product' is therefore a TRIPS-plus provision. The provision is designed to promote 'evergreening' of patents by allowing patent protection to be applied to trivial improvements to known processes or methods.[19]

14 B K Baker & K Geddes, 'Corporate Power Unbound: Investor-State Arbitration of IP Monopolies on Medicines-Eli Lilly v. Canada and the Trans-Pacific Partnership Agreement' (2015) *Journal of Intellectual Property Law* 1, 3.

15 TRIPS Agreement Article 1.

16 Ibid.

17 Office of the United States Trade Representative, Free Trade Agreement https://ustr.gov/trade-agreements/free-trade-agreements accessed 27 January 2019.

18 AUSFTA Article 17.9(1).

19 See O Owoeye, O Olatunji & Bukola Faturoti, 'Patents and the Trans-Pacific Partnership: How TPP-Style Intellectual Property Standards May Exacerbate the Access to Medicines Problem in

Under the TRIPS Agreement, WTO Members may exclude from patent protection, 'plants and animals other than micro-organisms, and essentially biological processes for the production of plants or animals other than non-biological and microbiological processes'.[20] This provision is excluded from the text of AUSFTA.

AUSFTA provides for the prohibition of parallel importation in the following terms:

> Each Party shall provide that the exclusive right of the patent owner to prevent importation of a patented product, or a product that results from a patented process, without the consent of the patent owner shall not be limited by the sale or distribution of that product outside its territory, at least where the patentee has placed restrictions on importation by contract or other means.[21]

This provision imposes a restrictive national exhaustion regime while Article 6 of the TRIPS Agreement explicitly provides that subject to the non-discrimination principles, nothing in the TRIPS Agreement shall be used to address the question of exhaustion of IP rights.

AUSFTA further provides that where a Party requires the submission of undisclosed test data as a condition for granting marketing approval for a pharmaceutical product, the Party shall not permit any third party to rely on such information for obtaining marketing approval for the same or similar products for five years without the consent of the owner of the test data.[22] This is another major TRIPS-plus provision under AUSFTA. The TRIPS Agreement requires the pharmaceutical product to involve the use of new chemical entities for the test data protection to apply. There is no such requirement under AUSFTA. In fact, AUSFTA defines a new product for the purposes of test data protection as 'one that does not contain a chemical entity that has been previously approved for marketing in the Party'. Thus, unlike TRIPS that requires some degree of novelty in chemical entities for the test data protection to apply, the newness requirement is satisfied under AUSFTA where the chemical entity was not previously approved for marketing within a Party's territory.

In addition, the test data protection regime under the TRIPS Agreement is designed to protect the data generally against unfair commercial use and the TRIPS Agreement allows the use of test data where such is necessary to protect the public. Under AUSFTA, no third party may be allowed to use test data without the consent of the Party that created the data and there are no public interest exceptions to the rule under AUSFTA although AUSFTA allows 'disclosure' by

the East African Community'. (2017) *International Trade Journal* 1–22 doi:10.1080/08853908.2017.1386143, p. 8.

20 TRIPS Agreement Article 27.3.

21 AUSFTA 17.9(4).

22 AUSFTA 17.10(1)(a).

a government entity provided measures are taken against any unfair commercial use of the 'disclosed' information.[23] AUSFTA therefore created a data exclusivity regime that clearly exceeds the requirements of the TRIPS Agreement.

8.3.2 US – Morocco Free Trade Agreement

The Morocco-US Free Trade Agreement (USMFTA) was signed on 15 June 2004 and it entered into force in 2006. The patent-related IP obligations under the Morocco-US Free Trade Agreement are very similar to AUSFTA with some minor variations. USMFTA like AUSFTA contains provisions that exceed the minimum standards available under the TRIPS Agreement. USMFTA's TRIPS-plus provisions have significant implications for access to medicines and public health in view of the fact that Morocco, unlike Australia, is a developing African country. The following are some of the TRIPS-plus provisions of USMFTA that have real implications for access to medicines.

USMFTA creates an obligation to make patents available for animals and plants.[24] Under the TRIPS Agreement, countries are at liberty to exclude animals and plants from patentability.

USMFTA further provides that 'patents shall be available for any new uses or methods of using a known product, including new uses of a known product for the treatment of humans and animals'. This is a TRIPS-plus provision that is likely to have a significant public health impact. Apart from the fact that the provision promotes evergreening of patents, it clearly derogates from Article 27.3(a) of the TRIPS Agreement which permits WTO Members to exclude from patentability, 'diagnostic, therapeutic and surgical methods for the treatment of humans or animals'.

With respect to exhaustion of IP rights, Article 15.9(4) of MUSFTA provides that 'the exclusive right of the patent owner to prevent importation of a patented product, or a product that results from patented process, without the consent of the patent owner shall not be limited by the sale or distribution of that product outside its territory'. The effect of this provision is that Parties to the trade agreement are barred from allowing the parallel importation of patented product within their territories. Parallel importation is one of the major flexibilities available under the TRIPS Agreement as Article 6 of the TRIPS Agreement removes issues relating to the exhaustion of IP rights from the adjudicatory power of the WTO Dispute Settlement Body to the extent that they do not run afoul of the non-discrimination principle. USMFTA however completely bars the parallel importation of products released by the patent owner into overseas markets. Thus, under USMFTA, the rights of the patent owner in relation to patents are not exhausted by sales overseas and parallel importation will only be lawful where it is done with the consent of the right holder.

23 AUSFTA 17.10(1)(e).
24 USMFTA 15.9(2).

With respect to test data protection, USMFTA imposes a data exclusivity regime by providing that Parties 'shall not permit third persons not having the consent of the person providing the information to market a product on the basis of the approval granted to the person submitting that information for at least five years for pharmaceutical products and ten years for agricultural chemical products from the date of approval'.[25] Again, this is another major provision that can constitute a real hurdle to the entry of generic pharmaceutical products. Data exclusivity applies under USMFTA where there is a new chemical entity that was not previously approved in a Party's territory.[26] Under the TRIPS Agreement, the definition of newness for test data protection purposes is not limited to chemical entities that were not previously approved in a Member's territory and protection is mainly available against unfair commercial uses.

In addition, USMFTA provides in relation to pharmaceutical patents that 'each Party shall make available an extension of the patent term to compensate the patent owner for unreasonable curtailment of the effective patent term as a result of the marketing approval process'.[27] This is a TRIPS-plus provision as the TRIPS Agreement has no such requirement for extending the patent term for pharmaceutical products.

The public health implications of USMFTA must have indeed been apparent to the negotiators of the Agreement as the Agreement contains a Side Letter on Public Health that is understood by Parties as forming an integral part of the IP rights chapter of MUSFTA. By a letter, annexed to USMFTA, from the US Trade Representative dated 15 June 2004, the Parties agreed as follows:

> The obligations of Chapter Fifteen of the Agreement do not affect the ability of either Party to take necessary measures to protect public health by promoting access to medicines for all, in particular concerning cases such as HIV/AIDS, tuberculosis, malaria, and other epidemics as well as circumstances of extreme urgency or national emergency.

The extent to which USMFTA's Side Letter on Public Health can allow measures to promote public health where such measures are not supported by the substantive provisions of the Agreement remains suspect. It is however unlikely that the high-level understanding expressed in the 'Side Letter' will carry the force of law should any measure contrary to USMFTA's TRIPS-plus provisions be adopted by Morocco. The language of the 'Side Letter on Public Health' suggests that the letter does not permit the doing of any act that is not allowed by the IP provisions of USMFTA. The 'Side Letter' particularly states as follows:

> ...if an amendment of the WTO Agreement on Trade-Related Aspects of Intellectual Property Rights enters into force with respect to the Parties and

25 USMFTA 15.10(1).

26 Ibid.

27 USMFTA 15.10(3).

> a Party's application of a measure in conformity with that amendment violates Chapter Fifteen of the Free Trade Agreement, our Governments shall immediately consult in order to adapt Chapter Fifteen as appropriate in the light of the amendment.

The statement above underscores the fact that no measure that runs contrary to the TRIPS-plus provisions of USMFTA would be permitted and any measure that may run contrary to the clear provisions of USMFTA would require further consultations and deliberations by Parties to the Agreement.

8.3.3 United States-Mexico-Canada Agreement

The United States-Mexico-Canada Free Trade Agreement (USMCFTA) was signed in November 2018. The Agreement, like other US free trade agreements, cover a wide range of issues including trade in goods, trade in services, IP, environment, labour, electronic commerce, financial services, sanitary and phytosanitary measures and public procurement. The IP chapter of the agreement is very detailed and like the earlier US trade agreements, it contains a number of TRIPS-plus provisions, and some of which are discussed below.

8.3.3.1 Evergreening of patents

The USMCFTA provides that patents shall be available for 'new uses of a known product, new methods of using a known product, or new processes of using a known product'.[28] As already mentioned earlier, this is a TRIPS-plus provision that makes it easy to patent inventions with trivial improvements over what is already known thereby promoting evergreening of patents.

8.3.3.2 Extension of patent term for pharmaceutical products

With respect to pharmaceutical products, USMCFTA provides for the extension of patent term to make allowance for any delay in marketing approval. The relevant provision provides thus:

> With respect to a pharmaceutical product that is subject to a patent, each Party shall make available an adjustment of the patent term to compensate the patent owner for unreasonable curtailment of the effective patent term as a result of the marketing approval process.[29]

This provision makes it possible to add to the minimum 20 years patent term required under the TRIPS Agreement where there has been some delay in obtaining marketing approval for a pharmaceutical product.

28 USMCFTA Article. 20.36(2).
29 USMCFTA Art. 20.46(2).

8.3.3.3 Data exclusivity

USMCFTA provides for a data exclusivity regime to be implemented by contracting parties in the following terms:

> a If a Party requires, as a condition for granting marketing approval for a new pharmaceutical product, the submission of undisclosed test or other data concerning the safety and efficacy of the product, that Party shall not permit third persons, without the consent of the person that previously submitted that information, to market the same or a similar product on the basis of:
>
> i that information, or
>
> ii the marketing approval granted to the person that submitted that information, for at least five years from the date of marketing approval of the new pharmaceutical product in the territory of the Party.[30]

It is pertinent to note that the TRIPS Agreement has no provision for a specified period of protection for test data. The USMCFTA, like other US free trade agreements also went beyond the language of the TRIPS Agreement by completely prohibiting the use of test data submitted by the original applicant by a third party. Under the TRIPS Agreement, such prohibition is only limited to cases of unfair commercial use.

Article 20.49 of USMCFTA deals with data exclusivity for biologics by providing as follows:

> With regard to protecting new biologics, a Party shall, with respect to the first marketing approval in a Party of a new pharmaceutical product that is, or contains, a biologic, provide effective market protection through the implementation of Article 20.48.1 (Protection of Undisclosed Test or Other Data) and Article 20.48.3 (Protection of Undisclosed Test or Other Data), mutatis mutandis, for a period of at least ten years from the date of first marketing approval of that product in that Party.

This is a major provision that introduces US local law on biologics' data protection for implementation by US trading partners. The data exclusivity regime for biologics is to subsist for a period of 10 years during which follow on biologics or biosimilars are not allowed to enter the market by relying on the originator's test data. Follow on biologics (also known as biosimilars) are the 'generic' versions of biologics. A biologic is defined by USMCFTA as referring to:

> ...a product that is produced using biotechnology processes and that is, or contains, a virus, therapeutic serum, toxin, antitoxin, vaccine, blood, blood

30 USMCFTA Article 20.48(1).

component or derivative, allergenic product, protein, or analogous product, for use in human beings for the prevention, treatment, or cure of a disease or condition.[31]

The strict provisions relating to test data protection for biologics can have grave implications for access to medicines and public health by making it almost impossible for biosimilars to enter the market for a period of 10 years even where no patent subsist in relation to the product. The Parties to USMCFTA included a provision to address the public health concerns by providing that notwithstanding the provisions of the Agreement, Parties reserve the right to take measures to safeguard public health in accordance with the Doha Declaration on TRIPS and Public Health and any waiver and amendment to the TRIPS Agreement with respect to the Doha Declaration on TRIPS and Public Health.[32]

8.3.3.4 Concluding remarks on RTAs

It is clear from the discussion on the different RTAs negotiated by the US that the US has consistently striven to include TRIPS-plus IP provisions in trade agreements negotiated with her trading partners. While Morocco is the only African country with a bilateral trade agreement with the US, it is important to note that the TRIPS-plus provisions implemented by countries with the capacity to manufacture and deliver drugs to low-income countries in Africa and Asia will inexorably impact on the ability of these countries to deliver drugs to third-world countries that lack the capacity to manufacture them. Canada for instance is the only country on record to export drugs to Africa under the waiver in force in relation to the TRIPS compulsory licensing provisions for exporting drugs to countries without significant pharmaceutical manufacturing capacity. With the current requirement to offer ten-year data exclusivity for biologics, it will become impossible for biosimilars to be approved in Canada for the period of data exclusivity and this will also affect the ability of Canada to manufacture such products for countries lacking the capacity to produce them.

8.4 Investor-state dispute settlement clauses and TRIPS flexibilities

Bilateral investment agreements, like free trade agreements, are agreements made to promote the inflow of foreign direct investments and to ensure the interest of foreign investors are sufficiently protected.[33] Investment agreements normally contain mechanisms for interstate and investor-state dispute settlement. Thus,

31 USMCFTA 20.49(2).

32 USMCFTA 20.48(3).

33 B K Baker & K Geddes, 'Corporate Power Unbound: Investor-State Arbitration of IP Monopolies on Medicines-Eli Lilly V. Canada and the Trans-Pacific Partnership Agreement' (2015) *Journal of Intellectual Property Law* 1, 3.

where a foreign investor believes their investment has been treated in a way that violates obligations under the investment agreement, they can launch an action against the offending state directly or through their home government.[34] Investment agreements often contain provisions that can curtail the ability of countries to adopt measures to address national issues especially in relation to access to medicines and public health. They may thus limit the ability of states to make maximum use of the flexibilities available under the TRIPS Agreement. The investment chapter of the US-Morocco Free Trade Agreement will be discussed to place a spotlight on some of the challenges that investment agreements may pose to the use of the TRIPS flexibilities to promote access to medicines.

8.4.1 Access to medicines and investor-state dispute settlement under the US-Morocco Free Trade Agreement

The USMFTA clearly provides that in the event of an inconsistency between the investment chapter of the agreement and any other chapter, including the IP chapter, the investment provisions will prevail.[35] USMFTA provides for the national treatment principle, the most-favoured-nation treatment and minimum standards of protection. With respect to national treatment, the agreement provides that investors and covered investments must be accorded no less favourable treatment than is given to local investors and investments 'with respect to the establishment, acquisition, expansion, management, conduct, operation, and sale or other disposition of investments'.[36] Thus, Morocco as a developing country under the agreement cannot adopt special measures to promote the local pharmaceutical industry under the agreement without running afoul of the investment provisions of USMFTA. That option would ordinarily be available under Articles 3 and 8 of the TRIPS Agreement. Thus, while countries may be able to adopt measures to protect public health and public interest by protecting local industries under the TRIPS Agreement as the TRIPS Agreement provides for exceptions to the national treatment principle pursuant to the Paris Convention, such exceptions do not apply under the USMFTA and other typical US bilateral trade and investment agreements.

With respect to the most-favoured-nation treatment principle, USMFTA provides that a Party shall accord no less favourable treatment to foreign investors and covered investments than it accords to any non-Party investors or investments 'with respect to the establishment, acquisition, expansion, management, conduct, operation, and sale or other disposition of investments'.[37] Morocco is an African country with trade relationships with other countries in North Africa and Sub-Saharan Africa. There are no exceptions to the most-favoured-nation treatment principle under the USMFTA unlike the exceptions available under

34 Ibid.
35 USMFTA Article 10.2(1).
36 USMFTA Article10.3.
37 USMFTA Article 10.4.

the WTO system. The most-favoured-nation treatment principle can be used by an investor to demand the application of the most favourable investment arrangement that has been negotiated with any other state.[38] The implication of the most-favoured-nation principle under the USMFTA is that products available in Morocco can be released into the market of all African countries that engage in trade with Morocco and that may affect measures to promote local production of pharmaceuticals in Africa generally. This will be the case where measures are put in place to limit foreign imports in other African countries who have trade agreements with Morocco. Morocco will, under the non-discrimination principles, be bound to introduce the products coming from foreign investments to all the markets where it trades.

With respect to minimum treatment, USMFTA makes it obligatory for the Parties to 'accord to covered investments treatment in accordance with customary international law, including fair and equitable treatment and full protection and security'.[39] The minimum treatment concepts of 'fair and equitable treatment' and 'full protection and security' are defined by USMFTA as follows:

a "fair and equitable treatment" includes the obligation not to deny justice in criminal, civil, or administrative adjudicatory proceedings in accordance with the principle of due process embodied in the principal legal systems of the world; and
b "full protection and security" requires each Party to provide the level of police protection required under customary international law.

The requirement to accord investments full protection and security as well as fair and equitable treatment can limit a country's ability to take legislative or administrative measures to promote access to pharmaceutical products protected by IP rights. Baker and Geddes aptly describe how the minimum standard requirement can pose a real barrier to measures to enhance access to patented pharmaceuticals thus:

> In the pharmaceutical context, foreign investors might claim that the "minimum standard of treatment" rule covers their reasonable expectations for future profits arising from the granting or even filing of intellectual property claims. Changing or re-interpreting substantive IP standards or guidelines judicially, administratively deciding pre- or post-grant patent oppositions in favor of challengers, or adjudicating exceptions to granted rights might all be interpreted as violations of minimum standards of treatment. In sum, whenever foreign IP rightholders disagree with judicial or administrative decisions or view those decisions as insufficiently transparent or candid,

38 B K Baker & K Geddes, 'Corporate Power Unbound: Investor-State Arbitration of IP Monopolies on Medicines-Eli Lilly V. Canada and the Trans-Pacific Partnership Agreement' (2015) *Journal of Intellectual Property Law* 1, 16.
39 USMFTA 10.5(1).

> the foreign rightholder could potentially bring investment chapter claims directly against that government without ever being required to exhaust appeal mechanisms.[40]

Of particular significance to this discussion are the performance requirements of the USMFTA. Article 10.8 (1)(a), (b), (c) and (f) set out the obligations of Parties in relation to the investment of foreign investors as follows:

> 1 Neither Party may, in connection with the establishment, acquisition, expansion, management, conduct, operation, or sale or other disposition of an investment of an investor of a Party or of a non-Party in its territory, impose or enforce any requirement or enforce any commitment or undertaking:
>
> a to export a given level or percentage of goods or services;
> b to achieve a given level or percentage of domestic content;
> c to purchase, use, or accord a preference to goods produced in its territory, or to purchase goods from persons in its territory;
> f to transfer a particular technology, a production process, or other proprietary knowledge to a person in its territory.

Paragraph 1(a) of Article 10.8 can create legal difficulties where pharmaceutical products are to be manufactured for exports to countries without the capacity to manufacture the drugs under the TRIPS compulsory licensing regime. Paragraph 1(b) prohibits local the use of local content requirements even where such is designed to help promote local manufacturing capacity. Under Paragraph 1(c) of the agreement, Parties are barred from adopting measures to protect local industries by imposing a requirement that favours the use of local products in any means. Thus, the agreement makes it more onerous to develop local capacity in sectors of vital importance to the economy without violating the terms of the Agreement. Paragraph 1(f) particularly prohibits countries from demanding a technology transfer arrangement with respect to the 'establishment, acquisition, expansion, management, conduct, operation, or sale or other disposition of an investment of an investor of a Party or of a non-Party'. This condition can pose a real challenge to a developing country like Morocco in the pursuit of technological sophistication and industrial development. In the access to medicines context, it would be particularly difficult to build local pharmaceutical manufacturing capacity without technology transfer agreements. It is pertinent to note that the TRIPS Agreement encourages WTO Members to promote technology transfer. Thus, Article 7 of the TRIPS Agreement provides thus:

> The protection and enforcement of intellectual property rights should contribute to the promotion of technological innovation and to the transfer

40 B K Baker & K Geddes, 'Corporate Power Unbound: Investor-State Arbitration of IP Monopolies On Medicines-Eli Lilly V. Canada and the Trans-Pacific Partnership Agreement' (2015) *Journal of Intellectual Property Law* 1, 25.

and dissemination of technology, to the mutual advantage of producers and users of technological knowledge and in a manner conducive to social and economic welfare, and to a balance of rights and obligations.

The effect of Article 10.8(1)(f) of the USMFTA is to prohibit a Party from insisting on technology transfer as a condition for investment agreements. Article 10.8(3)(b) however provides that the prohibition against technology transfer does not apply where a Party approves the use of patent right pursuant to the provisions of TRIPS on compulsory licensing or where measures for the disclosure of proprietary information are taken in accordance with the provisions of Article 39 of the TRIPS Agreement. These exceptions are apparently narrow and are designed to be restrictively applied. It seems the exceptions would only be applicable where compulsory licences are to be issued to address a public health emergency or a grave public interest intervention. The prohibition on the inclusion of technology transfer requirements in investment agreements can thus impede industrialisation and local manufacturing capacity in developing countries acceding to such investment agreements. It is noteworthy that the provisions discussed above represent the US approach to the negotiation of all investment treaties.[41]

Any breach of the obligations and terms of the investment agreement will invoke the application of the investor-state dispute settlement provisions. Under the USMFTA, Parties are encouraged to attempt to resolve investment disputes through negotiations and consultations.[42] However, where negotiations and consultations fail, the aggrieved Party may submit a claim to arbitration.[43] Generally, the national laws of a state do not carry substantial weight when matters are made subject to investor-state dispute settlement by arbitration. For instance, under Article 10.21(1) of the USMFTA, the governing law for any breach of the Agreement is the USMFTA and any relevant rules of international law. Article 10.21(2) provides that where there is a dispute relating to the breach of an investment authorisation or an investment agreement, the rules of law specified in the investment authorisation or the investment agreement will apply.[44] Where there are no specified rules of law, the domestic law of the respondent, including conflict of laws, principles and relevant rules of international law, will apply.[45]

An investment is defined as 'every asset that an investor owns or controls, directly or indirectly, that has the characteristics of an investment, including such characteristics as the commitment of capital or other resources, the expectation

41 Office of US Trade Representative, 'Summary of U.S. Bilateral Investment Treaty (BIT) Program' https://ustr.gov/archive/Trade_Agreements/BIT/Summary_of_US_Bilateral_Investment_Treaty_(BIT)_Program.html accessed 27 January 2019.

42 USMFTA Article 10.14.

43 USMFTA Article 10.15.

44 USMFTA Article 10.21(2)(a).

45 USMFTA Article 10.21(2)(b).

of gain or profit, or the assumption of risk'.[46] The USMFTA further states that an investment may take the form of IP rights.[47] Investment disputes under the USMFTA are to be pursued under the Convention nn the Settlement of Investment Disputes Between States and Nationals of Other States which is administered by the International Centre for Settlement of Investment Disputes (ICSID Convention), or; under the United Nations Commission on International Trade Law (UNCITRAL) Arbitration Rules or; any other arbitral rules or institution the Parties have agreed to approach in the event of a dispute occurring.[48]

8.4.2 **Eli Lily v Canada:** ***a case study on how investment clauses in RTAs may erode TRIPS flexibilities***

As mentioned earlier, IP rights are considered as investments that can be the subject of an investor-state dispute arbitral claim. A recent example is the Eli Lilly's investment arbitration against the Government of Canada. Eli Lily brought the claim against the Government of Canada for the invalidation of its drugs Strattera and Zyprexa by the Canadian courts.[49] Both patents were invalidated by the Canadian Courts for failing to satisfy the 'usefulness' requirement under Canadian patents law.[50] The claimant contended that the basis of the Canadian courts invalidation of the patents was their adoption of the 'promise utility doctrine' in the mid-2000s which the claimant considered to be 'new, arbitrary and discriminatory against pharmaceutical companies and products'.[51] The claimant contended that the application of the 'promise utility doctrine' was inconsistent with Canada's IP obligations under the North America Free Trade Agreement (NAFTA) and that it also amounted to unlawful expropriation under NAFTA.[52] They further argued that Canada's action was in breach of the minimum standard of treatment obligations under NAFTA.[53] Patent utility under Canadian patent law is based on two major elements; the first being that the invention must offer something of practical value and second, the disclosure in the patent specifications and claims must be detailed and sufficient enough to allow a person skilled in the relevant art to be able to put into effect 'the desired promise of the patent'.[54] Thus, if no specific result is promised in the specification, a 'mere scintilla' of usefulness will suffice.[55] However, where

46 USMFTA Article 10.27.
47 Ibid.
48 USMFTA 10.15(3).
49 *Eli Lilly and Company v Government of Canada* (Case No. UNCT/14/2) para 5.
50 Ibid.
51 Ibid.
52 Ibid.
53 Ibid.
54 Freedom-Kai Phillips, 'Promise Utility Doctrine and Compatibility Doctrine under NAFTA: Expropriation and Chapter 11 Considerations' (2016) 40(1) *Canada-United States Law Journal* 84, 93–94.
55 Ibid., 94.

a specific outcome is provided in the specification, utility is to be determined by that standard.[56]

The Zypreka (olanzapine) patent was filed on 24 April 1991 for the invention of a new organic compound capable of being used for the treatment of 'serious mental conditions such as schizophrenia and schizophreniform illnesses'.[57] The patent was issued on 14 July 1998.[58] Regulatory approval to market a generic version of Zypreka was granted to a Canadian drug manufacturer, Novopharm Limited, by Health Canada in June 2007.[59] Lilly Canada instituted a patent infringement action against Novopharm and the Canadian Federal Court dismissed the action and invalidated Lilly's patent for failing to describe an invention over and above what was already known.[60] In dismissing the action, the Federal Court noted thus:

> One does not have to discredit a product or those who make it in order to invalidate its patent. I am satisfied that olanzapine is a useful drug for the treatment of schizophrenia. However, Lilly had a patent for it that lasted from 1980 to 1997. It sought a separate and supplementary patent for it, no doubt, to try to recuperate some of its corporate investment in its neuroleptic programme ... But as the sun began to set on the '687 patent, it became important to try to extend the patent protection for olanzapine. The '113 patent was clearly drafted with a view of justifying a fresh patent. But the evidence just was not there, yet. Accordingly, I must conclude that the '113 is not a valid selection patent. The claims set out above are invalid.[61]

Lilly Canada appealed against the judgment to the Federal Court of Appeal and the court, in allowing the appeal, remitted the issues of utility and sufficiency of disclosure back to the Federal Court for reconsideration.[62] The Federal Court reconsidered the case as directed by the Federal Court of Appeal and found the patent invalid for lack of utility as the patent promise had not been demonstrated.[63] Lilly Canada's further appeal to the Federal Court was dismissed and leave to appeal to the Supreme Court of Canada was declined.[64]

With respect to the Strattera Patent (Atomoxetine), Eli Lilly Canada first obtained a patent for a class of chemical compounds including atomoxetine in 1979 for use as 'psychotropic agents' and antidepressants.[65] In 1985, Eli Lilly

56 Ibid., 94.

57 Eli Lilly and Company v Government of Canada (Case No. UNCT/14/2) Paragraph 73.

58 Ibid., Paragraph 78.

59 Ibid., Paragraph 79.

60 Ibid., Paragraph 80.

61 Eli Lilly Canada Inc. v. Novopharm Ltd., 2009 FC 1018, 154; quoted in Eli Lilly and Company v Government of Canada (Case No. UNCT/14/2) Paragraph 80.

62 Eli Lilly and Company v Government of Canada (Case No. UNCT/14/2) Paragraph 81.

63 Ibid., Paragraph 82.

64 Ibid., Paragraphs 83–84.

65 Ibid., Paragraph 85.

filed another patent for atomoxetine for use as an antidepressant.[66] In January 1996, Eli Lilly filed a 'new use' patent application for atomoxetine under the Patent Cooperation Treaty.[67] The Strattera patent claims the use of atomoxetine for treating a 'psychiatric disorder known as attention-deficit/hyperactivity disorder'.[68] The Strattera patent was issued in October 2002.[69] Novopharm brought an action challenging the validity of the Strattera Patent and the patent was invalidated by the Federal Court in September 2010 for lack of utility.[70] Eli Lilly's appeal to the Federal Court of Appeal was dismissed and leave to appeal to the Supreme Court of Canada was refused.[71] Thus, Eli Lilly instituted an investor-state dispute claim against the Government of Canada for the invalidation of its patents.

While the claimant strenuously contended in the investor-state dispute arbitration against Canada that the promise utility doctrine was new and applied to its patents retroactively, the Tribunal was not persuaded that this was the case and found the promise utility doctrine to have been part of the Canadian patent law jurisprudence since 1981.[72] In dismissing the entirety of Eli Lilly Canada's claim again the Government of Canada, the Tribunal thus opined:

> For the above reasons, the Tribunal holds that even if it were to accept Claimant's position regarding the legal standards applicable to its allegations of arbitrariness and discrimination, Claimant has failed to establish the factual premise on which its allegations of arbitrariness and discrimination are based. The Tribunal has already concluded that there was no fundamental or dramatic change in Canadian patent law. In the circumstances presented in these proceedings, the evolution of the Canadian legal framework relating to Claimant's patents cannot sustain a claim of arbitrariness or discrimination going to a violation of NAFTA Articles 1105(1) or 1110(1).[73]

The *Eli Lilly v Government of Canada's case* thus illustrates how investment clauses in free trade agreements may be used to challenge the right of states to adopt national measures to protect public health or promote local pharmaceutical innovation. In negotiating free trade agreements involving developing countries, it is very important for trade negotiators to protect their right to use the existing flexibilities available under the TRIPS Agreement and not accede to RTAs that may completely erode these flexibilities.

66 Ibid., Paragraph 86.
67 Ibid., Paragraph 88.
68 Ibid., Paragraph 88.
69 Ibid., Paragraph 91.
70 Ibid., Paragraph 93.
71 Ibid., Paragraph 94.
72 Ibid., Paragraphs 316–325.
73 Ibid., Paragraph 442.

8.5 Free trade agreements and access to medicines

Regional trade agreements have increased tremendously since the adoption of the GATT. Trade agreements in general have brought about the elimination of tariff and non-tariff barriers to trade with extraordinary outcomes for the global economy. Nonetheless, there have been grave concerns on the impact of trade agreements on global public health.[74] RTAs are able to enhance economic growth beyond the limits achievable through the WTO multilateral trade system and they provide an opportunity for the contracting parties to specially design trade rules that are suitable to their local circumstances.[75] A major concern is the fact that many trade agreements include provisions that limit the ability of countries to adopt national measures to address issues of vital importance to public interest, national economy or public health without running afoul of their obligations under multilateral, plurilateral or bilateral trade agreements.[76] There is a clear nexus between trade and health and the need to ensure that countries are not constrained from protecting public health due to multilateral trade obligations is well recognised in many WTO multilateral trade agreements including the GATT.[77]

In a similar vein, the WTO Agreement on Technical Barriers to Trade empowers countries to adopt measures for the protection of public health.[78] The WTO General Agreement on Trade in Services also recognises the right of WTO Members to adopt public health measures in relation to trade in services.[79]

This position is equally recognised in Article 8.1 of the TRIPS Agreement. There is also the WTO Agreement on the Application of Sanitary and Phytosanitary Measures (SPS Agreement) which confers on WTO Members 'the right to take sanitary and phytosanitary measures necessary for the protection of human, animal or plant life or health' provided such measures are not inconsistent with the SPS Agreement.[80] Despite the clear recognition of the need to protect the interest of states in implementing regulations that protect public health and the well-being of their citizens in the major multilateral trade agreements, trade rules are often implemented in a manner that undermines the sovereignty of states and their ability to adopt measure to regulate in public interest.[81]

74 J Libermand & A Mitchell, 'In Search of Coherence between Trade and Health: Inter-Institutional Opportunities' (2010) 25 *Maryland Journal of International Law* 143, 148–149.

75 S J Powell & T Low, 'Beyond Labor Rights: Which Core Human Rights Must Regional Trade Agreements Protect?' (2012) 12 *Richmond Journal of Global Law and Business* 91, 95.

76 J Libermand & A Mitchell, 'In Search of Coherence between Trade and Health: Inter-Institutional Opportunities' (2010) 25 *Maryland Journal of International Law* 143, 148–149.

77 GATT Article XX(b).

78 Agreement on Technical Barriers to Trade, Article 2.2.

79 General Agreement on Trade in Services Article XIV(b).

80 SPS Agreement Article 2.1.

81 J Libermand & A Mitchell, 'In Search of Coherence between Trade and Health: Inter-Institutional Opportunities' (2010) 25 *Maryland Journal of International Law* 143, 148–149.

It has been argued that the present deficiencies and failures in the protection of global public health internationally may be attributable to the 'absence of a legally consistent global health governance framework'.[82] The challenge with having a coherent legal framework for public health at the global level may also be due to the conceptual difficulty associated with the definition of health.[83] Health indeed can mean different things to different populations[84] and a perfect state of health is hardly attainable. While a legally consistent global framework for health governance may be particularly difficult to achieve given the fragmented nature of international economic law, there is a clear need to ensure RTAs do not unnecessary impede access to life-saving medications. This point was particularly accentuated in the report of the UN Secretary General's High-Level Panel on Access to Medicines published in September 2016. The UN High-Level Panel noted thus:

> Governments engaged in bilateral and regional trade and investment treaties should ensure that these agreements do not include provisions that interfere with their obligations to fulfil the right to health. As a first step, they must undertake public health impact assessments. These impact assessments should verify that the increased trade and economic benefits are not endangering or impeding the human rights and public health obligations of the nation and its people before entering into commitments. Such assessments should inform negotiations, be conducted transparently and made publicly available.[85]

The US-Morocco Free Trade Agreement is one RTA with significant public health implications. With the adoption of the African Continental Free Trade Agreement in 2018, the provisions of the Agreement may affect other African countries as the non-discrimination principles require Morocco not only to treat US goods and investments as it treats products and investments owned by Morocco, but also to accord all benefits and privileges accorded to African trading partners to US goods and investments. It is therefore very important for African trade negotiators to consider the potential public health impact of any RTA they negotiate before entering into binding commitments.

8.6 Conclusion

Trade liberalisation has played a significant role in enhancing economic growth and RTAs are used to facilitate trade liberalisation by building blocs for a

82 R J Neuwirth & A Svetlicinii, 'Law as a Social Medicine: Enhancing International Inter-Regime Regulatory Coopetition as a Means for the Establishment of a Global Health Governance Framework' (2015) 36 *Journal of Legal Medicine* 330, 333–334.

83 Ibid.

84 Ibid.

85 Report of the United Nations Secretary-General's High-Level Panel on Access to Medicines (September 2016) 9.

stronger and more transparent global economy.[86] Africa remains the world's least developed continent with more than 50% of African countries currently ranked as least developed countries by the UN. There is therefore no gainsaying the fact that Africa as a continent can benefit from trade liberalisation and the negotiation of RTAs with more advanced economies. The major concern however is the extent to which multilateral and regional trade agreements may pose a challenge to public health and access to medicines in African countries through the fetters that such agreements may impose on the ability of African countries to adopt measures to address issues of national interest especially as they affect public health objectives. The US-Morocco Free Trade Agreement is an example of an African RTA with provisions that substantially whittle down the existing flexibilities under the TRIPS Agreement and this may have implications for other African nations trading with Morocco given the non-discrimination principles entrenched in the USMFTA. As seen in the Eli Lilly's action against the Government of Canada, investment settlement clauses in free trade agreements may also make it possible to challenge national measures to make use of the TRIPS flexibilities before international arbitration tribunals where national laws may not be applicable. It is therefore very important for trade negotiators from developing countries to carefully consider the public health and pubic interest implications of obligations imposed by RTAs before acceding to them. It is also important for Africa as a continent to strengthen its existing economic communities so as to have a strong common front in the negotiation of RTAs with developed economies.

Bibliography

Baker B K & Geddes K, 'Corporate Power Unbound: Investor-State Arbitration of IP Monopolies on Medicines-Eli Lilly V. Canada and the Trans-Pacific Partnership Agreement' (2015) 23 *Journal of Intellectual Property Law* 1.

Libermand J & Mitchell A, 'In Search of Coherence between Trade and Health: Inter-Institutional Opportunities' (2010) 25 *Maryland Journal of International Law* 143.

Neuwirth R J & Svetlicinii A, 'Law as a Social Medicine: Enhancing International Inter-Regime Regulatory Coopetition as a Means for the Establishment of a Global Health Governance Framework' (2015) 36 *Journal of Legal Medicine* 330.

Office of the United States Trade Representative, Free Trade Agreement https://ustr.gov/trade-agreements/free-trade-agreements accessed 27 January 2019.

Office of United States Trade Representative, 'Summary of U.S. Bilateral Investment Treaty (BIT) Program' https://ustr.gov/archive/Trade_Agreements/BIT/Summary_of_US_Bilateral_Investment_Treaty_(BIT)_Program.html accessed 27 January 2019.

Owoeye O, Olatunji O & Faturoti B, 'Patents and the Trans-Pacific Partnership: How TPP-style intellectual property standards may exacerbate the access to medicines problem in the East African Community' (2017) *International Trade Journal* 1–22 doi:10.1080/08853908.2017.1386143 accessed 27 January 2019.

86 O Owoeye, 'Regionalism and WTO Multilateralism: The Case for an African Continental Free Trade Area' (2016) 50(6) *Journal of World Trade* 1085, 1090.

Owoeye O, 'Regionalism and WTO Multilateralism: The Case for an African Continental Free Trade Area' (2016) 50(6) *Journal of World Trade* 1085.

Phillips F-K, 'Promise Utility Doctrine and Compatibility Doctrine under NAFTA: Expropriation and Chapter 11 Considerations' (2016) 40(1) *Canada-United States Law Journal* 84.

Powell S J & Low T, 'Beyond Labor Rights: Which Core Human Rights Must Regional Trade Agreements Protect?' (2012) 12 *Richmond Journal of Global Law and Business* 91.

Sanders A K, "Intellectual Property, Free Trade Agreements and Economic Development" (2007) 23 *Georgia State University Law Review* 893.

9 Free trade and economic collaboration as paradigms for access to medicines

9.1 Introduction

A wide range of organisations and studies continue to accentuate the need for building local manufacturing capacity in the pharmaceutical sector in Africa. Achieving this will involve considerable financial investment in training, infrastructure and a viable market for pharmaceutical products. One current challenge that pharmaceutical companies in African countries encounter is the ability to market products in other countries within the region without significant market barriers.[1] The absence of strong structures for free trade in the continent presents, to this end, a major part of the access problem. It stands to reason that what Africa requires to address its current public health crisis in the continent is an economic alliance to foster free trade and enable parties to harness their resources to fund major investment projects like the development of a strong pharmaceutical manufacturing capacity. Such an economic alliance holds substantial benefits for African people if there is the political will to pursue it. Africa has long recognised the need for an economic collaboration within the continent to advance the socio-economic development of African nations and their people. This informed the adoption of the Treaty Establishing the African Economic Community in 1991 (Abuja Treaty).[2] In March 2018, the African Continental Free Trade Agreement (AfCFTA) was signed by 44 African countries in Kigali, Rwanda.[3] AfCFTA is to enter into force 'thirty (30) days after the deposit of the twenty second (22nd) instrument of ratification'.[4] As of 14 January 2019 and the date of writing, eight countries have ratified AfCFTA.[5] This chapter, building

1 I C Boulton, *Setting the Scene* (Forum for Africa-based Pharmaceutical Manufacturers and Potential Investors Kenya, 2011).

2 See e.g. Pan African Perspective, 'The African Economic Community' www.panafricanperspective.com/aec.htm accessed 27 January 2019.

3 See K Ighobor, *Africa Set for a Massive Free Trade Area, Africa Renewal*, August–November 2018 www.un.org/africarenewal/magazine/august-november-2018/africa-set-massive-free-trade-area accessed 27 January 2019.

4 African Continental Free Trade Agreement, Article 23.

5 African Union, *African Continental Free Trade Agreement Status List.* https://au.int/sites/default/files/treaties/34248-sl-agreement_establishing_the_african_continental_free_trade_area_1.pdf accessed 27 January 2019.

on conclusions derived from Chapters 1–8, uses the provisions on the Abuja Treaty to place a spotlight on how the creation of an African regional trade agreement (RTA) area can serve as a coalition strategy for promoting the interest of African countries in the World Trade Organization (WTO), and facilitate economic collaboration for the development of pharmaceutical manufacturing capacity in the continent. It also discusses how an African free-trade area can enhance the effective use of compulsory licences, the parallel importation of pharmaceuticals and the importation of generic drugs that are off-patent.

9.1.1 Intellectual property and free trade

The WTO TRIPS Agreement (The Agreement on Trade-Related Aspects of Intellectual Property Rights) was introduced into the Uruguay Round of the General Agreement on Tariffs and Trade (GATT) discussions in recognition of the fact that liberalising trade may have the effect of eroding Intellectual Property Rights (IPRs) in the absence of sufficient safeguards.[6] The connection between intellectual property (IP) and trade is well adumbrated in the following extract from a WTO briefing paper:

> The WTO's intellectual property agreement amounts to rules for trade and investment in ideas and creativity. The rules state how copyrights, patents, trademarks, geographical names used to identify products, industrial designs, integrated circuit layout-designs and undisclosed information such as trade secrets – "intellectual property" – should be protected when trade is involved.[7]

Osei Tutu has opined that trade-based IP has adopted a commodity-based approach without taking into cognisance the non-economic dimension to patent and copyright laws and she identifies a need for the global IP regime to embrace the diverse goals and values intrinsic in national IP systems.[8] This necessitates balancing the rights of IP holders with the public interest in accessing public goods such as essential medicines, books and modern inventions. However, the present trade-based international IP regime is unlikely to accommodate such significant changes soon. This is because the language of TRIPS only allows the protection of national interests to the extent that these do not derogate from the substantive rights protected by TRIPS. It is doubtful that any further amendments can successfully be made to TRIPS, given the experience with the attempt to amend Article 31, dealing with compulsory licensing.[9] As canvassed

6 See Chapter 2.
7 WTO, The WTO in Brief: Part 3 www.wto.org/english/thewto_e/whatis_e/inbrief_e/inbr03_e.htm accessed 27 January 2019.
8 J J Osei Tutu, 'Value Divergence in Global Intellectual Property' (2012) 87 *Indiana Law Journal* 1639, 1645–1646.
9 See Chapter 1.

in Chapter 5, an option with potentially greater prospect of success is to encourage the adoption of a more purposive interpretation of TRIPS to give greater force to the developmental interest of developing countries.

In the African context, a more pragmatic approach to the problem is to adopt the current flexibilities in the system into domestic legislation in a consistent manner across the continent, and use the paradigm of free trade to advance the cause of African nations in the global governance of IP. It has been noted that trade functions more efficiently when there is a uniform standard that applies in all jurisdictions.[10] This is particularly so in the case of custom unions which are free-trade areas with uniform external tariff. The problem, however, has always been how to determine what should be taken as the all-pervading standard. The essence of having an RTA is to promote economic efficiency and social welfare through optimum distribution of resources.

African nations have embraced the TRIPS Agreement without putting adequate structures in place for free trade in the continent. The consequence of this is that the prices of goods protected by IPRs in Africa are further affected by the current impediments to free trade such as tariffs and excise duties. The solution to the access to medicines problem should begin with real trade liberalisation in the continent followed by a collaborative arrangement for developing a strong local manufacturing capacity in the pharmaceutical sector. At present, the reasons for lack of access do not stem from the fact that most patented pharmaceuticals are protected in Africa. The first problem is that most countries in Africa do not have the capacity to make generic versions of such products even where there is a case of public health emergency. Another problem is the fact that the existing market barriers to goods such as customs and excise duties have significant implications for their affordability. There is accordingly need for African countries to expedite actions on the implementation of the Agreement Establishing the African Economic Community at least in so far as the establishment of a free-trade area in Africa is concerned. Section 9.2 provides some information on how the Abuja Treaty emerged in 1991.

9.2 The Treaty Establishing the African Economic Community (Abuja Treaty): a brief background

The Organisation of African Unity (OAU) was established in 1963 to facilitate unity, solidarity and cooperation among African states.[11] In July 1979, the now defunct OAU adopted the 'Monrovia Declaration of Commitment of the Heads of State and Government of the OAU'.[12] The Monrovia Declaration was

10 S Lester, 'The Role of the International Trade Regime in Global Governance' (2011) 16 *UCLA Journal of International Law and Foreign Affairs* 209, 262.

11 See Preamble of Charter of the Organization of African Unity, 479 UNTS 39 (entered into force 13 September 1963).

12 See Organization of African Unity, *Lagos Plan of Action for the Economic Development of Africa 1980–2000* (OAU, 1980) www.nepadst.org/doclibrary/pdfs/lagos_plan.pdf accessed 6 October 2013.

adopted in response to the serious economic problems in Africa and a general disenchantment with global development strategies.[13] The OAU further adopted the Lagos Plan of Action and Final Act of Lagos in 1980 to reinforce its commitment to the economic integration of African countries. The Lagos Plan of Action was implemented through the adoption in 1991 of the Treaty Establishing the African Economic Community (here-in-after called Abuja Treaty) which was signed by 51 African Heads of State and Government in Abuja, Nigeria. It entered into force on 12 May 1994. On 7 November 2000, the African Union was established to replace the OAU through the adoption of the African Union Constitutive Act.[14] A reason for the establishment of the African Union (AU) was to better facilitate the realisation of the ultimate objectives of the Abuja Treaty Establishing the African Economic Community.[15]

In furtherance of this objective, the AU adopted the Protocol to the Treaty Establishing the African Economic Community Relating to the Pan African Parliament on 2 March 2001 to facilitate discussions on the implementation of the Abuja Treaty. The Protocol entered into force on 14 December 2003.[16] Article 6 of the Abuja Treaty provides that the African Economic Community (AEC) shall be established over a transitional period not exceeding 34 years. However, 27 years after the adoption of the Abuja Treaty and 24 years after its entry into force, little has been done towards the establishment of the AEC. The implementation of some of the provisions of the Abuja Treaty, particularly in relation to the establishment of a free-trade area in Africa, could, however, go some way in addressing the African access to medicines problem.

9.2.1 The treaty establishing the African Economic Community and its provisions on economic collaboration in Africa

The relevant provisions of the Agreement are briefly examined below as a precursor to the formulation of recommendations on how best to pursue its implementation. Given its significance to the argument on free trade and economic collaboration in Africa, it is apposite to reproduce the objectives of the AEC as contained in Article 4(1) of the Abuja Treaty. Article 4(1) provides thus:

> The objectives of the community shall be:
>
> a To promote economic, social and cultural development and the integration of African economies in order to increase economic self-reliance and promote an endogenous and self-sustained development;

13 Ibid., 4.

14 See Article 33(1) of the Constitutive Act of the African Union opened for signature 11 July 2000 (entered into force on 26 May 2001).

15 Preamble to the Constitutive Act of the African Union.

16 See African Union, 'OAU/AU Treaties. Conventions, Protocols, & Charters' www.au.int/en/treaties accessed 27 January 2019.

b To establish, on a continental scale, a framework for the development, mobilisation and utilisation of the human and material resources of Africa in order to achieve a self-reliant development;
c To promote cooperation in all fields of human endeavour in order to raise the standard of living of African peoples, and maintain and enhance economic stability, foster close and peaceful relations among Member States and contribute to the progress, development and the economic integration of the Continent; and
d To coordinate and harmonize policies among existing and future economic communities in order to foster the gradual establishment of the Community.

Article 4(1) of the Abuja Treaty shows that the objective of the AEC is to promote interdependence and economic collaboration among Member States so as to advance the socio-economic development of the African people. The AEC, when established, should substantially reduce the current impediments to free trade in the region and, in line with its objective of mobilising and utilising the 'human and material resources of Africa', provide a feasible framework for the development of strong pharmaceutical manufacturing capacity in the continent.

By Article 6 of the Abuja Treaty, the AEC is expected to be established gradually in six stages of variable duration over a period of 36 years. The stages are summarised below:

1 strengthening of existing regional economic communities within the continent and establishment of such communities, within five years of entry into force of the Treaty, where they do not exist;
2 stabilising Tariff Barriers and non-tariff barriers, customs duties and internal taxes at the regional economic community level within a period of eight years and preparing a timetable for the removal of all such barriers to trade. The second stage also involves harmonisation and coordination of activities among the existing future and economic communities;
3 establishment of a free trade area within a period of ten years and the establishment of a Customs Union through the adoption of a common external tariff at the level of each regional economic community;
4 harmonisation of tariff and non-tariff systems among the various regional economic communities within a period of two years with a view to establishing a customs union for the continent and the adoption of a common external tariff;
5 establishment of an African Common Market within a period of 4 years, through the adoption of a common policy in various areas of trade, the harmonisation of fiscal policies, free movement of persons and common budgetary measures; and
6 consolidation of the African Common Market, integration of all sectors of the economy, the establishment of an African Central Bank and the adoption of a single African currency and the implementation of the final stage of the setting up of the legislative and executive structures of the community.

The Treaty provides that the cumulative transitional period must not exceed 40 years from the date of its entry into force.

The Abuja Treaty offers a platform for African countries to adopt cooperative and collective measures to reduce the barriers to free movement of goods and harness their resources to build multinational industries that are beyond the economic strength of individual nations through economic collaboration. To facilitate the free movement of goods, the Abuja Treaty recommends the establishment of a customs union for the continent. Article 32 provides for the progressive establishment of the customs union which is meant to begin at the level of regional economic communities and eventually culminate in the adoption of a continent-wide customs union.

With respect to cooperative and collective measures to build local industries in different sectors of the economy, the provision of Article 49 is particularly significant. Article 49(a) provides that in order to promote industrialisation and collective self-reliance within the continent, African countries shall ensure the development and modernisation of basic industries including both chemical and biotechnology industries.

Article 49(d) goes further to provide that Member States of the Community shall put structures in place at:

> regional and community levels for the establishment of African multinational industries particularly those whose construction cost and volumes of production exceed national financial and absorptive capacities.

Article 73 is pertinent in relation to cooperating to promote healthcare delivery in the continent. Article 73 enjoins Member States to encourage and foster cooperation in the area of health by collaborating in developing primary healthcare and facilitating medical research especially with respect to African traditional medicine and pharmacopoeia.

It appears that the Abuja Treaty has put in place a strong legal framework that can be used to facilitate the free movement of goods in Africa and thus to build a strong local pharmaceutical industry through the cooperative and collective efforts of Member States. There are now eight different Regional Economic Communities in Africa:[17]

1 the Community of Sahel-Saharan States (CEN-SAD);
2 the Common Market for Eastern and Southern Africa (COMESA);
3 the East African Community (EAC);
4 the Economic Community of Central African States (ECCAS);
5 the Economic Community Of West African States (ECOWAS);

17 United Nations, 'Regional Economic Communities of the African Union' www.un.org/en/africa/osaa/peace/recs.shtml accessed 27 January 2017.

6 the Intergovernmental Authority on Development (IGAD) in Eastern Africa;
7 the Southern African Development Community (SADC); and
8 the Union du Maghreb Arabe (UMA)

The implementation of the Abuja Treaty is currently at the third stage. AfCFTA was adopted in March 2018 but it is yet to enter into force.

9.2.2 The challenges of implementing the Abuja Treaty

The Abuja Treaty envisages the creation of a customs union and a 'borderless' Africa whereby people will be able to move freely and settle anywhere within the community. Article 43 provides:

> Member States agree to adopt, individually, at bilateral or regional levels, the necessary measures, in order to achieve progressively the free movement of persons, and to ensure the enjoyment of the right of residence and the right of establishment by their nationals within the Community.

It also contains significant provisions that entail a strong political alliance among African countries. This is probably one of its most problematic provisions as many African countries seem unprepared for the degree of political integration it envisages. The Abuja Treaty also proposes the adoption of a common fiscal policy for the continent so as to boost intra-community trade in goods and services.[18] The final stage of the implementation of the Treaty is expected to culminate in the creation of an African Central Bank and the adoption of a common African currency.[19] Given the highly ambitious scope of the Treaty, it is doubtful whether it will be capable of being given effect within the prescribed 40-year timeline. The Abuja Treaty entered into force over two decades ago but there is still a very long way to go for all its objectives to be actualised. Yet the current economic and health crisis in the continent and the deplorable state of human development makes the establishment of a free-trade area and customs union a priority task as this has the capacity to significantly ameliorate the African access to medicines problem. It is nonetheless conceded that the establishment of the AEC may not occur in the near future and even a customs union may not necessarily attract popular support at this stage. However, the creation of an African free-trade area as envisaged in the Abuja Treaty is a realistic goal especially with the current regional economic communities within the continent. The African Union (AU), to this end, could under its mandate take immediate steps to facilitate the process of encouraging Member States to ratify AfCFTA and implement it. The significance of a common front in negotiating international agreements on trade and IP cannot be overemphasised.

18 Treaty Establishing the African Economic Community, opened for signature 3 June 1991 (entered into force 12 May 1994), Article 44.

19 Ibid., Article 6(2)(f).

9.3 The role of the African Union

The AU has begun devising strategies for the full utilisation of compulsory licensing in Africa.[20] Its policy position, taken by 55 African Ministers of Health in the 2005 Gaborone Declaration, is

> ...to pursue, with the support of our partners, the local production of generic medicines on the Continent and make full use of flexibilities within the Trade and Related Aspects of Intellectual Property Rights (TRIPS) and Doha Declaration on TRIPS and Public Health.[21]

The AU's approach appears to place emphasis on national and regional efforts.[22] However, a continent-wide collaboration under the AU for every region in Africa is likely to be a more effective solution to the problem. The AU adopted a Pharmaceutical Manufacturing Plan for Africa to address this issue in 2007 which recommended that a Technical Committee be established to prepare a detailed report on the implications of local production of pharmaceuticals.[23] In its report, the Committee noted that local production of affordable medicines with quality, safety and efficacy would only be possible by collaboration.[24] Foreign aid has been a significant means of making drugs for the HIV pandemic available in Africa. According to a report on pharmaceutical innovation in Africa:

> Africa's capacity for pharmaceutical R&D and local drug production is among the lowest globally. Overall, 37 countries have some pharmaceutical production, and only South Africa has limited primary production of active pharmaceutical ingredient (API) and intermediates. Local production in Africa therefore relies on imported active ingredients. As a result, the sustainability of African pharmaceutical supply remains highly contingent on foreign funding and manufacturing.'[25]

However, to continue to rely on foreign aid without devising a means of finding a lasting solution to the access to medicines problem will result in a situation whereby healthcare delivery in the continent continually remains a far cry from

20 African Union, *Draft Pharmaceutical Manufacturing Plan for Africa*, Doc. CAMH/MIN/7(III), 6 (10–13 April 2007).

21 African Union, *Gaborone Declaration on a Roadmap Towards Universal Access to Prevention, Treatment and Care*, Doc. CAMH/Decl.1(II) 3 (10–14 October 2005).

22 M Berger, I Murugi, F Buch, C IJsselmuiden, M Moran, J Guzman, M Devlin & B Kubata, *Strengthening Pharmaceutical Innovation in Africa* (AU, COHRED and NEPAD, 2010) 58–59.

23 African Union Secretariat, *Draft Pharmaceutical Manufacturing Plan for Africa*, Doc. CAMH/MIN/7(III), 6 (10–13 April 2007).

24 African Union Secretariat, *Progress Report on the Pharmaceutical Manufacturing Plan for Africa*, Doc. MIN/Sp?AU?CAMH3/2, 12 (17 May 2008).

25 Berger et al., above n 22, 16.

what it should and could be. As a matter of fact, foreign aid to the continent is already dwindling as a result of the global economic recession.[26]

The time has come for Africa to come to Africa's aid. An objective of the Doha Paragraph-6 System is to encourage countries with insignificant manufacturing capacity in the pharmaceutical sector to aggregate their markets to make the development of a local pharmaceutical industry substantially easier.[27] The current state of local manufacturing capacity in Africa is such that 70% of pharmaceutical and medical products are imported from outside the continent.[28]

The development of a significant manufacturing capacity in Africa can be done by harnessing the existing resources to establish an intergovernmental body industry that is jointly owned by African countries. The development of significant manufacturing capacity in the pharmaceutical sector, coupled with the transitional provision in TRIPS enabling least developed countries to derogate from pharmaceutical patent obligations under TRIPS until 2033 will enable Africa to take full advantage of compulsory licensing and generic manufacturing in the continent pending the expiration of the transitional arrangement.

9.4 Access to medicines and free trade

It was noted earlier that Africa presently has eight regional economic communities. These communities could be amalgamated to constitute a free-trade area covering the whole of Africa, which could lead to a substantial removal of the barriers to trade within the continent while boosting local pharmaceutical manufacturing capacity. As noted by Peter Yu:

> To facilitate the supply of essential medicines to countries with insufficient or no manufacturing capacity, article 31bis (3) creates a special arrangement not only for the affected countries, but also for those belonging to a regional trade agreement. Such an arrangement allows less developed countries to aggregate their markets to generate the purchasing power needed to make the development of an indigenous pharmaceutical industry attractive. It also paves the way for the development of regional supply centres, procurement systems, and patent pools and institutions, while facilitating technical cooperation within the region.[29]

The Deputy Chairperson of the African Union Commission has emphasised the need for an African Common market to boost economic growth in the

26 International Finance Corporation. *Impact Annual Report* (2012) 58.

27 P K Yu, 'Access to Medicines, BRICS Alliances, and Collective Action' (2008) 34 *American Journal of Law and Medicine* 345, 346.

28 UNECA, Developing Africa's Pharmaceutical Sector Crucial, says ECA's Soteri, 1 August 2018 www.uneca.org/stories/developing-africa%E2%80%99s-pharmaceutical-sector-crucial-says-eca%E2%80%99s-soteri accessed 27 January 2019.

29 Yu above n 27, 346.

continent. In a statement made at the 6th Ordinary Session of AU Ministers of Trade in November 2010, he noted:

> We all know that in terms of population (with 38 of the 53 Member States of the AU having a population of 15 million people or less) and aggregate purchasing power, the size of the national market in most African countries is too small for competiveness in the global economy. Time has therefore come for us to speed up the establishment of the African Economic Community, which has been on the drawing board for almost two decades. A Pan-African Common Market of 1 billion people without internal borders will unleash the enormous economic growth and development potentials of Africa and strengthen economic independence of the continent.[30]

The AU adopted the 'Declaration on Boosting Intra African Trade and the Establishment of a free trade area' in January 2012. It noted that intra-African trade and deepened market integration could contribute considerably to sustainable economic growth, poverty reduction, industrial development and the integration of the continent into the world economy, and called for the establishment of a Continental Free-Trade Area by 2017.[31] Having a free-trade area for the WTO African region can, it may be argued, play a significant role in addressing the African access to medicines problem particularly in relation to the use of compulsory licences for importation of patented products into Africa and the parallel importation of such goods. It may also give African countries the economic and political leverage to make maximum use of the TRIPS flexibilities.

Of particular significance to African countries is Paragraph 6 of the Implementation Decision on Paragraph 6 of the Declaration on TRIPS and Public Health which reads:

> With a view to harnessing economies of scale for the purposes of enhancing purchasing power for, and facilitating the local production of, pharmaceutical products:
>
> i where a developing or least-developed country WTO Member is a party to a regional trade agreement within the meaning of Article XXIV of the GATT 1994 and the Decision of 28 November 1979 on Differential and More Favourable Treatment Reciprocity and Fuller Participation of Developing Countries (L/4903), at least half of the current membership of which is made up of countries presently on the United Nations list of least developed countries, the obligation of that Member under Article 31(f) of the TRIPS Agreement shall be waived to the extent necessary to enable a pharmaceutical product produced or imported under

30 Deputy Chairperson, *African Union Commission, Statement made at the 6th Ordinary Session of AU Ministers of Trade*, 1 November 2010, Kigali, Rwanda.

31 African Union, *Declaration on Boosting Intra African Trade and the Establishment of a Continental Free Trade Area (CFTA)*, Assembly/AU/Dec.1(XVIII).

> a compulsory licence in that Member to be exported to the markets of those other developing or least developed country parties to the regional trade agreement that share the health problem in question. It is understood that this will not prejudice the territorial nature of the patent rights in question.

Its upshot is that if African countries can establish a continent-wide regional trade zone, Africa will be able to take advantage of Paragraph 6 of the Decision to market drugs manufactured under a compulsory licence in one region over the entire continent. It will also make it easier for Africa to derive a greater degree of technical cooperation from developed countries in building its manufacturing capacity in the pharmaceutical sector.

It is expedient to move beyond economic communities and establish a continent-wide trade organisation that will enable Africa to benefit maximally from both the TRIPS parallel trade and compulsory licensing regime. The only eligibility condition contained in Paragraph 6 of the Decision – to benefit from the free movement of goods manufactured under compulsory licensing within a regional organisation – is that at least half of the member countries must be categorised as least developed countries by the UN. It is pertinent to note that 33 out of the 54 fully recognised sovereign states in Africa are currently on the UN list of least developed countries.

The public health crisis in Africa has attracted considerable attention and even spawned strong arguments for changing the existing legal order for international IP law to make it compatible with the developmental goals of developing countries. Developing countries have equally been urged to make maximum use of the existing flexibilities in the TRIPS Agreement for their benefit. Calls have been made for developed economies to domesticate the Protocol Amending the TRIPS Agreement[32] to enable them to manufacture products for export to developing countries under the TRIPS compulsory licensing regime.[33] The problem in Africa is, however, unlikely to be significantly ameliorated without putting all necessary structures for a durable solution to the problem on ground.

The access to medicines problem in Africa, as noted earlier, is not due to the fact that most patented pharmaceuticals are patented in Africa.[34] For instance, as of May 2012 only 238 patents had been granted in Rwanda since the nation's independence in 1966 with eight pending patent applications.[35] The country's accession to the Patent Cooperation Treaty in 2011 and its new IP law enacted in 2009 should, however, inevitably lead to an increase in patent applications over time. As already noted on various occasions in this book,[36] the problem

32 See Chapter 2 for discussion on the Protocol Amending the TRIPS Agreement.

33 See e.g. D Nicol & O Owoeye, 'Using TRIPS Flexibilities to Facilitate Access to Medicines' (2013) 91(7) 44 *Bulletin of the World Health Organisation* 533.

34 See Chapter 3.

35 Rwanda Development Board, 'Patent Information' Ref: RDB/3/DG/0504/5/12 dated 31 May 2002.

36 See Chapters 2, 3 and 4.

for most African countries is that they lack the capacity to manufacture generic pharmaceutical products, irrespective of whether they are patented or not. A 2012 study conducted under the auspices of the Results for Development Institute found that whilst IP might be a significant barrier to the production and uptake of affordable pharmaceuticals in developing countries, much would depend on whether the particular health technology being pursued could attract a large commercial market opportunity.[37] It therefore appears that the two major hurdles to having access to medicines in Africa are free trade and local pharmaceutical manufacturing capacity. The establishment of a common market and the creation of a stronger economic and political alliance such as the type envisaged in the Abuja Treaty can provide a strong structure for addressing the African access to medicines conundrum. To avoid isolation in the global governance of trade, there is need for Africa as a continent to embrace trade regionalism.

One of the fundamental principles of WTO law is the most-favoured-nation principle to the effect that with respect to any customs duties or charges of any kind in international trade, any advantage or privilege granted by a Member State to another Member State must be granted immediately and unconditionally to like products emanating from or destined for all other contracting states.[38] Free or preferential trade agreements are an exception to the most-favoured-nation treatment principle.[39] However, the criticism against the proliferation of free trade agreements seems to be based on protectionist bilateral or plurilateral agreements that tend to make it more difficult for non-members to trade with parties to such agreements. An African RTA does not have to make trading with African countries more onerous for non-parties. Rather, its aim should be to intensify economic collaboration and free trade in Africa whilst sufficiently empowering African countries to bargain for fair trade in the WTO multilateral system.

The GATT encourages the formation of free-trade areas and customs union for fostering trade and economic development. A free-trade area liberalises and eliminates barriers to trade within the area to a greater degree than that generally available under the WTO multilateral agreements. Article XXIV 8(b) defines a free-trade area as '*a group of two or more customs territories in which the duties and other restrictive regulations of commerce…are eliminated on substantially all the trade between the constituent territories in products originating in such territories*'. A custom union on the other hand does not only create a free-trade area but also entails the adoption of a uniform external protection standard. Thus, a customs union entails the substitution of one customs territory for two or more customs territories such that '*substantially the same duties and other regulations of commerce are applied by each of the members of the union to the trade of territories*

37 R Goulding & A Palriwala, *Patent Pools: Assessing their Value-Added for Global Health Innovation and Access* (Result for Development Institute, 2012) 5.

38 GATT Article I.

39 GATT Article XXIV 5.

not included in the union'.[40] The adoption of a common external policy is the distinguishing factor between a customs union and a free-trade area.

With the establishment of a free-trade area, the movement of goods within the continent will become easier, which will not only create a more viable market for local pharmaceutical industries in the continent, but also facilitate a more effective use of the existing flexibilities in the TRIPS Agreement. Even generic drugs that are completely off-patent can be easily imported into Africa and their free circulation within the proposed African free-trade area will increase their accessibility and affordability.

9.4.1 The benefits of an African free-trade area

For Africa to be able to benefit fully from the compulsory licensing regime, parallel trade and the social policy objectives of the TRIPS Agreement, a collaborative effort to boost local pharmaceutical manufacturing capacity is required. A recent study undertaken under the auspices of the WHO recommended the application of political pressure for differential pricing and the use of TRIPS flexibilities in relation to high-priced medicines especially where they are patented.[41] The effective use of such pressure for differential pricing and compulsory licensing in Africa could be enhanced through the formation of an African free-trade area.

Under the Doha Implementation Decision and Protocol Amending the TRIPS Agreement, where a developing or least developed country is a party to an RTA recognised by the WTO, it is permitted to export pharmaceutical products produced or imported under a compulsory licence in that Member to other developing or least developed country parties to the RTA. The other countries must however share the same health problem with that of the exporting country and half of the parties to the RTA have to be on the UN list of least developed countries for the exportation of such products within the trade zone to be possible.[42] As more than half of the countries in Africa are presently in the UN list of least developed countries,[43] Africa stands to benefit immensely from the establishment of an economic community in terms of forging a common front to develop a strong pharmaceutical manufacturing capacity whilst facilitating the free movement of drugs made pursuant to compulsory licences within the continent.

Such an economic alliance will give Africa a stronger voice in international politics, better economic leverage in international trade and the ability to

40 GATT Article XXIV 8(a)(ii).

41 World Health Organisation, *World Medicines Situation 2011: Medicines Prices, Availability and Affordability* (World Health Organisation, 2011).

42 World Trade Organisation, *Implementation of paragraph 6 of the Doha Declaration on the TRIPS Agreement and Public Health* WT/L/540 General Council Decision of 30 August 2003.

43 UN Office of the High Representative for the Least Developed Countries, Landlocked Developing Countries and Small Island Developing States(UN-OHRLLS), 'Least Developed Countries' http://unohrlls.org/custom-content/uploads/2018/12/list-of-least-developed-countries-rev1.pdf accessed 26 January 2019.

harness the resources of Member States to substantially advance socio-economic development in the continent. As observed by Stephen Powell and Trisha Low, '*RTAs provide poorer countries with mutual development gains through expanded markets, pooled resources, greater economic diversification, and increased regional investment and trade*'.[44] In addition, an African RTA will enable Africa to enter international markets and integrate into it on a regional scale with a resultant improvement in economic growth and human development.[45]

The significance of free trade to the access to medicines problem seems to have been well articulated in the following observation of Nuno Pires De Carvalho:

> If the populations of poor countries are being ravaged by diseases, it is not because of intellectual property rules, but because of poverty and their incapacity of affording medical treatment (including drugs). Diseases are not treated by reducing the TRIPS standards of protection of intellectual property rights. The real problem is that poor African countries may have acceded to the WTO but they have not acceded to international markets... Unfortunately for developing countries, major WTO partners have preferred to tackle a minor problem – whose practical consequences do not exist outside of a purely academic exercise which is essentially and ultimately anti-patent biased – than seeking a consensus on more serious, core issues, such as subsidies, SPS measures and competition law.[46]

Although Pires de Carvalho is correct in saying diseases are not treated by reducing TRIPS standards, that does not obviate the fact that there is a nexus between IPRs and the affordability of products protected by such rights.[47] Nonetheless, the statement that Africa has acceded to the WTO without a corresponding accession to international markets is true. The very problem that gives the global governance of IP an asymmetrical outlook that favours highly developed economies at the expense of developing and least developed ones also affects other major multilateral trade agreements under the WTO. That problem is simply the inability to mount sufficient bargaining power to ensure the global governance of trade does not continue to foster unequal equality. WTO countries may have equal status especially in respect of their sovereignty in international law, but the benefits they derive from the WTO system are far from equal. While fair trade is very germane to addressing the problem, it can be queried how it can be guaranteed with the current overwhelming bilateral and plurilateral trade agreements

44 S J Powell & T Low, 'Is the WTO Quietly Fading Away?: The New Regionalism and Global Trade Rules' (2011) 9 *Georgetown Journal of Law & Public Policy* 261, 267.

45 See O Owoeye, 'Regionalism and WTO Multilateralism: The Case for an African Continental Free Trade Area' (2016) 50 (6) *Journal of World Trade* 1085–1110.

46 N Pires De Carvalho, *The TRIPS Regime of Patent Rights* (Kluwwer Law International, 2nd ed., 2005) 337.

47 See C Brandi, C Ladenburger, & A Pegels, *Intellectual Property Rights as a Challenge to Providing Global Public Goods: The Cases of Public Health, Food Security and Climate Stability* (German Development Institute Discussion Paper 17/2010.

within the WTO. There are diverging views as to the role of regionalism or RTAs as against the WTO multilateral agreements in trade liberalisations.[48] Nevertheless, more countries in the WTO are currently embracing them.

Accession to international markets on terms that will be reasonably favourable to African countries inevitably requires a strong coalition strategy on the part of African countries. It has already been noted that the collective voice of developing countries exhibited through the use of a coalition strategy at the Doha Round is to be seen as an effective bargaining strategy that could ultimately be used to ensure the multilateral trade system takes sufficient account of the special circumstances of developing countries.[49] Whilst it is true that every RTA has a tendency to promote trade diversion that is detrimental to non-members, it is also true that RTAs can result in trade creation through significant growth in intra-regional trade. The World Bank has already stressed the point that '*security, bargaining power, cooperation, and lock-in are probably the main political motors for regional integration. Sometimes these motives receive a veneer of economic rationalization*'.[50]

There is, accordingly, a pressing need for the AU to take expeditious steps to facilitate the implementation of the Abuja Treaty at least in so far as the creation of a free-trade area through the implementation of AfCFTA is concerned. In sum, beyond their contribution to trade liberalisation, RTAs can have effects such as the improvement of production structures, higher degree of competition and economies of scale.[51] The consensus decision-making requirement of the WTO has made it considerably difficult for negotiations at the multilateral level to record significant progress, as the WTO Doha Round has shown. RTAs therefore remain indispensable to emerging economies seeking better access to international markets and Africa must join the trend to avoid fading into economic insignificance in the new era of trade multilateralism.

9.5 The patent pool option

The African access to medicines crisis is a multifaceted problem requiring a multidimensional solution. The contribution of international IP law to the conundrum can be substantially counterbalanced through the effective use of the available flexibilities and options in the TRIPS Agreement and the broader corpus of WTO law. Apart from the TRIPS flexibilities and the other options that may be explored in international law both within and outside the WTO box, a number of recommendations have been made on strategies that may be explored to address the access to medicines problem. Some of these options are discussed below. One is the patent pool option. A patent pool is generally defined as an

48 Powell & Low above n 44, 261.

49 J Oduwole, 'An Appraisal of Developing Country Coalition Strategy in the WTO Doha Round Agriculture Negotiations' (2012) 20 *Currents: International Trade Law Journal* 45, 54–55.

50 World Bank, *Trade Blocs* (2000) 124.

51 Powell & Low above n 44, 279.

arrangement whereby two or more patent holders pool their patents together in such a way that authorisation for use can be granted for all patents in the pool as a single package.[52] Patent pools can respond to challenges posed by patent thickets. A patent thicket is said to exist when two or more right holders hold intersecting patent rights that a manufacturer must obtain licences for in order to bring a product to the market without infringing on the patent holders' rights.[53]

Patent thickets may be strong or weak depending on how difficult the cross-licensing process is. It is believed that strong patent thickets are common in biomedical innovations[54] and most commercialised drugs use two or more patents for their formulation, delivery or production.[55] Research shows that where a patent thicket in the biopharmaceutical industry requires cross-licensing involving four or more patent holders, voluntary licensing is likely to become impossible.[56] With respect to the access to medicines debate, patent pools are particularly significant in view of the fact that they can facilitate the development of new drugs through the sharing of technical information among the members of the pooled patents as well as licences to the patent pool.[57]

While patent pools can serve the purpose of enhancing competition and making the licensing of IPRs less onerous, they may also have the anticompetitive effect of bringing the major competitors in an industry together to form an alliance to further fortify their market monopoly and make the process of breaking their patents more difficult.[58] Patent pools can also make the use of compulsory licensing more burdensome because any TRIPS-compliant compulsory licensing mechanism must make the issuance of such licences subject to judicial or administrative review. Patent pools can thus make patent holders more formidable in litigation and negotiating voluntary licences from a patent pool may limit the bargaining strength of the party seeking the authorisation given that licensees to a patent pool must negotiate with a stronger and more formidable monopoly scheme. For instance, a patent pool that existed in the US sewing machine industry from 1856 to 1877 was found to reduce innovation in the industry by '*intensifying the threat of litigation for outside firms*' and this was found to discourage innovation.[59] It has thus been argued that when a patent pool contains

52 D Nicol & J Nielsen, 'Opening the Dam: Patent Pools, Innovation and Access to Essential Medicines' in T Pogge, M Rimmer & K Rubenstein (eds.), *Incentives for Global Public Health: Patent Law and Access to Essential Medicines* (Cambridge University Press, 2010) 235, 237.

53 S Woolman, E Fishman & M Fisher, 'Evidence of Patent Thickets in Biopharmaceutical Technologies' (2013) 53 *Intellectual Property Review* 1, 2.

54 M A Heller, 'The Tragedy of the Anticommons: Property in the Transition from Marx to Markets' (1998) 111 *Harvard Law Review* 621, 688.

55 Woolman, Fishman & Fisher, above n 43, 27.

56 Ibid.

57 S Sher, J Lutinski & B Tennis, 'The Role of Antitrust in Evaluating the Competitive Impact of Patent Pooling Arrangements' (2012) 13 *Sedona Conference Journal* 111, 112–113.

58 S Carlson, Note, 'Patent Pools and the Antitrust Dilemma' (1999) 16 *Yale Journal of Regulation* 359, 388.

59 R Lampe & P Moser, 'Do Patent Pools Encourage Innovation?: Evidence from the 19th-Century Sewing Machine Industry' (2010) 70 *Journal of Economic History* 898, 899.

patent rights that are substitutable for one another, there is a tendency for the patent holders to use the pool to eliminate competition and use it as a platform for price-fixing.[60] Despite the risk of anticompetitive practices, patent pooling may still be useful where a combination of patents is required to facilitate the delivery of essential drugs such as HIV/AIDS.[61]

The Medicines Patent Pool, a UN-supported organisation, was founded in 2010 to ensure lower prices of HIV drugs and the development of such drugs for developing countries under the auspices of UNITAID.[62] The Medicines Patent Pool has signed agreements with up to 9 patent holders and 24 sublicensing agreements with generic manufacturers and product developers.[63]

The Medicines Patent Pool seems to hold great promises for developing countries, and African countries could, through a regional economic community, obtain licences from the pool to meet the health needs of HIV patients in the continent. The Medicines Patent Pool, however, deals only with HIV-related treatment and does not cover the myriad other diseases that afflict the African population like malaria, tuberculosis, typhoid, and yellow fever to mention a few. Nonetheless, the Medicines Patent Pool initiative can serve as a good model for other tropical diseases affecting people in Africa and patent pools can be created to facilitate the process of licensing patent rights for both government departments and pharmaceutical manufacturers that might be interested in such licences.

9.5.1 Other recommendations

Other recommendations include a proposal for the development of a practical mechanism that rewards biopharmaceutical innovations on the basis of its efficacy in reducing premature deaths and human morbidity provided the medicine is priced at the lowest realistic cost of production and delivery.[64] This is popularly referred to as the health impact fund. The health impact reward is to be funded by government as a public good under the scheme of an international agreement that would underpin the commitment of each country to the arrangement.[65] Thus, the health impact fund will allow patent holders to bring their patents under the scheme, sell at lower rates and receive incentives for their innovation from

60 Lutinski & Tennis, above n 57, 119–120.

61 Nicol &Nielsen, above n 52, 260.

62 Medicines Patent Pool, 'Who We Are' https://medicinespatentpool.org/who-we-are/ accessed 31 August 2013.

63 Medicines Patent Pool, *Update on Progress of Sublicensees* https://medicinespatentpool.org/what-we-do/global-licence-overview/update-on-progress-of-mpp-sublicensees/ accessed 27 January 2019.

64 T Pogge, 'The Health Impact Fund: Better Pharmaceutical Innovations at Much Lower Prices' in T Pogge, M Rimmer & K Rubenstein (eds.), *Incentives for Global Public Health: Patent Law and Access to Essential Medicines* (Cambridge University Press, 2010) 135, 149.

65 Ibid., 149–150.

the scheme.[66] Some of the major criticisms against the proposed scheme are the level of financial contributions from partner countries, criteria for patentability under the scheme, the merits of using patentability as a criterion for benefitting under the scheme and the measure of determining the contribution of a particular medicine to the reduction of the global disease burden.[67]

Another proposal makes a case for substituting or supplementing the patent system, as incentives to innovate, with a prize system funded by the government.[68] Such a system is believed to be capable of promoting competition and increasing access to medicines.[69] The government prize system also has some theoretical and practical challenges such as innovation for which the prizes should be available, balancing the rewards of pioneers and subsequent innovators and the form or value of the prize to be awarded.[70]

These examples reveal that there are other options than working within the WTO box, but they are not the main focus of this book. The major goal of the book is to explore options African countries can effectively explore to address their access to medicines problem. The health impact fund and research prize system both require a degree of infrastructural and administrative sophistication which does not presently exist in most African countries.

9.6 Conclusion

It seems African countries are not yet strategically positioned to take full advantage of the flexibilities and options available for facilitating access to medicines and ensuring adequate influence and relevance in international trade negotiations. The need for a free-trade area in Africa is long overdue. The implementation of TRIPS, it seems, will result in outcomes that are more onerous in circumstances where free trade is absent, as such countries will not only be paying IP royalties but additional customs and excise duties that will raise prices. The significant barriers to market entry makes the free movement of goods more difficult, which in turn is a considerable disincentive to manufacturers who want to be sure of the commercial viability of a capital intensive project before venturing into it. Africa, therefore, needs a free-trade area to provide a viable market for local pharmaceutical manufacturers.

In addition, a collaborative strategy can be used under the auspices of the African Union to facilitate the establishment or development of an African intergovernmental pharmaceutical company that will be saddled with the

66 K Liddell, 'The Health Impact Fund: A Critique' in T Pogge, M Rimmer & K Rubenstein (eds.), *Incentives for Global Public Health: Patent Law and Access to Essential Medicines* (Cambridge University Press, 2010) 155, 158.

67 Ibid., 180.

68 W W Fisher & T Syed, 'A Prize System as a Partial Solution to the Crisis in the Developing World' in T Pogge, M Rimmer & K Rubenstein (eds.), *Incentives for Global Public Health: Patent Law and Access to Essential Medicines* (Cambridge University Press, 2010) 181.

69 Ibid.

70 Ibid., 181–208.

responsibility of meeting the pharmaceutical needs of the continent. The full implementation of the Abuja Treaty may take longer to accomplish than envisaged by the makers of the Treaty. The Treaty nonetheless provides a legal framework for the establishment of an African free-trade area. Establishing a free-trade area in the continent will greatly facilitate easy movement of goods and a more effective use of the TRIPS compulsory licensing mechanism. The establishment of an African intergovernmental pharmaceutical industry is also strongly recommended. A free trade African area with a strong African pharmaceutical industry could significantly ameliorate the access to medicines problem in the continent. Such an arrangement may also make it considerably easier for Africa to take better advantage of other international arrangements for facilitating access to medicines such as patent pools and the international human rights framework that supports a human rights approach to IP protection.

The use of parallel trade, compulsory licensing and other TRIPS flexibilities under an African RTA can be supported under WTO law and the international framework for human rights protection. Strong reliance can be placed on the right to development and the right to health to justify the maximum use of the TRIPS flexibilities in the access to medicines campaign. Africa must be ready to summon the political will to harness all the resources at her disposal to address the continent's access to medicines conundrum.

This book has taken a broad and in-depth look at the implications of the TRIPS patent regime for access to medicines in Africa. It is acknowledged that the African access to medicines problem is not just about IP but the TRIPS patents regime does have significant implications for it. The book concedes the view that the access to medicines problem in Africa is a multifaceted problem requiring a multifaceted response. It is noted that there are flexibilities in the TRIPS Agreement that are meant to ameliorate its probable adverse effects on developing countries. The major flexibilities in the access to medicines context seem to be compulsory licensing and parallel importation. It is argued that whilst the conditions for the grant of compulsory licences do not make it possible for such licences to be available as a matter of course, compulsory licences nonetheless remain an essential part of the TRIPS flexibilities. It is noted that the Doha Paragraph-6 System does not hold much promise for countries with no pharmaceutical manufacturing capacity and Africa in particular may have to explore the option of building manufacturing capacity in the pharmaceutical sector through collaborative efforts.

It is further posited that there is nothing in TRIPS that restrains countries from adopting an exhaustion regime that accords with their socio-economic circumstances. Developing countries, especially in Africa, are encouraged to resist TRIPS-plus provisions that may take away the flexibilities available under TRIPS and an international exhaustion paradigm is recommended for Africa. The TRIPS data exclusivity regime may pose some problems for countries seeking access to medicines that are under test data protection. It is however contended that the circumstances in many African countries will adequately fall under the public interest exception under that provision and what is required is the political will to make use of the exception where necessary.

It is submitted that besides the flexibilities available by compulsory licensing and exhaustion of rights, human rights jurisprudence, particularly in relation to health and development, may be called in aid to give more life to the hortatory public interest provisions in the TRIPS Agreement. The book notes that with the waivers in place for least developed countries to delay implementation of pharmaceutical patents under the TRIPS Agreement until 2033, Africa can take advantage of these to develop a viable local pharmaceutical industry before it becomes more onerous for the continent to import drugs from Asia and elsewhere, as the world moves to a more protectionist global IP framework.

The book acknowledges the fact that developing a local manufacturing capacity would be a daunting goal for virtually any African country to independently pursue and for this reason a collaborative approach is recommended. The book makes a case for the immediate implementation of the AfCFTA through the creation of an African free-trade area in line with the objectives of the Abuja Treaty, to give Africa a better leverage in taking full advantage of the TRIPS flexibilities. The book recommends the harmonisation of the policies and administrative accoutrements of the existing African regional economic communities followed by their amalgamation to constitute an African Free Trade Zone. It is submitted that an economic coalition of this nature has become expedient in the African access to medicines cause.

Bibliography

African Union, *African Continental Free Trade Agreement Status List.* https://au.int/sites/default/files/treaties/34248-sl-agreement_establishing_the_african_continental_free_trade_area_1.pdf accessed 27 January 2019.

African Union, *Declaration on Boosting Intra African Trade and the Establishment of a Continental Free Trade Area (CFTA)*, Assembly/AU/Dec.1 (XVIII).

African Union, *Gaborone Declaration on a Roadmap Towards Universal Access to Prevention, Treatment and Care*, Doc. CAMH/Decl.1(II) 3 (10–14 October 2005).

African Union, *OAU/AU Treaties. Conventions, Protocols, & Charters*, www.au.int/en/treaties accessed 27 January 2019.

African Union Commission, *Deputy Chairperson's Statement made at the 6th Ordinary Session of AU Ministers of Trade*, 1 November 2010, Kigali, Rwanda.

African Union Secretariat, *Draft Pharmaceutical Manufacturing Plan for Africa*, Doc. CAMH/MIN/7(III), 6 (10–13 April 2007).

African Union Secretariat, *Progress Report on the Pharmaceutical Manufacturing Plan for Africa*, Doc. MIN/Sp?AU?CAMH3/2, 12 (17 May 2008).

Brandi C, Ladenburger C, & Pegels A, *Intellectual Property Rights as a Challenge to Providing Global Public Goods: The Cases of Public Health, Food Security and Climate Stability* (German Development Institute Discussion Paper 17/2010).

Berger M, Murugi I, Buch F, IJsselmuiden C, Moran M, Guzman J, Devlin M & Kubata B, *Strengthening Pharmaceutical Innovation in Africa* (AU, COHRED and NEPAD, 2010) 58–59.

Boulton I C, *Setting the Scene* (Forum for Africa-based Pharmaceutical Manufacturers and Potential Investors Kenya, 2011).

Carlson S, 'Note, Patent Pools and the Antitrust Dilemma' (1999) 16 *Yale Journal of Regulation* 359.

Fisher W W & Syed T, 'A Prize System as a Partial Solution to the Crisis in the Developing World' in T Pogge, M Rimmer & K Rubenstein (eds.), *Incentives for Global Public Health: Patent Law and Access to Essential Medicines* (Cambridge University Press, 2010).

Goulding R & Palriwala A, *Patent Pools: Assessing their Value-Added for Global Health Innovation and Access* (Result for Development Institute, Washington: 2012).

Heller M A, 'The Tragedy of the Anticommons: Property in the Transition from Marx to Markets' (1998) 111 *Harvard Law Review* 621, 688.

Ighobor K, *Africa Set for a Massive Free Trade Area, Africa Renewal*, August-November 2018 www.un.org/africarenewal/magazine/august-november-2018/africa-set-massive-free-trade-area accessed 27 January 2019.

International Finance Corporation, *Impact Annual Report* (2012).

Lampe R & Moser P, 'Do Patent Pools Encourage Innovation?: Evidence from the 19th-Century Sewing Machine Industry' (2010) 70 *Journal of Economic History* 898.

Lester S, 'The Role of the International Trade Regime in Global Governance' (2011) 16 *UCLA Journal of International Law and Foreign Affairs* 209.

Liddell K, 'The Health Impact Fund: A Critique' in T Pogge, M Rimmer & K Rubenstein (eds.) *Incentives for Global Public Health: Patent Law and Access to Essential Medicines* (Cambridge University Press, 2010).

Medicines Patent Pool, 'Update on Progress of Sublicensees' https://medicinespatentpool.org/what-we-do/global-licence-overview/update-on-progress-of-mpp-sublicensees/ accessed 27 January 2019.

Medicines Patent Pool, 'Who We Are' https://medicinespatentpool.org/who-we-are/ accessed 27 January 2019.

Nicol D & Nielsen J, 'Opening the Dam: Patent Pools, Innovation and Access to Essential Medicines' in T Pogge, M Rimmer & K Rubenstein (eds.), *Incentives for Global Public Health: Patent Law and Access to Essential Medicines* (Cambridge University Press, 2010).

Nicol D & Owoeye O, 'Using TRIPS Flexibilities to Facilitate Access to Medicines' (2013) 91(7) 44 *Bulletin of the World Health Organization*, 533.

Oduwole J, 'An Appraisal of Developing Country Coalition Strategy in the WTO Doha Round Agriculture Negotiations' (2012) 20 *Currents: International Trade Law Journal* 45.

Organization of African Unity, *Lagos Plan of Action for the economic development of Africa 1980–2000* (OAU, 1980).

Osei-Tutu J J, 'Value Divergence in Global Intellectual Property' (2012) 87 *Indiana Law Journal* 1639.

Owoeye O, 'Regionalism and WTO Multilateralism: The Case for an African Continental Free Trade Area' (2016) 50(6) *Journal of World Trade* 1085–1110.

Pan African Perspective, 'The African Economic Community' www.panafricanperspective.com/aec.htm accessed 27 January 2019.

Pires De Carvalho N, *The TRIPS Regime of Patent Rights* (Kluwwer Law International. 2nd ed., 2005) 337.

Pogge T, 'The Health Impact Fund: Better Pharmaceutical Innovations at Much Lower Prices' in T Pogge, M Rimmer & K Rubenstein (eds.), *Incentives for Global Public Health: Patent Law and Access to Essential Medicines* (Cambridge University Press, 2010) 135, 149.

Powell S J & Low T, 'Is the WTO Quietly Fading Away?: The New Regionalism and Global Trade Rules' (2011) 9 *Georgetown Journal of Law & Public Policy* 261, 267.

Rwanda Development Board, 'Patent Information' Ref: RDB/3/DG/0504/5/12 dated 31 May 2002.

Sher S, Lutinski J & Tennis B, 'The Role of Antitrust in Evaluating the Competitive Impact of Patent Pooling Arrangements' (2012) 13 *Sedona Conference Journal* 111, 112–113.

Small Island Developing States (UN-OHRLLS), 'Least Developed Countries' http://unohrlls.org/custom-content/uploads/2018/12/list-of-least-developed-countries-rev1.pdf accessed 26 January 2019.

UNECA, Developing Africa's Pharmaceutical Sector Crucial, says ECA's Soteri, 1 August 2018 www.uneca.org/stories/developing-africa%E2%80%99s-pharmaceutical-sector-crucial-says-eca%E2%80%99s-soteri accessed 27 January 2019.

United Nations, 'Regional Economic Communities of the African Union' www.un.org/en/africa/osaa/peace/recs.shtml accessed 27 January 2019.

UN Office of the High Representative for the Least Developed Countries, Landlocked Developing Countries and Small Island Developing States (UN-OHRLLS), 'Least Developed Countries' http://unohrlls.org/custom-content/uploads/2018/12/list-of-least-developed-countries-rev1.pdf accessed 26 January 2019.

Woolman S, Fishman E & Fisher M, 'Evidence of Patent Thickets in Biopharmaceutical Technologies' (2013) 53 *Intellectual Property Review* 1, 2.

World Bank, *Trade Blocs* (2000).

World Health Organisation, *World Medicines Situation 2011: Medicines Prices, Availability and Affordability* (World Health Organisation, 2011).

World Trade Organization, *The WTO in Brief: Part 3* www.wto.org/english/thewto_e/whatis_e/inbrief_e/inbr03_e.htm accessed 27 January 2019.

World Trade Organisation, *Implementation of paragraph 6 of the Doha Declaration on the TRIPS Agreement and Public Health*, WT/L/540 General Council Decision of 30 August 2003.

Yu P K, 'Access to Medicines, BRICS Alliances, and Collective Action' (2008) 34 *American Journal of Law and Medicine* 345,

Index

Note: Page numbers followed by "n" denote footnotes.

FSC
www.fsc.org
MIX
Papier | Fördert
gute Waldnutzung
FSC® C083411

Kolibri 360 GmbH
Ferdinand-Jühlke-Straße 7
99095 Erfurt, Deutschland
produktsicherheit@kolibri360.de